Praise for *Revolutionary New Jer*

MW00789518

"New Jersey Sons of the American Revolution and Daughters of the American Revolution: It is an honor for me to review *Revolutionary New Jersey*, the latest book by author and fellow SAR compatriot Bob Mayers. In it he explores the fascinating history of many critical war sites in our state that have been forgotten or overlooked in history. Many are familiar, but we are unaware of the full story of fierce struggles that occurred at these places during America's most important war. We should all support Bob Mayers' efforts to pass on the glorious story of the Revolutionary War in our home state."

— Clark D. McCullough, Past President, New Jersey Sons of the American Revolution,
President of the Elizabethtown Chapter #1

"*Revolutionary New Jersey* is well-researched, utilizing numerous valuable primary sources. It covers many locales in New Jersey associated with the war, telling of local landmarks and overlooked stories from our past. This book is a must-have for any Revolutionary War or New Jersey historian."

— Kelly Lindheimer, founder of the website www.thehistorygirl.com

"An exciting and insightful description into how New Jersey was ideally situated to be the major host of the American Revolutionary War. In *Revolutionary New Jersey: Forgotten Towns and Crossroads of the American Revolution*, Bob Meyers draws his readers' attention into the crucial role New Jersey citizens played in the winning of the war."

— Donald Johnstone Peck, historian, author, Trustee of the League of New Jersey Historical Societies

"Historian and author Bob Mayers' latest work, *Revolutionary New Jersey*, fills a major void in our known history of the American Revolution. The research and passion that Mr. Mayers has poured into this effort lays at our feet, facts and information sorely lacking in our common historic knowledge concerning the birth of our United States. I believe this book will be a 'must have' for every person's library interested in the founding of this great country."

— Cynthia Blumenkrantz, President, The Heritage Trail Association, Inc.

"This study is an area neglected in many of the standard works. Who knew in my own backyard? Places we drive by on the way to work or on vacation, all brought to life. Things that should be taught in schools are now relegated to living historians, reenactors, docents and labors of love like this."

—Kathy Faulks, Chairman, Washington-Rochambeau Revolutionary Route, NJ (W3R-NJ.org);
Secretary, Friends of the Abraham Strauss House, Inc.;
Commissioner, Somerset County Cultural and Heritage Commission, New Jersey

"A comprehensive study of New Jersey's role in the American Revolution on the local level, and a satisfying read for history buffs."

—Jeanne Floersheimer, President, North Jersey American Revolution Round Table

"I am delighted that Bob Mayers, fellow historian and compatriot Son of the American Revolution, has been able to 'fill in the blanks' about many of the under-appreciated battles and events of the American Revolution that transpired in New Jersey. Without thoughtful and prolific historians like Bob, these important events would stay in the shadows, and never reveal the enormous contribution of the citizen-soldiers who gave their all for the cause of Liberty. Without this book, it would be hard to imagine the true meaning and scope of so many key battles, whose physical sites have vanished underneath highways and homes. Bob has the unique ability to bring these places and events back to life, to help us value our heritage all the more."

—Warren C. Fristensky, SAR West Fields Chapter President

"New Jersey played a critical part in America's War for Independence. Nestled between New York and Philadelphia, the state truly became the 'Crossroads of the American Revolution.' Bob Mayers provides a needed examination of some of the state's little-known encounters and encampment sites that spanned the countryside during the crucial years of the war. This volume helps fill a much-needed gap in the state's Revolutionary history."

—Todd Braisted, author of *Grand Forage 1778: The Battleground Around New York City*

"*Revolutionary New Jersey* brings recognition to those places in New Jersey that once were significant in our national history but are today only dimly remembered. Bob Mayers' book renews our interest in these places, focusing attention on battlefields, towns, camps, and villages that played important roles in the creation of the American Republic. These sites provide a uniqueness of place to New Jersey and Mayers' book reminds us to preserve and protect these places. Further, we should take pride in the achievements and actions of the men and women his book has brought to light."

—Wade P. Catts, Historical Archeologist

"Many of us in New Jersey are residing in the midst of American Revolutionary War history without knowledge or appreciation of the many glorious events that occurred here and led to the formation of our nation. Our state has lagged behind in acknowledging many of the critical places where patriots fought, suffered and died. After reading *Revolutionary New Jersey* and reacting to its subtitle *Forgotten Towns and Crossroads*, I know these places will now be remembered—and thanks to Bob Mayers we will be able to say, 'I am proud to live here!'"

—Rich Rosenthal, Cofounder, with historian John T. Cunningham,
of the North Jersey American Revolution Roundtable

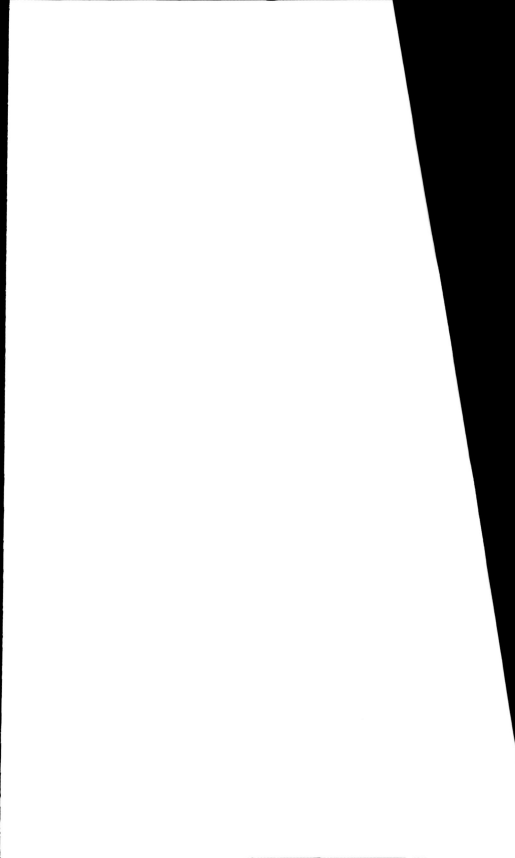

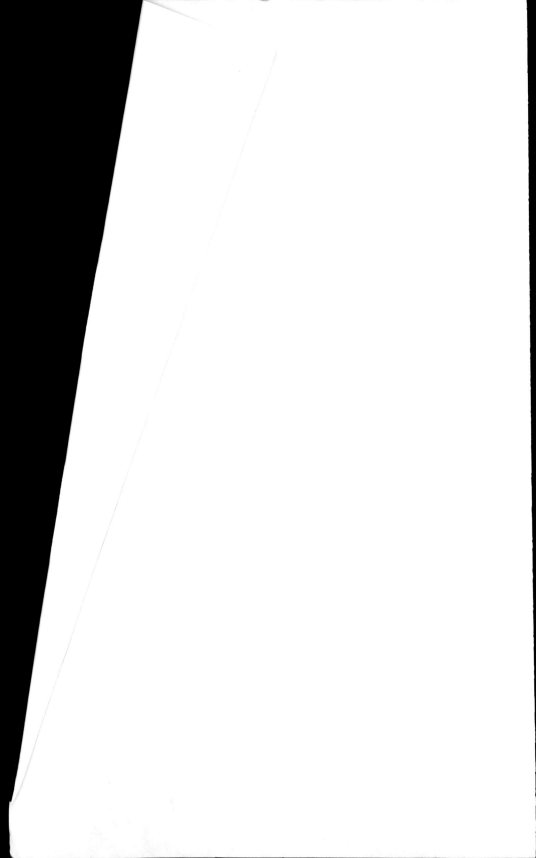

Revolutionary
NEW JERSEY

Revolutionary NEW JERSEY

Forgotten Towns and Crossroads
of the American Revolution

Robert A. Mayers

American History Press
Staunton Virginia

American History Press

Staunton, Virginia
(888) 521-1789
Visit us on the Internet at:
www.Americanhistorypress.com

First Printing June 2018

To schedule an event with the author or to inquire about
bulk discount sales please contact American History Press.

Library of Congress Cataloging-in-Publication Data

Names: Mayers, Robert A. (Robert Adrian), 1930- author.
Title: Revolutionary New Jersey : forgotten towns and crossroads of the
American Revolution / Robert A. Mayers.
Description: Staunton, Virginia : American History Press, 2018. | Includes
bibliographical references and index.
Identifiers: LCCN 2018016835 | ISBN 9781939995292 (pbk. : alk. paper)
Subjects: LCSH: New Jersey--History--Revolution, 1775-1783. | New
Jersey--History--Revolution, 1775-1783--Battlefields. | New
Jersey--History--Revolution, 1775-1783--Campaigns. | New Jersey--History,
Local.
Classification: LCC E263.N5 M39 2018 | DDC 974.9/03--dc23
LC record available at https://lccn.loc.gov/2018016835

Manufactured in the United States of America on acid-free paper.
This book exceeds all ANSO standards for archival quality.

DEDICATION

To my fellow authors and historians, John T. Cunningham, Tom Fleming, and John Nagy, who shared my obsession with the Revolutionary War and kindly mentored, supported and inspired me in my writing over several years. They are greatly missed and often in my thoughts.

Contents

Contents

THE WAR AT THE SHORE

NEW JERSEY REVOLUTIONARY CAMPGROUNDS

Contents

Introduction

Given the plethora of books devoted to the Revolutionary War in New Jersey, you might believe that every fascinating, unusual, and shocking detail of the war has already been discovered. Unfortunately, more often than not, the dreadful realities of warfare in the Garden State have been forgotten or concealed by bland accounts, dull statistics, and local development. Discovering the actual locales of critical events that occurred during America's important war is an adventurous voyage in time, and spinning the mysteries into a story is often like solving a real detective case.

I have been astonished that battlefields, encampments and sites of many significant events of the Revolutionary War in New Jersey have been lost or neglected by history. Places where Patriots fought and died are unmarked, shrouded in mystery and clouded in mythology. After more than two centuries, many of them have entirely disappeared while others languish unnoticed. Some are on private property or have been built over by developers and highway construction.

By walking in the footsteps of Revolutionary War soldiers and describing their lives I try to usher readers back in time so that they can feel, see, and hear the events that occurred over 200 years ago. The first thing that I observed during my quest was the impact of topography on the war, since mountains, waterways, hills, rivers, roads, cities, forests and coastlines created natural defenses. As a result, troop movements, battle sites, supply routes and the flow of action on land and sea were all affected by these features. While man-made changes in terrain in the Garden State have been enormous since the time of the American Revolution, the pervasive influence of natural features remains.

A visit during the season when a historic event occurred is the best way to grasp a sense of the circumstances surrounding it. Only by standing on Monmouth Battlefield on a sweltering summer day can you comprehend why just as many men perished of heatstroke as by musket fire, since the temperature remained above 100 degrees during the battle. Only by shivering on a bitter cold day in knee-deep snow at the Jockey Hollow encampment or standing on an icy Delaware River bank where the American Army crossed on a frigid Christmas night can you understand the appalling hardships endured by the American army.

I soon recognized that historians have given less acclaim to American defeats, regardless of the bloodshed and valor displayed, and tend to avoid mentioning places that evoke negative memories. My efforts to revive these forsaken locations with site visits and fresh research from original records have been described in my book, The Forgotten Revolution-Revisiting Critical Places of the American Revolution That Have Been Neglected by History. This work, published in 2014, recounts my adventures at several obscure Revolutionary War sites in the northeast.

I was amazed to find that many of these abandoned places were in my home state of New Jersey. This should not have surprised me. George Washington and his Continental Army spent more time here than in any other state, and the state has been called the "cockpit of the Revolution" and "crossroads of the Revolution." The state had more battles and skirmishes fought on its soil than any other due to its key geographical position at the center of the new nation and its position between the new nation's capital in Philadelphia and the stronghold of the British headquarters in New York. Subsequently, the opposing armies crossed and re-crossed it many times throughout the war.

The ravages of the Revolutionary War touched most New Jersey communities. The state united the new nation by providing a secure route between New England and the south, and many supply routes crossed the state. The ensuing pathways were also a burden for the Patriots as they provided an overland route for the marauding British Army.

The state's abundant resources were pillaged by both armies as scavenging parties from one or the other side scoured the countryside competing for food and forage. General combat between the armies, as well as local community discord, caused almost 300 significant military actions and hundreds of other skirmishes in New Jersey during the years of the war.

In 1775, the state's men marched north on the first large scale offensive campaign, the ill-fated Invasion of Canada. In the last months of 1776, after a series of defeats in New York, a decimated Continental Army was pursued across the state by the triumphant Redcoats. One month later, the tattered Americans turned on their overconfident adversaries and crushed the British and their Hessian mercenaries at Trenton and Princeton. From there the Patriots vanished into the Watchung Mountains to a secure winter camp at Morristown.

In June 1778, a rejuvenated American Army moved east from Valley Forge toward the Hudson Highlands. At the same time the Crown forces evacuated Philadelphia and headed for New York. The armies converged at Monmouth Courthouse (now Freehold, New Jersey), and engaged in the hardest fought and longest battle of the Revolutionary War. It was the last major engagement in the north and the only battle of the Revolutionary War fought in open field conditions where the main forces of both armies and the greater part of the highest and most renowned officers on both sides participated. Although it was a draw in a tactical sense, the Americans achieved a victory in terms of being able to fight on equal terms with the main British Army.

Off the New Jersey coast the thrilling war at sea also remains a neglected chapter in the state's history. The majority of the supplies needed by the British had to be transported by ship from England to their base in New York City. Throngs of enemy vessels cruised along the beaches of the 130-mile stretch of the state's coastline. Heavy shipping also traversed the Raritan Bay and New York Harbor. With its many bays and small ports, there was an abundance of vulnerable enemy vessels navigating the long New Jersey seacoast. These coves and inlets provided a sanctuary and an advantageous position for the Patriots to prey upon the vital enemy maritime supply lines.

Privateers were personally owned vessels whose goal was to capture British merchant ships and then sell the vessels and their cargoes at auction. New Jersey sailors also went out in whaleboats to capture British shipping or to make raids into British-occupied New York. Hundreds of small craft that crossed from the New Jersey bay shore to Staten Island, Long Island and Manhattan loaded with food and supplies from bountiful Loyalist farms were targets for the New Jersey privateers and whaleboats. American forces at sea were small in number, but the effect of their raids on British and Loyalist merchant vessels was a key factor in the Patriot victory.

Since the small towns along the shore were an abundant source of food and supplies, they attracted invaders. Accessible by water, they were often raided and sacked by the British. Skirmishing along the southern coast continued until the very end of the war in places such as Cedar Bridge in Ocean County, and Chestnut Neck (now Port Republic), on the Mullica River in Atlantic County.

The ridges of the Watchung Mountains provided the American forces with natural defenses. This high ground formed an impregnable fortress that blocked the British from encroaching west toward the interior of the state. During the so-called "forage war," which took place from January until March in 1777, they were only able to occupy a few towns between Princeton and Perth Amboy. The Watchung ridges also shielded the Continental Army during winter encampments by providing strategic sanctuaries, as well as serving as refuges for the aggressive New Jersey militia. Continental units used Pompton as a base three times and spent two winters at Middlebrook (today's Bridgewater). Both winters at Morristown tested the army's ability to survive. During these times the Americans were near defeat, but somehow they always managed to survive to fight another day.

New Jersey's civilian population was also drawn into the conflict, so in a sense the American Revolution was the first American civil war.

About one third of the population were Loyalists who sided with the British. Another third supported the fight for independence. The Quakers, about 20% of the population, were pacifists who tried to remain neutral. Others changed sides during the conflict, either for their own safety or to reap economic advantages.

New Jersey militiamen rallied to the Patriot cause in 1775 after the battles of Lexington and Concord. Every township was required to enlist men between the ages of sixteen and fifty years old in the militia. The fact that local New Jersey soldiers made up a large part of the fighting force at major engagements in the state is often forgotten. These citizen-soldiers provided vital support to the Continental Army when it counterattacked at Trenton, Princeton and Monmouth Courthouse.

Local militia units confined the enemy to a few towns during the "forage war" in 1777. At the Battle of Connecticut Farms (now Union Township), the combatants were all New Jersey militiamen, and at the Battle of Short Hills the defenders were largely General William Maxwell's New Jersey Continental Line Brigade. During the entire war the state troops remained active in opposing the gangs of armed Loyalists.

Finally, in 1781, the combined American and French forces assembled in New Jersey on the way to the final decisive victory at Yorktown in Virginia. They divided into three columns and marched through eight New Jersey counties to regroup as one unit at Middlebrook and continue south. After the successful siege the triumphant allied armies then retraced their steps though the state.

I hope that these accounts of remarkable places will be as thrilling for you as they were for me. It was enchanting to stand on the lookout at Washington's Rock in Greenbrook Township and to walk the windswept beaches of Sandy Hook. Some of these locales looked exactly as they must have appeared in the eighteenth century. When rediscovering the forgotten Battle of Navesink, where the outnumbered Patriots stood fast in 1777, I found the site overlooks an awe-inspiring thirty mile panoramic view of the coastline. I walked the golf course of the Plainfield Country Club, where, unknown to all but a few local historians, a battery of

American artillery held off the entire British Army. The cruel wind stung my face on a winter day in deep snow at Jockey Hollow. Grasping a rusted bayonet, hefting a cannon ball and discovering documents that had not been read in hundreds of years transported me back in time and made those forsaken places come alive once again.

The Continental Army spent almost a quarter of the entire war in New Jersey. May the description of these neglected sites inspire Garden State readers and out of state residents to pay a visit to those places they find the most intriguing.

Acknowledgements

This work was driven by my passion for onsite exploration of these awe-inspiring historical places as well as research of original 18th century documents. I had many fascinating adventures while visiting these sites and was delighted to locate the vast majority of my primary sources in a select group of major collections.

The New Jersey State Archives, the New Jersey and New York Historical Societies and the U.S. National Archives provided much source data. The collections dedicated to the American Revolution at the William I. Clements Library at the University of Michigan and the David Library of the American Revolution at Washington's Crossing, Pennsylvania were also invaluable. I am deeply indebted to these institutions for preserving the records of our nation's most important war and for their knowledgeable and patient staff who tolerated my sometimes assertive efforts to locate obscure documents.

In my travels to all of these locations the most enchanting experience of all was meeting the people who truly keep the spirit of America's most important war alive. These were the staff members of park sites, re-enactors, members of historical societies, participants at round tables, archeologists, and Daughters and Sons of the American Revolution. Many were caretakers of local history and were gracious about sharing their detailed knowledge. They also described events based on old eyewitness reports not found in history books. Some were private owners who live on the land and were descendants of the original settlers and soldiers who rest in local cemeteries.

Sincere thanks to the Watchung Writers. This group of talented authors was founded by novelist Gordon McLenithan and is currently led by Pat Rydberg. Surprisingly, these fiction writers and poets had the interest and enthusiasm to critique this military history. Those who contributed were Vivian Fransen, Roy Jarmon, David Kaplan, Phil Lear, Tom Melore, Craig Siti, Katie Taillon and Alan Wohl. Member J.R. Bale of Balefire Communications, LLC, provided guidance on graphics and internet issues, and created and continues to maintain my website/ blog at www.revolutionarydetective.com. All of my reviewers assured me that this book will be enjoyed by the average reader, and not only by military historians and academics.

My family members span across five generations and two continents, and they are among my most keen supporters. They have traveled with me to many of these awe-inspiring places and have attended my many speaking events in the northeast. We are descendants of Patriot soldier John Allison, so the war is personal for us. Special heartfelt thanks to my wife Norma who has endured my obsession with this history and my virtual absences when I vanish into the 18th century.

I often meet others who share my appetite for Revolutionary War history, and together we all share knowledge of this critical period for our nation. Although many people are enthralled by my accounts, some of these ardent fans of the era regret that during their school days they tuned out history as being distant and dull. I especially lament the inadequate effort to educate our young people about the history of our country. Perhaps this will change in the future. I certainly hope so!

The War
in the
Countryside

Chapter 1

Bloody Bound Brook and
the Lost Hessian Diary (1777)

Bound Brook, South Bound Brook, Bridgewater,
Franklin Township, Martinsville, New Brunswick, Piscataway

At dawn on Palm Sunday, April 13, 1777, in the third year of the American Revolution, a Hessian captain with his company of thirty Jägers faltered and fell as intense musket and cannon fire tore into them from an American redoubt. They fearlessly attempted a frontal assault over a stone bridge that crossed the Bound Brook at a New Jersey riverbank hamlet of the same name. The Hessians, German mercenaries, were the deadliest light infantry in the world at the time, elite special forces that were feared by their American opponents. Armed with short carbine-type German hunting rifles, they dressed in green and brown to blend in with their surroundings, as opposed to the blazing red wool uniforms of their British allies.[1]

That particular morning the small unit of Jägers was the advance party of a British force of 4,000 men. These Redcoat invaders were attempting a surprise attack on an exposed front-line outpost on the Raritan River. It was defended by a garrison of 500 Continental troops who were responsible for guarding the three bridges that crossed the Raritan River which were likely to be used by the British in moves against Washington's main army at Morristown.

Jäger Captain Johann von Ewald (1744-1813).
(C. A. Jensen, after a drawing by J. Aldenrath)

The Hessian commander, Captain Johann Ewald, sensed that something was dreadfully wrong. Although his rangers were had been specially combat trained for both rugged terrain and urban fighting, they were outnumbered and outgunned, and were being slaughtered as they charged into the thick gunfire at the fortification. Ewald was puzzled. Why had his small unit been ordered to lead this suicidal assault when thousands of troops of the main force would soon be arriving? By daybreak they were surrounded by hundreds of menacing Patriot soldiers. In the confusion that day his British commander had been vague about the mission and Ewald had misunderstood his orders. The Jägers had been directed only to divert attention from the main forces by a feint, not to engage in a hard-hitting attack. Thus began the battle of Bound Brook, New Jersey. The valiant German captain was later admonished for being too aggressive and alerting the Americans that a major British offensive had begun. Remarkably, the same day, he recorded the incident in his diary, but his vivid account of the action was lost for the next 200 years.[2]

The main British force arrived minutes after the fatal charge by the Jägers, and the battle then turned against the outnumbered Americans. Confronted by what was considered the best trained and equipped soldiers in the world, they swiftly retreated toward the mountains. The fighting at Bound Brook lasted ninety minutes before the speedy Patriot withdrawal. This action in Somerset County, New Jersey, was an early, though not severe, defeat. It has been regarded in history as a humiliating rout and largely overlooked by historians on both sides. American military observers often neglect depressing setbacks but amplify triumphs.[3]

The British side did not exploit their gain. Their objective of capturing an entire garrison was not met and an American general escaped to fight another day. The Redcoats returned to New Brunswick. However, this clash at the small riverbank outpost had a profound effect on the course of the entire war. It alerted General Washington, who, along with his 4,000 ragged men, the entire Continental Army, was in a secure encampment back in the mountains at Morristown, that there was a real possibility that the British army, with Hessian support, could sweep across central New Jersey. By doing so they could then take the American capital at Philadelphia in a campaign which could effectively end the War for Independence.

Aside from Ewald's objective narrative, the few surviving eyewitness accounts and newspapers are unabashedly spun to magnify the victory or minimize the loss, depending on the viewpoint of the observer.

The skirmish at Bound Brook was a pivotal event in the Revolutionary War and this intriguing but neglected event in New Jersey history is worth reexamining today. Two remarkable circumstances enhance the appreciation of the battle. The discovery of the intrepid Hessian Captain Ewald's diary provides a fresh perspective of the fray. What is even more rewarding is that the physical features of the battle site still exist and can be easily identified today. When you arrive in Bound Brook you are in the midst of the waterways, mountains and other landmarks that determined the flow of action. Moreover, structures that played a role in the clash and later events in the war, have been faithfully restored by dedicated residents of the area.[4]

Captain Johann von Ewald (1744–1813), the Hessian officer who led the bungled charge over the Stone Bridge, came to America in 1776 with the British military forces. A participant in many of the significant battles of the war, Ewald fought in the Philadelphia Campaign, the Battle of Monmouth and with Cornwallis at the Surrender of Yorktown in 1781. The captain was recognized by the British as one of the best light infantry officers in their service. This dedicated professional from Hesse-Cassel was provided on loan by the ruler of his province to the British to oppose the American uprising for independence. He was an expert in weaponry and an excellent leader of men in combat.[5] The diary of his experiences during the entire eight years of the Revolutionary War also contains several maps of the areas where he fought and shows the placement of troops and fortifications. He wrote it for his family and descendants, and it was never intended to be published.

The Lost Diary Discovered

Ewald's diary was accidentally discovered at the end of World War II by Major Joseph P. Tustin when he was working as a historian with the United States Occupation Forces in Germany. He found it in the possession of an impoverished clerk who had been a colonel in the German army. Tustin spent the next thirty years translating the work and verifying the facts. It was finally published in 1979 by Yale University Press, and the completed work included thirty-three of the original color maps from the diary's four volumes. Ewald's account of the battle of Bound Brook appears to have been written the same day, or soon after he returned to camp. His blunt depiction of the encounter provides a dramatic picture of the action that took place on April 13, 1777.

Bound Brook on the Pathway of the Revolution

Because of its strategic location between New York and Philadelphia, the Bound Brook area was crossed many times by the opposing armies.

Old Stone Bridge, Bound Brook, site of Ewald engagement. *(Author's collection)*

The most direct route toward Morristown passed through Bound Brook. George Washington twice encamped his army at Middlebrook—in June and July 1777, and in the winter of 1778–1779, a place located on the high ground on the first ridge of the Watchung Mountains above Bound Brook. Five houses were used by Washington and his generals as their headquarters during the Middlebrook Encampment, and several other sites in the area of the Encampment still remain intact.

The remnants of the Stone Arch Bridge, the one crossed by Ewald's men, still can be seen today. More recent versions of the two other strategic crossings, the Queen's Bridge and the Van Veghten Bridge, still span the Raritan River at their original battle locations. The Van Horne House, occupied by General Benjamin Lincoln on the day of the battle, played a significant role in the clash. It was later assigned to William Alexander (Lord Stirling), Washington's second-in-command. The Van Veghten House in Finderne, a section of Bridgewater Township, was occupied by Quartermaster General Nathanael Greene. The impeccably restored Abraham Staats House in South Bound Brook was occupied by Baron Friedrich Wilhelm von Steuben.[6]

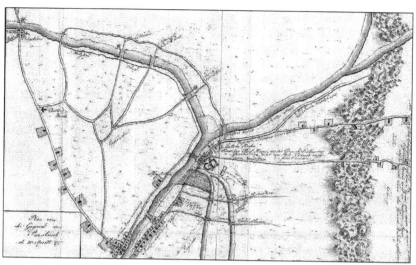

Map by Johann Ewald depicting Bound Brook area and plan of attack April 20, 1777. Bound Brook outpost is at the center. *(Author's collection)*

After the American victories at Trenton and Princeton in December 1776 and January 1777, the Continental Army entered winter quarters in Morristown, New Jersey. Washington's army had been weakened by the winter campaign since enlistments had expired, and many men had returned home. A smallpox epidemic then swept through the camp. The frigid winter weather, combined with an effort to prevent the enemy from foraging for supplies in the countryside, bought some time for the Americans to gain strength. A Patriot guerrilla war was waged by New Jersey Militia companies, often supported by Continental Army troops, during which they continually harassed enemy outposts and ambushed their foraging expeditions. But as spring approached spies reported that the British were planning to attack Morristown.

The British and their Hessian mercenaries were commanded by Generals William Howe and Charles Cornwallis. They decided to encamp for the winter in New Brunswick, New Jersey after learning that the Americans had removed all the boats along the Delaware River to prevent their crossing to Philadelphia. The British garrison of

17,000 soldiers in New Jersey was desperate for supplies and resorted to raids on local farmers and merchants in an effort to sustain its forces.

As a result, the people of Somerset County suffered severely during this winter from the British foraging parties. Prosperous farmers lived along the Raritan River and its tributaries, the Millstone and South Branch. Their well-filled barns, herds of livestock and well-furnished homes tempted the ravenous British soldiers. The Redcoat army met with resistance from the New Jersey Militia and were unsuccessful on foraging raids in January at Van Nest's Mill (near present-day Manville), Samptown (now South Plainfield), Quibbletown (now Piscataway), and as far north as Scotch Plains, Rahway and Woodbridge.

The relentless scavenging of the countryside continued through the winter. Patriot property was stolen or destroyed, and homes were plundered and burned by enemy troops seeking forage and supplies. Hundreds of families were forced to flee through the mountain passes or to build shelters on the wooded heights. Cornelius Vermeule established a militia post on Front street in today's town of Plainfield in late December 1776 to defend the Quibbletown Gap, a pass through the mountains at a lookout known today as Washington Rock.[7] This period of the war in New Jersey, the winter and early spring of 1777, has been called the "forage war."

Greatly overestimating the strength and condition of Washington's army, the English still found themselves on the defensive as April approached. Frustrated by the success of the Americans in blocking their raids, the British planned to retaliate with a concentrated attack on the garrison at Bound Brook. This assault could also provide the opportunity to search the area for food, fodder and anything else of value. The expedition was planned and carried out with so much secrecy that other units of the army and the people of New Brunswick did not learn of it until after the columns had departed.

The Bound Brook station, eight miles up the Raritan River west of New Brunswick, was nearest to the British army. The little force assigned there could briefly delay any thrust by the enemy toward

General Benjamin Lincoln (1733-1810). *(Portrait by Charles Willson Peale, 1784)*

Morristown and warn Washington and the main army of an impending invasion. The detachment could also block an English attempt to ferry supplies up the Raritan River.

The American line of patrol extended along the north bank of the Raritan River. It ran from the Van Veghten Bridge south to a bend in the river. From here any movements on the Raritan Landing bridge could be observed. Patrols extended five or six miles and covered the three bridges across the river. The detachment there was commanded by Major General Benjamin Lincoln. In February 1777, its outpost consisted of 1,000 men, but had been reduced by expiring militia enlistments to 500 men by mid-March. Since only Pennsylvania troops and a Continental artillery company remained, Lincoln was apprehensive. The nearest help was fifteen miles away in Morristown. He warned General Washington that there was no support to "render the least assistance to this post in case it is attacked." He added that he was keeping wagons ready in case a sudden departure was required.[8]

Redcoat Deception

In February 1777, British General Cornwallis, second in command at New Brunswick, asked the Hessian Jäger Captain Ewald to draft a plan of attack on Bound Brook. As Ewald recorded, "Lord Cornwallis showed his confidence in me by with entrusting me with drawing up a plan for a surprise attack on Bound Brook. But since it was necessary for a column to cross the Raritan above Bound Brook, the attack was postponed until spring."[9]

The winter drew on without incident, and Ewald complained about standing guard duty and patrolling up river in the deep snow. However, it was a comfortable winter in New Brunswick, for the British army and their German allies had been abundantly supplied from British-held New York City. The captain commented in his diary, "But the men lacked for nothing for most of the excellent provisions of salted beef and pork, peas, butter, rice and flower for bread, along with the best Englis [*sic*] beer. With the end of the month we watched the snow disappear and everything was green in a few days"[10] Ewald led a foraging raid on the town two weeks before the main action at Bound Brook, writing, "We drove the enemy outposts across the causeway into the town and returned without loss with booty of 15 head of oxen, which enemy soldiers had grazed on our side of the causeway."[11]

On the night of April 12, 1777 the Redcoats and Hessians at New Brunswick were poised to strike. The predawn, four-pronged strike was launched early the next day. Concealed by darkness with part of the assault force with cannons, the force moved up along present-day Easton Avenue to Raritan Landing, (now at Landing Lane in Johnson Park and the campus of Rutgers University). There the group split. Under Hessian Colonel Carl von Donop, the main body continued up the left, or Bound Brook, side of the river, and headed directly toward the Queen's Bridge that allowed access to the town across the Raritan River. To avoid detection, and to block a possible American route to retreat to Morristown, the other detachment, commanded by Major General James Grant and led by Ewald's Jägers, broke off and crossed the bridge at Raritan Landing. They advanced up River Road on the right side of the river toward Bound Brook, avoiding main roads while moving as stealthily as possible.

A third column on the left, commanded by Lord Cornwallis and Colonel William Harcourt, attacked from the west. It moved up through what today is Franklin and Piscataway Townships to Weston Canal Road. There it crossed the river on the Van Veghten Bridge to Finderne Road. The objective of this thrust was to capture American

General Benjamin Lincoln. This position was defended by Proctor's American artillery with three four-pounder cannons.

A fourth column of light infantry commanded by Major Maitland swept the east side through Piscataway and moved along the base of the Watchung Ridge to cut off any escape by the Americans to the hills in the north. By daybreak, all but this fourth detachment reached positions surrounding the outpost. Soon, the tranquil countryside would be shattered by volleys of cannon blasts and clattering musket fire.

The British plan was to surprise the American riverbank outpost at Bound Brook on April 13, 1777. They would then encircle the town and block the small garrison of Patriots from escaping into the Watchung Mountains. In the confusion they hoped that they might also be able to capture their commander, General Benjamin Lincoln. At first their strategy was completely successful. Four columns, a contingent of 7,000 Redcoats and their Hessian allies, marched seven miles from New Brunswick. The entire force, undetected by American sentries, arrived outside the town before sunrise, where they rested until daybreak. Their signal to launch the onslaught would be at the moment they heard the American sentries shouting, "All is well!" followed by the morning gunshot fired to confirm that all was secure.

Hessian Captain Ewald and his band of Jägers were the first to reach the town. He reported, "I was ordered to form the advanced guard of General Grant's column. At daybreak I came upon an enemy picket on this side of the stone causeway which led to Bound Brook through a marsh. . . ."[12] At this point he and his men had to cross over a stone arched bridge that spanned the Bound Brook itself on the edge of the town. A few yards from the end of the span the Patriots had built the "Half Moon Battery." This redoubt or small fortified position blocked entry into town. As the Hessian soldiers poured over the narrow span they were pinned down by deadly fire from the American soldiers in the redoubt.

Ewald wrote in his diary, "At daybreak I came upon an empty picket on this side of the stone causeway which led to Bound Brook through a marsh along the Raritan River for five or six hundred paces over two bridges. The picket received us spiritedly and withdrew under a steady fire. I tried to keep as close as possible to the enemy to get across the causeway into the town at the same time. This succeeded to the extent that I arrived at the second bridge at a distance of a hundred paces from the redoubt which covered it and the flying bridge (Queen's Bridge). The day dawned and I was exposed to murderous fire."[13]

Stunned Patriots Spring into Action

The resounding racket caused by the intense musket fire that ensued at the redoubt alerted the 500 Americans defending Bound Brook. Soon the elite force of Jägers were close to being annihilated, and after fifteen minutes their valiant assault faltered. They were saved by Hessian Colonel Donop's troops from the main column advancing north from New Brunswick along the side of the river where the D&R Canal is today. These reinforcements crossed the Queen's Bridge over the Raritan River a few yards from the redoubt and quickly overwhelmed the Half Moon position. As a result, the Americans were forced to abandon the battery. Ewald's survivors, together with the thousands of troops from Donop's column, then skirmished with the outnumbered Americans who stubbornly resisted their advance through the streets of Bound Brook.

Ewald wrote, "Luckily for us Colonel Donop's column appeared after a lapse of eight or ten minutes whereupon the Americans abandoned the Redoubt. We arrived in town with the garrison of the redoubt amidst a hard running fight and the greater part were either cut down or captured."[14]

Curiously, remnants of the Old Stone Arch Bridge where the Jägers were pinned down can still be seen today. Built in 1731, it is one of the few remaining battlefield resources in New Jersey for which a first-hand action account exists. The triple arch crossing was constructed as a link over the old channel of the Bound Brook. It was part of Old York Road, one of the main highways across New Jersey, connecting New York and Philadelphia in the 18th century. When a railroad was built nearby, the Bound Brook was diverted so it would no longer pass under this bridge. Since the early 1870s the Old Stone Arch Bridge has been almost completely buried by fill due to construction of the railroad embankment. It is exposed above the tops of the arches and underlies a more recent road. Local historians are understandably concerned that 18-wheeler trucks are allowed to regularly pass over the remains of the fragile structure. Its location is off South Main Street at the approach to an industrial zone. It was placed on the National Register of Historic Places in 2008.

General Cornwallis, commander of the entire operation, took a longer route to the south through Franklin and Piscataway Townships with a column of 2,000 men. He crossed the river over the Van Veghten Bridge onto Finderne Road in Bridgewater. By using this route he could attempt to encircle the town and score a twofold victory by both blocking an American retreat toward the mountains and capturing the headquarters of General Lincoln. Local historians dispute the identity of the house where General Lincoln was headquartered that morning. Some say it was in the house of Peter Williamson, known as the Battery house, situated in the eastern part of the village and at the half moon battery. Others maintain it was the Van Horne House in the same area. A short distance south of this house the Patriots had constructed a blockhouse surrounded by earthworks to prevent any river crossing from that direction. Proctor's Artillery Company manned this position with three four-pounder cannons.

At daybreak, the sentries who had been posted near the house heard the roll of drums and the report of cannon. The sudden appearance of the Redcoat dragoon grenadiers and light infantry startled the Americans, who only managed to shout, "To arms!" before they were overwhelmed. The frantic cries of the sentries awoke General Lincoln and his staff. They were stunned to see the enemy only 200 yards away from their house. Lincoln vaulted onto his horse without putting on his uniform and began leading his surviving soldiers out of the town between the gap of the rapidly closing British pincers. One of his aides was captured and all his baggage and records were taken. Hessian Colonel Von Donop reported that General Lincoln "must have retired *en Profond Négligé*" [profoundly undressed or naked].[15]

Ewald describes the incident: "In the evening Colonel Harcourt with 50 horse, two light infantry battalions and a battalion of British grenadiers crossed the Raritan River below the Van Veghten Bridge and arrived behind Horne's plantation where generals Lincoln and Wayne lay in their quarters under cover of three 4-pounders mounted in the rear of the enemy quarters. The guard was partly cut down and partly captured, the tree cannon seized and the two generals fled without their breeches."

The attack by Cornwallis's column prompted the Americans to begin abandoning the blockhouse where Proctor's artillery company had been decimated. Most of its men were killed or captured, and their cannons were seized. Had the alarm from the sentries come only a few minutes later or had the Cornwallis plan for surrounding the Americans been better organized, the entire American force at Bound Brook might have been encircled and captured. The British strategy was muddled by Ewald's early skirmishing, which alerted the Americans, as well as the late arrival of Major Maitland's column closing in from the north at Green Brook. The crown forces were not able to cut off the route to Morristown, and most of the 500-man garrison escaped into the mountains.[16] Ewald exaggerated American losses, "Every American who could took flight. But since the light infantry had not come up close enough around Green Brook only 300 men were captured, among whom were the adjutant of General Lincoln, one captain, and two officers."[17]

The escaping Americans swiftly fell back along current Vosseller Avenue toward the first ridge of the Watchung Mountains. They managed to maintain brisk musket fire as they retreated, and after reaching the higher ground they rallied and attempted to make a stand. After the overwhelming British forces began reforming and returning heavy fire, the Patriots continued their retreat to the safety of the mountains. The British looted the outpost at Bound Brook and captured Proctor's three cannons, along with ammunition and supplies. They returned to New Brunswick later that morning. Ewald's diary reads, ". . . afterward the place was ransacked and plundered because all the inhabitants were rebellious-minded, and then the entire corps withdrew along the road from Bound Brook to New Brunswick, and the enemy who had rushed support from Basking Ridge showed himself only at a distance."[18]

Aftermath

Washington responded immediately to the setback, and American reinforcements arrived in the town soon after the action. He also sent a large force from Basking Ridge under Major General Nathanael Greene to reoccupy Bound Brook. Although Greene hurried to support Lincoln, it was past midday when he reached the town, and the British had already left the area. However, Greene was able to send a detachment to harass the British rear guard, and his unit caught up with the Redcoats near Raritan Landing and killed eight and captured sixteen of the enemy.

In fact, thousands of British and Hessian soldiers had caught the American defenders at Bound Brook by surprise. Although the Patriots valiantly attempted to defend the town, in the end their efforts failed. The overwhelming numbers of the British and Hessian troops doomed the Americans, who soon withdrew into the hills with their commanding General Benjamin Lincoln. The British captured American artillery and a number of officers and men, but their triumph was essentially fruitless. Their four columns had not been able to close the trap and the shocked Americans took advantage of their brief time to resist and escape. 1 side reported that about thirty Americans were killed and eighty or ninety captured. Among the British and Hessians Howe claimed no deaths and seven men wounded. General Lincoln reported that sixty of his men were killed or wounded. The New Jersey Militia assigned to guard the Raritan River crossings was blamed for allowing the large enemy force to reach the town without detection.

Curiously, the valiant Captain Ewald, who both developed and led the successful attack, was admonished for his role in the battle. He was blamed for being too aggressive and alerting the Americans that a major British offensive had begun. He laments, "I learned later that I was accused of attacking too rashly. I should have been advised if this attack was to have been a faint, for then I would have only skirmished with the enemy picket. General Grant said to me, Captain Ewald, you know the area, I say nothing further to you. You know everything else."

It was quite normal for Ewald's Jägers to lead attacks and he was often in the front line of other skirmishes and battles in New Jersey, including an action at Mount Holly in 1778. His diary is a fascinating account of his adventures and was written ". . . with much toil and many a drop of sweat." Forgotten after its completion in 1791, it is a great contribution to the literature of the American Revolution and is the most significant work of any Hessian leader.

In May 1777 General Washington pulled back the garrison from Bound Brook but moved a large part of the Continental army from Morristown to a new camp at Middlebrook. This position was in the well protected hills overlooking the town. From this high ground the movement of the British army in the plains below and as far Perth Amboy and New Brunswick could be observed.

In June 1777 Howe and his entire force of 18,000 men attempted to draw Washington out of the Watchung Hills. Washington, outgunned and out manned, knew that defeat at the time would end the war in favor of the British. Thus he was unwilling to confront this superior force in a general engagement and refused to leave the security

The Battle of Bound Brook is reenacted each April with colonial crafters, encampment, children's activities, special programs and tours, all coordinated by the Friends of the Abraham Staats House. *(Author's collection)*

of Middlebrook. On June 26, Howe tried unsuccessfully to trap Lord Stirling's detachment at Woodbridge, Edison, Scotch Plains and Plainfield. This advance was repulsed at the Battle of Short Hills and the British army withdrew through Westfield, Rahway and Perth Amboy to Staten Island. By June 30, 1777 no Crown troops remained in New Jersey.

Bound Brook has always been a tenacious town and has survived the ravages of warfare as well as natural shocks. Its location on the confluence of waterways has pervaded its history. The Raritan River and its tributaries—the Middle Brook and Green Brook—which comprise the western and eastern boundaries of the town, made it a critical place during the Revolutionary War. However, the site of the town has been its misfortune. Over the past 200 years of recorded weather history frequent flooding repeatedly devastates the town and its environs.

Chapter 2

Mayhem on the Millstone (1777)

Manville, Millstone, Somerset, Franklin Township, Blackwell's Mills

Lieutenant Colonel Allan Maclean of the 84th Regiment of Foot, British Forces in America, wrote, "The Rebels have the whole winter gone upon a very prudent plan of constantly harassing our quarters with skirmishes and small parties, and always attacking our foraging parties. By this means they gradually accustom their men to look us in the face and stand fire which they never dared to attempt in the field." This Regiment was made up of Scottish soldiers who had served in the French and Indian War and then had stayed in America. It's officer corps was one of the oldest and most experienced of any regiment in North America.

General George Washington's army crossed the ice-choked Delaware on the night of December 25–26, 1776. Over the next ten days, the American forces won three critical battles. After Washington surprised and defeated a daunting outpost of Hessian mercenaries in Trenton on December 26, the Patriots were again victorious at the Second Battle of Trenton on January 2. A day later he executed a daring night march to achieve another coup at the Battle of Princeton. These victories against an enemy which the Americans had deemed invincible preserved the unity of the Continental army, reasserted American control of much of New Jersey, and greatly improved the waning morale of the troops and nation.

After these startling defeats, Cornwallis and the combined British and Hessian troops camped near Trenton and Princeton, then withdrew toward the north to regroup in New Brunswick and the adjacent villages of Bonhamtown and Piscatawaytown. This would allow the Crown forces to gather forage to feed their horses during the winter and subsist on provisions from the bountiful countryside that stretched ten miles west to the Watchung Mountains. They were now in a good strategic position, since it allowed the Redcoat army to either engage the Continental army or to withdraw back to their New York City headquarters.

Violent skirmishes occurred north and west of New Brunswick in the Raritan Valley and along the Millstone River during the first half of 1777 when the Americans assaulted foraging parties and raided the British front lines. Constant struggles occurred at Quibbletown and Samptown. Quibbletown (New Market area today) encompassed adjacent parts of Plainfield, South Plainfield. Dunellen, Middlesex, Bound Brook, Green Brook and Franklin Township. Samptown is today's town of South Plainfield. The massive effort to gain supplies and limit the enemy's access to provisions was the focus of most operations on both sides in New Jersey during the first half of 1777. Feeding and maintaining an army of 16,000 troops and civilian support personnel was a daunting challenge for the British.[1] This conflict over foraging has often been overlooked in the Revolutionary War histories of the Garden State.

No major battles occurred during the "forage war" of the winter of 1776–1777. But, for the Americans and their British adversaries, with their main armies gathered in New Jersey, it was an unusually dynamic time. After the losses at Trenton and Princeton and with supplies exhausted, the Crown forces were on the defensive. Their occupation was limited to the narrow corridor from Princeton to New Brunswick. Everywhere else they were vulnerable to the ambushes of a confrontational local militia defending their homes in nearby villages.

Opposing Armies Relocate North for the Winter

During the first week in January, the Continental Army withdrew
north of Princeton. This move placed Washington's troops in a
dangerous position where they could be trapped between the British
contingent remaining in Princeton and the rest of the British army in
New Brunswick. The American's only other option would be to go on
the offensive and attack the larger British force. But General
Washington, with his exhausted and outnumbered troops, decided to
move northwest, fifty miles up the Millstone River Valley toward the
security of the mountains surrounding Morristown, New Jersey.
Because of its geographic location this place could be strongly fortified
and used as winter quarters. There the Patriots would be protected by
the ridges of the Watchung Mountains and the impassible morass of
the Great Swamp. This encampment offered both maximum security
and a base to raid the British lines and harass their foraging parties.

Signs of British apprehension encouraged General Washington.
He considered their frantic foraging to be major evidence of their
distress. Their overall plan was to defeat the Continental Army in a
final decisive battle and occupy the critical crossroads state, but this
could not proceed without provisions and forage. The impending
action centered on the Raritan Valley, running north and west of New
Brunswick to the Millstone River Valley—bountiful flat land with
rich farms ripe for foraging.

On January 3, only a day after their defeat at Princeton, an
advanced Redcoat supply column began marching north toward New
Brunswick. Near Ten Mile Run, a tributary of the Millstone River,
the Redcoats stumbled into a New Jersey Militia cavalry unit, the
"Somerset Horse," commanded by Captain John Stryker, who was
killed later that year at the Battle of Brandywine. Some historical
accounts claim that the Americans surrounded and captured the
British wagons and promptly sent five of them which were loaded
with warm woolen clothing to Washington's freezing troops huddled

around campfires in Morristown. Captain Thomas Rodney of the Delaware Line, commanding a lead column that was heading towards Somerset Courthouse, recorded a completely different version of this event in his diary. "We then marched on to a little village called Stone Brook or Summerset Court House about 15 miles from Princeton where we arrived just at dusk. About an hour before we arrived here 150 of the enemy from Princeton and 50 which were stationed in this town went off with 20 wagons laden with clothing and Linen, and 400 of the Jersey Militia were afraid to fire on them and let them go off unmolested, and there were no troops in our army fresh enough to pursue them, or the whole might have been taken in a few hours."[2]

As British and Hessians accelerated their plundering there were more frequent attacks on their foraging raiders during the next week. This successful hit and run harassment spread to Newark and Rahway (then known as Spanktown), and Elizabethtown. However, a widespread resumption of the war during midwinter was not realistic for either side. Military activities typically came to a standstill during the winter months of the American Revolution. Hostilities would break off in the late fall when both sides would go into permanent winter camp for several months and suspend most activities until spring. With the harsh weather and energy requirements, armies needed a time to rest, recuperate and repair equipment.

General Washington also had his internal problems. At this time, lack of new enlistments and desertions had cut his effective fighting force to only about 2,500 men. The enlistment terms of many of his troops had ended so they returned home. A natural disaster also loomed to threaten the Patriots when a smallpox epidemic spread through the encampments surrounding Morristown.

Washington correctly perceived that harassing British supply lines and preventing foraging would stop the British from occupying and controlling New Jersey. He explained this to Major General Joseph Spencer of Connecticut, who was assigned to the Eastern Division of the Continental Army, writing "The enemy are very much distressed for provisions and forage and unless they make a push to extricate themselves, they must in a manner perish this winter."[3] On January 12, 1777, Washington sent this correspondence to the Continental Congress: "The Enemy have made no move since my last, by every Account they begin to be distressed, particularly for Forage, of which there is little or none remaining in the small circle they possess, except salt and hay."[4]

The Americans still needed protection on the plains below the Watchung Mountains. Passes through these natural defenses at Chimney Rock in Bridgwater, Quibbletown, Stony Brook and Scotch Plains allowed British access to western New Jersey. Washington placed a defense line of outposts along the waterway formed by the Bound Brook, the Green Brook and the Raritan River. These outlying stations could warn the Continental Army of any mass movement of the Crown forces to the west and attempt to delay their advance.

The British made repeated attempts to lure Washington's forces down onto the open plains during the first half of 1777. Whipping the debilitated Americans with superior forces in a European style battle on the open plains could be the final decisive battle of the war. Retaking the plains of central New Jersey and liberating the beleaguered civilian population which was suffering from the incessant constant plundering was a tempting prospect for Washington. Yet despite the urging of his more belligerent officers, he held back the Continental Army from venturing out of the Watchung Mountains.

Two significant engagements occurred along the line of outposts during the turbulent spring season of 1777. Actions at Bound Brook and the Short Hills, now Edison, Plainfield and Scotch Plains, were tactical defeats for the feeble Patriot army, but it survived to fight on.

British commanders retaliated against the devastating American attacks on their foragers by severe reprisals on all Somerset County farmers. Their troops indiscriminately pillaged the homes of both Loyalist civilians and Patriots. The Loyalists, abandoned by their British protectors, were then confronted by both hostile military forces and their vengeful American neighbors. This had the immediate effect of transforming the largely Loyalist population in the area into strong supporters of independence. Many Tories fighting with the British forces changed sides and citizens that had taken the oath of allegiance to the Crown swore loyalty to the Continental Congress. In the January 30, 1777 edition of the *Pennsylvania Evening Post*, a correspondent wrote: "Many of the inhabitants who received written protections, are now determined to return them to his Britannic Majesty's Commissioners in cartridges."[5]

A Nest of Hornets

A British officer described walking into an American ambush as stumbling into "a nest of hornets." During the first two weeks of January 1777 the morale of the New Jersey Militia and Continental troops was high, and they challenged every British sortie that was on the move, one of which ventured out five miles from Raritan Landing in New Brunswick to scout for foraging opportunities along the Raritan and Millstone rivers. Nearby American forces composed of 600 infantry troops from the 1st Connecticut Militia and the 8th Virginia occupied nearby Samptown and Quibbletown at this time. Their superior knowledge of the roads and terrain in the disputed locale was indispensable. Both armies roamed through the area on a daily basis, and frequently exchanged gunfire. When it appeared that encounters with the Redcoats were diminishing, emboldened Patriots began attacking British bases along the Raritan River.

Colonel Charles Scott, a local American commander, was a demanding officer, and his men hit the British hard. After being promoted to colonel in 1776, Scott's Virginia Regiment fought in the victory at Trenton and the subsequent Battle of Assunpink Creek (also known as the Second Battle of Trenton) on January 2, 1777. As Washington's main force prepared to spend the winter in Morristown,

Scott's regiment was based at nearby Chatham. From Chatham he could conduct light infantry raids against British foraging parties. The American army was also in desperate need of supplies during the hard winter months, so Scott's orders were to strip all the farms between the Watchung Mountains and the Raritan River of food, forage, livestock and wagons before the British could seize these items.[6] His forces successfully gathered supplies, but lacked the horses and wagons to transport them, so the plunder was stockpiled in Samptown and Quibbletown.

American foragers were reluctant to plunder Patriot civilians and were careful to provide them with receipts for purloined property. British officer Charles Stedman, a Loyalist who served under Howe and later as an examiner of Loyalist claims of the British government, had first-hand knowledge of many of the campaigns and the persons involved in the war. He complains about the treatment of Tories by American soldiers, "And it is but justice to say that the Americans never took anything from their friends, but in cases of necessity they uniformly gave receipts for what they did take, always living as long as they could upon their enemies, and never suffering their troops to plunder their friends with impunity. But at the same time it is to be noticed that the American troops were suffered to plunder the Loyalists, and to exercize with impunity every act of barbarity on that unfortunate class of people frequently inflicting on them even scorges and stripes." After the war property lost to the enemy was inventoried by the states but their claims were rarely followed up with any compensation

The ravenous Redcoats did not limit themselves with stealing forage; they stripped the homes of both Patriots and Tories of anything of value. A remarkable record of the property lost to their plundering can be found on claims filed after the war. As an example, the farm of Gabriel Compton of Woodbridge was raided in 1777. He lost one silver-hilted sword, one musket and bayonet, six acres of grain on the ground, three acres of good rotted flax, a post fence which was five rails high, and twenty tons of salt hay. His relative David Compton, a neighbor, also lost all his post and rail fencing. In addition, his fruit trees were stripped and destroyed, livestock was stolen, his barn was burned down, and his house heavily damaged. At the same time, James Ayers, also living nearby, had his house burned down and lost "seven tons of hay in the meadow," three guns with accoutrements, fencing, 100 apple trees and two acres of young timber.

The Crown Forces Grow Desperate

On January 13, a detachment of several hundred British and Hessian foragers advanced from New Brunswick. They marched west to Millstone, also known as Somerset Courthouse, which today is the town of East Millstone, in Somerset County. After staying in the village for about a week they withdrew back to New Brunswick. Along the route they burned houses, plundered property and stole livestock. This forceful incursion caused New Jersey Militia companies to assemble in support of Scott's Continental troops and to set up an outpost at Millstone. From that time onward, the area west of New Brunswick up to the Millstone and Raritan Rivers was considered hostile by both sides.

Captain Johann Ewald, the intrepid Hessian diarist, mentions the incident as an exchange of gunfire on January 13 at Bound Brook and Quibbletown, after which " . . . the jäger post duty now became quite serious, since Bound Brook and Quibbletown were less than an hour's march away. The teasing now occurred daily, and when they did not visit us, we rendered the honors to the Americans. Not only did the men have to stay dressed day and night, but they had to be kept together, the horses constantly saddled, and everything packed."[7]

On January 14, Washington again wrote to Congress from Morristown, this time reporting that the British were at "Amboy and Brunswick," and that "our Accounts still confirm their want of Forage, which I hope will increase."[8] On January 17, Washington advised

Congress that the British were "endeavouring to draw in all the Forage they can get, in the course of which, they have daily Skirmishes with our advanced parties."[9] The same day he wrote to Major General Joseph Spencer, saying, "The Enemy, by being drove back from most part of the province of Jersey, on which they depended for Subsistence, are much distressed for Provision and Forage, and unless they make a push to extricate themselves, they must in a Manner perish this Winter."[10]

Washington continued to revel over the fact that the Crown forces still appeared to be desperate for supplies and that his tactic of surprise harassment was disrupting their foraging efforts. Charles Stedman noted that, despite vastly outnumbering the Americans, the Redcoats by the end of January were restricted to occupying only New Brunswick and controlling the route to Perth Amboy: "By venturing out of this area they suffered great losses in skirmishes. The excursions that the garrison of Brunswick made for forage, were often attended with fatal consequences; and as the American army had extended their line of cantonments from Morris Town to Woodbridge, within three miles of Amboy, the provisions that were forced to be conveyed by land to Brunswick were often cut off by parties of the enemy, who were always on the watch, and to whom intelligence was regularly conveyed by those persons who inhabited the space of ground between Amboy and Brunswick."[11]

Stedman also lamented the wholesale plundering of civilians by his own army: "But no sooner had the army entered the Jerseys. Then the business of plunder began. The friend and the foe from the hand of rapine shared alike. The people's property was taken without being paid for or even a receipt given, which would have been evidence that such property was taken; leaving the payment or nonpayment to be determined by the issue of the war and the political merit of the parties. The British foraged indiscriminately, procuring considerable supplies of hay, oats, Indian corn, cattle and horses; which were never or very seldom paid for."[12]

An American Success at Van Nest's Mill

After the battles of Trenton and Princeton the New Jersey Militia harassed British foraging parties until only large groups of over 1,000 to 1,500 men dared to venture out from their base at New Brunswick. After enlistments for most of the Continental soldiers in Washington's army expired at the end of the year in 1776 the New Jersey Militia formed most of the armed forces in the state. Until his army was reformed in the spring General Washington fought a partisan war with a small cadre of men from the Continental Army who were supported by thousands of the state's citizen soldiers.

These part-time combatants incessantly attacked enemy outposts and foraging parties, often without the support of any Continental regulars. Instead of recuperating and repairing equipment during the winter of 1776–1777, the Crown forces had to man outposts and send out large forces to protect the foragers scouring the countryside for desperately needed supplies. Militia companies served only when there was an immediate and real threat. The Patriot citizens of the Raritan Valley proved they could effectively resist the plundering. The actions of these New Jersey state troops had such a devastating effect through the winter of 1777 that it changed the entire course of the war, and British General Howe abandoned his plans to march overland to take Philadelphia. Their aggressive behavior at the time is proof that their belief in the invincibility of the Redcoat regulars had been dispelled at Trenton and Princeton.

On January 20, 1777, General Philemon Dickinson led about 400 New Jersey militiamen and 50 Pennsylvania Continental Army soldiers in battle. The British suffered 25 killed or wounded and 12 taken prisoner. In addition, they lost 43 supply wagons, 104 irreplaceable horses, 115 head of cattle and 70 sheep.

That day began when a large British foraging party of about 500 men left New Brunswick and headed west toward the Millstone River. Lieutenant Colonel Robert Abercromby of the 37th Regiment of Foot led the raiding party. They moved out sluggishly, dragging along many empty wagons in hopes that they would return laden with captured provisions, forage and livestock. The British objective was to plunder the stores of a Patriot stockpile located at Van Nest's Mill in today's Weston section of Manville, about five miles north of Millstone. When Abercromby's raiders reached the mill, they planned to seize cattle, sheep, barrels of flour and other supplies, then quickly return to New Brunswick before the fearsome American militiamen arrived.

The Redcoat detachment reached the mill after plodding eight miles across the flat land of what today is Franklin Township. The gristmill sat close to a bridge over the Millstone River. Before moving up a road that led directly to the mill Abercromby posted a rear guard of Hessian soldiers with three cannons at the bridge. These defenders could stop the Americans from crossing the bridge to attack his marauders as they sacked the cache of supplies.

The militia companies stationed at Quibbletown had become more assertive and had gone on the offensive by assaulting enemy outposts near New Brunswick. Early that day, a network of patriotic citizens warned the militia that a large British foraging party was leaving New Brunswick and heading to the supply hoard at Van Nest's Mill. The militia had been recently reinforced by the company of 50 Pennsylvania riflemen from the Continental Army. This force was commanded by Philemon Dickinson.

Dickinson was commissioned as a colonel of the Hunterdon County militia at the beginning of the Revolutionary War. In 1776 he was elected as a delegate to New Jersey's Provincial Congress. He was destined to lead 400 militia troops in the punishing raid on a British foraging party near the Somerset Courthouse. This victorious action earned him an appointment as major general in command of all New Jersey Militia, a post he held throughout the rest of the war. Dickinson's militia took part in the Battle of Monmouth in 1778 and helped obstruct the retreat of the British to Sandy Hook. Dickinson and his brigade then fought well at the Battle of Springfield in June 1780. After the war he served as a U.S. Senator for New Jersey in 1790–93.[13]

When the New Jersey Militia with the Pennsylvania riflemen reached the approach to the bridge that led to the mill they faced the muzzles of the Hessian defense cannons. The weapons instantly erupted by spraying volleys of grapeshot into their ranks. Grapeshot was the prime anti- personnel ammunition. It transformed cannons into huge shotguns that had a devastating effect on infantry, especially at close range, Dickinson instantly recognized that trying to cross the heavily defended bridge was impossible. He ordered his men to follow the river bank until they were beyond the range of the hostile gunfire. Local men guided the American soldiers until they reached a place where they could wade waist deep into icy water to ford the turbulent river.

The enemy had completed loading their wagons with booty and was now in the process of leaving the mill. The Millstone River is normally about fifty yards wide and a couple of feet deep, but at this time of year the waterway, swelled by January thawing, was a torrent overflowing its ice-encrusted banks. As a result, the British column clashed with the frost-bitten soldiers as they emerged from the freezing water. The Redcoat raiders believed Dickinson's force had withdrawn after being brought to a standstill at the bridge and were astonished to see them suddenly reappear.

The Americans surprised the British wagon train in the lane near the mill before it reached the main road leading to the bridge. Their musket fire struck the first wagon and horses, and the entire procession came to an abrupt stop as the wagon drivers scattered. The British foragers fled toward the bridge and left their plunder behind.

American Samuel Sutphen, serving under William Houston, described the scene, "Our army got so timely to Millstone that by what I can learn we got 1/2 of the Enemy's wagons, and plunder; we took several of their English wagons, and others, likewise a great number of new Sacks of wheat, flour, meat, Horses, Cattle, sheep, Hay and several other Articles, which we found scattered every way along the streets and through the woods, where they had thrown them away, in their haste . . ."[14] A slave from Bridgewater, Sutphen served in the militia as a substitute for his master, who in return promised him freedom after the war. He was caught in the middle of the fighting and provided an unusually detailed and vivid description of the engagement when he applied for a pension many years after the war. He claimed to have guided the Americans to the fording place where they crossed to surprise the enemy at Van Nest's Mill. History has forgotten this heroic African American who fought in the battles of Long Island and Princeton and who was later shot in the leg during the Sullivan Campaign against the Iroquois Nations.

Unfortunately, his owner broke his promise and sold Sutphen to a new master after the war, where he remained in bondage for several more years. This was Private Samuel Sutphen's lucid recollection in 1834 when he was age eighty-seven:

In the spring following, probably March [the month should be January], *a party of the enemy from* N[ew] B[runswick] *came out to Van Ess mills on the Millstone. A party of militia under Lieut. Davis was stationed near the two bridges, when an express rider on a black horse from Col. Frelinghuysen gave tidings of the enemy at V. Ess mills. A party of Hessians, about 1 company (70), an escort for these teams from Brunswick, was discovered secreted behind a hedge with some 4 or 5 field pieces. They fired upon us and retreated. We followed on a piece, but Lt. Davis ordr'd us to retreat. Davis' Capt. Westcott from Cumberland had been left sick at Guysbert Bogert's, where he died, and was taken back to Cumberland Co. There was a large body of militia out, and Gen'l Dickinson commanded. The firing was principally across the river at the bridge.*

I piloted Davis' Co[mpany] and as many others as we could assemble to a fording place over the S[outh] branch, and hurried on to the mills. They had plundered the mill of grain and flour, and were on their way back to Brunswick, but had not got out of the lane leading from the mill to the great road. We headed them in the lane.

The team laden with the flour was the first we fell in with; the lane, 100 yards, was filled with 4-horse teams. Davis ordered us to fire, and then we shot part of the 1st team, which stopped the whole drove. The drivers left their teams and run. A guard escorting the teams made their escape. We took, as was said, about 40 horses, and all the waggons, about 10, which were all sent off under an escort to Morristown. A party of Hessians, about 1 company (70), an escort for these teams from Brunswick, was discovered secreted behind a hedge with some 4 or 5 field pieces. They fired upon us and retreated.

The ecstatic Dickinson wrote to Colonel John Nielson on January 23, "I have the pleasure to inform you that on Monday last with about 450 men, chiefly our militia, I attacked a foraging party near V. Nest Mills consisting of 500 men with 2 field pieces, which we routed after an engagement of 20 minutes and brought off 107 horses, 49 wagons, 115 cattle, 70 sheep, 40 barrels of flour—106 bags and many other things, 49 prisoners."[15]

An anonymous letter published in the *Pennsylvania Journal and Weekly Advertiser* on January 29, 1777 gives a more detailed account: "Last Monday a party of Jersey Militia, consisting of about 400, and about 50 of the Pennsylvania riflemen, marched to attack a body of the enemy, consisting of about 600, who were posted at a bridge at Millstone River, near Abraham Vannest's mill, which is two miles from Somerset Courthouse. In order more effectually to prevent our men from crossing, the enemy had placed three field pieces on a hill, about 50 yards from the bridge; when our men found it impossible to cross there, they went down the river, broke through the ice, waded across the river up to their middle. . . ."

General Washington, who often criticized the performance of the militia, wrote, "Genl Dickinsons behaviour reflects the highest honour upon him, for tho' his Troops were all raw, he lead them thro' the River, middle deep, and gave the Enemy so severe a charge, that, altho' supported by three field pieces, they gave way and left their Convoy . . . and only reported the taking of nine prisoners. . . ."[16]

Even the enemy commanders were amazed by the American feat. Archibald Robertson, a British officer, reported, "Lieutenant Colonel Abercromby with 500 men went on a foraging party towards Hillsborough. Part of this Corps was attacked by the Rebels, which occasion'd such disorder Amongst the Waggon Drivers that 42 Waggons were left behind." One British witness was "absolutely certain the attackers were not militia, they were sure that no militia would fight in that way."[17]

Captain Johann Ewald, the articulate Hessian diarist, does not mention the engagement at Van Nest's Mill, but notes a clash on January 13 at Bound Brook and Quibbletown, "The jäger post duty now became quite serious, since Bound Brook and Quibbletown were less than an hour's march away. The teasing now occurred daily, and when they did not visit us, we rendered the honors to the Americans. Not only did the men have to stay dressed day and night, but they had to be kept together, the horses constantly saddled, and everything packed."[18]

Finally, Washington again complimented the militia, when he reported to the Continental Congress, on January 22 1777, "I have the pleasure to inform you, that General Dickinson, with about 400 Militia, has defeated a foraging Party of the Enemy of an equal number, and has taken forty Waggons, and upwards of a hundred Horses, most of them of the English draft Breed, with a great number of Sheep and Cattle, which they had collected. The Enemy retreated with so much precipitation, that General Dickinson had only an opportunity of making nine prisoners, they were observed to carry off a good many dead and wounded in light Waggons. This Action happened near Somerset Courthouse, on Millstone River. Genl. Dickinsons behaviour reflects the highest honour upon him, for tho his Troops were all raw, he lead them thro the River, middle deep, and gave the Enemy so Severe a charge, that, although supported by three field pieces, they gave way and left their Convoy."[19]

Casualty reports from the action at Van Nest's Mill vary, and as usual were exaggerated by both sides to suit their individual purposes. The number of British soldiers killed, wounded, or captured appeared to have been about 30 according to press accounts. Dickinson claimed to have taken forty-nine prisoners and reported few militia casualties. The Americans lost four men and captured nine prisoners, and took about 40 wagons, 100 horses, 115 head of cattle, and 70 sheep.[20]

A Tory witness provided a wildly exaggerated estimate of American losses and was reluctant to admit the Americans were citizen soldiers of the militia, not the professional regulars of the Continental army. "A man who came from Brunswick this afternoon says, the enemy allow that they lost 35 or 36 men, but say the rebels lost 300. There were not more than 400 of our men crossed the river: The enemy reports that they were attacked by 3,000 of general Washington's troops there, and were absolutely certain that they were not militia, that they were sure that the militia would not fight in that way."[21]

Today, Millstone River Road runs along the west bank of the Millstone River between the towns of Manville and Millstone and is a busy thoroughfare that passes through the centers of both towns. Weston Canal Road follows the other side of the River, on the east bank, where the landscape is entirely different. There, the land bordering the river is heavily wooded, with a few farm houses and plowed fields, so the setting appears to look much as it did in 1777. Van Nest's Mill was in this vicinity at the time of the battle. The only current feature that was not here in 1777 is the Delaware and Raritan Canal, built between 1830 and 1834. This narrow man-made waterway parallels the river through this area but does little to change the appearance of the terrain.

The exact location of Van Nest's Mill can be found on two 18th century maps. *A map of the British outposts between Burlington and New Bridge, New Jersey in December* 1776 clearly identifies this place as "Vaness," a location is on the east side of the "Millstone Creek" about a mile south of the center of the present-day town of Manville, a town that did not exist in 1777. It is near a bridge. Hessian

Millstone River, ruins of Van Nest's Mill. (*Author's collection*)

Captain Ewald's map, *Plan of the Area of Bound Brook*, 20 *April 1777*, shows the entire region from Millstone to Bound Brook, and the area around the junction of the Millstone and Raritan Rivers. Ewald did not specifically point out Van Nest's Mill by name, but he does indicate a mill at the approach to the today's Wilbur Smith Bridge. This closely matches the place that appears on the December 1776 map. Elizabeth Menzies, in her book *Millstone Valley*, provides a 1968 photograph of a mill at Weston she claims the British targeted for "its flour and stores," and where they "were repulsed by General Dickinson's Continentals on January 21, 1777,"[22] but no details of its exact location are provided.

By using other landmarks, it appears that Van Nest's Mill was across the Millstone River on the eastern side next to the present-day

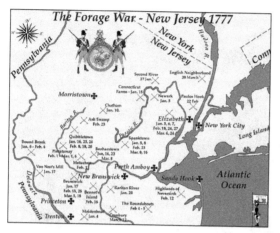

Locations of Forage War battles in New Jersey (*Courtesy Donald Moran, Sons of the American Revolution, Sons of Liberty Chapter, California Society*)

Wilbur Smith Bridge and across the river from the Sacred Heart Cemetery on Millstone River Road. The ruins of a structure lay beneath the Wilbur Smith Bridge, which would also support this location, and these remnants appear to be of 18th century construction. The Hessian cannons confronted Dickinson's force along this east bank of the Millstone River.

Where did the Americans ford the river to mount their surprise attack? We have the eyewitness account of the intrepid Samuel Sutphen. He reported leading Dickinson's troops about a mile from the bridge where they were able to wade across the river He claims that the crossing was made and across the south branch of the river. Since the Millstone River branches off the Raritan and flows south it can be considered a southern branch. Today the river widens and grows shallow about a mile north of the bridge. It is likely that the frigid crossing was made at that place.[23]

Chapter 3

Forage War Boils Over: Quibbletown, Samptown, and Spanktown (1777)

South Plainfield, Piscataway, Middlesex, Dunellen

The victorious engagement at Van Nest's Mill proved that General Washington was learning how to make use of the New Jersey Militia effectively. He encouraged the citizen soldiers to take the offense and attack in smaller units, tactics designed to disrupt the flanks of the enemy and exploit any weaknesses. Using this technique, they could suddenly attack a vulnerable target and withdraw quickly. By using surprise raids, sabotage and ambushes, the small and mobile militia groups, operating behind the enemy lines, could dominate the traditional larger and less flexible British army. Hundreds of small actions occurred after the action at Van Nest's Mill and continued through the spring of 1777.

The British responded by deploying infantry in greater numbers to support their plundering forays. Larger patrols, supported by cavalry, were specifically organized, trained, and equipped for this duty. Guerrilla tactics of the New Jersey Militia were so successful that on February 14, General Washington wrote to Major General William Heath, commander of forces in the Hudson River Highlands, "This would Oblige them to forage, with such large covering parties, that it would in a manner harass their Troops to death. We not only oblige them to forage with parties of 1500 and 2000 to cover, but every now and then, give them a sharp Brush."[1]

The British reacted swiftly after their humiliating rout at Van Nest's Mill. They knew their army would perish in New Jersey if they did not regain the initiative and the opportunity for unobstructed foraging, and they realized the need for immediate action along the Raritan and Millstone Rivers. British foraging parties had been random groups of lightly armed scavengers with trains of wagons loaded with pilfered supplies, but soon they became full expeditions of elite special forces with sufficient firepower to take offensive action. This chaotic period became known as the *petite guerre.*

British and Hessian troops withdrew from their posts in Elizabethtown and shifted to Perth Amboy, while the main army was billeted in New Brunswick to consolidate their forces. The army of American citizen farmers inspired by the victories at Trenton and Princeton kept the Crown forces isolated and enclosed in these towns. John Adams wrote to his wife Abigail on February 17, "Howe will repent his mad march through the Jersies. The People of the Commonwealth [New Jersey] begin to raise their spirits exceedingly, and to be firmer than ever. They are actuated by Resentment now and Resentment coinciding with Principle is a very powerful motive."[2]

Conditions for the Crown forces in the New Brunswick area were getting desperate. As the worst part of the winter began, Hessian Captain Ewald reported, "After a very exhausting campaign, these quarters, where the soldier could not even get straw for his bedding, were to serve for refreshing the troops. For this whole region has been completely sacked during the army's march during the past autumn and had been abandoned by all the inhabitants. The entire army has been stripped bare of shoes and stockings by the constant marching during the bad weather. Uniforms were torn, and the officers, especially those of the Jäger companies, had almost nothing on their bodies. The winter now began to set in severely, for snow had fallen for several days over a half-man deep."[3]

The most dynamic leader of the Continental Army during this *petite guerre* was General William Maxwell. One of George Washington's most capable generals, he had served well as commander of the New Jersey Continental Troops in several battles before the numerous engagements during the forage war. During 1775 he fought in Canada and then at Brandywine and Germantown. He served at the battles of Monmouth, the Short Hills, Connecticut Farms and Springfield. He was also with Sullivan in the campaign against the Iroquois Nations in 1779.

The *petite guerre* in central Jersey can better be understood today by reviewing the details and chronology of the most significant engagements that occurred in the winter and spring of 1777. The New Jersey Militia was elated by their success at Van Nest's Mill and quickly followed up by attacking two British Regiments near New Brunswick on January 23. This assault cost the Redcoats 30 to 40 men and several wounded.

Sir Henry Clinton, infuriated by being badly beaten by the part-time soldiers, sent 600 of his best troops, consisting of infantry and cavalry and a Hessian Jäger battalion, the next day. Their orders were to seize American supplies stored in Samptown. They marched ten miles from Raritan Landing at New Brunswick, through Piscataway, and looted farms along present day New Brunswick Avenue and New Market Road in South Plainfield.[4] The New Jersey Militia put up a strong defense but were unable to stop the British column that consisted of the finest professional soldiers in the Crown forces, and their outnumbered force was defeated near Quibbletown.

The British expedition was commanded by British Major General Alexander Leslie and Hessian Colonel Carl Emil Kirk von Donop. General Leslie reported that several men were killed and wounded on both sides, and that the Americans had suffered greater losses. General Washington later contradicted this claim in a letter to his brother, "Our scouts and the enemy's foraging parties have frequent skirmishes in which they always sustain the greatest loss in killed and wounded, owing to our superior skill in firearms."[5]

These British and Hessian commanders were among the best on the enemy side. After being promoted to brigadier general in 1776, Leslie fought in the Battle of Long Island, the landings at Kip's Bay, the Battle of White Plains, the Battle of Harlem Heights and at Princeton. He replaced Cornwallis as commander in the south in 1782. Von Donop was the senior German officer in southern New Jersey in late 1776 and was the commander of the Hessian garrisons and Jäger detachments in Trenton, Burlington and Bordentown. He was fatally wounded at the Battle of Red Bank, on October 22, 1777, which took place on the New Jersey side of the Delaware River just south of Philadelphia.

A Failed Redcoat Ambush Near Metuchen

Brigadier General Sir William Erskine recognized that direct engagement with the Patriots in places where they had the advantage of being familiar with the terrain were futile. He reasoned that an ambush might be a more

effective way to deal with the wily yeoman farmers. He sent a small party of foragers to Drake's Farm near Metuchen on February 1. Concealed behind a nearby hill was a combined force of a thousand British and Hessian troops. They included elite battalions of light infantry, grenadiers, and the 42nd Highlanders. This unit was supported by eight cannons. The 5th Virginia Regiment of the Continental Line, commanded by Brigadier General Charles Scott, fell into the trap; when they pounced on the small foraging party Erskine's force suddenly appeared as if out of nowhere.

Sir William Erskine, 1st Baronet. (messotint by Samuel William Reynolds, after Richard Cosway, early 19th century)

Instead of retreating, the Americans fought so fiercely that the much larger British force was driven back. The Virginians broke through the grenadier battalion by launching a vicious bayonet charge counterattack. Heavy cannon fire slowed the American advance, but the Patriots continued fighting until the British withdrew and fled back to New Brunswick. The British suffered 136 killed or wounded, and the Americans lost 30 to 40 men.[6]

This action was marked by an unfortunate incident. American Lieutenant William Kelly and six other wounded Americans were separated from the main force during the fighting. The frustrated British fell

General Charles Scott. (*Paul Sawyier (1865–1917), Kentucky Historical Society*)

upon the seven helpless men with bayonets and musket butts and slaughtered them all. When the Americans recovered the mangled bodies afterward they were infuriated. Brigadier General Adam Stephen exchanged angry letters with Erskine and wrote, "It is told that Sir William Erskine commanded the British troops covering the foraging party at Drake's farm, on Saturday the first instant, Is it possible that a gentleman, an officer so eminently distinguished for his bravery and experience, should allow troops under his command to murder the wounded after the manner of savages! . . . Mr. Kelly a brave officer in my brigade, and five other Virginians, slightly wounded in the muscular parts, were murdered, had their bodies mangled and their brains beat out, by troops of his Britanic Majesty. On Saturday the first instant."

Erskine denied all responsibility for the incident and replied,

However, I may mention that it is not to be wondered at if our soldiers are a little exasperated considering the many cruelities that have been late committed on them and their officers, even unarmed, passing singly from quarter to quarter.[7]

Despite this embarrassing defeat, Sir William Erskine was made Colonel of the 80th in March 1777. He led troops in the battles of Brandywine, Germantown and at Barren Hill, Pennsylvania, where a British force attempted to encircle a smaller American unit led by the Marquis de Lafayette. As Brigadier General, Erskine went on to lead troops at the Battle of Monmouth.

Brigadier General Adam Stephen, who wrote to Erskine, was a Scottish-born doctor and military officer who came to North America to serve in the Virginia Militia under George Washington during the French and Indian War. He continued to serve under Washington in the Revolutionary War, rising to lead a division of the Continental Army. In May 1777, he earned the censure of General Washington by reporting inflated casualty numbers from an incursion into the vicinity of Piscataway, New Jersey. After a friendly fire incident in the 1777 Battle of Germantown, Stephen was found to have been drunk during the battle and was subsequently cashiered out of the army.[8]

The Fox Stays in His Den

Lord Cornwallis decided to launch a massive invasion only a week later, on February 8. His plan was to march west across the flat land that stretched the ten miles between New Brunswick and the first ridge of the Watchung Mountains. It was here that General Washington and the Continental Army were encamped in the security of these hills. He left New Brunswick leading more than 6,000 men, in twelve regiments led by seven generals. This task force encompassed almost one quarter of all British troops in New Jersey.

Cornwallis had several objectives. The first was to lure Washington with the debilitated Continental Army down from the security of the hills at Middlebrook to defend the rich New Jersey countryside and engage in a general action. He could then engage the Americans with his superior force, and a victory there at that time would surely end the War for Independence.

By attaining military dominance in this breadbasket, Cornwallis would ensure that British foraging would again be productive enough to secure the supplies to sustain his huge force. The Patriots had stored substantial quantities of supplies in Quibbletown and Samptown. Capturing these goods would provide immediate relief to the starving Redcoats. Elsewhere, since the entire area had been totally stripped, there was nothing left to plunder, and Redcoat troops were subsisting on salt provisions imported from England. Thousands of men were crowded into the few remaining structures in the area, and on the filthy vermin-ridden transports docked on the river. Conditions grew worse over the winter and many soldiers became sick. Needless to say, these terrible conditions in the garrison towns depressed the spirits of the Crown Forces.[9]

The large British force fought their way into Quibbletown against heavy American resistance. Hessian Captain Johann Ewald describes the march from Raritan Landing and New Brunswick to the town.

The road leading from Raritan Landing to Quibbletown ran continuously through the woods, in which three devastated plantations were situated. At the first plantation, I ran into an enemy post of riflemen who withdrew after stubborn resistance, of whom several were killed and captured on their retreat. We followed this party so swiftly that we arrived with them before Quibbletown at the same time. The place lies on two hills between which a creek winds through a ravine that is spanned by two bridges. The stone walls around the gardens as well as the houses on both sides of the ravine were occupied by enemy riflemen who abandoned the village after strong resistance when artillery was brought up, and withdrew into the wood on the other side of the village.[10]

The attack on Quibbletown was two pronged. Cornwallis ordered General James Grant to drive toward Samptown with two regiments. Grant, an enemy officer despised by the Americans, has been described as the most vehemently anti-American officer of the Revolutionary War in these words: "Pompous, self-assured, dogmatic, obstinate, opinionated, these and more could adequately describe the obese Englishman whose hatred and low opinion of the Americans' ability to fight in the Revolutionary War probably did more to help the patriot cause than some of American generals."[11] Grant had begun degrading America's cause before the war while he was a member of Parliament, and his subsequent comments enraged the colonists and caused many who were neutral to become Patriots. His poor leadership of the British and German outposts in New Jersey aided Washington's successful attack on Trenton and Princeton as well as their success during the forage wars.

Although Brigadier General Charles Scott's men resisted bravely, they were forced to surrender their entire store of provisions. The Americans fell back into the Watchung Hills and General Washington avoided losing a battle with a force that was superior in numbers and weapons. As the columns of Lord Cornwallis withdrew to their base in New Brunswick, the Patriots inflicted heavy losses on the flanks and rear. In many ways this retreat was similar to the British retreat from Lexington and Concord to Boston two years earlier. Thirty British soldiers were killed and 30 were wounded. The Americans loss included 6 killed, 20 wounded and 6 captured.[12]

The most dynamic Continental officer during this action was General William Maxwell, who had taken over command of the militia in Morristown in late December 1776. He was directed, "therewith to give all the protection you can to the Country, and distress to the Enemy by harassing of them in their Quarters & cutting off their Convoys."[13] Washington also encouraged Maxwell to recruit soldiers for the New Jersey Continental regiments because one-year enlistments in that outfit were expiring. Maxwell's mobilization of the New Jersey Militia preceded the Continental Army's encampment in Morristown in January 1777, preparing them for a series of small scale battles between British foraging parties and New Jersey Militia coordinating with Continentals. Maxwell proved to be adept at this "hit-and-run open style of warfare" which the militia "successfully practiced against the British."[14]

American Brigadier General Henry Knox had nothing but praise for the response of the militia to the British offensive. "Nothing could exceed the spirit shown on this occasion by the much-injured people of the Jerseys," he said. "Not an atom of the lethargic spirit that possessed them last winter—all fire, all revenge."[15]

The Battle of Spanktown and a Violent Encounter at Bonhamtown

British Colonel Charles Mawhood commanded an elite force of grenadiers and light infantry. Mawhood had shown superior leadership at the Battle of Princeton, and his regiment was admired by the entire British army as one of its top units. His objective was to "surprise, surround and extirpate the Rebel army or at least a large piece of it."[16] He headed into harm's way on February 23, 1777 when he moved to attack what he believed was lightly defended Spanktown, which was a ten-mile march from Perth Amboy.

As the special forces approached the town, they came across a small detachment of New Jersey Militia herding cattle and sheep along the in the vicinity of a waterway called Robinson's Branch on the North Branch of the Rahway River. Mawhood ordered his captain, John Peebles, who led the Grenadier Company of the 42nd Highlanders, to lead an attack on the American's flank. As they rushed in, a force of Maxwell's Continentals sprang up from a concealed position and fired a crashing volley of musket fire into the Redcoats. This ambush completely surprised the Grenadiers, and although they bravely tried to rally, they were slaughtered. American General William Maxwell appears to have anticipated Mawhood's aggressive tactics based on his reputation and was able to turn this to an advantage.

Maxwell's Continental Army troops that arrived to support the militia included his New Jersey Brigade, Colonel Edward Hand's and

Colonel Daniel Brodhead's Pennsylvania Regiments, and Lieutenant Colonel George Stricker's Maryland Regiment. They drove back the British assault in an intense engagement, and after 26 grenadiers fell the British soldiers took flight back to Amboy. The empty wagons they had brought to carry away captured supplies were instead loaded with their wounded men.

Captain Peebles describes this horrific scene in vivid detail in one of the finest dairies to come out of the American Revolution, The Scottish grenadiers fought valiantly, but were "gall'd by fire and began dropping fast." In the thick of the fighting, Peebles found himself standing alone, as all of his men had fallen or fled. He admits to taking to his heels while the survivors of his unit scrambled for cover. "In this situation the men were dropping fast when they [his supporting troops] got orders to retire, which I heard nothing. I remained at my post until I had no one man left near me except John Carr lying wounded and fired away all my cartridges, when seeing the Rebels coming pretty close up, I took to my heels and ran back to the company. Under heavy fire which Thank God I escaped-in this affair, we had the worst of it for want of that support we had reason to expect from the rear."[17] The battle raged on for twelve hours with the Rebels beating off the British, who lost almost one hundred men.

Two different accounts were published the following week in Pennsylvania newspaper. Their casualty figures differ, and both list much higher casualties for the British than the Americans. It was typical of pro-Independence newspapers to inflate American numbers but minimize casualties. The following extracts of a letters dated February 26, 1777 was printed in the *Pennsylvania Journal and Weekly Advertiser*:

I was at Gen. Dickenson's last evening when he received the following intelligence—that on Sunday last, about 1000 of our army, under command of General Maxwell, were attacked near Spank Town by near four times their number of the enemy from Perth

The house of Annie Van Liew, occupied by Howe and Cornwallis, as it appears today. (Courtesy *Gordon Bond*)

Amboy, and after an obstinate engagement the enemy were obliged to retreat, with the loss of fifty killed, one hundred wounded, and nine taken prisoners: Our loss is but five killed and nine wounded.

[British soldiers] *were out on Sunday last upon a foraging party with three field pieces, when they were attacked by about 600 of our people at eleven in the morning near Spank-town. The firing continued from that time with some short intermission until night, by the best accounts we can get the enemy's loss amounted to upwards of a hundred men killed and wounded; we took ten prisoners; our loss was eight killed and wounded."*[18]

The British retreated through what is today Woodbridge Township. Their path, now Route 35, was heavily wooded and difficult to break through. Peebles estimated that the trek was twenty-eight or thirty miles when actually it was less than ten miles. The Americans took full advantage of this terrain by constantly sniping at Mawhood's columns from all sides as they fled down the rough trail. By the time they reached Perth Amboy, they had lost between 75 and 100 men. American losses at the battle of Spanktown were five killed and nine wounded. Two weeks later, on March 8, the Redcoats went on the offense again, but encountered what they later referred to as a bunch of "American hornets."

The Americans were growing stronger and making incursions with large forces deep into British held territory in the belt stretching from New Brunswick to Amboy. On April 10, a Redcoat detachment on the front lines was approached at Bonhamtown, now Edison, by Maxwell's brigade of 2,000 troops. The best account of this clash comes from Archibald Robertson, who served as a Lieutenant-General in the Royal Engineers: "Between four and five in the evening the rebels, in a body of about 2000 under Brigadier Generals Stephens and Maxwell, attacked Piscataway, where the 42nd regiment is cantoned, who beat them back nearly three miles to their camp near the heights near Metuchen, with the loss of 6 privates and 3 sergeants killed, 2 officers, 2 sergeants and 15 privates wounded. The Rebels lost a great number and had a captain and 21 taken by the 42nd and 11 taken by the light infantry who had a sergeant wounded."[19]

This incessant combat increased the expertise and confidence of both the militia troops and the Continentals. British Lieutenant General Sir Charles Stuart wrote, "The rebel soldiers, from being accustomed to peril in their skirmishes, begin to have more confidence. The wounding and killing of many of our rear guards, gives them the notion of victory and habituates them to the profession."[20]

The Redcoats Withdraw to Amboy

General Cornwallis interposed these late winter skirmishes with a surprise attack on the Continental Army outpost at Bound Brook on April 13, 1777, and very nearly captured its commander, General Benjamin Lincoln. The Americans were outnumbered 2,000 to 500. The Crown forces met stubborn resistance from the riflemen of the 8th Pennsylvania Regiment. Although the British captured three 3-pound guns and 20 or 30 men, and killed six Americans, the bulk of

Lincoln's force escaped into the hills near Middlebrook. This engagement is described in detail earlier in this book.

By May, constant raids by both sides over the preceding four months had left both Patriot and Loyalist farms from the Raritan River Valley north to Elizabethtown stripped bare of food, forage and anything else of value. Military action then became more conventional warfare. Both sides focused on attacking outposts and engaging in random skirmishing on the front lines. At this time, General Washington recognized the need to consolidate his army at the Middlebrook Encampment. In May he ordered that Samptown and Quibbletown be abandoned, and on June 1 a British patrol entered Samptown and reported that it was completely deserted.

General Howe began moving his army of almost 17,000 troops to Amboy on June 12. The procession included 1,000 wagons and stretched out for twelve miles. Crown forces also formed a nine-mile front along Amwell Road from New Brunswick through Middlebush (now Franklin Township), to Millstone. The cavalry of the New Jersey Militia incessantly harassed the Redcoats, and it took them three days to march the ten miles from New Brunswick to Millstone. Once there, Howe positioned his forces to encircle Washington's Army if it could be lured down from the Middlebrook Hills.

Howe and Cornwallis set up their headquarters at the home of Annie Van Liew in the village. The house, built in 1752 by Cornelius Van Liew, still stands on the east side of the Millstone River on Amwell Road in East Millstone. It later became a tavern known as the Franklin Inn but was shut down with the start of Prohibition in 1916. It later operated as a used book store, but in 2012 it was flooded by Hurricane Sandy and forced to close.

The British and Hessians spent the five days from June 14 to 19 building nine redoubts along this front from New Brunswick to Middlebush. To protect his left flank, Howe ordered that Samptown be occupied by a company of the Hessian Kessel Jägers commanded by the ubiquitous Captain Johann Ewald. The Germans had the misfortune of blundering into Continental troops as they reoccupied the town. He described the incident in his diary "On the 20th I was ordered to relieve the light infantry of the English Guards at Samptown with 80 Jäger and an amusette [small cannon]. The post was situated in front of the Army's center and covered a defile which ran through a wood, On the 21st and 22nd all our outposts were alarmed and harassed by the enemy both day and night. I had two men badly wounded in a skirmish on the 22nd. General Washington had advanced with his army and ordered the exits at Bound Brook Quibbletown and Samptown occupied with light troops, by which one could see that he was well informed of everything that was happening. At daybreak on the 23rd, our army set out for Amboy. The Hessians escaped to Bonhamtown to rejoin the main army on its withdrawal to Perth Amboy."[21]

Howe's Army reluctantly left for Amboy during the night when it became apparent that Washington could not be tempted down from the Middlebrook Heights. A victory on the plains of New Jersey would have forced the small, poorly equipped Americans to fight the superior Crown Forces. On the march New Brunswick to Amboy the flames of burning houses illuminated the way for miles around. Captain Ewald reported that "all the plantations of the disloyal inhabitants, numbering perhaps 50 persons, were sacrificed to fire and devastation."[22]

A Near Fatal Call, the Battle of the Short Hills and the Withdrawal of the Main British army from New Jersey

In the days that followed, Washington believed that the British were retreating to Staten Island. He relaxed, allowed the militiamen to return to their homes and moved the main body of the American Army into camp around Samptown. He realized that from that location they might be able to attack when the enemy was vulnerable as they attempted to cross over the Arthur Kill to Staten Island. General William Alexander's divisions were sent beyond Samptown to what is now Plainfield to shadow the Crown forces as they departed and to protect the American Army's left flank.

On June 26, 1777, Washington received a dreadful shock. More than 16,000 British soldiers emerged from Perth Amboy and began marching back toward the direction of Samptown. However, General Stirling warned him about their surprising turnabout, so the main body of the Continental Army was able to make a hasty retreat back into the hills. At the junction of the Oak Tree and New Dover Roads in present day Edison Township, the British turned north, and a pitched battle raged over the grounds of what is now the Plainfield Country Club. The outnumbered Americans fell back into Scotch Plains and the victorious Cornwallis and his army marched through Westfield on their return to Amboy. This engagement was referred to as the Battle of the Short Hills.

After the British had retreated to Staten Island, they went by ship into the Chesapeake Bay to attack Philadelphia. The New Jersey Militia was given the task to defend the state, as Washington's Army rushed to protect Philadelphia and the New York Highlands. The militia of the Garden State again responded in force in September 1777 when the British raided Bergen County. For the remainder of the war, northern and coastal New Jersey continued to be the site of many skirmishes with the British forces who occupied New York City.

A Lesson Learned from the Forage Wars

About thirty-five battles and skirmishes occurred between January 4 and March 21, 1777. One low estimate is that the British forces lost about 900 men, killed, wounded, captured or missing, and American losses were considered to be less than half of that number. American Generals Washington and Greene maintained that enemy losses were much higher, perhaps between 2,000 and 3,000 men.

American commanders learned a precious lesson from the foraging warfare in central New Jersey that changed their strategy in the years that followed—a strong local militia with competent leadership could be of tremendous value. More than 100,000 men served in the Continental Army during the Revolutionary War, but probably twice that number soldiered as militiamen. Before this time the militia had been disparagingly referred to by Thomas Paine, in his iconic essay, *The American Crisis,* as "summer soldiers," since they often went home to plant in the spring, rejoined the army, then left again for the fall harvest.

General Washington was never a great champion of the militia. He complained that they had failed to exhibit "a brave & manly opposition" while engaging British or Hessian regulars in the early tragic campaigns of 1776 in Manhattan and on Long Island. At the Battle of Brooklyn Heights in August 1776, thousands of militiamen fled from the battlefield. Washington believed that their sniping at the enemy from behind stone walls was not the way to defeat an organized enemy trained in European-style tactics. But, after the New Jersey foraging engagements the citizen soldiers were employed more effectively.

The part-time soldiers swelled the American ranks before most major battles. When Washington marched to Yorktown in 1781, he left the militia to protect New Jersey, even with the threat of half of the entire British army in nearby New York. The militiamen served as the military government by opposing and punishing Loyalists, often with tar and feathers. They forced reluctant citizens to sign oaths of allegiance and intimidated merchants who were supplying the enemy or refusing to accept continental currency. Many citizens served as guards for British prisoners of war and gathered provisions or drove herds of cattle to supply the regular army. While the militia could not have won the war alone, the war probably could not have been won without them. During the New Jersey forage war, the enemy also gained an appreciation for the fighting skill of the citizen soldiers.

Nearly forty percent of soldiers serving under Washington in his legendary Christmas night victory at Trenton in 1776 were militiamen. The decisive victories at Bennington in 1777, and King's Mountain in 1780, were both fought solely by militia being led by experienced officers without any help from the Continental Army. Half of the American forces in the wildly successful Saratoga Campaign of 1777 were militiamen. At that great American victory, the militia poured in after the Continentals had fought the British army to a standstill. Their huge numbers tipped the balance and convinced General John Burgoyne that his position was hopeless, so surrender was his only option.

The popular conception of the Revolutionary War is that it consisted of only a few major battles, the ones that we all read about in history books. The forage conflict in New Jersey proves that the war was a composite of numerous actions. There were 1,331 military engagements in the war throughout the colonies.[23] In New Jersey alone, at least 500 separate military incidents have been identified.[24] The Revolutionary War was a steady onslaught of engagements between standing armies and citizen soldiers on both sides. More Americans died in this series of New Jersey skirmishes than were killed in the most renowned battles of the war.

Other intriguing insights can be gained from these foraging actions in central New Jersey. Curiously, this action intimately identifies and recognizes the presence of many "second tier" Revolutionary War officers, leaders who commanded American, British and Hessian soldiers but have been forgotten or neglected in history. Several, especially on the British side, provide firsthand accounts describing their personal participation in events. The diaries of Captain Johann Ewald and Major John Peebles are ranked among the best that have survived from the entire war. Others, including the valiant militia leader Philemon Dickinson, have been ignored for the most part, and even omitted from recent accounts of the war in New Jersey. Behavioral traits, both good and bad, often explain their actions in combat. This enhances the historian's appreciation of this six-month period in American military history better than most other times in the eight-year war.

The American luminary in all this critical but largely forgotten action was the exemplary William Maxwell. His soldiers affectionately called him "Scotch Willie" because of his thick Ulster accent. In

August 1777, General George Washington prepared for the next campaign season by assigning Maxwell to organize and command a Corps of Light Infantry. This is perhaps the greatest example of Washington's confidence in the ability of any of his generals.

Maxwell formed this new elite force was by culling 100 of the best troops from each of the army's ten brigades. Their mission was not to engage in a general action, but to observe and report on enemy activities and movements and fight only when necessary. Maxwell commanded this light infantry at the battle of Brandywine and Germantown. This force formed the advanced skirmish line in the defense of Philadelphia and spent the winter at Valley Forge. Unfortunately, Maxwell tendered his resignation to Congress in 1780 feeling he was inadequately recognized for his contributions.

Chapter 4

The Short Hills & Beyond (1777)

*The Amboys, Woodbridge, Edison, Metuchen,
Plainfield, Watchung, Scotch Plains, Westfield, Rahway, Metuchen*

The Battle of the Short Hills occurred on June 26, 1777, after Crown forces had advanced from New Brunswick to Perth Amboy. Their objective was to envelop and destroy the Continental Army at Samptown and Quibbletown, but the opposing forces clashed in Woodbridge, Edison, Plainfield and Scotch Plains in engagements that lasted only a few hours. In the course of their victory, the superior forces commanded by Sir William Howe and Lord Cornwallis drove an American detachment led by Lord Stirling from the field, and also captured three cannons.

While this was a small triumph for the British, it served to divert them from their primary campaign objective—to defeat the main Continental Army. The action gave Washington the time to withdraw his forces to the security of the heights of Middlebrook to fight another day. In fact, the digression of Howe's forces at the Short Hills had great strategic impact on the course of the entire war. Unfortunately, this critical event in the Revolutionary War has been largely forgotten, and the locations of the action are now spread over a heavily developed area traversed by numerous highways. Regrettably, the name Short Hills has caused confusion over the years. Many New Jersey residents, even today, assume that this battle occurred in a different New Jersey town with the same name located ten miles away.

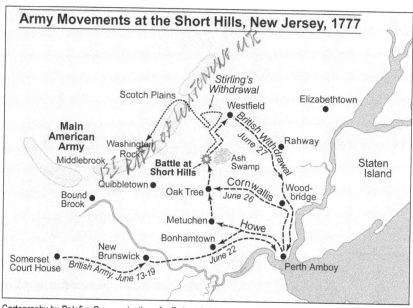

Cartography by Balefire Communications for Robert A. Mayers

The forces under the command of Sir William Howe which participated in this battle were composed of about 16,000 British regulars and Hessians, soldiers that were principally drawn from the German state of Hesse-Kassel. This was twice the size of the American forces. Following the defeats at Trenton on December 26, 1776 and Princeton on January 3, 1777, Howe's forces abandoned much of New Jersey but encamped around New Brunswick. The Americans who wintered at Morristown raided the British garrisons and obstructed their foraging forays, but no large-scale military actions occurred during the winter months.

Continental Army in Secure Encampment at Middlebrook

In May 1777, Washington moved his army, composed of both Continental troops and state militia, to a secure position at Middlebrook on the first ridge of the Watchung Mountains above the town of Bound Brook. The Middlebrook position provided easy access to the western mountains if a retreat became necessary and was within seven miles of the British front lines at New Brunswick. This natural fortress placed the American forces on the right flank and rear of Howe's Army, if it moved across the state to capture Philadelphia, a principal objective at that time. But the arrival of Washington's forces at Middlebrook offered General Howe the fortunate opportunity to attempt to engage the entire Continental Army in an ultimate decisive battle. A British victory here would end the war.

By June, British forces had occupied New Jersey for seven months. During this time General Howe had failed to lure Washington with the Continental army down from their position in the Watchung Mountains. A general action on the flat ground around the Millstone River west of New Brunswick would assure a defeat for the comparatively weak Patriots. British General James Grant lamented, "Remaining longer in the Jerseys could of course answer no good end. It was therefore thought expedient to return . . . to Brunswick & to proceed from thence on the more important operations of the Campaign."[1]

Howe decided it was time to move on. His army left New Brunswick on June 22 and marched fifteen miles to Amboy. There he prepared a crossing to Staten Island, where the fleet would carry him and the Crown forces south to Chesapeake Bay. From a secure position at the head of the bay the campaign to take Philadelphia could be launched.

In the last week of June 1777, American lookouts on the crest of the first ridge of the Watchung Mountains observed a welcome sight. The Crown Forces appeared to be evacuating Amboy and crossing the Arthur Kill to Staten Island. This was a sure sign that the entire British army was abandoning New Jersey. While British sources of the time deny it, this major withdrawal appeared to have been another feint to deceive the wary Americans and was Howe's final attempt to coax Washington out of his mountain stronghold at Middlebrook. This time his scheme worked.

The abandonment of central New Jersey would allow the Patriots to reoccupy this Tory-infested land. Washington was apprehensive, and at first hesitated to move the army out of the mountains, but he finally yielded to his more zealous officers who tactfully scorned him for lack of aggressiveness. On the day before he left the safety of Middlebrook, he wrote to Joseph Reed, his secretary and aide-de-camp, "I cannot say that the move I am about to make towards Amboy accords altogether with my opinion, not that I am under any other apprehension than that of being obliged to lose ground again, which would indeed be no small misfortune as the spirit of our troops and the county is greatly revived (and I presume) the enemy's not a little depressed, by their late retrograde emotions"

The Americans were delighted to see the apparent withdrawal of the Crown forces. Washington jubilantly observed the evacuation from his perch on a rock outcropping on the crest of the first Watchung Mountain. He became so confident the enemy was withdrawing permanently from the state that he allowed the militiamen to disband and return home. He then moved American forces down to the plains at Samptown (South Plainfield) and Quibbletown (Piscataway) and fanned out his regiments in a ten-mile arc to defend New Jersey from a possible counterattack. The American lines on the plains of central New Jersey extended from Quibbletown, north to the Short Hills and Ash Swamp (now Plainfield and Scotch Plains).

Washington Protects His Northern Flank

General Washington recognized a flaw in his defenses. The northern flank of the American forces with passes through the hills at Watchung, Scotch Plains and Springfield needed protection. They were in the critical Short Hills-Ash Swamp area in what is today Plainfield and Scotch Plains, where the ground rises to the west of Oak Tree Road in Edison and reaches its highest point at the present-day Plainfield Country Club. The Short Hills are appropriately named since they are low and inconspicuous compared to the first ridge of the Watchung Mountains that rise above them a few miles to the west.

Washington assigned Brigadier General William Alexander, one of his most experienced combat officers, to this vital mission. Stirling left his post at Vermeule's farm in Plainfield on June 24 with a force of 1,798 soldiers and moved to the Short Hills-Ash Swamp area to protect the flank of the American army. He set up his headquarters at a central location along today's Inman Avenue in Scotch Plains. His division was composed of Pennsylvanians under Thomas Conway and William Maxwell's Jersey Brigade.

Still observing the withdrawal of the Crown forces to Staten Island, Washington cautiously brought his army down from the heights of Middlebrook. An American deserter alerted the British commanders that Washington had finally come down from the hills, and it appeared that his army was ready to challenge the Redcoats on the flatlands of Piscataway and South Plainfield. Howe had been eagerly awaiting this opportunity, and his forces immediately reversed course. British and Hessian troops were ferried back from Staten Island to begin an assault on the Continental Army.

The Crown Forces Strike

Howe divided his army of 18,000 British and Hessian troops into two columns. On the night of June 25, they marched from Perth Amboy to engage Stirling and force Washington into an action. Howe planned a surprise attack, using his superior numbers and field artillery to first wipe out Stirling, and then encircle and crush Washington's army. Stirling's detachment, then, was the only obstacle between the Crown forces and Washington.

One of Howe's columns, commanded by Cornwallis, marched from Perth Amboy through Woodbridge while the other, led by Howe, marched toward Metuchen. Their combined objective was to reunite in order to encircle the vulnerable Continental Army and cut off its withdrawal to the heights of Middlebrook. The left column, under General John Vaughan, proceeded through Metuchen but would not reach Oak Tree Road in time to take part in the fighting.

On the evening of June 25, General Washington conferred with his officers to plan a defensive strategy. Their meeting took place at the Drake house on West Front Street in Plainfield (the original farmhouse has been preserved and today it is a public museum administered by the Historical Society of Plainfield). The next morning, at about 6:00 A.M., Colonel Daniel Morgan's riflemen, part of Lord Stirling's command, encountered Cornwallis's advance on what is now Green Street in Woodbridge. The sounds of gunfire coming from this skirmish cost the British the advantage of surprise. The outnumbered American riflemen fell back and Cornwallis continued to advance west along Oak Tree Road toward the Short Hills.

Lord Stirling alerted the main American Army after the fighting erupted. His warning, combined with the stubborn resistance of his outnumbered forces, provided Washington with enough time for an orderly withdrawal to the more secure high ground at Middlebrook. The encirclement of the Continental Army and its annihilation in a major battle were avoided, a defeat that would have likely ended the American War for Independence.

As the fighting continued, Brigadier General Thomas Conway's Brigade of about 700 Pennsylvania German volunteers opposed the Redcoats. Conway was forced to retreat toward the Short Hills. When Cornwallis reached New Dover Road his forces were again attacked by Ottendorf's Corps, comprised of men from eastern Pennsylvania. The fighting continued along Oak Tree Road, then turned west and headed up the slope of the Short Hills toward Scotch Plains. The main action then began with an assault by Maxwell's New Jersey Brigade. The battle raged for the next two hours between Oak Tree Road, Woodland Avenue and Tingley Lane. During the battle the Americans lost, recaptured, and lost again three French cannons.

The severe British cannon fire and their strength in numbers forced Stirling and his retreating Americans to lead both of the armies into the Ash Swamp in Scotch Plains. The Americans made a final stand there while they continued to withdraw toward Westfield. The British, suffering from the extreme heat of the day, broke off the fighting and continued to Westfield. Eventually the battered Americans retreated through Scotch Plains to the gap in the Watchung Mountains at Bonnie Burn Road. From there they returned to the main army at the Middlebrook Encampment, through Watchung and Warren, using the protection of the first Watchung ridge. Howe's aide, Friedrich von Munchausen, counted thirty-seven rebel wagons filled with wounded struggling up a winding hill on the road, and for many years after that area was known as Bloody Gap.

British Colonel Charles Stuart provided this concise description of the combat two weeks after the engagement had taken place:

On our arrival at Amboy every preparation was made for embarking the Troops, and one Brigade of Hessians had actually embarked. This induced Washington to quit his hold in order to attack us, on hearing which Gen. Howe ordered those Troops to disembark, and at daybreak the next morning march'd in two columns; the right hand one, commanded by Cornwallis and Grant, were to pass by Woodbridge to Westfield, and the left by Bowen Town [Bonhamtown] to the same place. Washington's army was drawn up about 3 miles from the Mountains, his left at Sparkston, [Samptown] and his right extending towards Boundbrook. Upon the alarms of our movements, Washington retired to the post he before occupied. Lord Cornwallis, falling in with Stirling, near Matonaking [Metuchen], after a slight skirmish obliged him to retire. In this confusion, we took 60 men, and 3 pieces of cannon; our loss was Capt. Finch, of the Guards, killed, and 30 men killed and wounded, besides 20 men who dropp'd down dead from the heat or fatigue.[2]

British Forces Withdraw

Later in the day, Howe assessed the position of the American Army, now dug in on the high ground at Middlebrook, and decided against attacking this strong Patriot position. The gaps through the first ridge of the Watchungs, along present Route 22, were also heavily guarded and easily defended. Concluding that any further assault would be futile, the Crown Forces retreated north toward Westfield. Howe commented, "The enemy was pursued as far as Westfield with little effect, the day proving so intensely hot, that the soldiers could with difficulty continue their march thither: in the meantime, it gave opportunity for those flying to escape by skulking in the thick woods, until night favored their retreat to the mountain."[3]

As Stirling's troops withdrew, a cannonball struck the side of a house in the center of Scotch Plains. It is believed that an American artilleryman attempting to fire his cannon at the pursuing British, misdirected his shot and hit this house. Since that time this dwelling has been called the "Cannonball House," and it has been meticulously restored by the historical society of that town.

On the route to Westfield after the battle British General Cornwallis, lured by the enticing smell of baking bread from the nearby Frazee house, stopped his column. Tradition claims that Cornwallis introduced himself and asked Betty Frazee if he could have some bread for his troops. She replied, "Sir, I will give you this bread through fear, not in love." Cornwallis politely declined to take any bread, supposedly saying, "Not a man in my command shall touch a single loaf," but his ravenous soldiers did proceed to take livestock and household goods before resuming their march. The Frazee House still stands near the corner of Terrill and Raritan Roads. The historic dwelling was in an advanced state of disrepair, but a complete restoration is now underway, backed by the Scotch Plains-Fanwood Rotary Frazee House, Inc. as its Rotary International Centennial Project. Betty and her husband Gershom are buried in the Cemetery of the First Presbyterian Church in Westfield.

The thirsty Redcoats continued their plundering after discovering and imbibing three barrels of applejack at Lambert's Mills on Old Raritan Road. In James Lambert's subsequent claim for damages he listed the amount stolen as 20 gallons.[4] British troops also drank the Terry well, located at the intersection of Rahway and Cooper Roads, completely dry on that scorching day in late June.

An Angry Army Ravages the Countryside from Westfield to Amboy

British columns, now unopposed, continued north from Scotch Plains to Westfield. The town was beyond the reach of British foraging parties during the winter of 1777, so was spared the destruction that occurred at farms and properties in Amboy, Brunswick, Bound Brook, and other places along the Raritan River. The British commanders were frustrated by their failure to draw the American army into battle, and their men, normally well-disciplined and restrained by their officers, became looters and destroyers of civilian property. Claims recorded by many residents detail the extensive damage done to civilian homes and property.[5] The Westfield Presbyterian Meeting House at Broad and Mountain Avenues frantically tolled its bell to warn of the approach of thousands of Redcoats and Hessians. The word quickly spread to evacuate, but there was no time to gather possessions or cattle.

This extract from a Philadelphia newspaper describes the scene as Howe's army moved to Westfield. Morristown, July 5, 1777: "The British army burnt, stripped and destroyed all as they went along. Women and children were left without food to eat or raiment to put on. Three hundred barrels of flour were sent down towards Westfield and the Ash Swamp, by order of his Excellency [General Washington] to be distributed among the poor sufferers. The enemy destroyed all the Bibles and books of divinity they came across."[6]

The enemy forces viewed the Presbyterian Church in Westfield as a symbol of radical patriotism, so they camped on the church grounds. Despite marching fifteen miles from Amboy and fighting in

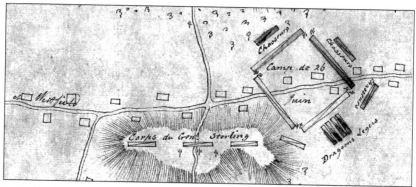

Detail of the British encampment at Westfield. (Detail from "Plan de l'affaire de Westfield & du camp de Raway" by Friedrich Adam Julius Von Wangenheim, 1777)

the extreme heat, Howe's troops soon continued their ruthless pillaging in the Westfield neighborhood.[7]

While the present Presbyterian church structure dates to 1862, it is the same height as the older structure that stood on the grounds where the British army bivouacked on the night of June 26, 1777. Jacob Ludlow, a New Jersey militiaman, reported that "the British filled the church with sheep and put a ram's head in the pulpit and slaughtered a great number of hogs, sheep and cattle. They threw down the bell from the steeple and slaughtered sheep and cattle in the building."[8]

Other jubilant Redcoats camped overnight in another section of Westfield along today's Willow Grove Road and Central Avenue and initiated a long night of feasting and drinking. The reveling soldiers cooked the freshly slaughtered livestock in camp kettles hung from the branches of walnut trees along Broad Street.[9] Many of the Redcoats even spent the night in the homes and shops of the Patriot residents.

Based on their claims later filed by Westfield homeowners with the State of New Jersey, Crown troops looted and destroyed at least ninety-two houses in Westfield and plundered a staggering 11,000 individual items in the town.[10] They also tore down over 2,000 fence rails and posts for fuel to cook their food. In addition, they stole all the cash in the town. During the melee, a slave seized the opportunity to escape from his American master. Pitifully, he is listed fourth on an inventory of plundered items, after "2 excellent milk cows, 1 two year old heifer, and 2 large fat hogs." Although his value was listed as 80 pounds, his name and age were not given.[11] Even British Major John Andre, who would later be hung as a spy, lamented that on June 27, "the spirit of depravation was too present on these marches."[12]

The British army left Westfield by 9:00 A.M. on June 27, marched south toward Rahway following today's Grand and Rahway Avenues, and finally camped that night along the Rahway River. They had absconded with about 500 cattle and several wagonloads of looted property. Major John Andre confirmed this in his journal, "At 9 in the morning we marched by the left bringing with us about 60 prisoners picked up in different places and driving the cattle we met on the road"[13] The prisoners were American soldiers captured during the battle, and some unfortunate civilians apprehended during the trek to Rahway. All were initially imprisoned in the notorious Sugar House in New York City, but many were later transferred to ghastly prison ships moored off Brooklyn in Wallabout Bay, which became a death sentence for many of them.

Not long after, American soldiers under Colonel Israel Shreve of the 2nd New Jersey Regiment entered Westfield. Shreve reported:

They made shocking havock, Distroying almost Everything before them, the house where Gen. How stayed which was Capt. Clarks he promised Protection to If Mrs. Clark would use him well and Cook for him & his Attendance, which she Did as Chearful as she Could, Just before they went off Mr. how Rode out, when a No. of his soldiers Come in And plunder[ed] the Woman of Everything in the house, Breaking And Destroying what they Could not take Away, they Even tore up the floor of the house, this Proves him the Scoundrel, and not the Gentleman, Gen. Lesley took his Quarters At Parson Woodruffs [and] Protected his property in Doors, the Doctor fled [but] his Wife and famaly Remained, the meetinghouse a Desent Building they made a sheep pen of threw Down the Bell,

and took it of . . . they Drove of[f] All the Horses, Cattle, Sheep &
hogs they Could Git—I saw many famalys who Declared they had
Not one mouthful to Eat, [nor any] bed or beding Left, or [a] Stitch
of Wearing Apparel to put on, only what they happened to have on,
and would not afoard Crying Children a mouthfull of Bread Or
Water Dureing their stay.[14]

From Rahway the Redcoats returned to Perth Amboy, again
pillaging and burning Patriot homes along the way. Then the Crown
forces crossed over the Arthur Kill to Staten Island. For the first time
since November 1776, no large force of British or Hessians occupied
New Jersey. Two days after the British left, General Washington moved
the army from Middlebrook to an even more secure place, at Pompton,
sixty miles further inland. This first Middlebrook encampment lasted
thirty-five days, from May 28 to July 2, 1777. The Continental Army
returned seventeen months later, in November 1778.

Alexander Hamilton, while serving as an aide to General
Washington, wrote this description of the aftermath of the battle to
Governor Robert R. Livingston:

Head Quarters Camp, at Middlebrook, June 28th 1777. Lord
Stirling's party was near being surrounded: but after a smart skirmish
with the enemy's main body, made their retreat good to Westfield,
and ascended the pass of the mountains back of Scotch Plains. The
other parties after the skirmish on their flanks came off to join the
main body and take possession of the heights. The enemy continued
their march towards our left as far as Westfield, and there halted. In
the meantime, it was judged prudent to return with the army to the
mountains, lest it should be their intention to get into them and force
us to fight them on their own terms.

They remained at Westfield till the next day, and perceiving their
views disappointed have again returned to Amboy, plundering and

burning as usual. We had parties, hanging about them in their return; but they were so much on their guard no favourable opportunity could be found of giving them any material annoyance. Their loss we cannot ascertain; and our own, in men, is inconsiderable, though we have as yet received no returns of the missing. I have no doubt they have lost more men than we; but unfortunately, I won't say from what cause, they got three field pieces from us, which will give them room for vapouring, [boasting] and embellish their excursion, in the eyes of those, who make every trifle a matter of importance. . . . [15]

The Scene Today

Today, the Short Hills are located on the ridge along the southern edge of the Plainfield Country Club, which was the high ground occupied by Stirling's defenders and where Patriot cannons fired down the slope toward Oak Tree Road. This site offers a commanding view over the former battlefield and the surrounding landscape. Contemporary descriptions of the landscape described woodlots and cultivated fields, and the battlefield area remained as farmland until the early 20th century, when suburban development spread. The northern portion of the land was converted to a golf course in the first quarter of the 20th century, and this location is still occupied by the Plainfield Country Club. [16]

The long open vista sweeps over built up areas, busy roads and wooded areas, and in no way resembles the appearance of the 18th century agricultural landscape. The panoramic view to the northwest from the country club grounds to the first ridge of the Watchung Mountains also looks over a heavily developed area, but most signs of manmade activity are obscured by treetops, so it remains similar to the terrain as it appeared in 1777. [17]

Historical descriptions and maps that show the major roads over which the troops on both sides advanced still exist. Oak Tree Road, the route that Cornwallis's column followed west from Woodbridge,

View toward the first Watchung Mountain, facing west from the Plainfield Country Club. *(Courtesy of Wade P. Catts, Historical Archeologist)*

does not appear on any early maps. But it can be traced by damage claims filed by property owners along the road and extensive geographic systems mapping.[18] Present day Main Street in Metuchen and Plainfield Road in South Plainfield are located on the route of advance for the southern or left column of the Crown forces. This unit arrived too late to participate in the fighting but joined Cornwallis when his forces returned to Amboy.

At the Short Hills, both sides had casualties in excess of 100 men. While the British gained a tactical victory, they failed to destroy the brigades under the command of Lord Stirling. The main Continental Army, located to the southwest, was able to make a hasty withdrawal from Quibbletown to the hills of Middlebrook. Once again, the Continental forces had escaped destruction as they had done the previous August on Long Island. The engagement at the Short Hills was indecisive but was the end of campaigning for the Crown forces in New Jersey. The event also marked the beginning of the Delaware Valley campaign that ended with the capture of Philadelphia in September 1777.

Historians consider this battle a strategic victory for the Americans. The stand taken by Stirling's forces at the Short Hills and Ash Swamp had saved Washington's Army. The British had failed in their attempt to gain entry into the interior of New Jersey, and their final evacuation was a welcomed relief to civilians throughout the state.

The inability of Howe to force a decisive battle or outmaneuver Washington in New Jersey resulted in the movement by sea of the balance of Crown forces from Staten Island to Head of Elk (now Elkton) in Maryland in preparation for launching the Philadelphia campaign. This maneuver away from New York City and the Hudson River Valley, contributed to the eventual halt and defeat of Sir John Burgoyne's army at Saratoga, since Howe's forces were in no position to support that advance.

Chapter 5

Crosswicks in the Crosshairs
(1778)

Haddonfield, Moorestown, Cherry Hill, Mount Laurel, Mount Holly,
Bordentown, Columbus, Mansfield, Crosswicks, Allentown, Holmdel, Hopewell,
Kingston, Cranbury, Englishtown, Freehold

After the devastating defeat of the Continental Army at the Battle of Brandywine in September 1777, the new nation was further demoralized when the British army occupied its capital at Philadelphia. By spring 1778, however, their forces had begun preparations to leave the city. The residents of Philadelphia observed the last of the occupation forces departing on the morning of June 18 when the British army, along with its baggage, artillery and civilian followers, crossed the Delaware River to Gloucester Point, New Jersey in a 12-mile-long procession. This colossal column headed northeast across the Garden State toward their destination of New York City. It would travel largely unopposed for thirty-five miles to the hamlet of Crosswicks, near Bordentown, New Jersey, where it would encounter the first stiff resistance from a Patriot force.

The massive convoy included 11,000 Redcoat soldiers and Hessian troops and more than 1,000 Loyalist refugees. Hundreds of camp followers trailed at the rear of the line. Straining oxen and horses hauled a baggage train of 1,500 wagons, overloaded with weapons, equipment, supplies, personal baggage and booty stolen from Patriot homes and businesses. For days the exposed column plodded along at an average of only four miles each day over the sandy roads of southern New Jersey, often following remote paths to avoid the many swamps and streams along the way. The Crown forces trudged through ankle-deep sand or swampy marshes under burning sun and driving rain. The soldiers, drenched with sweat, wore tight, heavy woolen clothes and carried packs that weighted 60 to 100 pounds.

The weary Redcoats had to constantly build new bridges to replace the ones destroyed by Patriot partisans or local militia. They cleared trees felled across roads to block their way. In brutal return, the invaders ransacked local homes and businesses, stole food and livestock, and ravaged Patriot women. Captain Johann Ewald, a German mercenary serving with the British wrote, "Skirmishing was constant, and the heat was deadly. Many men fell and lost their lives because of the intense heat, and due to the sandy ground, which we crossed through a pathless wood where there was no water to be found on the entire march."[1] More than 500 men deserted along the way, the equivalent of an entire battalion. Most of the runaways, about 450 men, were Hessians who decided to make America their home. Many of them joined American regiments or returned to the girlfriends they left behind in Philadelphia.

The vast procession's 90-mile journey to New York passed through many New Jersey towns in Burlington, Monmouth and Ocean Counties. Along the way the British invaders were confronted by a rejuvenated American defense force and forced to engage in the last great battle of the Revolutionary War in the north at Monmouth Court House (now Freehold), New Jersey.

During that same winter the British army spent in Philadelphia, General George Washington and the American Army were only about 20 miles away at Valley Forge, Pennsylvania. The camp was located in a strategic location. It was close enough for General George Washington to observe the British troops and still be in a strong defensive position should the British decide to attack. Unfortunately, it did not have the supplies to sustain the Patriots over the winter months. General Washington expected to be attacked at Valley Forge but suspected that the Crown Forces would head across New Jersey. He wrote the following to Major General Philemon Dickinson:

Valley forge May 24th 1778 11 O'Clock P.M.

Dr Sir From some intelligence received since I wrote you to day, it would seem that the Enemy have a Land movement in view, but where or what their object is, is entirely a matter of incertainty. Some reports say they mean to make a push against us here and that this is the most common opinion—Others that their intention is to pass through Jersey. Lest the Latter should be their object, I think it will be highly expedient to prepare the Militia for assembling themselves on the shortest notice, and for this purpose, that it will be advisable to fix on certain Signals by which they may be the more expeditiously summoned. The Tree near prince Town, which is well known to you & to most people appear very proper to hoist Beacons on.

It seems incredible that the British did not make a sustained attempt to attack the beleaguered American campground during the harsh winter of 1777–1778. It was a lost opportunity to end the rebellion. Desolate Valley Forge, with its starving and freezing army, replete with desertions and expired enlistments, was only a day's march away. If the British had surrounded that campground the struggling Patriots would have been forced to capitulate in a few days.

Why did the British army undertake this incredible risky trek through New Jersey? It would be strung out over many miles and exposed in an unknown and hostile area over grueling terrain. With most of the Crown forces in Philadelphia, British leaders became apprehensive as the spring of 1778 approached. France had entered the war six months earlier, and it would be possible for the French Fleet to blockade the mouth of Delaware Bay and intercept the supply ships that sustained the occupation force. Since the British were supplied from the sea, they would an easy target for the American Army which could then come down from Valley Forge and besiege the city.

The occupation of Philadelphia was further weakened when British regiments were dispatched to Florida and the West Indies. British commanders lamented that they did not have enough troops to continue to occupy the city. A substantial part of the British expeditionary force in America, 18,000 troops, was in the New York City area. However, this location was also considered to be vulnerable, so plans were made to abandon New York, if the position became untenable, and withdraw to Quebec. The army was considered to be at a distinct strategic disadvantage by being divided between America's two major cities. British strategists in London and America were alarmed when a French Fleet was spotted heading for the mouth of Delaware Bay. They decided it was time to move out of Philadelphia and maximize the strength of His Majesty's forces by massing them in one place—New York City.

Sir William Howe, senior British army commander in America, came to recognize the failure of the strategy to end the war for independence by capturing the capital of the new nation. He left all his problems behind by resigning and sailing back to England. Howe was replaced in May 1778 by Sir Henry Clinton. Sir Henry, age forty, was a cautious but courageous officer who often placed himself in danger while leading his troops in combat. His first major challenge was to move the army out of Philadelphia in order to join the other British forces in New York City. He was compelled to lead what amounted to the most massive retreat of the Revolutionary War after being in command for less than a month.[2]

Sir Henry would have preferred transporting his army by sea, but there were too few ships available at the time. He did load 3,000 Loyalist refugees, along with all men, women and children unfit to march, on the vessels that were on hand. Two Hessian regiments, about 1,000 men, with a mutinous reputation, also were sent with them.

Clinton believed that this approach would be less risky if these people were confined onboard ships. Nevertheless, many of the German soldiers who had married or formed strong relationships with American ladies hid until the ships departed. The plan was that the main army and everyone else would take a land route through New Jersey.

General Washington called his commanders together for a council of war, since he had expected Clinton to evacuate his troops from Philadelphia. During the earlier years of the war, the American Commander-in-Chief wanted to avoid a total showdown with a stronger army that had the capacity to outman and outgun his forces. But now he perceived that his odds were better. The rejuvenated Continental Army, trained by Baron von Steuben at Valley Forge, had experienced a surge in new enlistments, and was not greatly outnumbered by the British. The foe was fleeing from an occupied city, without a battle, to open country where they would be highly vulnerable. Washington decided to abandon the practice of strategic withdrawal to preserve his army and to pursue the British forces as they crossed the Garden State. The two armies converged at Monmouth Court House on June 28, 1778 in the Battle of Monmouth, the longest continuous battle of the war.

The hardships and warfare that occurred on the arduous ten-day evacuation of the Crown Forces with their entourage of Loyalist civilians and camp followers from Philadelphia to Monmouth has been neglected in New Jersey history. The details of these events can only be found in contemporary military documents, journals and correspondence, and most of the accounts are from British or Hessian records. The order book of Lieutenant Colonel Alured Clarke, commander of the 7th Regiment of Foot, is one comprehensive primary source containing daily details of the march. The document was found on the Monmouth Battlefield and is now housed in the collection of the Historical Society of Pennsylvania. The British exodus moved through the present day towns of Haddonfield, Cherry Hill, Mount Laurel, and Moorestown to arrive three days later, on

June 20, at Mount Holly. The column then proceeded on through Bordentown, Crosswicks and Allentown to the Monmouth Battlefield.

A Reluctant Departure from Philadelphia

Before departing from Philadelphia British commanders had first prepared a staging area in New Jersey directly across the river on Coopers Creek at Gloucester Point, four miles below Camden. The evacuation across the Delaware River in flatboats began on June 18. The British navy blockaded the southern side of the ferry route to protect the defenseless flatboats. The 17,000 officers, men and civilians hastily left the city after reluctantly bidding farewell to their Loyalist supporters, with whom they had spent a comfortable and festive winter. The many partings from the local ladies with whom romantic relationships had developed were especially poignant. The army scurried to the river bank without making any noise, as it was feared that the Americans would attack if alerted by sounds of a clamor.

Captain John Peebles, an officer in the grenadier company of the Royal Highlanders, known as the Black Watch, described leaving the city on the morning of June 18: "At the break of day the troops got under arms at the lines, and marched down by the Skirts of the Town to Glocester point, having evacuated the redoubts & called in the Troops that were in Town where they embarked in flatboats and crossed over to Glocester, by several trips the whole over by the forenoon. . . ."[3]

Sir Henry Clinton expected the worst and correctly anticipated that his columns would be constantly harassed by local militia and the mobile light infantry units of the Continental Army as it passed through New Jersey. As a precaution, he divided the armed units of his forces into two parts, each led by his two top commanders, Lord Charles Cornwallis and Hessian General Wilhelm von Knyphausen. Half the soldiers marched in front of the wagon train and the other half followed in the rear as the vast parade headed out from Gloucester

Point. Hessian Jägers, elite special forces, were sent ahead six miles inland to seize the town of Haddonfield, the first town in the Garden State on the route of the British forces, and the town was taken without resistance. By the first night the main body of the army along with their baggage and supplies had reached Haddonfield.

Peebles reported, "The Troops marched to within 2 miles of Haddonfield where they encamped in the usual manner, viz, wigwams, strict orders against plundering & a Proclamation [were] given out to encourage the People in the Jerseys to supply the army with fresh provision & forage & remain at home."[4] Haddonfield was a Quaker town. The Society of Friends avoided taking sides during the war, which may explain why the Redcoats entered the place unopposed.

The British set up their campsite near the Indian King Tavern on Kings Highway. Constructed in 1750, the inn is where the New Jersey Legislature met during the Revolutionary War to avoid contact with the British forces. In 1777 it declared New Jersey to be an independent state. Today the tavern is a state historical site and museum.

General Clinton was intensely opposed to the plundering of American civilians and declared the offense to be punishable by death, but the camp followers who trailed behind the British army were vigorous pillagers. They slipped away unnoticed and stripped homes along the route of anything of value. Even worse, they were accused of returning to the column infected with smallpox. The women were punished with the same sentences given to the soldiers, the most common of which was a severe flogging.

One such example of punishment was discovered in British army War Office Court Martial Records. Mary Colethrate and Elizabeth Clarke, "followers of the army," were brought before the court and accused of plundering. Major John Antill of the New Jersey volunteers (a Loyalist regiment) deposed that on the march, a farmer came up to him and begged for protection as some women were in the act of plundering and destroying his house. When the farmer entered his home, he found between thirty and forty women cutting open his feather beds and destroying other property. He pointed out Mary Colethrate and Elizabeth Clarke as being the ringleaders. Both women appeared to have something in their aprons, which turned out to be flour. Clarke was removing clothing from a closet. The farmer's wife claimed she was beaten and her children stripped of their clothing. The defendants returned several times to remove other items of value. Both women admitted to being in the home, but made various excuses and denied any looting.

The Court Martial issued this verdict: "The Court having considered the evidence against the prisoners, together with what they had to offer in their defense, it is our opinion that Mary Colethrate is not guilty of the crime laid to her charge but Elizabeth Clarke is guilty of the Crime. I doth therefore adjudge the said Elizabeth Clarke to receive one hundred lashes on her bare back with cats of nine tails, and then to be drummed out of the Army in the most public manner possible. Norman Lamont, Lieut Col.,Confirmed by H.Clinton"[5]

Why did General Clinton value relations with enemy civilians so highly? He correctly surmised that many were Loyalists and would offer support by providing supplies to the hungry column. Friendly locals could also offer intelligence with regard to Patriot troop activity and directions to navigate through the arduous and unknown terrain of swampy southern New Jersey. Fearing widespread plundering of civilians and desertions by soldiers returning to their girlfriends in Philadelphia, he issued his first general order:

Head Quarters Haddenfield June 18th, 1778

The Commanding Officers of Corps will strictly inform all others relating to Discipline and good Order, and it being the General's intention to have the Army as amply Supplied as there Situation can admit of, he desires that it be understood that he is fully determined to execute upon the spot every man directed in marauding or who shall quit his company upon the march, or should be found beyond the outposts of the camp without permission.

Reports of the impending British departure from Philadelphia began arriving at Valley Forge weeks before the British forces crossed the Delaware River. Curiously, no military action was taken to prevent the British forces from gaining a beachhead in New Jersey, when they would be most vulnerable. General William Maxwell and commanding general of the New Jersey Militia, Philemon Dickinson, were nearby in Burlington County with a force of 1,800 troops, and Washington, with the main body of the Continental Army, was only twenty miles away, less than a two-day march.

General Washington wrote to Brigadier General William Maxwell on May 25 from Valley Forge:

> *Sir,*
> *You are immediately to proceed with the two remaining regiments of your Brigade, to Mount Holly in the Jerseys, and order the other two regiments under Col: Shrieve to join you. In order to this, you will take the shortest route towards Coryel's ferry, there cross the Delaware and repair to the place of your destination. You are to keep your Brigade when assembled, in such a situation as will be most consistent with its security, and best calculated to cover the country and annoy the enemy, should they attempt to pass through the Jerseys, which there are many powerful reasons to suspect they intend.*

The Continental Army Departs from Valley Forge

The American Army left Valley Forge only three days after the last British troops left Philadelphia. In retrospect, they might have easily headed for the crossing area a few days earlier and pounced on the enemy when it was in such a helpless state. This action could have been of great significance and tilted the rest of the war in favor of the Americans.

On the long road that lay ahead Generals Maxwell and Dickinson had labored hard to sabotage the route. Along the way the British were picked off by the steady musket fire of scattered Americans concealed in the verdant spring foliage on both sides of the sandy trail. The Americans did not dig in to halt the advance until it arrived at Crosswicks Creek near Bordentown.

Opposing Armies Draw Together on the Path to Battle Evesham

An advanced party of German special forces at Haddonfield was sent six miles north to the little hamlet of Evesham on the morning of June 19, 1778. As they approached the town they were jolted by a small party of New Jersey Militia who dashed out of the woods and ambushed them. This resistance was the first opposition that the Crown Forces encountered in New Jersey during the march. The British apparently considered it to be inconsequential since no mention of it appears in their records.[6] The German advance burned the homes of Patriots leaders in the village, and Militia Captain Jonathan Beesley of the First Battalion, Cumberland County Militia, was severely wounded by a Jäger sharpshooter and taken prisoner.

The dying officer was persistently interrogated in an effort to learn the future movements of the Continental Army. The brave Beesley tenaciously refused to disclose any information and died later in the day. General Clinton commented that Beesley was a brave man and should not be treated with indignity, and indeed the enemy buried him with full military honors. This unusual custom and display of respect was observed by both sides at that time. Beesley's body was disinterred and moved to the Quaker cemetery in Haddonfield soon thereafter.

Later that morning, Clinton departed Haddonfield with his large force consisting of three brigades and followed the advanced party along Kings Highway to Evesham. The next day this main British column headed for Mount Holly through a heavy rainstorm, followed by a period of intense heat. Burdened by stiff uniforms and heavy backpacks, the British and Hessian regulars suffered much more than the lighter-clad and lesser-equipped Americans soldiers.

The British forces arose each morning at 3:00 A.M. and attempted to complete as much marching as possible before the heat became intolerable. Dr. Johann Schoepff, a Hessian surgeon, struggled to treat the many cases of heat stroke. He remarked that blood gushed from the mouth and nostrils of the victims and reported, "The Remarkable heat and fatigue enveloped our men in heavy woolen garments and tight leggings and carrying the entire weight of a gun, sixty cartridges, knapsack and rations, they cannot but suffer doubly from all the discomforts of such days"[7] The greater portion of the entire march through the Jerseys was undertaken on days of high humidity, severe rain storms or scorching sun.

MOORESTOWN

Most of the main army had moved eight miles north on a parallel route through what today is Cherry Hill. The Crown forces and their civilian followers camped at Moorestown at the Chester Meeting House of the Society of Friends. The invaders plundered everything they could find along the way, helping themselves to household goods, grain, horses and cattle. Many of the villagers had the foresight to hide their property in the swamps.

MOUNT HOLLY

On June 22, the British columns advanced ten miles more to Mount Holly, where they found the town deserted. Having been previously raided, residents knew how to prepare for the swarm of ravenous Redcoats and their retinue, and had fled with their possessions.[8] The British had passed through the town going in the opposite

The Friends
Meeting House at
Crosswicks.
*(Courtesy of West
Jersey History
Project-Historic
Images of
Burlington County)*

direction while pursuing the vanquished Continental Army after the fall of

New York City in 1776. When the invaders had reached Mount Holly they destroyed the iron works, the town's only industry, and they burned the home of Colonel Israel Shreve, commanding officer of the 2nd New Jersey Regiment. This time, the commissary department occupied the Friends Meeting House. General Clinton's warnings to everyone about plundering were completely ignored, and the pillaging of homes along the route continued unabated. He reprimanded his troops again and repeated his threat to execute violators:

Crosswicks June 23

The houses of Mr Shreve and Mr Tallman having been burnt this morning, the Commander–in-chief will give a reward 25 guineas to anyone who will discover the person or persons who set fire to the above houses, so they may be brought to the punishment due to acts, so disgraceful to the army. Any person that may hereafter be found committing such disorders will be delivered to the Provost Marshall for immediate execution.[9]

Crosswicks Creek
Bridge as it
appeared in 1917.
*(West Jersey History
Project)*

COLUMBUS, MANSFIELD (SLABTOWN and BLACK HORSE)

All the Crown forces came together at Mount Holly on June 22, and
combined army continued north through terrain consisting of a
patchwork of streams and swamps. The New Jersey Militia forces had
destroyed every bridge along the way, so a full corps of British
engineers had to be put to work building new bridges and causeways.
Patriot saboteurs along the route had also filled in the local wells, and
men in the stalled ranks began to suffer from the oppressive heat and
thirst. After a march of seven miles the columns reached Slabtown
and Black Horse (Columbus and Mansfield). At that point they
learned the ominous news that General Washington's army had
abandoned Valley Forge and was heading east on a parallel path
destined to converge with their route.

Sir Henry Clinton conferred with Lord Cornwallis as they rode at
the head of the procession, and the two generals agreed that their army,
encumbered by its vast entourage, was at a grave disadvantage. Greater
mobility was needed to oppose the flexible American infantry, so they
considered divesting the train of everything that was not essential to
combat. The 1,500 wagons of the train were loaded with plunder and
baggage. Portable bakeries, laundries, blacksmith shops, large quantities

of hospital supplies, boats hoisted onto wagons, and collapsible bridges were all being dragged along by teams of oxen. This burden was followed by the vast mob of Tory refugees, camp followers and sutlers, civilian merchants who sold provisions to the soldiers from the backs of wagons or tents. Clinton reluctantly decided to continue with the entire ponderous parade, figuring that abandoning the civilians and jettisoning the surplus equipment would be a strong signal of weakness to his soldiers and would completely demoralize them.[10]

Bordentown and Crosswicks in the Crosshairs

After marching fifteen miles north, advance units of Hessian Jägers and British Dragoons of the 5th Brigade entered Bordentown on the morning of June 23. After passing through the town they continued on to the small Quaker village of Crosswicks (now within Chesterfield Township). Hessian Captain Johann Ewald's Jäger Company headed for the drawbridge over Crosswicks Creek at Watson's Ford. Ewald mentioned in his journal that along the way his men were picked off by the steady musket fire from scattered Americans concealed in the brush on both sides of the road. Adding to their misery, the German soldiers suffered from the intense heat and humidity, and were surrounded by swarms of mosquitoes. Ewald found that the planking on all the bridges over local waterways had been removed, and wells in the vicinity had been filled in or intentionally polluted.[11]

When the Jägers reached the deserted bridge at Watson's Ford they found the planking had indeed been removed and the drawbridge had been raised. It was a essential for the bridge to be workable for the thousands of troops that were following behind, so an attempt was made to repair the bridge with planks torn from a nearby barn.

The Crown forces soon met with intimidating organized resistance, and were stunned to find that American troops were prepared to defend the site, as evidenced by the redoubts and entrenchments that had been dug at the crossing by the New Jersey Militia. Colonel Israel Shreve's First Burlington Regiment, along with the First Hunterdon under Colonel Joseph Phillips, occupied the high ground on the north side of the creek, now called Yardville Heights. The Patriots poured volleys of musket and cannon fire on the British sappers (engineers) while they were desperately trying to replace the bridge planks.

Attempts to repair the bridge were given up after four Redcoat soldiers fell and several more were wounded. The Americans then struggled to complete the destruction of the bridge before the main enemy army had a chance to reach it. Job Clevenger, a young militiaman, bravely, or perhaps foolishly, hacked away at the bridge supports, urged on by the cheers of his comrades. He soon became the target for British snipers and was shot in the head by a musket ball as he cut through the last stanchion. His body then splashed into the creek.

A total of about 900 New Jersey Militia guarded the bridges along Crosswicks Creek. Vastly outnumbered by the approaching enemy, their orders were to only delay and harass the invaders, and not attempt to attack or to hold their positions. The main force consisting of thousands of British and Hessians them began congregating at the bridge and soon engulfed the defenders. Redcoat sappers were able to make repairs over the next day to allow the main army to file over the patched up structure. Others followed an old abandoned road and entered the rear of the village. The remains of the American redoubts at the site were still visible in 1899, and remnants of the bridge still can be viewed today.[12]

Another column of British dragoons passed through Bordentown at dawn the next day and arrived two miles east at another bridge over Crosswicks Creek. Today Route 130, in Yardville, crosses over the creek at this place. Lieutenant Colonel John Simcoe, leading the Queen's Rangers, was stopped by the 2nd New Jersey and the 12th Pennsylvania Regiments. The Americans used their 3-pounder cannons effectively, but the superior force of Rangers eventually captured the bridge after losing five men. These clashes at the Crosswicks Creek crossings must have been considered trivial by the British army as no mention of the skirmishes appears in official military documents. The events are briefly described in two officer's accounts.

Grenadier Captain John Peebles regarded the action as insignificant. He wrote in his journal: "Tuesday 23d. The army marched at 4 o'clock in three divisions. . . . We, the middle division came by the Sign of the Rising Sun to Crosswicks about 6 miles. The advanced corps had a little skirmish at the creek where a party of Rebels had partly broke up the bridge and made a little stand with some cannon, but were soon drove off and pursued with little loss. The Queens rangers had a Captn. wounded."[13]

Major John Andre, before his grim end on the gallows a year later, reported in his journal: "At Crosswicks a piquet of the enemy fired at the head of the column and retired to join a body on the other side of the creek the bridge over which they hastily destroyed. The Queens rangers followed them very soon. But they retreated with great speed after firing a few shot across the riverlet. A Captain of Sincos was dangerously wounded. One or two of the enemy [all other reports state that the cannons were American and that it was British soldiers that fell] were killed by grapeshot from a 3 pounder brought on a height in front of Crosswicks whilst the bridge was repairing. The 16th Dragoons supported by a brigade of light infantry was pushed in pursuit 2 miles on the Allentown Road as far as another creek where the enemy were at work destroying the bridge."[14]

Much of the British army encamped that night around Crosswicks. Slumbering Redcoats rested along Ellisdale Road several miles south of Allentown. A new bridge, eight miles to the east, at Wainford, was constructed for the larger part of the column being led by Cornwallis and Knyphausen. The British crossed over it and continued on to Imlaystown and Allentown.

The Rising Sun Tavern, in nearby Mansfield, was opened in 1761 and was used as a Hessian outpost in 1776. Three cannon balls fired by the Americans during these engagements struck the north wall of the Friends Meeting House in Crosswicks. One of the rounds left a crater on the brick wall. This cannonball was saved and later mortared into the wall where it hit. Hessian soldiers used the building as a barracks. Marks from their bayonets and musket muzzles are still visible on its floor and benches.

With their towns enveloped in the fighting, the war became difficult for the pacifist Quakers, but they continued to assemble at their meeting house, even when it was occupied by armed forces. Its use as a wartime barracks, an overt contradiction to their creed, was especially offensive for the Society.

Sir Henry Clinton made his headquarters at Mrs. Bunting's house in the village of Crosswicks. Apparently, he had begun to yield to the intense pressure of the forced march and went to bed drunk on the night of June 23. During the night he had a nightmare and was seen running from the house, but was subdued and forcibly returned to bed by his aides. Mrs. Bunting's remarkable eyewitness account of the incident has survived:[15]

But she [Mrs Bunting] was not allowed to indulge in her sad reflections for many moments before she was summoned to the room below with bucket, clothes and all the things necessary to remove the mud from the august person of the British General. He, it seemed, had an attack of nightmare caused by the carouse of the evening and probably imagining that the Yankees were upon him, had started from his bed and rushing through the door, which was opened on account of the heat, dashed down the hill and before the astonished sentinel could decide whether he had seen a ghost or not, his noble commander was floundering knee deep among the mud and mallows of the little creek. The plunge awakened him, and his loud outcries brought officers and soldiers rushing from their tents in full expectation of finding themselves attacked by the Rebel army. The shouts and curses, the confusion the rushing here and there of half dressed men, formed a scene at once alarming and ridiculous. But the cause being at length

discovered, the discomfited General was led back to his quarters, and
with Mrs. Buntings aid was cleansed, and half stupefied as he still
was, placed again in the clean comfortable bed which he had occupied.
Order was restored in the camp, and silence reigned unbroken until
reveille aroused the slumbering host.

ALLENTOWN

An advance force was sent to reconnoiter, clear the way, and repair
roads and bridges the day before the wagon train left Crosswicks for
Allentown. The zealous Redcoats assumed that the devastation of the
local countryside was also part of their mission. Homes, barns and
outbuildings of prominent Patriots were looted and ignited from a
mile west of Allentown to the present-day town of Holmdel. Silverware
was stolen, furniture was burned or carried away, hay and straw were
incinerated, and the entire area was stripped of cattle, pigs and
poultry. Hundreds of the enemy soldiers deserted at this time, but the
hatred of the local people remained, and was so intense that none of
them was allowed to settle in the area after the war.[16]

More than thirty women were assaulted, often by British officers
and men in full uniform. While violators were summarily tried by
court martial in accordance with General Clinton's orders, even those
who offered a simple defense were not punished. Sarah Willis accused
soldier Thomas Gormon of raping her and reported the crime to
authorities. He offered the usual denial at his trial and, predictably,
was not found guilty:

The prisoner [Gormon] being put up on his defense said that he did
not deny his having carnal knowledge of Sarah Willis but that she
was as willing as he was, that when he went to her house at 7 oclock
that evening, she asked him to come there at night and that she told
him to pretend he came with a press-gang and if her husband should

happen to be at home it would frighten him an make him run away and he might then come in, that he had had carnal knowledge of her before and particularly on the night she acknowledges that he came to bed to her, and he supposes it was from the jealousy of her husband that she has been induced to accuse him, tho she has told him that she was not married and that he once gave her a Dollar and has always been welcomed at the house.[17]

The Fork in the Road and a Fateful Decision

The next morning the entire army continued north about ten miles to Allentown on June 24 and came upon a fork in the road. The northern route followed the path of the present-day New Jersey Turnpike and led to New Brunswick, the Raritan River and the Amboys, where there was a crossing to Staten Island. The other route was a single sandy path that led east through Monmouth Courthouse and continued through Middletown, Navesink and Highlands to Sandy Hook. Clinton had to decide which route to follow. His mission was to get his army safely to New York.

A reconnaissance party sent ahead to scout out the shorter northern route reported that Washington's Army was blocking the way to the Raritan River, and was lying in wait in expectation that the British forces would come that way. Considering that the Americans were nearer to the river, they could cross over first, then strike the vulnerable entourage as it attempted to to the same. Clinton's bountiful baggage train would be an especially valuable prize for the needy Americans. The scouts also found that the land on the way to New Brunswick was swampy and thus would be difficult for the army to cross. Lastly, no local Monmouth County guides could be found who knew the way north.

As a result the road to Sandy Hook appeared to be the best way to avoid converging with the emboldened American Army, and Clinton issued orders to turn east. This was a bad decision, and it would result in a heated battle. The route ran through Monmouth Courthouse, a small village with less than 100 inhabitants (today's Freehold). Clinton's plan was to load the long column of soldiers on ships to cross the few miles over Lower New York Bay to the safety of Staten Island and Manhattan.

The Bloody Day at Monmouth Courthouse

The cumbersome 12-mile-long procession, hampered by its long train of overloaded wagons and trailing civilians, began the 18-mile march from Allentown to Monmouth Courthouse on June 25. The parade was led by British armed forces on foot and horseback, followed by the artillery, provision train, baggage train, private carriages and baggage-carrying horses. Portable bakeries, laundries, blacksmith shops on wheels, hospital supplies and transportable bridges followed. Thousands of camp followers, Loyalist refugees and everything of value that had been looted from Philadelphia and places along the way made up the rear of the immense train.[18]

As the British columns staggered over dusty Monmouth County roads the heat became much more intense, and soon reached 100 degrees. Almost a third of the Hessian's were overcome by the soaring temperatures and collapsed along the roadside. Some even died of sunstroke. Surprise raids on the column by detachments of the American advanced force intensified. A force under Major Joseph Bloomfield of the 3rd New Jersey Regiment made repeated strikes on the British rear and took fifteen Hessian prisoners. The procession stopped for the night about four miles from Freehold. General Clinton made his headquarters at the Rising Sun Tavern in Millstone, midway between Allentown and Freehold. Millstone is located about four miles north of today's Six Flags Great Adventure Amusement Park.

On occasion, General Washington also used the Rising Sun Tavern as an outpost during the war. The tavern was our first place of business, accommodating such travelers as Benjamin Franklin and

Joseph Bonaparte. It was located on a stagecoach route, it was used by many weary travelers on the main route to Philadelphia and the direct route to Freehold. Unfortunately, this valuable historic building was torn down many years ago.

In the spring of 1778, while at Valley Forge, General Washington had become optimistic. His army had survived the winter, there was a wave of new enlistments coming in, and supplies began to flow into the encampment. Baron Von Steuben's incessant drilling had energized and improved the morale of his ragged soldiers. Washington began making plans to go on the offensive as the Crown forces moved through New Jersey. On July 1, he wrote to Henry Laurens, President of the Continental Congress:

On the appearance of the enemy's intention to march through Jersey becoming serious, I detached General Maxwell's brigade, in conjunction with the militia of that state. To interrupt and impede their progress by every obstruction in their power, so as to give time to the army under my command to come up with them and take advantage of every favorable circumstances that might present themselves. Having proceeded to Coryel's Ferry [Lambertville] I immediately detached Col. Morgan with a select corps of 600 men, to reinforce General Maxwell, and marched with the main body toward Princeton.[19]

As the British army approached Monmouth Courthouse, the entire American Army was massing and preparing for action at Hopewell, about eight miles from Princeton. It was then that General Washington became aware that Clinton was taking the southerly route to Sandy Hook. As muskets were being cleaned and two days of extra rations were being cooked, Washington called his generals together again for a council of war. They met at the Stout house, an elegant brick building that still stands at the corner of Hopewell-Rocky Hill Road and Hopewell-Amwell Road.

The plan was for a large advanced force to attack the British rear, with the main body of the army following closely in support. While he gave his generals the opportunity to voice their opinions, Washington's hidden agenda at this time was to maneuver his army into a full-scale battle at Monmouth Courthouse within a few days. Five months had passed since France had joined the American cause, and for most of that time all these new allies had experienced was a diminishing Continental Army which barely survived the harsh winter at Valley Forge. Washington desperately needed a victory, or even a show of strength, to renew French confidence and offer hope to his fellow countrymen. The open country of Monmouth County also ensured that a major engagement would be fought on terrain that was not advantageous to the enemy in any way. If they were allowed to continue on their route, in only one day the British would reach the high ground at Middletown and Navesink, a place where they would have a tactical advantage.

On June 25 American detachments were beginning to swarm around the rear of the British column. Stragglers lagging behind were captured, while the marauding American soldiers were verbally abused by weary and irritable British camp followers. The exhausted British army lumbered into Monmouth Court House on June 26.[20]

Washington described their position before the battle in his July 1 report to Laurens:

The Enemy were now encamped in a strong position, with their right extending about a Mile and an half beyond the Court House, in the parting of the Roads leading to Shrewsbury and Middletown, and their left along the Road from Allen Town to Monmouth, about three miles on this side the Court House. Their Right flank lay on the skirt of a small wood, while their left was secured by a very thick one, a Morass running towards their Rear, and their whole front covered by a wood, and for a considerable extent towards the left with a Morass. In this situation they halted till the morning of the 28th.

The American forces left Hopewell and moved ten miles to Kingston, where they abandoned their excess baggage and heavy equipment. From there they marched through Cranbury and Englishtown, twenty miles closer to Monmouth Courthouse. Orders were given for an assault to begin up Monmouth Road.

On the morning of Sunday, June 28, the British camped along Dutch Lane on the Freehold-Mount Holly Road while the main American Army was camped at Manalapan Bridge, four miles west of Englishtown. Washington sent orders to Major General Charles Lee to immediately begin an assault to bring the British column to a halt. He then planned to bring up the main strength of the American army to support him. Sir Henry Clinton soon realized that Washington was preparing to attack him with all his forces. The unwieldy supply and ammunition wagons, with their accompanying mobs of unruly camp followers, along with the train of heavy artillery, were sent on ahead of the fighting forces. Hessian General Knyphausen began to advance up the Middletown road. Soon the Battle of Monmouth Courthouse had begun.

It is surprising that Washington's forces missed their chance to wreak havoc and destruction on the vulnerable British procession as it moved through New Jersey. Some historians argue that an opportune time for a major battle would have been at Crosswicks Creek, a place where the high ground occupied by the Americans offered more advantageous terrain than at Monmouth.

Apparently, General Washington did not fully comprehend the difficulties that his enemy were encountering as they were strung out in their long column. Other than the minor stands at Crosswicks, and Bloomfield's attack beyond Allentown, most of the action by the Patriots had been limited to sporadic raids by small detachments, and the obstruction of bridges and roads. The Continentals lost valuable time when they halted at Hopewell. Combined brigades of Dickinson and Maxwell, with the strength of 1,800 men, were roaming close to the slow-moving enemy columns. Once their adversary reached

Bordentown, the main body of the American Army was never more than twenty-five miles away

Many questions remain about the Crown forces crossing New Jersey before the Battle of Monmouth. Why didn't King George's mighty army in America attack the emaciated Continental Army, less than half its size, at Valley Forge? Why were the Crown forces allowed to cross the Delaware River in flimsy flatboats when they could have been blasted out of the water by American cannons along the river bank? Why was a slow miles-long column, interspersed with supply trains and undisciplined civilians, allowed to pass, largely unopposed, over fifty miles of New Jersey terrain? Whatever the case, for Washington's rejuvenated troops Monmouth Courthouse was a two-day march, and it led up to one of the most important battles in American history.

Chapter 6

Washington Rocks: Perches of the American Eagle (1777-1778)

*Bound Brook, Martinsville, Bridgewater, Green Brook,
Plainfield, South Plainfield, Warren*

I t is difficult today to imagine the significance that the Watchung Mountains held during the Revolutionary War. Washington Rock, located in present-day Green Brook Township, is the location of the best known of several Revolutionary War observation posts that may be found on the crest of the first ridge of the Watchung Mountains. Historians and local residents claim that General George Washington used all of these sites to scan the countryside and observe the movements of British troops on the plains of central New Jersey, Staten Island and New York City.

I first selected Washington Rock as a critical site of the Revolutionary War that has been neglected in the history of the Garden State. However, while today it is typically acknowledged as being the *only* lookout, my research has recently revealed that it was one of *several* places along the first ridge of the Watchung Mountains used by General Washington during the war as an observation post.

The first ridge provides a 60-mile panoramic view of central New Jersey, stretching from Newark to Trenton. Troop movements in the British-occupied areas around New Brunswick, Perth Amboy,

Charles Willson Peale's sketch of Washington at today's Washington Rock State Park, drawn while he was viewing the Battle of Short Hills, 26 June 1777.

Elizabeth, Staten Island and New York Harbor could be closely watched from its several vantage points. These lookouts, at an elevation of between 400 and 500 feet above the central plains of New Jersey, provided the American Army with a unique sight advantage. An early warning to American troops would allow time to prepare and plan tactics and strategy to counter the invaders. In the 18th century the land below the Watchung Hills was mostly plowed fields and open pastures, thus allowing an almost unobstructed view from the lookouts.

My expanded study encompassed all the known Washington Rock locations in New Jersey. Most of these sites became obscure over time and were seldom identified in historical accounts. One of the most important places had been forgotten and unacknowledged for over 150 years, which led to my exciting rediscovery of a rocky ledge that has not been visited, to my knowledge, by any historian since 1851. It was found above the Middlebrook Encampment near Chimney Rock in Martinsville.

Strategic Situation

During the winter of 1776–1777, Washington kept the Continental Army encamped at Morristown, New Jersey. In April 1777, when the outpost garrison at Bound Brook was attacked and the American troops were routed, he moved his army to the Middlebrook Encampment on the heights above the town of Bound Brook. This location was twenty miles closer to the British lines around New Brunswick. He arrived at Middlebrook with the troops on May 28 and remained there until July 2, 1777.

A total of 8,298 Continental troops were encamped in the Watchung hills between Bridgewater and Green Brook Townships, which included 2,660 sick and disabled men who were unable to fight. This extended stay by the Patriots is known as "The First Middlebrook Encampment." Massing the American troops in these mountains at this turbulent time would prove to be a superb strategy.

British forces in and about New Brunswick had been reinforced to an overwhelming 17,000 men. The Redcoats were seasoned troops, well trained and equipped with state of the art weapons, including a small number of repeating rifles. Much of Washington's poorly clad army were raw militia with worn muskets often brought from home.

Washington could observe the enemy troop movements from anywhere along the crest of the first Watchung ridge, from Middlebrook to Scotch Plains. The Continental Army was in a naturally fortified position. From there they could counteract any hostile repositioning and have a significant effect on British campaign planning in America.

In early 1777 constant military action occurred on the plains below the lookout rocks, and skirmishes took place almost daily. These incidents included a clash at Spanktown (now Rahway) on January 5 and another on February 1 near the Millstone River at what is today Franklin Township. In April and May there was fighting near Perth Amboy and Piscataway. During this time there were also encounters on the roads from Elizabeth to Morristown and near Springfield and Scotch Plains.

British commander William Howe had two options at this time that could end the war with a British victory. He could advance directly across New Jersey by land to take the nation's capital of Philadelphia. He then could move up the Hudson River to join General Burgoyne, who was moving southward from Canada by way of Lake Champlain. This action would split New England from the other states, severely limiting the ability of America to wage war.

Or he could move to Amboy to embark at Staten Island and proceed by sea. This voyage would require sailing up the Chesapeake Bay and marching north to reach Philadelphia. The threat of an attack by the Continental Army from the hills at Middlebrook could force him to take the safer, but much slower, sea route from New York to Chesapeake Bay. This trip could cause a long delay which would completely upset Howe's strategy and affect the course of the entire war for Great Britain.

Two weeks after General Washington had moved from Morristown to occupy the heights of Middlebrook, he began to notice activity in the British lines. He observed the main body of the British army moving out during the night of June 13 and marching toward Somerset Courthouse, now present-day Somerville. In Middlebush (now Franklin Township), they threw up earthworks and tried to tempt the Americans to move down from their impenetrable position to engage in a European-style action on open ground, where the Redcoats would have all the advantages.[1]

The British continued to hold their position at Middlebush after June 15. British General Howe marched and countermarched his army, making feints. These false movements failed to draw Washington from the security of the Watchung heights to fight on the plains of Quibbletown (today's South Plainfield and Piscataway). Washington tenaciously refused to leave the security of his mountain stronghold to confront an enemy that had him outmanned and outgunned.

During this time, the British forces and their Hessian mercenaries indiscriminately plundered the farms of both Patriots and Loyalist inhabitants. The whole region of the Raritan and Millstone was stripped. The farmers threshed their wheat and then hid it under the straw in the barn in order to preserve it from the greedy enemy. In many instances not enough seed was saved to serve for replanting in the autumn. Cellars, houses, pig pens and hen roosts were all raided, and everything desirable was carried off.

At the Somerset Courthouse, British soldiers set fire to the Presbyterian and Dutch Churches, burned farmhouses and attempted to destroy every building between there and New Brunswick. Despite these provocations, the American general could not be lured from his stronghold on the first ridge above Bound Brook. He simply advanced his forces to the south side of the mountain, which he could more readily defend

On June 19, Howe finally appeared to abandon this strategy to engage the American in battle and began a general withdrawal from New Brunswick to Perth Amboy and Staten Island. Washington spotted the move from his rock ledge lookout on the first ridge at Middlebrook and detached three brigades under General Nathanael Greene to hassle the rear guard of the retreating Redcoats. He rejoiced when he observed the evacuation of the British forces and assuming the enemy would not return, and soon released militia units to return home.

General Washington perceived that he was witnessing an orderly withdrawal of the enemy from Amboy across the Arthur Kill to Staten Island, so he sent his army down from the heights of Middlebrook to liberate the oppressed farmers of central New Jersey. The Patriot forces gathered at a weak and exposed place, Quibbletown, now the New Market section of Piscataway Township. He did take one vital precaution by sending a force of 1,500 men, led by New Jersey Generals Stirling and Maxwell, to protect the flank at Edison, Plainfield and Scotch Plains.

The retreat of General Howe's forces from New Brunswick to Amboy has been viewed by many historians as only a deception to induce Washington to draw the American army down from its strong position in the hills at Middlebrook. There they could theoretically engage in a final decisive battle of the war, a fight in which the Americans where would be outnumbered and outgunned. But his original report shows his initial objective was simply to move his army to Staten Island for embarkation, not as a move to deceive Washington: "On finding their [the Americans] intention to keep a position—which it would not have been prudent to attack, I determined, without loss of time, to pursue the principal objects of the campaign by withdrawing the army from Jersey, and in consequence of this determination returned to the camp at Brunswick on the 19th, and marched from thence to Amboy intending to cross to Staten Island, from whence the embarkation was to take place."[2]

The intelligence that Washington had left his fortified camp in the hills was immediately reported by Tory spies to General Howe at Amboy. When he heard this news he ordered the British army to about-face and rapidly deploy to Quibbletown, where he hoped to surprise Washington in his unprotected position

Howe continued in his letter to Germain:

The necessary preparations being finished for crossing the troops to Staten Island, intelligence was received that the enemy had moved down from the mountain [heights at Middlebrook] and taken post at Quibbletown, intending, as it was given out, to attack the rear of the army removing from Amboy; that two corps had also advanced to their left—one of three thousand men and eight pieces of cannon, under the command of Lord Stirling, Gens. Maxwell and Conway, the last said to be a captain in the French service; the other corps consisted of about seven hundred men, with only one piece of cannon. In this situation, it was judged advisable to make a movement that might lead to an attack, which was done on the 26th, in the morning, in two columns.

Washington was warned by Stirling of the impending surprise attack, so he hastily withdrew back into the hills without any losses.

But Stirling and his vastly outnumbered detachment took heavy losses while holding off the entire British army. This valiant stand at Edison, Plainfield and Scotch Plains saved the American forces from a disastrous defeat that would have certainly ended the war. This critical but largely forgotten engagement has come down in history as The Battle of the Short Hills, as already discussed.

The battered survivors of Stirling's detachment retreated to Middlebrook through the Borough of Watchung and Warren Township, where they were secure behind the first ridge. The English generals then assessed their position and decided that the Watchung ridges were impregnable. This kept the American Army secure and difficult to attack, and when added to the strength of the formidable New Jersey Militia units, this prevented Howe from marching across New Jersey to take Philadelphia. Instead, he was forced to take the longer and more difficult sea route to Chesapeake Bay.

Washington's last glimpse of the enemy was from Washington Rock in Green Brook Township. He watched the English forces moving out of New Jersey through Westfield, Rahway and Amboy to Staten Island for the voyage to Chesapeake Bay to begin the Philadelphia campaign. They departed Amboy on the last day of June 1777, and this final exodus left the Garden State in possession of the Americans for the remainder of the war. The American army evacuated its position at Middlebrook two days later and moved northward to Pompton, a locale which provided even greater security, and a better position to protect the Hudson River Valley.[3]

Washington Rock at Green Brook

Today the first ridge of the Watchung Mountains in Union and Somerset Counties looks down on US Route 22. During the Revolutionary War this stretch of high ground was known as the "Blue Hills." The first settlers on the plains below gave it that name because of the blue haze that can still be observed cloaking these mountains today. Nestled in these hills were the sites of training schools, supply depots and hospitals. The three ridges of the Watchungs provided the security for Washington's Continental Army to encamp two winters at Middlebrook. Lookout stations and a string of signal beacons on the crest of the first ridge served the American Army as the main line of defense in New Jersey during the entire war.

Washington Rock, in Green Brook Township, the best known of the lookout posts, is in a scenic 52-acre state park. After more than two centuries of housing and roadway development in the region the landscape surrounding the park has been altered. Today it takes little time or effort to drive through these hills. We do not appreciate the fact that in the 18th century, when only men or horses provided the strength to haul wagons and cannons, the Watchung Mountains were major obstacles to troop movements and all other types of transportation. The ridges of the Watchungs provided layers of protection that stretched for over forty miles, from Mahwah to Somerset County, and formed a natural barrier that protected New Jersey from a British invasion westward.

The passes through these mountains were guarded by the New Jersey Militia from several counties. These citizen-soldiers assembled and drilled on the farm of Cornelius and Frederich Vermeule at the base of the first ridge along the Green Brook, in today's town of Plainfield. Washington Rock at Green Brook lies on the ridge directly above the Vermeule Farm. General Washington ordered that a camp be established here when he reached New Brunswick early in December 1777. It would serve as an assembly place for the New Jersey Militia who could fan out over the central part of the state to protect inhabitants from the plundering bands of British and Hessian soldiers.[4]

The militia of Hunterdon, Morris and Sussex Counties, the First Essex Regiment, the First Somerset Regiment under Colonel Frederick Frelinghuysen, and the First Middlesex Regiment, under Colonel John Webster, were stationed at the Vermeule Camp. "General

Wind's brigade," the nucleus of the garrison, totaled more than 1,200 men. The entire garrison of this post swelled to 2,000 men at various times, which made it half as large as Washington's entire Continental Army during the winter of 1776 and 1777.

This large militia post was built along the east bank of the Green Brook between what is now Clinton and West End Avenues. Its present address is 614 Green Brook Road in North Plainfield, New Jersey. It consisted of ninety-five acres and a large fort that guarded the main road from Scotch Plains to Quibbletown, present-day Front Street in Plainfield. Although the Plainfield area was mostly open farm land at that time, with a population of only about fifty residents, the location of the post had significant military importance. It served as the approach to the two vital passes through the first ridge—the Quibbletown Gap, now an abandoned roadbed, parallels Warrrenville Road, and the pass at Stony Brook, now Somerset Street in Watchung.

General Washington ordered troops to guard the main gaps through the southern section of the first Watchung Ridge as early as the fall of 1776. These gaps were at Middlebrook, where today Chimney Rock Road cuts through the ridge, the Quibbletown Gap, the pass at Stoney Brook, and at Scotch Plains where Bonnie Burn Road now ascends the first ridge. The battles at Bound Brook and the Short Hills, in the spring of 1777, were attempts by the British to penetrate American defenses by punching through these passes to get behind the ridge. These attacks were not successful, but their small raiding parties often caused havoc.

The British incursion that captured Major General Charles Lee at Widow White's Tavern in Basking Ridge, New Jersey was the most notable of the smaller forays. During the retreat across New Jersey in December 1776, General Charles Lee, second in command of the Continental Army, placed his troops near Morristown rather than join General Washington on the west side of the Delaware River. While sleeping in the tavern of the Widow White, Lee was taken prisoner by the troops of General Charles Cornwallis. The removal of Lee, a frequent critic of Washington, may have actually led to Washington's success at Trenton and Princeton. There had been conflicting rumors as to why General Lee was even at the Widow Whites Tavern; some historians allege that he went there in search of female sociability, or perhaps to visit Widow White herself. The tavern's original location was on what is now the corner of South Finley Avenue and Colonial Drive in Basking Ridge.

When the British army began moving from New Brunswick to Amboy after June 19, 1777, Washington followed suit by shifting his observation post north of Middlebrook to Green Brook, an easy move along the crest of the ridge. Parts of the trail that he took are still visible, although most of the route has been covered by residential development. Local tradition is that the general spent five days away from the Middlebrook Camp visiting the rock. This visit likely occurred during the end of June when the fighting took place at the Short Hills.

At Green Brook he was nearer to any hostile action that might develop and was closer to the Vermeule Camp. He remained in this immediate area and is known to have visited both the camp and the house of Nathaniel Drake. It was at the Drake House that General Washington consulted with his officers during and after the Battle of Short Hills, which was fought over the entire Plainfield area between June 25 and 27, 1777.[5] Washington observed the clash from the Rock and may have sent orders to the beleaguered General Stirling using semaphore flags.

One can imagine the stress Washington must have endured while looking down on the action with his "glass." He could see the troops of Stirling, outnumbered six to one, being beaten back toward Westfield and the wagons loaded with American wounded escaping up Bonnie Burn Road. Would the victorious British army then attempt to break through one of the passes and attack him from the rear? He must have been elated to see the Redcoats withdraw and not continue to press the assault.

After the war, in the early 1800s, Washington Rock at Green Brook became a popular tourist attraction. About 2,500 area residents visited the rock on July 4, 1831, to celebrate the 75th anniversary of the nation's independence. To accommodate the influx of travelers, a road called Cardinal Lane was constructed for stage coaches to shuttle tourists between the Plainfield Railway Station and Washington Rock. Families would spend the day picnicking on the grounds near the rock, and in the years that followed inns and hotels were opened nearby. Cardinal Lane remains today as an unpaved hiking trail. In the decades following the American Revolution, community leaders made many attempts to identify Washington Rock with a monument. This proved difficult as ownership of the property frequently shifted.

The earliest public reference to the Washington Rock at Green Brook was in 1844, sixty years after the War. This description is given in Barber and Howe's *Historical Collections of the State of New Jersey*:

> *At an elevation of about 400 feet on the brow of the mountain in the rear of Plainfield stands Washington's Rock. It is one of very large size, being about 25 feet in height and from 30 to 40 in circumference. The bold projection, which nature has given it from the surface of the eminence, renders it a fine position for taking an extensive view of the country below.*

In June, 1777 the American Army was stationed at various places on the plain below. After the retreat of Sir William Howe from New Brunswick, Washington retreated to the heights in rather than confront the enemy. The advance guard of the British army led by Cornwallis fell in with Lord Stirling's Division on June 27, 1777.

Barber and Howe further reported:

> *At various times he [General Washington] resorted to this place to ascertain the movements of the enemy. This circumstance has given the Rock a sacred character to the people of the present day, which, in connection with the beautiful prospect it affords, has made it a place of resort for parties of pleasure.*

The scene is one of uncommon beauty. The whole country, apparently, lies as level as a map at the feet of the spectator, for a circuit of 60 miles. On the left appear the spires of New York City, part of the bay, Newark, Elizabeth, Rahway and New Brighton [Edison]. Directly in front are Amboy and Raritan Bays. To the right New Brunswick and the heights of Princeton and Trenton; and far to the southeast the eye stretches over the plains of Monmouth to the heights of Navesink. Beautiful villages bedeck the plain; and cultivated fields, farm houses and numerous groves of verdant trees are spread around in pleasant profusion.[6]

Proof that General Washington used the Rock as an observation post was verified in 1897 when evidence of an eyewitness account was found. This account was related to George W. Fitz-Randolph by two local farmers, Ephraim and Josiah Vail, before 1830. Fitz-Randolph, a descendant of the Vail family who owned several farms below the Rock in Green Brook:

In the year 1777 or '78 Washington, with 6,000 men was encamped on the Ridge at Middlebrook near and west of Bound Brook. The British army were encamped at New Brunswick, Rahway and Perth Amboy, making incursions into the surrounding country. Doubtless, with an intent of guarding against a serious incursion or surprise, Washington was on his way to the top of the mountain back of Green Brook.

Be that as it may, he, with an aide-de-camp, mounted, rode in the gateway and up to a group of men standing between the house and the barn on the farm, now known as the Jonah Vail farm. Washington said: "Can any of you gentlemen guide me to some spot on the mountains from whence a good view of the plain below can be obtained?" Edward Fitz-Randolph, one of the group, said: "I know of the best point on the mountains for that purpose" and added that, if he had his horse, he would take him to it. Thereupon the General requested his aide to dismount and await his return. Fitz-Randolph, mounted upon the aide's horse, piloted the General to the Rock, which today bears the historic name of 'Washington's Rock'.

I have given the above nearly word for word, as given to me by Ephraim Vail, who died a few years since aged 90 and over, on the farm where he was born and raised. Josiah Vail gave me the same version of the incident; Indeed any of the old residents of Green Brook would corroborate the same, were they alive. All these Vails were Quakers, owning adjoining farms, and their word is reliable.[7]

George Fitz-Randolph again confirmed Washington's presence at the Rock shortly before he died in 1830. Fitz-Randolph reported that Washington observed the British Fleet preparing to sail to Chesapeake Bay: "Looking through his glass, Washington rejoiced at finally watching the British fleet of 270 transports leave Amboy bay heading to sea and leaving Jersey forever.

The development of the rail line below the Rock in 1838 accelerated the development of the towns below. Westley H. Ott, the unofficial historian of Dunellen, reported that the Rock was a popular spot for political rallies as early as 1840. Rail service was provided between Elizabethtown and Plainfield at that time and was later extended to Bound Brook in 1843.[8]

The Rock has long been a landmark and site for day trips for Central Jersey residents. As early as 1840, residents from nearby towns began climbing up to the Rock to admire the view and have picnics. Rebecca Vail, a Quaker farm wife of Green Brook, kept a diary for a brief period in her life. That fragment of journal records that in 1847 she made a picnic trip to the Rock.

Historian Ott also reported that on the 75th anniversary of Independence in 1851, more than 2,500 spectators visited Washington Rock. He also described the Washington Rock Mountain House, erected in 1852, as a "large three-story building" with a full-length porch. This hotel burned to the ground in a raging fire in 1883.

Curiously, in 1851, the famous historian Benson Lossing visited New Jersey and inquired about the location of "Washington Rock." At the time local residents assumed that the Rock was the rocky ledge above the Middlebrook Encampment near Chimney Rock, not Green Brook. While Lossing mentions the Green Brook Rock, residents apparently regarded it as less historically important than the other lookout in the years after the war.

Lossing provided this brief mention of the Green Brook Rock after a lengthy detailed description of the large stone at Middlebrook: "In the rear of Plainfield, at an equal elevation, and upon the same range of hills, is another rock bearing a similar appellation, and from the same cause. It is near the brow of the mountain, but, unlike the one under consideration, it stands quite alone, and rises from a slope of the hill, about twenty-five showing. From this latter lofty position, it is said, Washington watched the movements of the enemy in the summer of 1777."[9]

An 1860 real estate map titled "Washington Rock to Newark Bay," part of a collection found at the Cannonball House in Scotch Plains, shows two hotels at the site. In the 1870s, a stage coach regularly ran two miles between the Dunellen Station and the Rock. After the Civil War, John W. Laing, a Plainfield stableman, dutifully climbed the mountain each year to give the Rock a coat of whitewash.[10]

The Constitutionalist, Plainfield's leading newspaper from 1868 to 1911, reported that repainting the Rock each year had become a notable annual event.[11] In 1898 *The Constitutionalist* proclaimed that Washington Rock was to be defended, not against the assaults of a Spanish Army, but by the ravages of time: "It is really but right that that historical spot should be looked after especially at such a time as this. For years, it has been the custom of some patriotic citizens to whitewash the Rock so that it can be seen for miles around. Constable William N. Pangborn and Edward Conshee are leading a group to ensure that the Rock receives a coat of whitewash and the brush cleared around it."[12]

With the approach of the Centennial, a group of citizens formed the Washington Monument and Historical State Association in 1867. The group included many members of the local Masonic lodge in Plainfield, since George Washington was an active Mason all his life and served as the Grand Master of his fraternity. The association began raising funds to build a 100-foot observation tower on the mountain behind the Rock. The tower, was to be "a monumental shaft dedicated to immortal Washington which greets the rising sun from yonder mountain brow." The Masons provided the motto "New Jersey gratefully remembers her defenders in the dark and bloody days of the Revolution."[3] Although the foundation and cornerstone were laid, mortgages held on the land prevented the association from getting a clear title, and the project was eventually abandoned.

While the tower monument was never built, the ceremonies, parades, speeches, fireworks and displays held on July 4, 1876, were extensive. A band played on all day at the huge dancing platform constructed at the Rock. In the evening, the grove and the hotel were brilliantly illuminated, music was provided for more dancing, and a grand Centennial supper for 6,000 guests was served.

There was still interest in erecting some sort of memorial at the Rock, and finally the Daughters of the American Revolution (DAR) Continental Chapter started raising funds in 1879. A.L.C. Marsh, a New York City architect who designed "country homes," and lived in Plainfield, donated a design plan to the DAR for the memorial. It called for building a stone cairn on the foundation of the tower that had been built forty years before by the Masons, and adding a native stone retaining wall to join the two rocks on the site. This plan was never put into action, however, due to lack of funding. In 1909 the property was purchased by Mr. Charles McCutchen of North Plainfield, who understood its historical significance, and held it in trust for the people of Plainfield and North Plainfield.

Finally, in 1912, a small cube-shaped one room stone building was erected by the DAR at the cost of $3,000. The monument now stands approximately twenty feet above the rock and is surmounted by a high flagpole. On March 27, 1913, the New Jersey Senate and State Assembly passed an act to acquire Washington Rock and adjoining lands as a gift from McCutchen. The act also called for the appointment of a commission to improve and maintain the site as a public park.

Washington Rock in Green Brook is currently being managed by the Somerset County Park Commission. Today Washington Rock State Park encompasses two large rock outcrops that stand about eighty feet apart. One is called "Lafayette Rock" in honor of the young French general who frequently accompanied Washington and who is reported to have perched on it in 1777. The park is currently operated and maintained by the New Jersey Division of Parks and Forestry.[14]

The Washington Rock at Middlebrook and Other Lookouts

General Washington apparently utilized many locations along the first Watchung Ridge to observe the British and to plan troop movements. My tracing of the history of Washington Rock in Green Brook, led to a fascinating discovery when I came across a reference to another rock observation post along the ridge in a British account written in 1785. This document mentions Washington's observation post as being on a rock on the south side of Middlebrook Heights, which would place it on the first ridge about five miles southwest of Green Brook in the Middlebrook Encampment, in what is now Martinsville.

General Washington relocated the American army from Morristown to Middlebrook after learning that British forces under Howe might be preparing to move across New Jersey to capture the nation's capital at Philadelphia. American troops began arriving in May 1777 and remained until early July. This become known as the First Middlebrook Encampment. From Middlebrook Washington could quickly maneuver his forces to strike the flank of the enemy columns if they attempted to move anywhere in New Jersey. These

Washington Rock at Middlebrook
Campground, Martinsville, N.J. 1851
(*Drawing by Benson J. Lossing in*
The Pictorial Field-Book of the
Revolution)

tumultuous seven weeks in the spring of 1777 were a time of uncertainty and indecision for the Americans. What would be the next move if the mighty 16,000-man British force billeted around New Brunswick? Would they move south to take Philadelphia? Would they move west to occupy the entire state? Or would they cross over the Arthur Kill to Staten Island and return to New York?

A lookout post at Middlebrook would provide a sweeping view of the area from New Brunswick, seven miles away, to Amboy. Enemy activity could be observed on the Raritan River and on the road to Pluckemin to the west. It would be logical for General Washington to have an observation post close to the British lines. The lookout, at Green Brook Rock, two miles north, would only have value if the Redcoat army moved in that direction.

More recent references reported that the Middlebrook Rock was actually Chimney Rock, an iconic landmark that has been notable throughout the state's history. This natural rock outcrop resembles a chimney stack, hence its name. It is identified on current maps as Hawk's Watch and is now a place frequented by bird watchers. I ruled it out as being the Middlebrook Washington Rock after noticing that the view from there is through a valley and is restricted by hills on each side.

Another early reference to the Middlebrook Rock was from local historian, Rev. Dr. Abraham Messier, pastor of the nearby First Church of Raritan. He described the rock outcrop in the 1830s but did not disclose its exact location. He reported, "On the apex of the Round Top, on the left of the gorge in which Chimney Rock stands, there are yet to be seen the rude remains of a hut which Washington sometimes frequented during those anxious months of 1777. On the east side of the gorge, also, fronting the plain north of Middlebrook, there is a rock which has been named 'Washington Rock,' because there he often stood to gaze anxiously upon the scene it overlooks."[15]

I found very few references in documents written in the next 150 years that mention a lookout site somewhere along the ridge, so its exact location had been lost in history. One account reported that it was covered by a swimming pool, but it provided no further details. In 1975, local historian and archeologist A. A. Boom reported that the location of the Middlebrook Washington Rock was mentioned in a book by historian Benson Lossing.[16]

Lossing had actually visited the site in 1851, so I conducted a search of his journal. This proved to be an abundant source of information, because it stated that the rock was at the end of the old steep road over the mountain. Not only did he describe the location in lucid detail, but he also drew a sketch of the rocky ledge which was identified by local residents as "Washington Rock." Lossing's account of his visit to the Middlebrook Rock provided enough detail for me to find the approximate location using existing landmarks:

Returning to the village, we proceeded to visit the campground, which is upon the left of the main road over the mountains to Pluckemin; also 'Washington's Rock.' The former [at Green Brook] exhibits nothing worthy of particular attention; but the latter, situated upon the highest point of the mountain in the rear of Middlebrook, is a locality, independent of the associations which hallow it, that must ever impress the visitor with pleasant recollections of the view obtained from that lofty observatory.

We left our wagon at a point half way up the mountain, and made our way up the steep declivities along the remains of the old road [Vossellor Avenue]. How loaded wagons were managed in ascending or descending this mountain road is quite inconceivable, for it is a difficult journey for a foot-passenger to make. In many places not even the advantage of a zigzag course along the hillsides was employed, but a line as straight as possible was made up the mountain. Along this difficult way the artillery troops that were stationed at Pluckemin crossed the mountain, and over that steep and rugged road heavy cannons were dragged.

Having reached the summit, we made our way through a narrow and tangled path [Miller Lane] to the bold rock seen in the picture on the next page. It is at an elevation of nearly four hundred feet above the plain below, and commands a magnificent view of the surrounding country included in the segment of a circle of sixty miles, having its rundle southward.

At our feet spread out the beautiful rolling plains like a map, through which course the winding Raritan and the Delaware and Hudson Canal. Little villages and neat farmhouses dotted the picture in every direction. Southward, the spires of New Brunswick shot up above the intervening forests, and on the left, as seen in the picture, was spread the expanse of Raritan and Amboy Bays, with

many white sails upon their bosoms. Beyond were seen the swelling
hills of Staten the Island, and the more abrupt heights of Neversink
or Navesink Mountains, at Sandy Hook. Upon this lofty rock
Washington often stood, with his telescope, and reconnoitered the
vicinity. He overlooked his camp at his feet, and could have descried
the marchings of the enemy at a great distance upon the plain, or
the evolutions of a fleet in the waters beyond."[17]

I was able to match Lossing's description with a 1777 map drawn
for General Washington by Captain William Scull.[18] The map shows
the locations of the Continental Army units during the First
Encampment in 1777, as well as both Vosseller Avenue and Chimney
Rock Roads. An icon marks the exact location of Wayne's Regiment,
which occupied the hilltop. With this additional information, I could
now closely identify where the rock should be.

I returned to Middlebrook with these clues, along with a copy of
Lossing's sketch. I left Route 22 West and drove up the hill on
Vossellor Avenue to the crest of the first ridge, then turned left onto
Miller Lane. Here I began looking out for the rocky ledge depicted in
Lossing's sketch. I soon noticed a sign—"Eagle's Nest Museum-
Herbert M. Patullo."

Nearby was a large barn and a private home. The barn appeared
to contain antiques. Adjacent to these structures was a grassy plot
with a flagpole that overlooked a vast panoramic view. I knew at once
that this was the vista described by Lossing. I was soon greeted by
Herb Patullo, owner of the premises. He examined Lossing's sketch of
rock outcrop and noted that it looked very familiar and might be close
by. We tramped through the woods for about fifty yards to a rock
outcropping which resembled Washington Rock at Middlebrook as
described by Benson Lossing in 1851.

Mr. Patullo, owner and operator of the Eagle's Nest Museum, told
me he has lived his entire life in Bound Brook and for many years was
a restaurateur in the town. He has served the community as a leader in

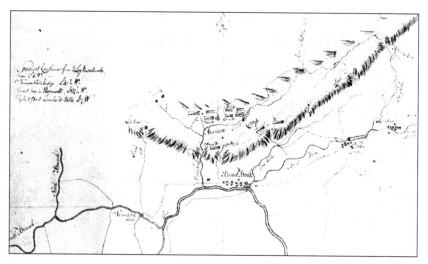

Map by Captain Scull of the 11th Pennsylvania Regiment, 1778. Route 22 now runs along the base of the thick dark line. Note label for Bound brook.

many cultural and historical activities, including serving as past President of the Washington Campground Association. As a child his father instilled in him an awareness that their town and the heights above it provided the setting for many critical events during the American Revolution. As a result, he is an astute local historian, and has a comprehensive knowledge of the history of the Bound Brook area and the Middlebrook Encampment. This historical awareness led to his lifelong interest and efforts to preserve the historic encampment site from desecration by commercial and residential development.

This land on the heights around Bound Brook, now part of Martinsville, was the nucleus of the two Middlebrook Encampments; in many ways is more significant than other renowned Continental Army camp sites such as Valley Forge and Jockey Hollow. It was a natural fortress for placement of artillery positions to guard the pass that is now Chimney Rock Road. The site provided a view of the countryside that General Washington needed to observe the activities of the British in New York and New Brunswick; it was a position from which he could attack if they attempted to cross New Jersey to Philadelphia.

Washington placed his best armed and trained brigade in this position of honor in advance of the main Army. The Pennsylvania Brigade, commanded by General Anthony Wayne, was recognized as an elite fighting unit. It camped here in an area that extended from the intersection of Vosseller Avenue and Hillcrest Road towards Chimney Rock. The position secured the strategic road passes through the mountain and guarded the rest of the army that was spread out in the Washington Valley behind the ridge. Wayne's Brigade was made up of four Pennsylvania Regiments, most of whom were armed with .69 caliber Charleville muskets from France. Many of the Pennsylvanians were veterans of the Trenton-Princeton campaign and the earlier operations in New York State.[19]

The historical significance of this land had been completely forgotten until relatively recently. The land had been owned by an adjacent quarry operation since the late 19th century. In the early 1970s the property was occupied by a single dilapidated building that housed a county home for the indigent. Herb Patullo became worried that encroaching commercial and residential development would soon envelop this historic place. When the county home was closed in 1974, he purchased the building and the 3-acre lot on which it stood. Later, in 1988, he acquired the forty acres that span along the ridge between Chimney Rock Road and Vossellor Avenue. This large swath covered the entire hilltop of the Revolutionary War campsite. He built his home on the site twelve years later and eventually sold the remainder of the property back to Somerset County. The county added the historic land to the adjoining Washington Valley Park in 1994.

The Eagles Nest Museum is open to the public and houses a modest eclectic collection of historic memorabilia, as well as items from Patullo's time as a Machinists Mate in the US Navy during the Korean War. Two original paintings by local artist Victor Temporra are also on display, both of which portray scenes of the camp during the time when it was occupied by Washington's Army. Many of the details depicted in the paintings were provided by Patullo. The museum is open to the public, and visitors remain enthralled by the view from the premises.

Another Middlebrook Rock

I was asked to be the speaker at the annual meeting of the Washington Campground Association in February 2017. I took this opportunity to venture the possibility that the Rock at Middlebrook on the Patullo property was the observation post along the ridge mentioned in the British account of 1785, and the same one visited by Lossing in 1851. Soon afterward I was contacted by local historian Don McBride. He claimed to have found another observation rock that more closely matched Lossing's sketch, one that was only 1,000 yards north of the Patullo Rock and nearer to Vosseller Avenue.

McBride lives on the ridge adjacent to the former campground, and for many years has explored the area on foot. He has identified remnants of trenches and stone walls and has cleared paths to the crest of the ridge. I stopped by to join McBride to visit the Vosseller Avenue Rock a few weeks after my talk. We tramped through the foliage to the edge of the cliff and stood on the Rock to observe its field of view. We found the same sweeping panoramic 60-mile vista. We then descended about fifty feet down the hill to the base of the cliff to observe the lookout from below. We then compared the two Rock observation posts to the Lossing sketch and narrative.

The Vosseller Avenue rock formation looks much more like Lossing's drawing. Its location atop a distinct cliff closely resembles his sketch, and the site is closer to the road (Vosseller Avenue), as described by Lossing. In addition, the site is where Wayne Brigade was camped, and its elevation is 375 feet, 65 feet higher than the Patullo Rock. However, if trees were removed, the view from Petullo's Eagles Nest would be better to the South-South East toward New Brunswick. Moving down the ridge toward Petullo's home also allows a better view of the Sandy Hook area.

You can move about 100 yards down the ridge to get a view of Sandy Hook in the winter when there are no leaves on the trees. It is impossible to see the Vosseller Avenue Rock in profile looking south towards New

McBride's Rock. *(Author's collection)*

Brunswick, so it is likely that Lossing used some artistic license in his illustration. It is also probable that General Washington moved to several places along the ridge between Vosseller Avenue and Patullo's Eagles Nest in 1777 to detect the movement of his Redcoat adversaries.

The Middlebrook Encampment has never been regarded as a significant New Jersey tourist attraction. Most people that are acquainted with it are residents of nearby towns who attend a July 4th ceremony each year held at a commemorative park which is maintained by the Washington Campground Association located on Middlebrook Road east of Vosseller Avenue.

In 1888 the LaMonte family donated twenty acres near the camp to the Washington Campground Association. The LaMontes donated the land on the condition that the Declaration of Independence be read every 4th of July, and that the 13-star version of the American flag be flown twenty-four hours a day. They also stipulated that the land would revert back to the heirs of the family if these requirements were not fulfilled. Since the Association had clear title and it could be easily reached via Vossellor Avenue, the area was suitable for a commemorative park. The Association has faithfully respected the wishes of the LaMonte family each year since that time. Unfortunately, few visitors are aware that the park is not on land occupied by the Middlebrook Encampment; it was actually positioned about a quarter of a mile away.

In the 1990s, the Somerset County Cultural and Heritage Commission explored the feasibility of establishing some historical landmarks in the area south of Miller Lane. They considered retaining Hunter Research, an archaeological investigative firm, to perform a study in the area near Middlebrook Washington Rock to determine if there was any evidence of remains from Revolutionary War encampments. This effort did not play out, but in a way this may be fortunate since this forgotten place remains undisturbed to this day, and the Middlebrook Washington Rock appears very close to the way it did in 1777.

More Washington Rocks Along the First Watchung Ridge

Another Revolutionary War lookout post was located above Montclair State University at the intersection of the Great Notch area of Little Falls and the Montclair Heights section of Clifton. Eagle Rock in West Orange served as a lookout site as well. Two other places on the South Mountain Reservation, in central Maplewood, Millburn and West Orange have been reported, one of which is marked with two stone pillars.

In June 1780, sentries at these northern lookout stations reported the dreaded news that the British had finally launched a westward attack. The assault moved toward the Hobart Gap, the pass through Chatham and Madison which is now Route 24. This corridor led west to Jockey Hollow, Morristown, the winter encampment of the Continental Army. A breakthrough would have been devastating to the debilitated Continental Army, which was recovering from one of the most brutal winters ever recorded.

Five thousand enemy troops advanced through Union Township. A British column rushed along Galloping Hill Road while Hessian troops were under the command of Hessian Lieutenant General Wilhelm von Knyphausen pressed up Vaux Hall Road. This joint attack was vigorously repelled at Connecticut Farms by the

Continental Army and New Jersey Militia forces under the command of General William Maxwell and at Springfield on June 23, sixteen days later. The warnings provided by the observation posts along the First Ridge of the Watchung Mountains in New Jersey were critical to stopping an American defeat and an early end to the War.

Chapter 7

Dashing Through New Jersey (1781)

Counties of Bergen, Passaic, Essex, Union, Morris, Somerset, Middlesex, Mercer

The entire French Army of 7,000 soldiers, along with 2,000 horses and 700 draft oxen, swarmed down the main streets of New Jersey hamlets, hurrying south through the New Jersey countryside. Young French noblemen wearing plumed silver helmets were mounted on splendid steeds, commanded their columns. A unit of 600 mounted Huzzars, an elite light-cavalry unit used for scouting, wore tall black hats and sky-blue jackets adorned with gold loops and braid along with bright yellow breeches. Their ornate uniforms were modeled on a 15th century Hungarian light-horse corps.

The farm families lining the dirt roads along the route were dumbfounded by this spectacle, and were fascinated by the splendid parade of superbly-clad soldiers speaking an exotic foreign language accompanied by bands playing martial music. Amid their wild cheers they offered the soldiers freshly baked bread, jellies, cheese, cider, and liqueur made from cherries. Flirtatious country lasses approached the marching soldiers. The Count de Clermont-Crevecoeur commented, "Enchanting to find charming young ladies in our midst. We had the musicians play each evening and invited the girls to dance. Thus we relaxed from the fatigues of the day."

Many interesting and delightful accounts of the 5-day march through New Jersey by foreign troops on the way to Yorktown come from these French officers and their men. They viewed New Jersey as an exciting wonderland filled with surprises. On the other hand, few descriptions of the march were left by American soldiers. For them the terrain, towns and people were familiar, and were so similar to the places they lived that they were not worth describing in writing.

Strategic Situation

The Continental Army had been devastated and demoralized by the difficult winter of 1779–1780 spent at Jockey Hollow, Morristown, and the Hudson Highlands. At the start of the new year the Pennsylvania brigade could not endure the harsh conditions, so its members finally mutinied in Morristown. Terms of an agreement to end this rebellion were reached on January 9. The mutineers were given back pay, were furloughed until March, and allowed additional accommodations.

Three weeks later, the men of the New Jersey Line demanded the same concessions after they mutinied in Pompton. Understandably, General Washington was alarmed. He feared that if these insurrections continued this would be the end of the War for Independence. He therefore crushed the New Jersey rebellion using extreme force by executing two of its ringleaders at Federal Hill near Pompton. As spring of 1781 approached, the Continental Army continued to weaken by desertions while British forces moved almost unopposed across the southern states. In desperation, General Washington wrote on April 9, 1780, "We are at the end of our tether, and . . . now or never our deliverance must come."[1] A successful campaign in 1781 was the army's only chance to achieve independence.

The presence of the French army and fleet in North America between 1778–80, along with the assurance of their support in the coming campaign season, lifted morale throughout the new nation.

Jean-Baptiste-Donatien de Vimeur, Comte de
Rochambeau, Marechal De France. *(Charles-
Phillippe Larivière, Palace of Versailles)*

Washington's aide, Tench Tilghman, wrote to Congressman Robert Morris from New Windsor, New York on May 17 that he was planning, "to set out tomorrow with His Excellency for Weathersfield [Connecticut] where he is to have an interview with the Comte de Rochambeau. ... The expectations of the people are high and perhaps they may expect a change more suddenly than it is possible to affect one."[2]

Rochambeau was advised by the American leaders to draw up plans for the coming campaign with Admiral de Grasse, who had left France for the Caribbean on April 5, but who might be able to provide naval support. At Wethersfield in May 1781 Washington and Rochambeau decided to join forces on the Hudson River and make plans to attack New York City. The city had been occupied by the British for the past six years and served as their headquarters in America.

The main arena for operations during 1780 and 1781 shifted to the southern states. British General Cornwallis captured Savannah, Georgia and followed up with victories at Charleston and Camden, South Carolina. Outnumbered American forces under Generals Nathanael Greene and the Marquis de Lafayette avoided a final decisive battle and continued to weaken the enemy by luring them inland in an attempt to stretch out their supply lines. This Patriot strategy paid off with victories at Cowpens, Guilford Courthouse and Kings Mountain in the Carolinas.

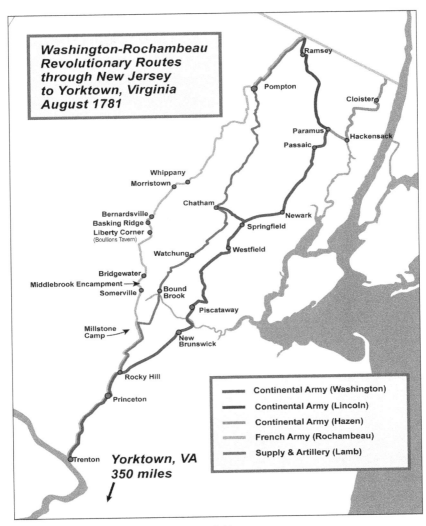

Cartography by Balefire Communications for Robert A. Mayers

Sir Henry Clinton, the top English commander, who had his headquarters in New York City, now ordered Cornwallis to establish a permanent camp for the winter at a port in the mid-Atlantic states. Cornwallis selected Yorktown, a small seaport at the tip of the York Peninsula in Virginia. He arrived there during the summer with the British southern army of 8,300 men.

Yorktown seemed to be an ideal location, protected and supplied by the British Fleet and reinforced by sea from New York. If threatened, an army could easily be evacuated by the nearby fleet. But in retrospect the selection of Yorktown as a base was the biggest British blunder in the entire eight years of the Revolutionary War since Cornwallis had overlooked the possibility that his army could be entrapped.

The main forces of both opposing armies in the north had been stalemated for two years around New York City. There, Washington's force of 9,000 was massed above the city along the Hudson River confronting 14,000 Crown troops in Manhattan. During the time the Redcoats had held this area they had become well entrenched and fortified, with a perimeter of defenses north of the city and on Long Island, where they were strongly supported by the large Loyalist population. The formidable English fleet could protect the city from incursion from the sea. A successful American assault against this mighty British bastion in America could win the war for the new nation, but a defeat would surely be the end of the American rebellion. The losses would be appalling, and the dream of independence would vanish forever.

The French Expeditionary Force had arrived in Rhode Island a year earlier with 7,800 men and a powerful French Fleet under the command of Count de Grasse. The French joined the Continental Army at Dobbs Ferry, New York in July 1781. Washington now had superior numbers and incredible resources at his disposal. The allied army was now in a position to assault the British fortifications at Kingsbridge, across the Harlem River from Manhattan, and on Long Island. The long-awaited siege of New York could begin.

The French Arrive in New York- Dobbs Ferry, July 8, 1781

General Washington reviewed the French forces encamped near Phillipsburg (near present-day Tarrytown, New York). The following day, American officers were invited to inspect the French Army. The French soldiers "appeared in the grandest parade uniform. M. de Rochambeau took his place in front of the white flag of his oldest regiment and saluted General Washington. . . . Our general received the greatest compliments for the beauty of his troops. It is true that without doubt those that we have with us were superb at our departure from France.[3]

The following day, after Rochambeau and his officers had reviewed the Americans, they were shocked. Baron Von Closen commented, "I had a chance to see the American army, man for man. It was really painful to see these brave men, almost naked with only some trousers and little linen jackets, most of them without stockings, but would you believe it? Very cheerful and healthy in appearance. A quarter of them were Negroes, merry, confident, and sturdy. . . . Three quarters of the Rhode Island regiment consists of Negroes, and that regiment is the most neatly dressed, the best under arms, and the most precise in its maneuvers."[4] The Comte de Clermont-Crèvecoeur "was surprised by, not by its smart appearance, but by its deprivation, The men were without uniforms and covered with rags; most of them were barefoot. They were of all sizes, down to children who could not have been over fourteen."[5]

Washington weighed the odds of a successful siege against New York after a thorough reconnaissance of the city in July. The strength of the outer ring of defenses was evaluated and found to be formidable. Washington's then began to focus attention on Cornwallis in the south. On August 1, he wrote that he, "could scarce see a ground upon which to continue my preparations against New York, and therefore I turned my views more seriously (than I had before done) to an operation to the southward."[6] But the two generals had to wait in a no-man's land, just north of New York City, for news from Admiral de Grasse, whose fleet would determine the place of attack. On August 14, when the frigate *Concorde* brought news de Grasse was headed for the Chesapeake and could support the allied armies in the Chesapeake Bay area, but not New York, plans to move south were finalized.

We Will Go South

General Washington settled on a strategy after conferring with Comte de Rochambeau. This plan was so daring and fraught with so many risks and uncertainties that it seemed ridiculous. Washington was at first reluctant to abandon his long carefully planned strategy of an assault on New York City from the north, but the availability of the French fleet changed his mind. Why not try to trap the southern British army at Yorktown, rather than sustain possible appalling losses and risk defeat by attacking New York City?

The success of a Virginia campaign depended on a series of uncontrollable events that had to occur with precise timing. The allied Franco-American army would have to travel up to 600 miles in seven weeks to reach the battlefield. When they arrived, there was no certainty that the British would still be there. The French Fleet had sail south to take up positions to block the British warships from evacuating or reinforcing Cornwallis. Due to the vagaries of weather, there was no certainty that the French would appear on the coast at the right time. Lafayette, with the southern American army, had to reach Yorktown from the Carolinas to increase the size of the American forces. Meanwhile, it Sir Henry Clinton discovered that the allied armies had left New York, leaving only a small force at West Point, he could invade north up the Hudson River all the way to Canada and divide the states. Separating New England from the other states would effectively end the war. As a result, a feint was necessary to convince Clinton the attack would come from Staten Island.

The entire venture would depend on a surprise attack. The combined armies would have to move south secretly across nine states in a race against time. If the British side discovered any indication that the allied troops were leaving New York, the British fleet would sail south to evacuate or strengthen the beleaguered Cornwallis. Both armies immediately headed south.

The combined army first crossed to the west bank of the Hudson

River fifteen miles north of Dobbs Ferry, at Kings Ferry, near Haverstraw, New York. Since there were few boats available to ferry such a large force across the Hudson the going was extremely slow, and it was feared that the British would send frigates up the river to prevent the crossing. It took seven days for the joint forces to cross with supply wagons, cannons and horses, but the British did not approach them.

The haggard soldiers of the Continental Army came first. Most had bare feet and were clad only in the remnants of tattered uniforms or ragged civilian clothes. After three days, the French began arriving. In sharp contrast, they were well disciplined and fully equipped infantry wearing immaculate white uniforms with blue, pink or green facing. The allied armies began their epic march to Virginia from Haverstraw. The area on the west side of the river, along present-day Route 9W, served as a staging area. The American Army of 2,720 officers and men, and more than 600 horses and 300 oxen, started out on the long, perilous, 500-mile march south on August 22, 1781. Three days later they crossed over into New Jersey.

The Grand Secret

After crossing into New Jersey, the army headed south toward Princeton, leaving only a small force behind to maintain the deception that the anticipated invasion of New York City by an amphibious landing from Staten Island was in progress. Secrecy was of utmost importance so that deserters or Loyalists in New Jersey would not alert the enemy of the intended target of Yorktown, Virginia.

Concealment was vital for the success of the plan. In early August, before the armies entered New Jersey, General Washington had leaked word that New York was about to be invaded. He first informed Patriots but was fully aware that the message would soon reach the Loyalists, who in turn would relay it to the British Headquarters in

New York. To encourage the ruse, he issued false dispatches, marked "Secret," to give advance notice to both the American and French forces. His officers issued contracts for provisions to be delivered in New Jersey, and sent letters about such details via the most hazardous routes with the intent that they would fall into enemy hands. This bogus information lent credence that the plan was for an imminent amphibious attack on New York from Staten Island.

In the French and American armies only a few trusted officers were informed of the decision to march to Virginia. The hoax was so convincing that even Rochambeau was completely confused. American General James Clinton was irate because he did not know about the real plan until the end of August when his New York Brigade reached Trenton. The Americans also set up false encampments along the New Jersey side of the Hudson River. British spies and Tory informants reported that both armies, as well as the French Fleet, were heading to a place on the lower Hudson River.

What seemed to be irrefutable evidence that the allies were about to launch an amphibious invasion of New York was the presence of boats. Several flatboats, known as bateaux, that could hold up to forty soldiers, were dragged along on oxcarts. Colonel Philip Van Cortlandt, 2nd New York Regiment, accompanied the bateaux. A crossing of the Arthur Kill between New Jersey and New York or an assault directly across the Hudson River seemed imminent. Word had also spread that the Franco-American forces might attempt both of these assaults. Sir Henry Clinton began setting up defenses to prepare for this two-pronged attack.

Fifteen impeccably uniformed French soldiers appeared at Chatham, New Jersey on August 4, and they were assumed to be an advanced party for the New York invasion. This detachment had orders to establish a complete army base with warehouses that would hold the supplies for the "attack" on New York. What amazed everyone was that they began building rows of brick ovens under a 65-foot-long shed along the eastern bank of the Passaic River. At the same time French soldiers canvassed the area for provisions and brought in large quantities of supplies. The residents of Chatham were thoroughly convinced that their town would be the staging area for the assault on New York.

In less than a week the Frenchmen built a bakery that produced 3,000 loaves of bread each day. Both Patriot and Loyalist civilians were completely convinced that a large invading army must be approaching. To protect this base at Chatham, Washington stationed three regiments on the heights between Chatham and Springfield on August 19. At this time the top British commander, Sir Henry Clinton, must have been assured that the attack was only a few days away. The allies armies would attempt a landing supported by a French Fleet that would enter New York Harbor to bombard New York City.

On August 27 the *New York Mercury,* a Loyalist newspaper, reported that more than 6,000 troops had arrived in Chatham, and ominously pointed out that the town was only about nine miles from Staten Island. Washington arrived at Chatham from Pompton with a supply column on August 27 and stayed for two days before leaving to continue down what is today's Morris Avenue to Springfield. The hoax was so successful that Sir Henry did not know the allied army was heading to Virginia until most of the troops had crossed the Delaware River. What is even more astonishing is that many French and American officers would learn about their destination at the same time. Once Trenton was reached, there could no longer be any doubt that Lord Cornwallis's army at Yorktown was the target of the campaign.

The five days that the armies took to move through New Jersey have been obscured in the history of the state, having taken a back seat to the major battles fought there. For the French the advance was much easier than their march through New England since the roads were better and the summer heat had given way to the cooler fall weather. Once the crossing of the Hudson was completed and the march through New Jersey had begun, the Continental Army settled into a routine. They were assembled to march at 4:00 A.M., and the campsite for the day was reached in the early afternoon, at the latest.

Next came the distribution of food, especially beef, to the men. Meals were eaten together by members of the same unit. i.e. messes, and food for each mess was cooked together in a common kettle.[7]

On August 25, the advance guard of the Continental Army entered New Jersey and moved south through Paramus, Acquackanonk (Passaic) and Springfield. This American light Infantry force stayed close to the Hudson River to protect the entire left flank of the dispersed allied forces which would be exposed if the deception failed. This column is referred to on some contemporary maps as the "route of the Continental Army."

The French army, accompanied by the 2nd New York Regiment and Lamb's Artillery Regiment, formed a "supply column." They left one day later and took a more westerly route. General Washington rode with Lamb's Artillery but later rejoined the Continental Army infantry column at Springfield. The 2nd New York guarded the forty bateaux, the invasion landing craft which were being pulled by oxen. The boats would be used to cross waterways along the route and also serve as false evidence that New York was the primary objective. These western forces camped for a night at Suffern, New York, before entering New Jersey.

In his memoirs, John Hudson of the 2nd New York Regiment, who had just celebrated his 13th birthday on June 12, 1781, wrote "We carried on our march boats so large that it took a wagon and eight horses to draw them and two inch plank in quantities, by the same conveyance. These were to enable us to form flotillas to cross our troops upon the water courses which lay in our route." That means that this regiment alone had 272 horses just for the wagons transporting the boats.[8]

Three Columns Rush Through New Jersey

The armies advanced through the state in three columns. Unfortunately, the American forces left few descriptions of what they observed and experienced during their five days in New Jersey. An examination of known accounts during this time yields little information. The official papers of Washington, Pickering, Knox, and Lincoln, as well as the orderly books of Colonel Lamb's Artillery and the Van Cortlandt's 2nd New York regiment, contain nothing about the ordeals of the soldiers. The diaries of Samuel Tallmadge and the memoirs of Philip Van Cortlandt, John Hudson, or Sergeant-Major Hawkins do not tell us anything about the towns the troops marched through or the people they met. For the American military, the land was very similar to their homes, so everything seemed to be familiar and hardly worth recording.

Congress, in 2000, authorized a resource study of the 600-mile route through Connecticut, Delaware, Maryland, Massachusetts, New Jersey, New York, Pennsylvania, Rhode Island, and Virginia, the route traveled by George Washington and General Rochambeau during the American Revolution. This bill allocated federal funds to the National Park Service to carry out a study that began in late 2001 and was completed in 2006, in time for the 225th Anniversary of the march of the Franco-American armies to victory at Yorktown. This comprehensive report contains a section titled *The Washington-Rochambeau Revolutionary Route in the State of New Jersey, 1781–1783.* which provides an exceptionally thorough analysis in tracing the movement of the allied armies through the Garden State. It also verifies the route of march as noted by military records, various references, and early landmarks.[9]

The Jerseys-A Beautiful Country

For the French officers and foreigners who served with the allied armies, New Jersey was a region filled with natural wonders and fascinating inhabitants, a place they would most likely never see again. Much of what they witnessed was new and exciting, and was worth describing in their journals, but was not noted in military records. It is from these diaries, memoirs and letters of foreign nationals that we can learn much about life in Revolutionary War New Jersey.

The amount of detail each writer covers varies greatly. It ranges from simple notations of dates and places to narratives such as the one Abbé Robin's wrote at Princeton on September 1, 1781:

Wholly different from [the country] we have hitherto traversed: it is not, like Connecticut, covered with small hills lying close together, which render travelling difficult, obstruct the view, and prevent one from forming a clear idea of the whole scene. Many ridges of mountains, which seem to be branches of the Appalachian, stretch from north east to south west, and from intervals of vast and beautiful plains, which the hand of the geometrician seems to have smoothed to a level. These plains are adorned with large and handsome edifices; and the country abounds with orchards, fields of wheat, rye, barley, Indian corn, and flourishing woods. The inhabitants, for the most part of Alsacian and Dutch descent, are gay, easy and engaging in their manners, and resemble the happy region they inhabit. Provisions are brought into our camp from all quarters; and those that bring them are commonly wealthy people, and very unlike our traders in fruits and pulse. You will often see the women decked with their headdresses and gauzes, riding in their farm waggons to market, drawn by the most elegant horses.[10]

Baron Ludwig von Closen, a French officer, provides us with this exuberant picture:

The Jerseys, where we are now (beautiful country!) abound in all kinds of produce. The inhabitants (who are of Dutch origin) have kept it neat and have retained their gentle and peaceful customs, and have been very friendly towards the army. It is a land of milk and honey, with game, fish, vegetables, poultry, etc. after leaving New York state, where misery is written on the brows of the inhabitants, the affluence in the state of the Jerseys seems to be much greater. There are also some lead and copper mines in the area near

Elizabethtown, but, since the war, operations have been suspended; and, in general, North Americans do not care at all for labor underground, which the people of Peru and Chile like very much.[11]

The People of New Jersey-Equality, the Ladies and Deserters

Rochambeau's troops marveled at the people which Georg Daniel Flohr described in his journal, saying "all inhabitants are wealthy and well. One does not see a difference between rich and poor. Here one does not see a difference between the Sunday clothes and their workday clothes," and women were "always dressed like ladies of the nobility." Flohr was puzzled, "I wondered where their wealth came from since they don't work at all." He came to the conclusion that this equality was created by more equitable ownership of land, "where the absence of tenancy leveled social distinctions based on birthright and noble privilege." Americans were "not haughty at all. They talk to everybody, whether he be rich or poor," and common folk live "more ostentatious than the nobility in Europe."[12]

Another interesting eyewitness account of New Jersey's flirtatious ladies comes from an anonymous American who passed through Oakland, a small town adjacent to Pompton. "In this area males are very welcome since we did not meet many of them, where one entered into a house there the first thing they did ask whether one did not want to stay with them, they would hide you until the French were gone, one also encountered everywhere Hessian soldiers who had deserted."[13]

Louis Eberhard von Esebeck, a lieutenant-colonel in the Royal Deux-Ponts Regiment, observed that "no one could live more happily than here. There is a freedom here the like of which is found nowhere else."[14]

For the landless sons of poor peasants in France the exotic New World was a strong temptation to desert. As a result, there were 316 deserters from Rochambeau's corps, 186 of whom were German-speaking subjects of the king of France who came mostly from Alsace and Lorraine. Many of them deserted around New York and during the march through Pennsylvania. Flohr wrote, "half of the regiment met friends and relatives anxious to help a fellow countryman disappear." The French soldiers were delighted when they occasionally met with French-speaking Americans. These people were descendants of Huguenot refugees who had settled in New York State in the early 1700s. Relatively few Frenchmen deserted, however, since they were reluctant to venture into a country inhabited by locals who were handed cash rewards for returning deserters to their units.[15]

The French Column (Rochambeau)

The French divisions left Suffern, New York and marched twenty miles to Pompton, New Jersey along present-day Route 202. Cromot du Bourg, a French officer, reported on the march that day, "We went from Sufferns to Pompton, the road is superb. This is an open and well cultivated country, inhabited by Dutch people who are almost all quite rich. We arrived in good season and the camps being set and the troops arrived, I thought I could do no better than to go to Totawa to see a cataract [the Paterson Falls] which is considered to be one of the most curious sights in this part of the country."[16]

French army columns were considerably longer than that of the Americans. Hundreds of horses and oxen accompanied the thousands of troops. Eighty horses drew twenty staff wagons the artillery added about 500 horses, while mounted Hussars rode 300 steeds. About 400 officers had at least three horses each for their use, which added another 1,200 animals to the columns. Eyewitnesses would remember the spectacle for the rest of their lives. A similar British column after the Battle of Monmouth was described in detail by Sir Henry Clinton.[17] Rochambeau crossed New Jersey in two regiments of 1,000 men each, accompanied by their staffs, servants, wagons, and artillery supplements. Estimating 125 wagons per mile and allowing for delays and gaps in the column it is likely that the column stretched three miles, or more, along the roads. The daily marching distance was between ten and fifteen miles.

The columns passed through Oakland, New Jersey, then crossed the Pompton River and set up camp in Wayne Township on the Newark Pompton Turnpike, just north of the Pompton Meeting House and the Reformed Church of Pompton Plains. Washington stayed nearby that night at the Schuyler-Colfax House in Wayne. Most historic buildings in that area have survived the years and are splendidly preserved and well maintained, and several remain private residences.

The next day the French trudged twelve miles south through Pompton Plains, Lincoln Park, Montville, Lake Hiawatha and Hanover Township to Whippany. The location of their campsite in Whippany was on Whippany Road, on what was until recently Lucent Technologies Park. In 1781, Whippany consisted of about thirty houses and 200 inhabitants. It is quite possible that on August 28 and 29 of 1781 close to 5,000 officers and men camped there, along with their 2,000 horses and 700 oxen that grazed on the outskirts of the little town.

These numbers created logistical issues. The French had hard currency, while Washington's purchasing agents could only offer Continental dollars or letters of credit; thus American farmers always preferred to sell to the French. Colonel James Hendricks of the 1st Virginia Regiment wrote to General Washington from Alexandria on September 21, 1781, stating that as long as French agents can pay with specie, "the American Army will be starved."

The French Advance South

The French experience and their reactions to the places, people and culture of the Garden State countryside were vividly described in many eyewitness accounts and recorded in journals, diaries and military documents. George Daniel Flohr, a German, was an enlisted man in the French Army. He kept an extensive journal but confined his descriptions to a sentence or two, for instance, "On the 26th we broke camp again 14 miles to Pompton, a Gentleman's manor; this region is heavily settled by Dutch, but one also meets here and there a German already."[18] Flohr described Whippany as "a small town in the mountains in a beautiful area; there we had a rest day and again numerous visits from the inhabitants." Cromot du Bourg, Rochambeau's aide, describes leaving Pompton on August 27, "we marched to Whippany by a fine road. Whippany is quite a large place; a river of the same name, which is fordable, passes through it." Compared with the British, the Hessians, and even the Americans, the soldiers of the French regiments were very disciplined. No civilian reports of pillaging or theft have ever been discovered.[19]

Following a rest day at Whippany, Rochambeau's divisions arose early and tramped fifteen miles through Morristown, Basking Ridge and Bullion's Tavern (Liberty Corner). Cromot du Bourg, described Morristown on August 29 as "a very pretty town; it is situated on a little hill and in a very pleasant situation. It has sixty or eighty well-built houses. . . . the road to Bullion's Tavern [NJ Route 202] is fine and level; the troops arrived there early." Flohr also left us with his favorable impression of the town, "Morristown, Moritz-Stadt, also a beautiful little town in a pleasant region, where one met here and there German inhabitants," Captain Louis Comte de Lauberdière, another Rochambeau aide, called Morristown a "petite ville assez jolie" (a little village tolerably pretty). The French camp at Bullion's Tavern is now the site of a gas station at Route 78 West, Exit 36. From there, it was a one day march to Bound Brook, and there the French Army rejoined Lamb's supply column and the main Continental Army.

General Washington, traveling with Lamb's supply column, headed east to Springfield to rejoin the Continental Army, but paused at Chatham to update Congress:

Head Quarters, Chatham, August 27, 1781
Sir: I have the Honor to inform Congress, that my Expectation of
the Arrival of the Fleet of Monsr. De Grasse, in the Chesapeak Bay,

with some other Circumstances, of which Congress were informed in my Letter of the 2d. Augst., and in which very little Alterations have since taken place, have induced me to make an Alteration in the concerted Operations of this Campaign. I am now on my March with a very considerable Detachment of the American Army, and the whole of the French Troops, for Virginia.

As I expect a few Days will bring me to Philadelphia, I shall then have the Honor to open my Motives and Intentions to Congress, more fully than it may be prudent to do by Letter at this Distance. I have the Honor etc.

Washington also wrote to Rochambeau from Chatham on August 27, "Sir: By intelligence which I have received since my arrival at this place, I find that the enemy have been throwing Troops upon Staten Island. This circumstance, and a desire of bringing up the rear of the two Armies will induce me to halt the American Troops one day at Springfield, as I pray your Excellency to do those of the French at Whippany."

Montresor does not learn that he was on the way to Virginia until he reaches Bullion's Tavern:

We halted on the 29th. Until then we had been marching down river and we believed we were bound for Staten Island. What confirmed us in this belief was the fact that the American Army and the Lansun Legion had made a reconnaissance in this vicinity. A dummy camp had been pitched facing Staten Island, where fires were kept burning for several nights in order to screen our march and to keep the English thinking that we planned to besiege New York. We were much surprised when General Rochambeau left for Philadelphia, thus upsetting our forecasts.[20]

On August 30, Cromot marched with the First Brigade and reported, "to Somerset Court House, [Millstone] the distance to which is only twelve miles, over fine roads." Flohr described Somerset Court House as "a little town in the plains and completely surrounded by fruit trees, a large number of them." His use of the words "little town" probably denotes seven or eight houses as opposed to the thirty-some houses of Whippany, which Cromot du Bourg called "quite a large place."

On the same day General Washington received a dispatch from General Lafayette in Virginia. The Marquis reported that Cornwallis was fortifying the Yorktown Peninsula and it appeared that he was either waiting for reinforcements, or for the British fleet, to rescue him. This was a strong indication that the Franco-American expedition now had a possibility of success

On August 31 French forces marched south along the banks of the Millstone River from Somerset Courthouse. They crossed the Millstone River at Griggstown, and then continued south to Rocky Hill and Princeton on today's Route 206. Camp was set up along Nassau Street.[21]

Flohr describes Princeton as "a pleasant little town in the plains, which little town is graced with a pretty college." The Abbé Robin, a French Army chaplain, provided more details, writing, "The village of Princeton is inconsiderable, but remarkable for its charming situation, elegant houses, and above all a college built of stone, four stories high, having twenty-five windows in the front, in each story. In the college I saw two grand performances of mechanism; one of which represents the motions of the heavenly bodies, according to the system of Newton and Copernicus. The inventor is an American, and resides in Philadelphia."[22]

The entire Franco-American task force assembled at Trenton. Clermont-Crèvecoeur described the place as follows: "The town is larger than Princeton but less well buidt and not as pretty. On its outskirts there is a large creek that is a branch of the Delaware and is spanned by a bridge. The Delaware, where there is both ford and ferry, is half a mile beyond the place; the river of the same name, which is fordable, passes through it." The Allied forces then crossed the Delaware River and marched south to the last major battle for both sides on the continent of North America, a battle which turned out to be a brilliant military campaign.

Accounts of enlisted men's experiences during this campaign are extremely rare; only three are known to exist. One kept by an anonymous grenadier in the Bourbonnais Regiment recorded nothing more than the stations of the march through New Jersey. The other account, kept by André Amblard of the Saintonge Regiment, also contains no details about the march itself, though the one sentence Amblard penned about New Jersey is worth quoting: "La fertilite & la beaute de cette province la fait nommer le jardin de l'Amerique, elle est ce Partie habitée par des Hollandois et des Allemands." (The fertility and beauty of that province causes it to be called the garden of America, it is that part inhabited by the Dutch and Germans). In his journal, the French commander Vicomte de Rochambeau drew this erroneous conclusion from his journey through New Jersey: "Here agriculture is followed and brought to perfection. But no great market centers will ever be established here because the two great cities of New York and Philadelphia are too near. The inhabitants of this section will never be more than the commission merchants for the dealers in these large cities."[23]

Count William de Deux-Ponts, second in command of the Royal Deux-Ponts regiment, provided a typical brief record of the French campsites in New Jersey:

On the 26th of August, we marched to Pompton.

On the 27th of August, we encamped at Hanover or Whippany, near Morristown.

On the 29th of August, we encamped at Bullion's Tavern.

On the 30th of August, at Somerset.

On the 31st of August, at Princeton.

On the 1st of September, we marched to Trenton, where we cross the Delaware. We keep our tents, but today the trains ford the river. Tomorrow morning the troops go over in boats. The establishment of a bakery and other store houses at Chatham, 4 miles distant from Staten Island, was strong evidence of an impending siege of New York.

With General Washington In New Jersey, August 1781

The American Armies had advanced through New Jersey in two columns, with the French following a route from Pompton through Morristown. The American infantry regiments took the route closest to the Hudson River, in case the deception failed. On the third day, all of the allied armies assembled in Trenton, on the Delaware River. All but a handful of troops had been left along the shores of the Hudson, tending hundreds of campfires to maintain the massive ruse. Sir Henry Clinton, therefore, remained convinced that New York was the target until after the combined forces had crossed the Delaware River.

The "Supply and Artillery Column" (Lamb) left Pompton and traveled toward Chatham and Summit, where they turned south. Entrusted with all the supplies, provisions and heavy weapons for the campaign, they chose a more secure route further inland and behind the first ridge of the Watchung Mountains. Washington and his staff rode with this column until it reached Summit, where he continued straight to Springfield to join the Continental Army infantry regiments for the march south. Aside from military strategy, these divided routes took into account the logistics of providing thousands of men with food, forage, firewood and shelter. This made it necessary for the Franco-American forces to follow separate routes as well. Even Philadelphia, America's largest city with 28,000 inhabitants, could not support the allied forces and their thousands of animals.

The thorough analysis conducted by the *Washington-Rochambeau Revolutionary Route* study provides a guide to the itinerary by matching military records with contemporary maps. Orderly books of the regiments not only recorded daily orders; they also mentioned the place where the regiment was at the time, and where it planned to march that day and set up camp the next evening.[24] Matching orderly books with the detailed maps of the Erskine-DeWitt Collection at the New York Historical Society is the best way to trace the roads the army followed. DeWitt's maps are drawn to scale and include indicators for many mile markers. They do not show the campsites, but do show numerous landmarks such as inns, churches, grist mills, fords, ironworks, and other structures, as well as terrain features.[25]

In addition, numerous plaques, markers and monuments have been placed along the way over more than two centuries since the 1781 march. Many are remarkably accurate and are in places where they have been verified by the knowledge and eyewitness accounts that have been passed down in local legend and history. Federal, state, and local authorities, as well as patriotic organizations such as the Daughters of the American Revolution (DAR), the Sons of the American Revolution (SAR), the Society of the Cincinnati, historical societies and civic organizations such as Rotary Clubs have been responsible for their erection.

For clarity, in tracing the routes of Washington's army through New Jersey, present day names of the towns are used to identify towns along the way. Maps of that era show the old names, many of which have changed. In addition, some of these sites were not unidentified with names at the time.

The Route of the Infantry Column-Continental Army with General George Washington

On its march through New Jersey the American Army was split into two main columns—the supply column of equipment and artillery commanded by Colonel John Lamb, and the Continental Army column, which consisted of mostly infantry regiments. While Lamb's men stayed well inland to take advantage of the protection of mountains and waterways, the Continental Army infantry's route of march remained as close as ten miles from the Hudson River. If the British attacked, they would probably cross the river from New York City, and by positioning themselves on the eastern flank the Continentals served as protection for the supply column.

The infantry column itself initially split into two units when it crossed over from New York into Bergen County, New Jersey. Each was led by Brigadier General Moses Hazen and Major General Benjamin Lincoln, respectively. Hazen's Brigade first passed through the town of Closter, five miles south of the New York border, continued for another three miles to Cresskill and Dumont, and then turned east toward the Hackensack River. The brigade then followed the river south until it reached New Bridge Landing, where it then crossed the river. New Bridge was a prosperous mill hamlet, clustered around a bridge strategically placed at a narrow point on the Hackensack River. New Bridge Landing, a narrow dock built of logs, could accommodate sloops of up to forty tons burden. Local products were shipped south, including iron, which was shipped overland from Ringwood and Long Pond Ironworks.

The "New Bridge" had been built in 1744. The bridge saved the American Army in 1776 when General Washington led his men across New Jersey while retreating from British forces after the fall of Fort Washington and the abandonment of New York City. Describing the American retreat from Fort Lee on November 20, 1776, eyewitness Thomas Paine wrote, "Our first objective was to secure the bridge over the Hackensack. . . ." This strategic crossing was in constant conflict during the war because it was the first bridge above Newark Bay. New Bridge served as a battleground, fort, encampment, military headquarters and intelligence-gathering post during every year of the American Revolution. The current draw bridge on the site was built in 1888 and added to the National register of Historic Places in 1989.

New Bridge is the site of "The Steuben House," a five-room cottage built in 1752. During the Revolutionary War, its owners, the Zabriskie Family, were Loyalists who fled to British-held Manhattan. Washington made the house his headquarters for ten days in 1780. After the war, in 1783, Congress granted Baron von Steuben a lifetime annuity for his contributions to the American cause, and the baron restored the war-damaged home. The Steuben House was purchased by the State of

New Jersey in 1928. In 1939, the Bergen County Historical Society was invited to display its collections in the house's museum. The society purchased an adjacent eight acres in 1944 to preserve the original look of the Bergen Dutch countryside. The house is an artifact that memorializes the "Drill Master of the American Revolution," Major General Baron von Steuben, whose valuable wartime services have been described as second in importance to those of George Washington.

After crossing at New Bridge, Hazen's brigade continued about two miles to Paramus, where it joined Lincoln's Brigade. After having entered New Jersey, Lincoln's group first passed through Ramsey in Bergen County and then moved south through Allendale and Waldwick to Paramus. The merged infantry columns camped around the old Paramus Reformed Church in Ridgewood. The original Paramus Reformed Church building at this location was built in 1735. During the Revolutionary War, it was used at various times as a headquarters for General Washington, a barracks for American troops, a hospital and a prison. The original church building was replaced in 1800 by the building that can be seen today. It was constructed in part from stones from the original church.

The merged infantry column left Paramus and proceeded south through the present-day towns of Lodi, Garfield and Passaic. At Passaic they began following the course of the Passaic River through Nutley and Belleville until reaching Newark. From Newark they turned west and moved up Springfield Avenue to pass through Irvington, where the road becomes Vauxhall Road. This brought the Infantry Column to Springfield, where they were joined by General Washington. Here they set up camp on the night of August 29.

On August 29, while at Springfield, Sergeant-Major Hawkins made this entry in his journal: "At Half past two this Morning the Revelie beat, which was followed between three and four oClock by the beat of the General when the Baggage was loaded and the Regt under Arms and marched and just at fair day Break our Regt arrived at the Foundation of the burnt Church at Springfield." The first drum command referred to "reveille," which was beat at dawn. If the army was to march the "reveiller" was replaced with the beating of the "general." The burned church which Hawkins referred to was Presbyterian Church on Morris Avenue, which had been torched by the British on June 23, 1780, during the Battle of Springfield. The church was targeted by British and Loyalist troops passing through the town since it had been used to store ammunition for the Continental Army. It was rebuilt by 1791 and still stands today in downtown Springfield.[26]

After breaking camp in Springfield, the Continental Army column turned south toward Mountainside. They followed present Route 22 for five miles, then turned toward Westfield. Sergeant-Major Hawkins records in his journal, "Park [carts], Boats, Baggage, and Stores of every kind, as well as the Sappers and Miners passed thro the Village called the Scotch Plains and about 12 oClock arrived at Quibble-Town, where they halted and rested three Hours. Our Destination is kept so secret that our Officers are at a loss to know where they are going."

The body of men then headed toward Samptown, today's South Plainfield. From Samptown they marched twelve miles to Bound Brook on the Old Raritan Road, which today is a railroad line. Hawkins stated that camp was set up at Bound Brook: "When the troops proceeded on, and passed through a scattered old fashioned Village called Bound Brook, adjoining to which halted and encamped in a field at Middle Brook, about an hour before dark."

From their camp at the foot of the first ridge of the Watchung Mountains at Middlebrook the column doubled back through the town of Bound Brook and crossed the Raritan River over the Queens Bridge. They then marched along the Raritan River on Easton Avenue and camped at Raritan Landing at the site of what is now Buccleuch Park, between Easton Avenue and the Raritan River in New Brunswick. The infantry regiments then turned west to pass through Somerset and Franklin Township to arrive at Millstone. They followed the Millstone River south for eight miles to Griggstown, where they crossed the river and continued two miles to the borough of Rocky Hill.

Lieutenant Cromot du Bourg, an aide to Rochambeau, reported that he marched with the troops of the 1st Brigade of the Continental Army column to Millstone on August 30, and that the twelve miles they covered were over "fine roads."

Cromot was ordered to deliver a letter to Rochambeau in Philadelphia. He described the road to from Millstone to Princeton as leading, "through some very disagreeable woods," but described the town of about eighty houses as being "well built and pleasantly situated." Most French officers whose accounts have survived took the opportunity to explore nearby battlefields. At Princeton Cromot traced the course of the battle; he also did this in Trenton, which he found "not so pretty" as Princeton.

At Rocky Hill all allied forces all came together. The Continental Army infantry column, the French column and the supply column merged as one to begin their long journey to Virginia. From Rocky Hill the Franco-American Army marched two miles to Princeton, where they camped near Nassau Hall. The next day they moved fifteen miles to Trenton. This completed their march through New Jersey.

At Trenton the allied forces camped along Broad Street. A ferry was at the end of what was then appropriately called Ferry Street (today's South Warren Street). It was commandeered by the army for crossing the river, and appeals were also sent for miles around requesting every type of boat that could be gathered.[27] During the 1780s, Trenton Landing on today's Lamberton Street, between modern Landing and Lalor Streets, was the location of several wharves. It was the most likely place of embarkation for the allied forces. A fording place was also found for the artillery to cross.[28]

After struggling with the bateaux for seventy miles from New York over the rough New Jersey backroads, the men of the 2nd New York Regiment were given a welcome reward when they reached the Delaware River at Trenton. While most of the army trudged south they launched their boats and sailed fifty miles down the Delaware River to Wilmington, Delaware.

George Washington at
the Siege of Yorktown.
*(Engraving in C. Edwards
Lester's* History of the
United States, *1883)*

Thousands of men and wagons traveled along New Jersey roads during the five days in August 1781. The uninterrupted journey of the French column and the American supply and infantry columns through New Jersey depended on vigilant secrecy, precise logistical planning and mapping, and an extensive intelligence network. The large force that moved rapidly from the New York border to the Delaware River at Trenton required meticulous coordination and apparently was fully supported by the residents of the Garden State. New Jersey citizens contributed directly to the victory at Yorktown by providing food, shelter, transportation and forage along the way. The armies passed through many villages and touched the lives of patriotic people who greeted them along the roads.

The loss of Britain's operational field army in the siege at Yorktown proved to Parliament that the war in America could never be won. Shortly thereafter, peace negotiations commenced, and fifteen months later the Treaty of Paris was signed and America's independence was finally recognized.

New Jersey has the right to be proud of her contribution to the success of the Yorktown Campaign. New Jersey's geographic position as the only land route from New York to Philadelphia placed it in an essential position for the march of the allied armies to Yorktown in 1781. The route through the Garden State was a critical segment of the exceptional strategy that resulted in the final decisive victory of the Revolutionary War.

The War
at the Shore

Chapter 8

The Shadowy Skeletons of Sandy Hook (1776-1783)

Sea Bright, Highlands, Middletown, Freehold, Lincroft

For centuries, Sandy Hook, New Jersey, has abounded with strange stories of skeletal remains having been unearthed in the area. These tales, a mixture of fact and fiction, are part of the rich folklore of one of America's most fascinating historical sites. Most of these incidents seem to hail from the turbulent time of the American Revolution, when this strategic location was the setting for the violent acts of occupying hostile forces. The origins of these strange and bizarre mysteries are revealed by a careful review of the site's history based on original documents from that time. A few eyewitness accounts survive as well, and new archeological evidence is still being found in more recent times.

The first landmark that can be seen from ships headed to New York Harbor are the Highlands of the Navesink and extending from the base of these headlands is the low-lying piece of land known as Sandy Hook. A lighthouse at the north end of the Hook is the only structure of any height for several miles along this stretch of land, technically known as a "barrier spit." This peninsula, which separates the mainland from the Atlantic Ocean for seven miles along the coast, has always been a navigational hazard for ships attempting to enter

New York Harbor. After several shipwrecks in the early 1700s, New York merchants insisted on providing a way to warn their ships from running aground on its treacherous shoals. The Sandy Hook Lighthouse, first lit in June 1764, is a 90-foot-high brick and masonry structure with eight feet thick walls. It is the oldest standing lighthouse tower in the United States, as well as the oldest operating lighthouse in the United States.

During the American Revolution, the strategic location of the lighthouse south of the Hudson River made Sandy Hook a critical site of military importance. Early in the war, the New York Congress decided the lighthouse should be destroyed to prevent it from falling into enemy hands. American Army Major William Malcolm received orders on March 6, 1776 to use his best discretion "to render the lighthouse entirely useless."[1] Nevertheless, British forces occupied the Hook for the entire eight years of the war, the longest span of time for any place in the colonies.

The British landed less than three months after Malcolm had received his directive. They repaired the lighthouse, and soon it resumed operation. Soon afterward American Colonel Benjamin Tupper led a daring attack to attempt to destroy it with cannon fire. But after an hour of volleys, he "found his cannon balls could not penetrate the walls." Tupper reported, "This Morning about 4 o'clock we attacked the Light House with about 300 Men; they were strongly reinforced being (as I saw a Boat go on board from Long-Island) previously informed of our Design. I continued the Attack for two Hours with Field Pieces and small Arms, being all that Time between two smart Fires from the Ship-ping and the Light House, but could make no Impression on the Walls." The apparently quite sturdy lighthouse remained under British control for the remaining seven years of the war.[2] Solomon Nash, a soldier from Massachusetts provided another eyewitness account of the attack in his diary.[3]

A Beacon for Ships

The Sandy Hook Lighthouse was declared a National Historic Landmark on June 11, 1964, the 200th anniversary of its first lighting, today it still serves its original function as a beacon for ships coming in and out of New York Harbor. It is now lit twenty-four hours a day with a powerful modern light maintained by the United States Coast Guard, which is visible for nineteen miles on a clear night.

At the time of the Revolutionary War the lighthouse stood only 500 feet from the northern tip of Sandy Hook. Since that time ocean currents have moved sand up the coast, extending the tip farther out into the harbor. The structure now stands about one and one-half miles from the shore.

Sandy Hook served as a sanctuary for local Loyalist refugees and escaped slaves throughout the Revolutionary War. These bands, commonly referred to as "Tory refugees," supported the British cause. They established a village near the lighthouse and used it as a base of operation from which they raided Patriot farms as far inland as the present-day town of Tinton Falls. The locale was jammed with soldiers during the week following the June 1782 Battle of Monmouth, one of the major engagements of the war. At that time the entire British army of 16,000 troops had marched to Sandy Hook and were being evacuated by ship to New York City.

Ghostly Folklore and Skeletal Remains

Veiled in mystery and ghostly folklore, Sandy Hook and its lighthouse are best known for the preceding events. A mythology has sprung up in the area, much of which can be traced back to the tumultuous events during the Revolutionary War. Due to the many skeletal remains unearthed over the years along this spit of sand, the Hook has a reputation for eerie tales and gruesome secrets.

According to New Jersey legend, Captain Kidd, the infamous pirate, buried his treasure trove among the pines of Sandy Hook. Stories about Kidd persist to this day, and children are told about his gaunt crew anchoring their phantom vessel, the *Adventure Galley,* and roaming the shore in search of their lost loot. The ghost of Patriot Captain Joshua Huddy, a Patriot officer, is also said to be a frequent spectral visitor. Huddy was hanged from a tree by the British in 1782 in the nearby borough of Highlands. Ever since his tragic death, the rumor is that the vengeful Captain Huddy wanders the shores of Sandy Hook in full uniform. Another old tale tells of a secret cellar that was discovered in the 1860s beneath the lighthouse. Once opened, it was found to contain a skeleton seated at a table before a fireplace.

A crumbling brick burial vault, constructed during the Revolutionary War, was unearthed in April 1909. Discovered by workers who were excavating for a new road, it contained the bones of as many as fifty men. Evidence indicates these bones were the remains of wounded British soldiers who were carried away from the Battle of Monmouth and died during the mass evacuation of the Redcoat army from Sandy Hook in 1778.

Fortunately, many original American and British military records survive from the time of the American Revolution, so with conscientious searching in the archives it is still possible to determine the credibility of these haunting tales.

The British army Evacuates To New York From Sandy Hook

The Battle of Monmouth at Freehold, New Jersey, ended in a standoff. The exhausted British soldiers were allowed to rest for a few hours after the fighting broke off in the evening. They evacuated during the night and headed to Sandy Hook, where they awaited ships to carry them to New York City. The Crown forces were unable to bring along many of their severely wounded men, so they left them behind in Freehold with their dead. Four wounded officers and forty soldiers, along with a British surgeon, were left to the mercy of the American forces. Sir Henry Clinton, the senior British commander, left a note of appreciation in anticipation that the Americans would be compassionate.

Other wounded Redcoats were transported to nearby Tennant Church, which served as a makeshift hospital, and cared for alongside American soldiers. British soldiers killed on the battlefield were collected and buried in the Tennant Churchyard. Those who died from wounds in the town were buried together in a pit near the village center.

Clinton withdrew his army so stealthily that it was already well on their way when the American sentinels discovered its flight. By the next morning Clinton had left a gap of six hours between the two armies, and the British had advanced three miles to a place beyond the town of Lincroft called Nut Swamp, where they set up camp. During the afternoon Clinton even took the time to send Washington a message, under a flag of truce, thanking him for caring for his wounded men.

Scottish Grenadier Captain John Peebles, best described the hasty and quiet departure of the British during the night and the removal of their wounded: "Sunday 28th June . . . it was thought improper to advance any farther upon the Enemy who were strongly posted, & the Troops were accordingly order'd to retire to cover the Village of Monmouth where the Wounded & Sick were brought to in the Evening—where we remained till near 12 oclock at night, & leaving those of the wounded that were too ill to remove, with a Surgeon & flag. We march'd forwards to join the other divisions of the Army whom we overtook near to Middletown about 9 o'clock of the morning of the 29th."[4]

The night after the battle, the American army lay with their arms, ready to renew the conflict in the morning, but Washington decided not to pursue the enemy after it was discovered that they had slipped away. They knew the retreating British forces would soon reach a strong defensive position on the high ground at Middletown, which ascends into the Highlands of the Navesink. Hostile Loyalists controlled much of this area, and as the Redcoats neared Sandy Hook they would come under the protection of the guns of their fleet.

One week after the battle, Sir Henry Clinton reported in his narrative of the war, "the King's army descended from the High[lands] of Navesink, where I caused them to encamp, and embarking in transports (off Horse Shoe Cove) were conveyed to their respective stations on Staten, York, and Long Islands."[5]

The British were probably able to take many more ambulatory wounded men along with them. It is likely that many of them perished during the grueling 25-mile march over the rough dirt road from Freehold to Sandy Hook in the intense heat. Those still surviving remained in a makeshift field hospital which was set up during the week the army waited to embark for New York. The skeletons found in the brick vault were the remains of some of the soldiers who died during the evacuation.

The crumbling walls of the vault were unearthed in 1909 at Fort Hancock, a US Army fort on Sandy Hook which was constructed between 1857–67. It was first believed that the walls were the foundation of an old water tank of the Jersey Central Railroad that had at one time run through the military reservation. The ancient vault was penetrated by the picks of workers ten feet below the surface, and within minutes human bones began turning up, along with pieces of lead that later proved to be bullets. Fragments of human skulls soon verified that they had struck a burial vault.

Curiously, the diggers did not find any buttons or remains of weapons in the vault, which would have proven the identity of the remains. But there was little doubt that the vault dated from the time of the Revolutionary War, since its bricks were of old English type and were of the same composition and pattern as those used to construct the lighthouse in 1765.

A 1909 *New York Times* account reported that Colonel Henry L. Harris of the Coast Artillery Corps would continue the search of the vault and care for the bones, pending orders from the War Department as to their deposition. If the remains proved to be British, they would be respectfully reinterred or would be shipped to England at the British government's request. But some mysteries still remained. Since the transient British forces were on the Hook for only a few days, it would seem likely they would have simply buried the dead in the ground. Why would they take time to construct a brick vault, especially during the extreme summer heat? One theory states that since British forces continued to occupy the Hook for the next five years, they would have had ample time to construct a permanent mausoleum to reinter their fallen comrades in a more honorable grave.

After these remains were unearthed the British government was duly notified. In March 1909 the bones were respectfully reinterred in a single grave in the Cypress Hills National Cemetery for Veterans in Brooklyn, New York. Later, in 1939, a large granite monument was erected there by the British navy in memory of these soldiers who perished after the Battle of Monmouth.

The Halyburton Tragedy

In April 1908 the *Red Bank Register* reported that a vault containing sixteen human skeletons had been unearthed by workmen who were grading for an extension of the railroad at Sandy Hook.[6] The bones were found near an old roundhouse of the Central Railroad that had not been used for several years and was covered by several feet of sand.

So began the tragic Halyburton story. It was soon determined that these bones were the remains of two officers and eleven marines who had were sent ashore in December 1783 from a British man-of-war on a mission to capture five deserters.

In the final years of the War for Independence Americans openly encouraged British sailors to desert their ships to escape the brutal discipline and harsh conditions of life at sea. Royal Navy Captain

Workmen grading an army railroad bed in 1908 found the lost crypt from the Halyburton Tragedy. *(Courtesy Gateway National Park Area)*

Brenton complained, "In the whole of our intercourse with them from the year 1783 to 1812, insult and injury constantly attended the arrival of every British ship in what were called 'the waters of the United States.' If a boat landed, the seamen were enticed to desert, and often openly paraded the streets in defiance of their officers; the magistrates of the republic refused to interfere and exulted in the mortification of their hated and unwelcome visitors."[7]

It was New Year's Eve, 1783, when British forces were evacuated from New York City as part of their final withdrawal from the city after the peace treaty that ended the Revolutionary War had been signed. The warship *Assistance,* with its hull full of some of these men, was anchored in Horseshoe Cove on the bay side of Sandy Hook when a tragic misfortune occurred when six seamen deserted the ship in a launch and fled to shore. Captain Bentinck ordered Hamilton Douglas Halyburton, a twenty-year-old 1st Lieutenant, to lead a party of twelve other junior officers and seamen to apprehend the missing men. The search party set out in heavy seas on a small flat-bottomed barge and headed for the beach, but it soon capsized in the gale force winds of the prevailing storm.

The next morning, both the launch and the barge were found aground on the beach. A local person at the site reported that the deserters had landed safely and escaped, and they were never apprehended. Since their pursuers were not with the beached boats it was assumed that they were also safe. But the searchers soon came upon an appalling scene when they came upon ten frozen snow-covered bodies lying face down in a salt marsh along the shore. Three men remained missing, but their rigid corpses were soon found, and all thirteen men were buried by local inhabitants on Sandy Hook. This dreadful event might have been lost in history, except that Halyburton was the son of an earl and his untimely death made news in his homeland of Scotland. This eyewitness account was published in an Edinburgh newspaper in January 1784:[8]

> *Extract from the letter of a gentleman, dated on board his majesty's ship Assistance, arrived at Sandy Hook.*

> *On the 31st ult.*[December 1783], *about 3 o'clock, six seamen of this ship being sent in the longboat, under the command of a midshipman, to fetch water casks. The men overpowered the midshipman, cut the rope they were again to be hauled ahead by, and made for the Jersey shore. A number of gentlemen insisted on putting off in pursuit contrary to the intention of their commander. . . . But soon after they put off, the weather thickened with snow and the wind freshened so as very soon to blow hard. The Assistance fired a gun every half hour to guide the men back, but finally assumed they had landed safely and would remain on the shore until the weather improved. The gale continued with snow and sleet.*

These brief entries appear in Captain Bentinck's log of the HMS Assistance for December 30, 1783:

> *. . . Employed getting water, five men deserted from the boat ashore.*

> *December 31 At 3 Six seamen runaway with the launce in going for water. Sent the barge after her in which was 1st Lieut, Lieut. of Marines* [Halyburton], *11 midshipmen and one seaman.*

January 2nd 1784 A.M. light Breezes and clear, sent the Cutter on Shore in Search of the Launch & Barge

Jan. 3rd at 4 the Cutter returned with the Barge. informing us that the Barge had swampt all perished. Sent on Board the Hermione & Sophie for Carpenters employed making coffins, at 10 A.M. sent the deceased bodies on Shore to be buried.[9]

The New York *Independent Gazette* of January 10, 1784 reported that a funeral held at the lighthouse was attended by several men from the ship. The bodies of the young men were buried "with the honors of war" in ten separate coffins and placed in a common grave. Most of them came from prominent English families and were younger than twenty years old.

Hamilton Douglas Halyburton was from a distinguished and wealthy family of Scottish nobility. Soon after, sometime between 1785 and 1788, his mother Katherine, the Dowager Countess of Morton, had a marble monument erected on the west side of Sandy Hook to the memory of her Royal navy son and the boat's crew. These poignant words were inscribed on its plaque:

Here lie the remains of the Honorable Hamilton Douglass Haliburton, son of Shoto Charles, Earl of Morton, and heir of the ancient family of Haliburton, of Pitcurr in Scotland, who perished on this coast, with twelve more young gentlemen and one common sailor, in the spirited discharge of duty, the 30th or 31st of December, 1783-born October the 10th, 1763: a youth who in contempt of hardship and danger, though possessed of an ample fortune, served seven years in the British navy, with a manly courage. He seemed to be deserving of a better fate. To his dear memory, and that of his unfortunate companions, this monumental stone is erected, by his unhappy mother Katherine Countess Dowager of Morton.[10]

A few years later, in 1808, during the Napoleonic Wars, the monument was destroyed by the crew of a French warship and the location of the graves was lost. It was reported by authors Barber and Howe in 1844, "About the year 1808 a French vessel-of- war landed and destroyed this beautiful monument of maternal affection, but some traces of it still exist."[11] Any remnants of it were completely destroyed when the bed for the New Jersey Southern Railroad was built over the gravesite.[12] A second marble memorial from Halyburton's mother hangs in Trinity Church in Manhattan. It has a similar text to the monument at Sandy Hook, and appears to have been installed around the same time as the Sandy Hook monument, but there is no record of how this memorial ended up in Trinity Church.

Civilian Conservation Corps/WPA marker commemorating the death of Honorable Hamilton Douglas Halyburton, 1st Lieutenant, Royal Navy, and 13 crewmembers of the HMS *Assistance* at Fort Hancock, Sandy Hook, NJ. *(U.S. National Park Service)*

Over the years the burial place of the sailors on Sandy Hook was covered with sand, disappeared entirely, and was forgotten. A century later, in 1908, workmen grading the army railroad bed uncovered the crypt. The 18 x 20-foot vault was nine feet deep with walls two feet thick. The remains of the young men were reinterred at Cypress Hills National Cemetery in Brooklyn near their comrades who had perished two years earlier after the Battle of Monmouth.

The current Halyburton Memorial stands along the roadside a mile south of the lighthouse. It was built in 1937 by the Civilian Conservation Corps (CCC), and a plaque was installed on it in 1939 as part of the preparation for the visit of Queen Elizabeth and King George VI of England to the United States. The royal couple passed by the monument during their brief visit to Sandy Hook, less than three months before the onset of World War II.[13]

Sandy Hook is replete with other evidence of skeletal remains. As recently as the 1960s the Army Corps of Engineers unearthed the remains of four men and one woman buried near the base of the lighthouse. One theory is that they could have been Loyalist guerillas who established the town near the base of the lighthouse and used it as a stronghold throughout the Revolutionary War.

Lying close to shore on Spermacetti Cove, on the bay side of the Hook, is beautiful strip of pristine beach that rivals anything in the Caribbean. It has become a mecca for boaters. Curiously the place is named Skeleton Hill Island.

Chapter 9

Havoc on the Highlands (1777)

Navesink, Highlands, Middletown, Rumson

The month of February in 1777 was a dreadful period for the American cause for independence. General Washington, with a depleted Continental Army that was hungry, ill-clad and paralyzed by a smallpox epidemic, was encamped at Morristown for the winter. The British army occupied western New Jersey to the north of Princeton and had begun moving their troops from New Brunswick to the Amboys on their way to Staten Island and then New York City. The Redcoat hoards and their Hessian mercenaries pillaged civilians along the way and attempted to lure the American forces down from the security of the Watchung Mountains to fight a final battle on the plains of central New Jersey. Outmanned and outgunned, Washington wisely remained in the hills to live to fight another day.

On the New Jersey coast, bitter cold and a severe snowstorm swept through the Navesink Highlands in Monmouth County. There the militia, composed of the citizen soldiers farmers of the local area, endured a brutal defeat, when over half of the American force was lost. Twenty-five Americans were killed and seventy-two taken prisoner during this obscure engagement. The action is remembered by the few who call it the Battle of Navesink.

Only two brief contemporary British accounts of the battle have survived. By comparing this sparse information to public records, oral histories and traditions in the area, a reasonable correct description of

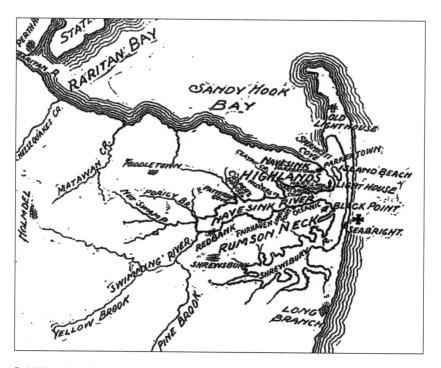

Probable position of the wreck of English victualling ship, cast ashore February, 1777. *(Murray M. C. Hyde, "The Battle of the Navesink," New York Times, February 23, 1896)*

the event and its tragic aftermath can be pieced together, one which culminates in a trail of events leading up to the present day. The thousands of summer tourists who swarm to the pristine beaches of Sandy Hook are unaware of what happened here as they pass by the site on Route 36 before it crosses over the Highlands-Sea Bright Bridge.

Surprisingly, this saga begins with a shipwreck. On the first day of February in 1777 an English supply ship heading for New York was driven ashore on the southern end of Sandy Hook during a blinding blizzard amidst heavy gale winds. The beach where it came ashore is where the Hook joins the present-day town of Sea Bright.

A small Monmouth County Militia outpost, under the command of Colonel Nathaniel Scudder, was stationed nearby at Black Point when the ship floundered. Now called Barley Point, it is located on the Rumson side of the Navesink River where it joins the Shrewsbury River. From Black Point the American soldiers were able to observe the British forces on occupied Sandy Hook, about a mile away. The Crown troops had taken possession of the Hook and its lighthouse in 1776, and remained there for the remaining seven years of the war.

Scudder's men observed the troubled vessel and rushed to the scene as soon as it ran aground to recover its trove of valuable supplies. After rescuing a Frenchman onboard whom the British had taken prisoner, they alerted the main force of Americans who had assembled on the heights of the Navesink, about two miles away. This high ground overlooks Sandy Hook and the waters around it and lies along Route 36 on the approach bridge that joins Sandy Hook to the mainland. Esek Hartshorne had built a sturdy house here in 1762, and it was commandeered by the Monmouth County Militia for an outpost and guard station. A strong stone outbuilding near the house served as a powder magazine for the Patriots. From this outpost all activities of the enemy forces on the Hook, as well as movements of the British Fleet offshore, could be easily observed.

Five companies of militia, about 200 men, hurried in from the nearby towns of Middletown, Holmdel and Shrewsbury to gather at the Hartshorne house. They prepared to move down the hill and out to the Hook to join Scudder's men at the wreck site in an attempt to salvage the contents of the stricken vessel. Their pathway to the beach is now spanned by the Highlands-Sea Bright Bridge, opened in 2013.

Among the first of Scudder's men to arrive at the wreck was a Loyalist spy named McClees. He managed to slip away and hike to the Sandy Hook lighthouse, about a six-mile trek north, where he reported the wreck of the vital supply ship to the British authorities. The alarming news that the "vitualing ship" had run aground was quickly relayed to the British headquarters on Staten Island. The command center responded quickly by sending the warship *Syren* to the site of the wreck on Sandy Hook. The *New York Gazette and Weekly Mercury,* a Loyalist newspaper, reported that a British assault force of 170 soldiers and marines commanded by Major Andrew Gordon from the 26th Regiment was immediately dispatched from Corlis Ferry, Staten Island.[1]

The only primary sources for the Battle of Navesink are two brief contemporary accounts found in the *New York Gazette and Weekly Mercury*. These are dated February 7 and February 24, 1777. M.C. Murray Hyde, a local historian whose ancestors were among the early families in Monmouth County, wrote an extensive account of the event for the *New York Times* in 1896. She quoted from the *Gazette* accounts and add details gleaned from the oral history and traditions of Monmouth County.[2] Written 120 years after the battle, it is vague with regard to descriptions of locations and geography. In 2001 John P. King provided a description of the battle in Highlands in his book *The Making of America-Highlands New Jersey*.[3] To my knowledge, these two historians are the only ones who have studied the battle and written commentaries about it since 1777. Although both rely on the brief newspaper accounts, they disagree on the exact location where the event occurred. Hyde maintains that the fighting took place at a different house altogether—the home of Richard Hartshorne, which was situated on a cove off the Navesink River, located on the back of the high hill that overlooks the Hook.

Coincidentally, as a waterfront home owner on the Shrewsbury River, in Highlands, close to the battle site, and an active boater and fisherman, this author has first-hand knowledge of this immediate area and its surrounding waters. I offer this account of the Battle of Navesink based on personal familiarity with the natural features of the surrounding area, examination of primary historical sources and period maps, as well as a review of the versions presented by Hyde and King.

A relentless winter storm and heavy seas made it impossible for the *Syren* to approach the area for three days, but the man-of-war was finally able to enter the mouth of the Shrewsbury River through a narrow inlet called "the gut." This feature had recently been cut through when the ocean breached the base of the Hook where it joins present day Sea Bright. It is likely that the ship anchored inside near this entrance since it was near the wreck site. Positioned at the confluence of the Navesink and Shrewsbury Rivers, the 32-gun *Syren* could prevent any intervention while the provisions were recovered from the wreck using the ship's boats.

The British force is reported to have waded ashore early in the morning in waist-deep water "two miles below the rebel post as far as the fishing village of Parkertown," now the Borough of Highlands near Island Beach. After the landing party had made it ashore, local Tory civilians informed them that the garrison of Americans camped on the hill above the town was preparing to move out to the beach and the stranded ship the next day. As the Redcoats moved down the beach toward Parkertown they surprised the first American sentries they happened upon and seized them without firing a shot. The British assault force then split into two columns to attempt a double pronged pincer attack to surround the American troops billeted around the house. The main column likely pressed on, directly up the hill onto present Route 36 as it approaches the new bridge, and advanced north.

The flanking column moved to the right along the Gravelly Point Beach through Parkertown, and ascended the hill on Linden Avenue to reach Route 36. These flankers, however, did not reach the action at the house until after it was over. The main British troops remained concealed by the underbrush as they moved along Route 36. The slumbering American garrison was not alerted until the oncoming British ran into other sentries only 200 yards from the house.

A Battle or a Massacre?

When the attackers reached the Esek Hartshorne house they surprised the majority of dozing Americans. These inexperienced and outnumbered citizen-soldiers of the Monmouth County Militia were completely overrun by the seasoned British soldiers. Few shots were fired. The Patriots attempted to rally and made a brave stand but soon fell under an onslaught of bayonets. The appalling losses during the ensuing struggle suggest bitter hand-to-hand fighting, but more likely what occurred was the wanton slaughter of vulnerable defenders. Some enemy troops were slowed by dense foliage and snow as they ascended the hills, which enabled some of the defenders to escape. Most of those who were able to escape were wounded. The British force then deployed and retraced their path back to the grounded ship, where they were able to capture the Americans who were guarding it.

An account written by a British officer describes the assault: "A little before day they [the British] marched and surprised the advanced guard without firing a shot. From thence they proceeded about a mile to the house of one Hartshorne [Esek Hartshorne] at which they were approaching by two different ways (the flanking companies taking to the right) a guard posted about 200 yards from the house was first alarmed. These after firing a few shots, together with their main body, who at first affected to form and make a stand, being pushed by the battalion, fled too soon, for the grenadiers and light infantry to come up time enough to cut off their retreat. Between 30 and 40 escaped. We found several dead bodies in the woods, which were buried by our soldiers."[4] The British lost only one soldier in this mismatched fight that was actually a massacre.

The Americans did not give up in their attempt to capture the contents of the stranded ship. An American force of about 250 men under David Forman, with two 6-pounder cannon, made an attempt to recapture the grounded ship after the battle, but their cannons proved to be too light and they were driven off by the guns of the *Syren*.

The *New York Gazette and Weekly Mercury* reported on March 8, 1777, "about 250 of the rebels made an attack on the lighthouse at sandy hook. By the bravery of the men posted there and by the cannon of the *Syren* anchored near the spot, they were beaten off with some loss. The [British] troops had not a man either killed or wounded." The cargo of the wreck was successfully unloaded but the vessel soon broke up in the surf. The Gazette later verified this by reporting that "the victualing ship which was lately cast away on Sandy Hook is lost, but almost the whole of her cargo is saved."

The captured Americans were taken on board the *Syren* and transported to New York. They were kept in one of the notorious makeshift "Sugar House" prisons, where many died there within a few weeks from wounds, starvation or disease. Survivors were later removed to prison ships in Wallabout Bay, where many more perished. At least 17,500 are estimated to have perished in the sugar houses and prison ships over the course of the war, more than double that of casualties from battle.[5]

Revolutionary war veterans and their widows were granted pensions starting in 1818. A handful of these pension applications describe the sad fate of a few men that fought at the Battle of Navesink. The fact that many died as prisoners in the sugar house prisons soon after the battle probably indicated that they had received bayonet wounds. This weapon had a triangular blade that inflicted injuries that could not be sutured, which soon became infected and turned fatal. These pension documents can be found at the Monmouth County Archives in Freehold. John Whitlock, 1st Lieutenant, age forty-four, was killed at the Navesink Highlands. He managed to kill the man who took his life. His body lay in the snow for eight days. He left his wife Lydia and seven children. An eighth child was born five months after his death. Whitlock is buried in the Holmdel Church Memorial Cemetery in Holmdel, the only known grave of a soldier killed in the Battle of Navesink.[6]

Mathais Rue, a militiaman from Scudder's Regiment, was taken prisoner at the battle and jailed in New York, where he afterward died. A pension application was filed by his widow Elizabeth in 1780. In it, a man named William Johnson swore that he was taken prisoner along with Rue, and that he witnessed his death on February 28, 1777. That he died only two weeks after the battle indicates that he had most likely been wounded.

James Crawford, a militiaman with Scudder's Regiment, was killed during the engagement. He left a widow Margaret and seven children. She applied for a pension in June 1780. Alexander Clark was killed on February 13, 1777 in the action at the Navesink Highlands. Obadiah Stillwell was taken prisoner. "John Goodenough a fellow prisoner saw him die two months later in New York in April 1777." He left a wife named Mary. William Cole was taken prisoner. His death was also witnessed by John Goodenough in New York in March 1777. James Winter, Joseph Davis, James Hibberts and Lambert Johnson all were taken prisoner during the action. All perished in March 1777 in the Sugar House prison in New York.

The Highlands and the Heights of the Navesink remained in a no-man's land following the massacre. The Monmouth County Militia forces and the Continental Army had established inland bases at more secure locations at Middletown and Tinton Falls. As the years passed the tragic incident and the slaughter of the citizen-soldiers in 1777 on Route 36 in the Borough of Highlands have been shrouded in mystery and legend.

The Water Witch House

For the remaining six years of the Revolution the Esek Hartshorne house served as an outpost for American forces. Its commanding view of the bay allowed the Patriots to observe the movements of the British troops and shipping along the entire length of Sandy Hook, Esek and his family returned to their home after the war, and when he died in 1797 the house was sold to Nimrod Woodward, who opened a hotel on the premises. He was forced to close the hotel in 1812 when war again broke out with Great Britain. At that time the army again built a fortification at the strategic site, and eight companies of artillery and riflemen were stationed there along with a battery of heavy 32-pounder cannons. When peace was declared in December 1814 Woodward returned and resumed his hotel business.

In the years that followed the legendary house achieved fame once again. James Fenimore Cooper, America's first true novelist, was a frequent visitor to Highlands. During the 1820s he spent a many delightful days vacationing at the ambient New Jersey bay shore. He described the area as "the most beautiful combination of land and water in America." These fond memories served as the background for his novel *The Water-Witch*. Its setting is a hotel called "Lust for Rust," which was none other than the old house built by Esek Hartshorne. The fictional ship *Water-Witch* cruised the Sandy Hook Bay at the foot of the Navesink highlands. This book is considered one of America's finest sea legends.

The venerable hotel-fortress was known for many years as "The Water-Witch House." Today the site lies along Route 36 where it passes Waddell and Riker Streets on the approach to the bridge, and a few remnants of the building could still viewed as recently as 1913. The house had a massive brick fireplace and chimney, which were the only parts of the structure that survived a fire there in the 1800s. A radar scientist, Dr. Fields, built a summer home on Marine Place in Highlands in the 1900s. He removed the bricks from the Hartshorne fireplace and repurposed them in his home. In 2013 that house was severely damaged in Hurricane *Sandy*, and being beyond repair, it was slated for demolition. Its owner offered the chimney and fireplace to the Historic Society of Highlands in the hopes that it might be preserved.

Society President Russell Card, whose family has lived in Highlands for eight generations, requested the assistance of the Monmouth County Park System to have the 35-foot-tall fireplace and chimney moved to a more suitable location. Moving this structure would be a formidable task and the historical society reluctantly acknowledged that lack of time and money made any proposal infeasible. The last remnant of the Esek Hartshorne House was dismantled in April 2015.

Today the house site is heavily built over with private residences and no evidence of the structure remains. A nearby railroad station abandoned in the 1940s was once marked with the sign "Water Witch." The only reminder of the tragic Battle of Navesink and the other remarkable events that occurred here is a street named Waterwitch Avenue which runs adjacent to the former site of the house down to the lower part of town, and a coffee shop on that street called Water Witch Coffee.

Chapter 10

The Patriot and the
Pine Tree Robber (1775-1782)

Shrewsbury, Sandy Hook, Highlands, Rumson, Sea Bright,
Toms River, Colts Neck, Tinton Falls, Red Bank, Oceanport,
Monmouth Beach, Eatontown, Fairhaven

C uriously, two incredible heroes of the American Revolution in New Jersey remain obscure in the history of their home state. Colonel Tye, a feared and respected guerrilla leader, was a slave who escaped and fought for the British. He became one of the most successful and dreaded Loyalist commanders of the Revolution. His adversary, Captain Joshua Huddy, was a devoted Patriot who led raids against the Loyalists and captured and executed their leaders. Both were known for their swashbuckling exploits in what was, in reality, a civil war in the shore area of the state. Tye grew up in bondage. Huddy was from a family of prosperous landowners. Tye was black. Huddy was white. Their paths were destined to cross, and on a fateful day in September 1780 one fatally shot the other.

Captain Joshua Huddy

Joshua Huddy was born November 8, 1735 to a wealthy Quaker family in Salem County. As a young adult he was often in trouble. He was tried and convicted several times for assault and theft and was frequently in debt. He was expelled for "dissolute behavior" from the Society of Friends in 1757 when he was in his early twenties. His unruly behavior continued into adulthood when he was forced to sell his 300-acre farm to pay his debts, and later served time in debtor's prison. Huddy proved that he was physically tough at an early age. It is said that he survived a boating accident in Delaware Bay by swimming for three hours.

In 1764, he married Mary Borden and the couple eventually had two daughters, Martha and Elizabeth. After Mary died in the 1770s, Huddy moved to Colts Neck in Monmouth County, where on October 27, 1778, he married his second wife, Catherine Applegate Hart, a widowed owner of a tavern she had inherited from her first husband. Huddy and Catherine soon became estranged. He was then accused by the Monmouth County sheriff of trying to commit fraud by acquiring the tavern, forcing his wife and her children out onto the street, and selling their possessions.[1]

Court records show that during these years Huddy was in civil and criminal court many times as both a plaintiff and a defendant. He was arrested for assault in 1778.[2] He was again accused of livestock theft in 1781.[3]

When the Revolutionary War broke out Huddy volunteered to become captain of a privateering ship. The mission of the *Black Snake* was to prey on British merchant ships cruising along the New Jersey coast. By his commission, the Continental Congress authorized Huddy to "set forth in a warlike manner" against the British in "the Armed boat called Black Snake." The tiny vessel only weighed ten tons, far below the average size for an American privateering ship. It had a single swivel gun and a 14-man crew. The success of the armed boat, the *Black Snake,* is unknown, but Huddy's courage in confronting the world's greatest naval power with a single swivel gun attests to his patriotism—or perhaps to his impulsive nature.

A month later, in September 1777, Huddy chose shore duty and was soon appointed as a captain of artillery in the New Jersey Militia.

He fought at the Battle of Germantown, Pennsylvania later that year and went on to lead a group of mounted militiamen at the Battle of Monmouth in the summer of 1778 under David Forman, Brigadier General of the New Jersey Militia. In the aftermath of that decisive battle, Huddy and his men busied themselves harassing the British rear after they left Freehold and made their way to Sandy Hook for an evacuation to New York City.

After the British army withdrew from the Monmouth County area, which then encompassed Ocean County, it became a no-man's land. This shore area was terrorized by the bands of Loyalist partisans who murdered Patriots and plundered and destroyed their homes. These Tory marauders were known as "refugees," "cowboys" or "pine tree robbers." After the raids these pillagers could easily evade capture by disappearing into the nearby swamps and forests or by retreating to the protection of the British stronghold on Sandy Hook.

Captain Huddy conducted retaliatory attacks against these outlaws, and any other Monmouth County citizens who remained loyal to Great Britain. In 1780 he joined the Retaliators, a vigilante group that terrorized Loyalists and suspected Loyalists. He soon became revered by the Patriot community, which recognized him as their greatest protector during that troubled time. Huddy's assaults on the Tories were marked by barbarity and revenge executions, so he was intensely loathed by his Loyalist enemies. He was responsible for hanging Stephen Edwards, the first Loyalist to die in the county, and fourteen other Tories. His fierce opposition against British sympathizers was to continue even after the war officially ended.

Huddy's personal life was equally turbulent. In September 1780 an attempt was made by some refugees to capture him at his home in Colts Neck. His Large saltbox-style house was used as a post for a detachment of American militia. It stood across the road from the Colts Neck Inn, the tavern his wife had inherited. The inn opened in 1717 and a flourishing restaurant/hotel operates near the site today.

An Attempt to Capture Huddy

In September 1780 a refugee party of seventy-two men led by the intrepid Colonel Tye surrounded Huddy's house in an attempt to capture him. He was at home with a twenty-year-old woman named Lucretia Emmons, who was reported to be his mistress. Huddy fired at the raiders while Lucretia loaded several muskets left behind by the militia. He moved from window to window, firing at the attackers and creating the impression that a large number of defenders were in the house. Using this tactic, the pair managed to repel the enemy for two hours.

Huddy was able to wound several of the "refugees." Colonel Tye was shot through the wrist. After their assault failed, Tye tried setting fire to the house, and Huddy and Lucretia became trapped as the fire spread. They offered to surrender if Tye's men would agree to help extinguish the fire and allow Lucretia to escape. The attackers were enraged when they discovered only two people had held them off, so after plundering the house they allowed it to burn to the ground. The wounded Tye and his band of Tories then took Huddy prisoner and retreated to the Shrewsbury River to make their escape to New York.

The gunfire at Huddy's house alerted a nearby force of militia who pursued Tye's raiders as they fled with their prized captive. They headed for Black Point, a peninsula between the Shrewsbury and Navesink Rivers in Rumson. As they launched boats which they had hidden nearby they were soon overtaken by the militia. As the militia opened fire, the boat carrying Huddy capsized in the fracas, but he was able to escape and swim toward shore. But as he neared the riverbank, he was shot in the thigh by friendly fire. After he raised his hand and shouted, "I am Huddy! I am Huddy!" his compatriots brought him safely to the beach.[4]

Colonel Tye's wound from Huddy's musket ball seemed to be a minor one at first, but the injury soon turned into a tetanus infection. A few days later it proved to be fatal. Tye's valiant reputation lived on among his comrades, as well as with the Americans. The Patriots admitted that much of the bitter fighting among neighbors in Monmouth County would have

Captain Huddy led from prison to be hanged. *(Engraving from* Our Greatest Country, *1901, U.S. Library of Congress Collections)*

been unnecessary if Tye had been enlisted on their side. After his death, Colonel Stephen Blucke of the Black Pioneers (an all-black unit) replaced him as the leader of his raiders, and attacks on the Patriots continued well after the final decisive British defeat at Yorktown in late 1781.

For the next two years Huddy continued to harass the Loyalists of Monmouth County. In February 1782 the forty-seven-year-old captain was given command of the blockhouse at the village of Toms River in present day Ocean County. This small fort, manned by twenty-five men, was built to protect the local saltworks that were essential to cure meat for Washington's Continental Army. Toms River also served as an important base for American ships. Its inlet provided a deep anchorage for Patriot privateers who captured British merchant vessels sailing along the coast to supply the British forces in New York.[5]

The Loss of the Blockhouse at Toms River

In March, a force of between 100 and 200 Loyalists and refugees were organized under the direction of Governor William Franklin to attack the blockhouse. William was the illegitimate son of Benjamin Franklin and served as governor of New Jersey from 1763 until 1776. The Tory newspaper, *Rivington's Royal Gazette*, published in New York City, wrote the following account on March 20, 1782:

> *Lieutenant Blanchard, of the armed whale boats, and about eighty men belonging to them, with Captain Thomas and Lieutenant Roberts, both of the late Bucks County Volunteers, and between thirty and forty other Refugee loyalists, the whole under the command of Lieutenant Blanchard, proceeded to Sandy Hook under the convoy of Captain Stewart Ross, in the armed brig Arrogant, where they were detained by unfavorable winds until the 23d."* About midnight of the 23rd this party landed near the mouth of Toms River *(probably near present-day Ortley Beach).* Garret Irons, who was on patrol, ran seven miles to the blockhouse to alert the 25 or 26 defenders. By daylight of the 24th, the Loyalist force reached the blockhouse. Lieutenant Blanchard demanded the surrender of the blockhouse and those inside, which was refused.

As the Loyalist force assaulted the blockhouse, Huddy and his small band gallantly defended the position until their ammunition ran out. The defenders, outnumbered five to one, continued their resistance using long spears called pikes. In the fierce hand-to-hand fighting that followed the Patriots lost nine men killed while twelve who were taken prisoner. The attackers ordered Huddy to surrender, but his reply was, "Come and take us!" Eventually Huddy and his men were overwhelmed, and some of the survivors were viciously bayoneted afterward. The Tories then burned the blockhouse and the dozen houses in the village.

At Toms River they also destroyed the tavern, the blacksmith shop, the salt warehouses, a sawmill and a gristmill.[6]

The men of the town were either killed or captured, and over a hundred women and children were left without food or shelter. Huddy managed to escape but was captured with two of his soldiers while hiding in a nearby mill later that day. He was taken prisoner aboard the *Arrogant* and brought to New York with twelve other Americans captured at Toms River. They were all imprisoned there in the notorious Sugar House.

During the British occupation of New York (1776–1783) the Rhinelander Sugar House was turned into a notorious prison. This was a brick warehouse into which American prisoners of war and private citizens were thrown when suspected of assisting the Patriots. Sanitary conditions were primitive, and starvation was a constant threat, all of which resulted in an unbelievably high death rate. After the war, it still stood in a slum area near today's southwest corner of Rose and Duane Streets. For well over a century the deserted warehouse was considered to be haunted. The Sugar House was finally demolished in 1892, but a barred window of the original building and some of the old bricks were set into the wall of the modern building that replaced it along with a descriptive plaque which can be seen to this day. A section of the old Sugar House wall and a barred window also were transported to Van Cortlandt Park in the Bronx.

Today in downtown Toms River there is a replica blockhouse standing in the small waterfront Huddy Park. In 1782, the surrounding areas had a number of saltworks, all of which were very important to American troops because they were used to preserve meat rations. The British knew that interrupting the flow of salt would be a critical blow to the local Patriot effort. The original blockhouse, larger than the replica found in the park today, was built nearby on the hill of current day Robbins Street.

Most Toms River residents aren't aware that a battle took place in their town. The action was significant because it made more colonists vilify the Loyalists and gave the French more incentive to help the

Patriots. Huddy's dedication to his cause and the bravery he displayed during his last hours transformed him into a martyr and local legend, motivating more people to stand up and fight. Reenactments of the battle are sometimes performed in the park during the late spring or early summer.

Huddy's Tragic End

The captive Huddy was soon abducted from the British prison by a group of New Jersey Loyalists headed by Captain Richard Lippincott. They claimed he would be used for a prisoner exchange, but their real purpose was to execute him in revenge for the death of Phillip White, one of their leaders. White was a Tory from Shrewsbury who was captured and killed while trying to escape from the American militia, and because Lippincott was White's brother-in-law he wanted vengeance. In addition to this, he also had a personal grudge against Huddy, who was once his neighbor. Governor William Franklin approved the execution of Huddy to retaliate for the killing of White. Huddy, with irons on his hands and feet, was taken by Lippincott in the hold of the sloop *Britannia* to Sandy Hook and then rowed over to Highlands.

At Gravelly Point in Highlands in the morning of 12 April 1782 a gallows was erected and a barrel was placed under it. Resigned to his fate, Huddy made out his will, then stepped up on the barrel. A label was attached to Captain Huddy's breast, that read:

> *We, the refugees, having long held with grief the cruel murders of our brethren, and finding nothing but such measures daily carrying into execution; we therefore determine not to suffer without taking vengeance for the numerous cruelties, and thus begin, having made use of Captain Huddy as the first object to present to your view, and determine to hang man for man while there is a refugee existing. Up Goes Huddy for Phillip White.*

According to local tradition the hanging actually took place from a tree that stood within a few hundred feet of the Waterwitch Railroad Station in the Borough of Highlands. The site is now on the corner of Waterwitch Avenue and Shore Drive. The tree was still standing in 1867. Huddy left all his possessions to his daughters from his first marriage. His will is now preserved in the collection of the New Jersey Historical Society in Newark:[7]

In the name of God, Amen, I, Joshua Huddy of Middletown in the County of Monmouth of sound mind and memory, but expecting shortly to depart this life, do declare this last will and testament. First I commend my soul into the hands of almighty God, hoping he may receive it in mercy and next I commend my body to the earth. I do appoint my trusty friend Samuel Forman to be my Lawful executor and after all my just debts are paid desire that he do divide the rest of my substance, whether by book debt, bonds or notes or whatever effects belonging to me equally between my children Elizabeth and Martha Huddy In witness thereof I have unto signed my name this Twelfth day of April in the year of our Lord, One thousand and seven hundred and eighty two. Joshua Huddy

It was reported that Huddy died calmly and bravely, declaring that he would "die innocent and in a good cause." His body was left hanging until afternoon and then was taken to Freehold, where Huddy was buried in an unmarked grave in the Old Tennent Church churchyard with full military honors on April 15, 1782. More than 400 people gathered to protest his execution and a petition was sent to General George Washington demanding retribution by surrendering Lippincott or another British officer of similar rank for hanging.

Sir Charles Asgill. *(Charles Turner, after 1822 portrait by Thomas Phillips, R.A.)*

Retaliation

Patriotic sentiment ran high following the death of Huddy. In an effort to avert reprisals by the New Jersey Militia, General Washington agreed to select a British prisoner of war for retaliatory execution. Straws were drawn and a hapless young British officer, Captain Charles Asgill, drew the short straw. He would be executed if Lippincott was not turned over to the Patriots.

The situation was complicated. Asgill and all other captive British officers were actually protected under the peace terms that were then being negotiated, so if he hung it would be a clear violation of the agreement. The British managed to delay Asgill's retaliatory execution by holding their own court martial of Lippincott for abducting Huddy. It came as no surprise when Captain Lippincott was found not guilty on the grounds that he was just following orders. It would later be learned that the man Joshua Huddy was accused of murdering, Loyalist raider Phillip White, was likely killed after Huddy had been captured. The accusation was likely fabricated so that the British had justification for the execution.

This delay allowed time for Asgill's mother to appeal for the intercession of the American's French allies. The matter was referred to the highest level, all the way to King Louis XVI and his wife, Marie Antoinette. In addition, Catherine Hart, Huddy's spurned widow, also stated Asgill's life should be spared since he was an innocent victim. The matter was turned over to the Continental Congress, which agreed to free Asgill. In return, the commander of British forces in New York, General Sir Henry Clinton, condemned the hanging of Huddy and prohibited the Loyalists from seizing other Patriot prisoners.

In 1836, Huddy's surviving daughter, Martha Piatt, wrote to Congress that the nation had never expressed its gratitude to Huddy's family. She demanded money and land, but the bill was never acted upon. Huddy was largely forgotten until the Bicentennial Celebration in the 1970s, which renewed interest in Monmouth County's fascinating history during the Revolutionary War.

There are few tributes to the memory of this brash hero in Monmouth County. A monument bearing a plaque to Captain Joshua Huddy now stands in the small park that bears his name at the foot of Waterwitch Avenue in Highlands, near the spot where he was hanged: "Here, Captain Joshua Huddy of the Monmouth County Artillery, A prisoner of war, Captured March 4, 1782, while defending the Blockhouse at Toms River, was hung by Tories without warrant April 12, 1782. The British repudiated, but did not atone for that crime. The Sons of the American Revolution in New Jersey have set up this stone to the memory of the patriotic victim."

In 1950 the Daughters of the American Revolution (DAR) erected and dedicated a bronze plaque to Captain Joshua Huddy that is embedded in a large natural rock on the approximate site of the blockhouse at Toms River. The U.S. Army Department placed a marker in the Old Tennent Cemetery in 1962 with Captain Joshua Huddy's name on it. However, he does not lie at that exact spot, since he was buried elsewhere in the cemetery in an unmarked grave and the location has been lost to time.

Captain Joshua Huddy's story is a reminder that the Revolutionary War in Monmouth County, New Jersey was really a civil war. Patriots and Loyalists continued to attack each other for the entire eight years of the war, and even after the main armies had stopped fighting and peace had been officially declared. This violence was often initiated to retaliate for previous events, of which Huddy's death was one of the last that occurred before the Treaty of Paris was signed in 1783. His sacrifice was a tragic example of a regrettable and continuing pattern that divided the people of the new nation and caused Loyalist land

and property to be confiscated. Those loyal to the English mother country were driven out of the country, and they settled in Canada, Nova Scotia and the Bahamas.

The Pine Tree Robber

The British had an even grander agenda for welcoming African-Americans into their armed forces. The American rebellion in New Jersey and elsewhere was supported and financed to a great extent by a plantation economy, one that would be paralyzed by the loss of slave labor. Destruction of this oppressive agricultural system could effectively end the war if states would be compelled to recall their militia forces from military service to maintain a hold over rebellious slaves.

Tye escaped from his brutal, hot-tempered master the day after Dunmore's Proclamation was issued, and soon joined the flood of Monmouth County blacks who sought refuge with the British and became soldiers, sailors and workers. He memorized a map and fled down the coast to Norfolk, Virginia. He claimed to be a freed man, did odd jobs along the way and changed his name to Tye. Corlis posted a reward for Titus's capture and return, and this advertisement provides a rare glimpse of Tye's appearance:

THREE POUNDS REWARD

RUN away from the subscriber, living in Shrewsbury, in the county of Monmouth, New-Jersey, a NEGROE man, named TITUS, but may probably change his name; he is about 21 years of age, not very black, near 6 feet high; had on a grey homespun coat, brown breeches, blue and white stockings, and took with him a wallet, drawn up at one end with a string, in which was a quantity of clothes. Whoever takes up said Negroe, and secures him in any gaol, or brings him to me, shall be entitled to the above reward of Three Pounds proc. and all reasonable charges, paid by Nov. 8, 1775. JOHN CORLIS.

THREE POUNDS Reward.

RUN away from the subscriber, living in Shrewsbury, in the county of Monmouth, New-Jersey, a NEGROE man, named TITUS, but may probably change his name; he is about 21 years of age, not very black, near 6 feet high; had on a grey homespun coat, brown breeches, blue and white stockings, and took with him a wallet, drawn up at one end with a string, in which was a quantity of clothes. Whoever takes up said Negroe, and secures him in any goal, or brings him to me, shall be entitled to the above reward of *Three Pounds* proc. and all reasonable charges, paid by

Nov. 8, 1775.   §   JOHN CORLIS.

John Corlis's runaway advertisement for Tye.

When Tye arrived in Virginia he enlisted in "Lord Dunmore's Ethiopian Regiment" with 300 other escaped African American slaves, the first black regiment to serve the Crown during the American Revolution. This elite corps wore a uniform with sashes containing the inscription "Liberty to Slaves." The unit was of tremendous propaganda value of the British and soon grew to be an effective fighting force of 800 men. This black regiment in British service was a symbol of hope for all enslaved African Americans who interpreted the War for Independence as a cause committed to maintaining slavery. Terrified Patriot military leaders regarded the all black regiment as a major threat and enraged slave owners denounced it as a "diabolical scheme."

Tye and his comrades believed they were fighting not just for their own individual freedom, but for the freedom of enslaved blacks in North America. Being trained by the world's best army to bear arms and kill their oppressors was a radical idea at the time.

British officers soon began to recognize Tye's potential as a leader, and he was promoted to captain. While the British army did not officially commission black officers, it often bestowed titles out of respect. He had his first taste of combat near his original home in New Jersey at the Battle of Monmouth. Tye was involved in the thick of the fighting and is credited with capturing a Monmouth County Militia captain.

Conditions in Monmouth County provided a perfect storm for African-Americans to rebel and band together into armed groups. The Continental Army consistently failed to offer assistance to the local militia against Loyalist raiders. The proximity of the British stronghold on Sandy Hook offered support and a sanctuary for the refugees. Over a third of the residents remained loyal to the Crown and could be counted on for aid and encouragement.

Gaining freedom was not always the primary motivation for preying on the defenseless Patriot land owners. Revenge on former masters, plunder, and even bounty rewards from his Redcoat supporters were compelling inducements. The British army was elated by this direct military intervention and often rewarded the partisans with a standard payment of five gold guineas, a large sum in those days, roughly equivalent to $2,500 today.

Tye Terrorizes Monmouth County

Colonel Tye's in-depth familiarity with the people, land, and waterways of Monmouth County, in combination with his bold leadership, made him a familiar and feared Loyalist guerrilla commander over the course of the next two years. His marauders, about 800 black and white fighters, targeted the most affluent Patriot land owners, often burning their homes and looting their property. Slaveholders were especially prized as targets, and after being immediately freed they often joined their liberators. If being captured during raids, militia officers or civilian leaders were frequently executed, and other captives were dispatched to the Sugar House Prison in New York City.

Tye employed Indian-style tactics while attacking and plundering Patriot homes. He struck by surprise and then quickly disappeared into nearby swamps or forests. A refugee village on Sandy Hook, close to the lighthouse, also provided a sanctuary for combatants and their families. Tye's leadership instilled confidence in New Jersey's African-

Americans and many of them joined him, while others escaped and fled to the British-occupied territory of New York City. Some even formed their own guerrilla bands. For over two years Tye's raiders kept the New Jersey shore in turmoil; he was feared more than any other Loyalist military leader, black or white.

In July 1779 Tye's party launched a daring raid on his hometown of Shrewsbury. His force freed several slaves and carried away clothing, furniture, horses and cattle. By 1780 Tye, now recognized as a colonel, had become an important military force in destabilizing the entire Monmouth County region. During one week in June, he led two actions in the county. On June 9 Tye and his men murdered Joseph Murray, a man hated by the Loyalists for his summary execution of captured Tories under a local vigilante law. On June 12 Tye's band launched a daring attack on the home of Barnes Smock. Tye captured the prominent militia leader along with twelve of his men and destroyed their cannons. This bold action struck fear into the hearts of local Patriots, and even greater numbers of African-Americans began fleeing to join their British protectors in New York.

During the severe winter of 1779, when Washington's Continental Army froze and starved at Jockey Hollow, Tye and twenty-four of his men served as part of the Queen's Rangers, a crack unit of special forces who protected New York City and conducted raids for food and fuel on Patriot farms throughout New Jersey.

By 1780 Colonel Tye and the refugees had created what in effect was a civil war along the New Jersey shore. Governor Livingston, New Jersey's wartime governor, who curiously had tried to abolish slavery in the state, invoked martial law to stabilize the turmoil. This measure proved totally ineffective and an even greater number of blacks, encouraged by news of Tye's feats, fled to British-held New York.

In a series of raids throughout the summer, Tye continued to debilitate and demoralize the Patriot forces. In a single day, he and his band captured eight militiamen (including the second in command), plundered their homes, and transported them to imprisonment in

New York. He was able to do this virtually undetected and without suffering a single casualty.

In September 1780 Tye decided to pursue Captain Joshua Huddy, the scourge of Loyalists in the shore area, an adversary they had tried to kill or capture for years. As mentioned, the surprise attack on the Patriot leader's home in Colt's Neck led to Tye's untimely death. Huddy and his friend Lucretia Emmons held off the attackers for two hours until the Loyalists flushed them out by setting the house afire. During the skirmish, Tye was shot in the wrist by Huddy. What was thought to be a minor wound turned fatal a few days later when Colonel Tye developed tetanus and gangrene as a result of the wound. This soon caused his death at age twenty-seven, three years before the end of the war. His burial place is unknown.

After his death, Colonel Stephen Blucke of the Black Pioneers replaced him as the leader of Monmouth County's refugee force.[8] Attacks on the patriot population diminished with the loss of the charismatic Tye, but still continued sporadically after the British defeat at Yorktown. Tye's reputation lived on among his comrades, as well as among his enemies. Many Americans contended that the war at the New Jersey shore would have been won much sooner had Tye been enlisted on their side. Others observed that had he lived on for the rest of the war, it would have been a disaster for the Patriots of Monmouth County. Ironically, Tye and other African-American Loyalists fought against the Patriots not because of their loyalty to the Crown but for many of the same freedoms the Patriots had demanded from the King.

Chapter 11

The Whaleboat War (1776-1782)

South Amboy, New Brunswick, Matawan, Sandy Hook,
Bradley Beach, Neptune, Manasquan

After the crushing defeat in November 1776 at Fort Washington, near the north end of Manhattan (now part of the New York City neighborhood of Washington Heights), American forces evacuated the greater New York area. For the remainder of the Revolutionary War that region remained under British control. New York City at that time consisted of only the southern tip of Manhattan Island. It was from here that the British controlled political and military operations in all North America.

The waters around New York teamed with British ships. Huge fleets of merchant ships under the escort of British warships crossed the Atlantic and made landfall under the Highlands of the Navesink before anchoring in New York Harbor. Swarms of enemy vessels cruised along the 130-mile New Jersey coastline from Sandy Hook to Cape May. Others crisscrossed Raritan Bay and New York Harbor. Every day speedy schooners from the West Indies carrying rum, salt and sugar cruised along New Jersey beaches.

Before they arrived at New York, ships often paused near Sandy Hook or off of Staten Island, where they were sheltered from storms and defended by warships and shore batteries. Innumerable small boats supplied and tended these ships while they sat in port. Hundreds of small craft crossed from the New Jersey bay shore, Staten Island

and Long Island to Manhattan loaded with food and supplies from bountiful Loyalist farms. New Jersey was within sight of this abundance of vulnerable enemy shipping and was in an unusually advantageous position to prey upon it.

Almost everything that the British army needed had to be brought by ship to America. This may be difficult to understand since the adjacent countryside was an abundant source of food and most raw materials. The British government initially assumed that their army of occupation would soon become self-sufficient and live off this land. But they found the population to be more hostile than expected, and their army had more people in it than most American cities. As the war continued they were additionally joined by many women and children, Loyalist refugees, prisoners of war, runaway slaves and Native Americans. During the war this combined group averaged 34,000 people and consumed thirty-seven tons of food each day. The round-trip voyage between America and Britain took as long as four months. Storms, shipwrecks and ships gone missing were commonplace. For the most part the British armed forces continued to rely on supplies from Britain, which accounted for the abundance of maritime traffic along the New Jersey coast.

At first, single merchant ships sailed alone, but in 1775, the first year of the war, the British found themselves assaulted on land and sea by men venturing out on the open sea in small boats from the New Jersey coast to attack them. These losses became so frequent that supply ships began sailing in convoys escorted by British ships of war. This protection was formidable, since British navy three-deck ships of the line had tiers of heavy cannons. Fast sailing and maneuverable, armed frigates and smaller sloops of war provided a screen for the largest men-of-war.

This profusion of British shipping in New Jersey waters provided plenty of easy marks, but the problem was that the new nation had no way to take advantage of this water-borne prey. Prior to the Revolutionary War, the British fleet had protected American colonists, so the colonies had no need to construct their own warships. The Americans had no navy or other armed floating force to disrupt British shipping by seizing their commercial or military prizes in coastal waters. The Americans corrected this limitation with Yankee ingenuity and a spirit of entrepreneurship. The Continental Congress and state legislatures authorized the practice of privateering. This authorized individual citizens to operate their privately-owned ships in campaigns against enemy shipping. The publicly-declared reason for participating in this legal piracy was patriotism, but the rich cash awards that came from the sale of captured ships and cargo were what really motivated American sailors.

The Privateers

On March 23, 1776, several months before the signing of the Declaration of Independence, Congress authorized the issuance of "letters of marque and reprisal." A letter of marque authorized armed merchant ships to challenge any likely enemy vessel that crossed its path. These commissions were issued to vessels called privateers whose mission was to disrupt enemy shipping. The ideal target for a privateer was an unarmed, or lightly armed, commercial ship. The practice continued during the entire American Revolution, and while those involved risked their lives and resources, financial gains could be substantial. The lowest members in the crewman hierarchy could make a fortune if their ship successfully captured prizes.[1]

For ships lacking a letter of marque privateering activities were looked upon as acts of piracy and were subject to prosecution. If an approved privateer captured an enemy ship an admiralty court had to approve the seizure. Then the proceeds from the sale of the prize and its cargo auction were shared among the owners and crew of the privateer according to a pre-arranged contract.

Privateers achieved their best results if they could trick an opponent into believing opposition was pointless. When this ruse failed the

A modern copy of a traditional whaleboat on display at Mystic Seaport, Mystic, Connecticut. (*Wikipedia.org*)

result was often violent combat, and many privateers were captured or sunk when they challenged ships of greater strength.

Despite the dangers involved, the effort by privateers to cripple Britain's commercial fleet was highly effective. While the Continental Army was having a difficult time getting men to enlist, privateers had more than enough volunteers due to the prize money. American privateers actually did much more damage to British shipping than the miniscule U.S. Navy, which was greatly outnumbered and outgunned by Britain's Royal Navy. The practice of privateering was not outlawed by the international community until the Declaration of Paris in 1856.[2]

The Garden State stood at the hub of all this nautical action. In November 1778 New Jersey Governor William Livingston wrote to Congress, "as the Spirit of privateering seems to increase amongst us we need more blank bonds for letters of marque." Motivating these legal pirates or privateers was a combination of ideological support for the Revolution, a need to defend their own homes against the British and Loyalists, and the unique opportunity for even the poorest sailor to become prosperous.

Privateers ventured out all along the Atlantic seaboard, from New England to the Carolinas. To capture merchant ships in the waters along the New Jersey coast and take advantage of being close to the British in New York, these ships usually sailed out from small port towns. In the 18th century, rivers and inlets were much wider and deeper than they are today, so places that today have been forgotten or are now landlocked were once havens for privateers. New Brunswick and Matawan Creek were on Raritan Bay. The mouth of the Shrewsbury River ran directly into the ocean at the base of Sandy Hook. Deal Lake was open to the sea. Duck Creek and Fletcher Lake in Bradley Beach are now closed in by land, but Shark River, Manasquan, Toms River, Little Egg Harbor and some Delaware River ports remain open today. From those vanished harbors, courageous New Jersey sailors sailed out in fast and maneuverable sloops and whaleboats to both capture hostile shipping or raid enemy territory in New York.[3]

Whaleboat Warfare

The whaleboat was usually the vessel of choice for New Jersey privateers. The small craft was between twenty-six and thirty feet long. They were broad-beamed open boats with a shallow draft and sharp double ends. They looked very much like typical ocean liner lifeboats, only longer. They were rowed by pairs of fourteen to twenty-four men at the oars and could be moved quickly and quietly, and even carried for short distances over land. One or two masts could be raised to allow for swift sailing. Their occupants were usually local people, often fishermen, who knew the coastline and inlets. Whaleboat men armed themselves with boarding pikes and muskets, but the weapons they relied on most were pistols and cutlasses for close hand-to-hand combat.

Larger whaleboats carried a single piece of artillery—a small swivel gun mounted on the bow or the stern. This swivel gun was really a large musket fastened to a rotating mount. It was too small to be a cannon but it could conveniently fire a quarter pound ball in almost all directions.[4]

Whaleboat privateers had to rely on swift, shocking attacks in order for their raids to be successful. They had to swarm onto the decks of their astonished enemies, take immediate control, capture the crew, then quickly sail away with the prize. To escape to safety, whaleboat privateers navigated across treacherous shoals and up winding channels where heavier armed, deeper-drafted war ships could not pursue them. The privateers took captured enemy ships back to port where they sold the ship and cargo, then divided the profits between the backers, the officers and crew, and the government.

The Whaleboat Captains

CAPTAIN WILLIAM MARRINER

Hundreds of seafaring men operated American privateers from small port towns along the New Jersey coast, among them men with names like Hendrickson, Browne, Burge, Schenck, Van Pelt and Roberts. Two captains stand out for their bold exploits and contributions to the Patriot cause. The fittingly named Captain William Marriner and Captain Adam Hyler challenged the occupying British on sea and land in both New York and New Jersey. They aggressively hunted British ships and also conducted raids on land to take hostages to exchange for imprisoned Patriots. Both came from New Brunswick, a town advantageously situated in the heart of the maritime action around New York Harbor. The details of their bold exploits can be followed from day to day in contemporary newspapers, a rich source of historical information.[5]

According to local tradition Marriner was "a tall man with a large body and possessed great physical strength." Early in the Revolutionary War, he served as a private in the New Jersey regiment of William Alexander. Marriner left the army in 1777 and opened a tavern on the banks of the Raritan River near New Brunswick. General George

Washington knew William Marriner as a tavern keeper. Patriot spies, informers, and whaleboat men used this tavern as an informal headquarters where customers could share their information and plans to usurp the British.

British commanders in New York City at that time believed the most effective way to defeat the Patriots in New Jersey was to capture their leaders. Tory spies knew the rebel leaders personally. They also knew where they lived, so Loyalist raiders advanced through the countryside in Middlesex and Monmouth Counties and snatched unsuspecting Patriots from their homes. Many of them were then transported to New York and confined in the diseased holds of prison ships anchored in Wallabout Bay in Brooklyn, where most starved to death or died of disease.

The only way to get a captive American released was to exchange them for an influential British or Loyalist prisoner. Unfortunately, the American side had few important prisoners to use as pawns to swap. After deciding that the best strategy was to kidnap important Tory leaders in whaleboat raids, General Washington called on the New Jersey captains.

In 1777, Captain Marriner asked John Schenck, a local militia officer, to join him in organizing a whaleboat raiding expedition on the Long Island shore at Flatbush, a place where many Tory leaders owned country homes. Schenck had frequently visited that area and knew it well. On June 11, 1777, these men conducted the most daring and successful whaleboat raid of the war when they attacked these Tory homes and captured Loyalist leaders.

Marriner and Schenck, along with twenty-six hand-picked men, set out in two whaleboats. The privateers left Matawan Creek on the southwestern shore of Raritan Bay to avoid being spotted by British patrols. They stayed close to the shoreline, where they would be concealed by the late afternoon shadow, and then headed across the bay to Long Island. The sky was overcast, and the strong east wind swept in from the open ocean with waves that battered the sides of the whaleboats. When they were north of the mouth of the Raritan River, the whaleboats steered toward Prince's Bay on the Staten Island shore and clawed north along the shore toward New York. It was reported that here one of Captain Schenck's militiamen became audibly seasick. Intent on his mission, Captain Marriner ordered his whaleboat men to throw the man overboard if the noisy gagging continued.[6]

The whaleboats then crossed the Narrows, the channel that separates Staten Island from Long Island and connects upper and lower New York Harbor. This stretch of water is now spanned by the Verrazano Narrows Bridge. They grounded their whaleboats at what is now Fort Hamilton along the Belt Parkway and concealed them in the bushes. After leaving one man to guard them, they stationed three pickets on the road so their escape route could not be blocked. The remaining men crept inland five miles without being detected, to what is now the Flatbush area of Brooklyn. Once there, they hid in the shadows of the Dutch Reformed Church on the corner of Flatbush Avenue and Church Street. The 1793 church that now stands here is the third house of worship on the site.

Marriner and Schenck had a list of Tories marked for capture. New York City's Mayor David Matthews topped the list. Other targets were Miles Sherbrook, a wealthy Tory merchant, Jacob Suydam, an affluent land owner, Colonel William Axtell, a member of the Governor's Council, and Theophylact Bache, president of the New York Chamber of Commerce. At the church, the Patriot raiders divided into four squads. Each squad carried a heavy plank to use as a battering ram. If the mission worked as planned, each group would strike a different home at the same time. After seizing their prisoners, they would return to the church, reunite, and make their way back to their boats as a group.

Fortunately for the Americans, during that evening several parties were in full swing. These social vents distracted local residents, and the merriment allowed the whaleboat raiders to remain undetected, so the roundup commenced. Captain Marriner's men were disappointed when they discovered that Mayor Matthews and Colonel Axtell were in New York City and would not return until the next morning. At the Suydam house they discovered Captain Alexander Gradon, an American officer who had been taken prisoner in the capture of Fort Washington in November 1776. He was under house arrest at the Suydam home while awaiting a prisoner exchange. He was immediately freed by his countrymen. They found Theophylact Bache sleeping in his bed and dragged him away. In a nearby home, Captain Marriner discovered Miles Sherbrook hiding behind a Dutch chimney. Sherbrook hadn't had time to put on his pants before Captain Marriner prodded him along to the church, where the other raiding parties had gathered before making a hasty departure. The stunned Tory leaders were then led to the whaleboats.

The whaleboat privateers had struck quickly and stealthily, and no alarm had been sounded in Flatbush. The privateers quickly launched their boats, headed directly across New York Bay, and set course for Matawan Creek. On the return voyage they were helped by a following sea and wind, and an incoming tide also carried them along. The whaleboats raced across lower New York Bay and reached Matawan Creek and Keyport only an hour-and-a-quarter later. While the whaleboat raiders had not captured all of the Tories on their list, they had captured at least two men to exchange for Patriot leaders, and they had returned safely without losing any losses.

During a subsequent raid onto Long Island Marriner was captured, but he was soon paroled and returned to his tavern in New Brunswick. A year later, on April 24, 1781, he wrote a letter to British officials. They had reported that he was responsible for another raid and he wanted to set the record straight: "In a New York newspaper it is said I was concerned in taking a sloop, Such a report is without foundation. I am on parole, which I shall give the strictest attention to. She was taken by Hyler and Dickie."[7] This is one of the first mentions of Hyler, whose achievements in the whaleboats surpassed even those of Marriner.

Little is known about the life of Marriner after the war, except that he moved to Harlem, New York and lived there for many years.

CAPTAIN ADAM HYLER

Adam Hyler was born in Germany around 1735. He was the son of Philip Hyler, who emigrated from Baden, Germany, to New Brunswick, New Jersey in 1752. Adam Hyler went to sea at an early age, and for a time he was forced to serve in the British navy after being captured by a "press gang." Impressment was the practice of forcing men into a navy by compulsion, and without notice. When the Revolutionary War began, Hyler was operating his own small fleet of sloops and carrying cargo from his home town of New Brunswick to New York City. Little else is known about his personal life except that he lived in a large log and frame house in New Brunswick and married twenty-three-year-old Ann Nafey after his first wife died.

Hyler served in Marriner's whaleboat fleet during the earlier years of the war, but nothing is known of these activities. In November 1780 Hyler led a raiding party of whaleboat men on a successful foray along the Staten Island coast and captured an anchored sloop. On August 5, 1781, he duplicated Marriner' previous feat by crossing to Long Island on a prisoner-hunting raid. The *New Jersey Gazette* in Trenton reported that he marched three-and-a-half miles into enemy territory and captured a high-ranking Loyalist militia colonel and a British ship captain, and then returned safely back to New Brunswick with his prisoners.[8] His name began to appear in the newspapers of the day and he was soon regarded as Marriner's successor and the foremost whaleboat captain on the New Jersey coast.

These actions were only the prelude to Hyler's exploits while commanding whaleboats. On October 5, 1781 a Patriot courier arrived at Marriner's tavern and reported that a fleet rich in potential prizes was anchored inside the sheltering arm of Sandy Hook in Horseshoe Cove. Hyler hastily alerted his whaleboat crews and they launched a tiny armada of three whaleboats. He led the whaleboats with a small sloop that he had christened the *Revenge*. The little flotilla sailed out over shoal-cluttered Raritan Bay and waited for darkness off South Amboy, at the mouth of the Raritan River. From there they headed east toward Horseshoe Cove.

When Hyler's little fleet arrived at the cove they found themselves within range of the guns of a mighty British ship-of-the line. Tiers of gun decks rose up her black sides. This guard ship protected a convoy of five smaller vessels anchored nearby. Three of the anchored ships were merchantmen, but the other two were armed vessels, each with firepower exceeding the *Revenge* and her whaleboats. One was a sloop that mounted a 3-pounder cannon and six swivel guns. The other boat was even larger and carried four 6-pounder cannons. This floating arsenal was backed up by a battery of cannons on shore at the base of the Sandy Hook lighthouse, less than a half-mile away. The guns of this log redoubt were trained out over Horseshoe Cove and were prepared to defend the anchored ships.

Hyler's small flotilla remained undetected by British lookouts as it approached the enemy fleet in the inky darkness. He dispatched one of the whaleboats to drift among the moored ships to determine their state of readiness. The reconnoitering whaleboat returned with encouraging news. Nobody seemed to be on watch on the large guard ship, and the nearby merchantmen also looked deserted. Apparently, most of the British sailors had gone ashore and only a skeleton crew remained on board. Since nobody was on watch, there were no challenges or alarms.

As the American whaleboats drifted down on their targets, Hyler took advantage of the element of surprise and struck immediately, and so he ordered the whaleboat crews to board the deserted merchantmen and the armed sloops. The *Revenge* attacked the stronger-armed sloop first. As they slid alongside they tossed grappling hooks to catch and hold the British vessels. Hyler's men then swarmed over the sides. The slumbering sentries, now alerted, began shouting warnings, and a few of the defenders charged the boarders with cutlasses and pistols. Most of the enemy crews were trapped below decks, but several were able to escape by diving overboard and fleeing in a longboat. The entire fleet of five ships was swiftly captured. All resistance soon came to a halt, and no American whaleboat men had been lost.

But the Americans were still confronted by the shore batteries and the immense guard ship. The British sailors who had fled ashore alerted the soldiers in the log redoubt, but there was still no activity on the guard ship. Hyler and his men worked fast to remove the cargo from the captured vessels. Plundered guns, sails and supplies were swiftly tossed over the side into the whaleboats.

At that time, the twelve swivel guns mounted on the log redoubt began firing. Fortunately, they were out of range, and the darkness prevented them from finding their mark. But the noise of the gunfire alerted the men on the guard ship, which prepared to open fire. The whaleboat men set four of the ships on fire but spared one on which they found a woman and four children. The *Revenge* and the other whaleboats were silhouetted by the burning vessels and struck by shot from the huge cannons of the guard ship but were able to slip away unharmed into the darkness. Hyler and his whaleboat crews made a hasty departure and sped away toward the safety of Raritan Bay under full sail.

The American whaleboats arrived triumphantly at New Brunswick at daybreak. The *New Jersey Gazette* reported joyfully that the small fleet had come back laden with prisoners, sails, and cordage that had been stripped from the captured vessels. Other booty included 250 bushels of wheat, a quantity of cheese and several swivel guns. Hyler immediately set out again and captured two enemy fishing boats near the Narrows. Two weeks later, with three whaleboats under his command, he attacked a heavily gunned Royal Navy galley off Prince's Bay on Staten Island. This time he was not so fortunate. The galley, a large sailing ship with oars, returned fire and hit the stern of one of Hyler's boats with an 18-pound shot. The crew managed to ground the stricken vessel and get ashore, but they were immediately made prisoners. Shortly thereafter, Hyler landed at the scene with his own men and managed to overpower the Redcoat captors and rescue the

American crew. With his two remaining boats, he escaped into Raritan Bay, but his bad luck followed him. Six miles away, off South Amboy, another British galley blocked his course and sank his boat with a huge 24-pound shot. Hyler's and his surviving men struggled aboard the remaining boat and fled home safely to New Brunswick.[9]

In 1782, Hyler became seriously ill. He reportedly suffered "a tedious and painful illness" from an accidental leg wound. Another quite different version recounts that "a Tory tavern wench" in South Amboy slipped poison into the drink of the intrepid whaleboat captain. He died three months later at age forty-seven at his home in New Brunswick on September 6, 1782. He was buried in the old Dutch burial ground. Ten days later, his wife, Ann, bore him a son who was named Adam, and grew up to become a captain on the waters of New York Harbor.

Many other whaleboat men in New Jersey served their state and country well and took the war to the British by capturing vitally needed supplies, war material and prisoners for exchange. Whaleboat men were awesome fighters of the sea, especially when led by captains such as Marriner and Hyler, who had the seamanship and the ability to inspire blind faith in their leadership. Nowhere did these traditions count for so much as on the exposed deck of a whaleboat.

Chapter 12

The Nest of Pirates,
Little Egg Harbor Disaster (1778)

Little Egg Harbor, Beach Haven, Stafford Township,
Batsto Village, Port Republic, Brigantine, Absecon, Atlantic City

T*he New Englanders are fitting out light vessels of war. By which it is hoped we shall not only clear the seas and bays here of everything below the size of a ship of war, but that they will visit the coasts of Europe and distress the British trade in every part of the world. The adventurous genius and intrepidity of these people is amazing.*

– Thomas Jefferson July, 1775

Little Egg Harbor, a bay separated from the Atlantic Ocean by a narrow sand dune, lies along the shore of Burlington County, New Jersey. Many people pass it on their way to Atlantic City, fifteen miles south, and have no idea that this place off Exit 58 of the Garden State Parkway has a violent and unusual history. During the first years of the Revolutionary War this now isolated area of the Pinelands was critical to the American's war at sea and was regarded by British military leaders as a notorious "nest of rebel pirates." The British and American commanders wrote comprehensive accounts of the engagements which took place in the vicinity in reports to their superiors, and these have been preserved in the military archives and are quoted in this narrative.[1]

The most recent account of the events at Little Egg Harbor was written by J. Anthony Harness, a local historian and Little Egg Harbor resident. His work appeared in the Atlantic County Historical Society Year Book for the year 2016. This comprehensive and flawlessly documented work relies on primary sources in the form of comments and excerpts from the correspondence of contemporary British and American military leaders. Especially interesting is the overview of the military and political events at the time of the Little Egg Harbor action.

Sea-faring Patriots from the nearby shore area were known as privateers. They were able to slip out of the bay in small, swift boats to capture many richly laden merchant vessels sailing from England or between New York Harbor and other ports on the East Coast. They brought their prizes, which carried a vast amount of supplies destined for the British army, into Little Egg Harbor a crucial port on the southern New Jersey coast.[2] The profits from the sale of the vessels and their cargos were distributed among the daring crews. This haven for these legal buccaneers sheltered as many as thirty of their armed sloops at one time, all lying in wait for some bountiful enemy vessel sailing along the New Jersey coastline.

Privateering was a stroke of luck for the destitute new government. It provided a way to disrupt enemy commerce without expending resources and money on warships or crews. Although the Continental Navy had few vessels, it was able to intercept the supplies of food, clothing, arms and ammunition needed by the British armed forces. The bankrupt Continental Congress issued licenses called "letters of marque" authorizing owners, captains, officers, and crews of privateers to capture or destroy British shipping.

These privately-owned warships, many of which were based at Little Egg Harbor, were in an excellent position to attack enemy shipping anywhere along the east coast. American investors were able to help the war effort by financing privateers, and captured vessels were often refitted and used as American men-of-war. Congress issued 1,697 letters of marque during the war, and about 55,000 men served at one time or another as sailors on these ships. These men captured about 2,300 enemy ships; in comparison, the Continental Navy had only 64 vessels and captured less than 200 enemy ships.[3]

This windfall for the Americans was devastating for their adversary. The Crown forces in America depended almost totally on shipments of supplies from England. To prevent the severing of their vital trade routes, Great Britain was forced to divert their warships to protect merchant ships. The entire British economy began to suffer as shipping insurance rates soared. The situation became serious enough to consider changing the course of the entire war. On March 8, 1778 Lord George Germain, British Secretary of State for the Colonies, sent secret orders to Sir Henry Clinton, directing him to curtail his land operations and to attack ports from New York to Nova Scotia in order to destroy these legal pirates.[4]

The low draft American ships could navigate shallow waterways to hide and escape from pursuers. Their crews were made up of impoverished fishermen and farm laborers who lived in a harsh environment where it was a constant struggle to survive. These economically disadvantaged Patriots were unusually skilled sailors and this hazardous, but lucrative, seafaring venture presented an opportunity for them to both serve their nation and improve the quality of their lives. They were a strong breed who valued their independence from a distant and intolerant government.

When an enemy vessel was captured it was sailed to an authorized port. There the cargo was inventoried, and both the ship and the cargo were stored until an Admiralty Court ordered its disposition. The vessel, was called the "prize," and its cargo were usually disposed of by auction. Cargo unloaded from captured ships in Little Egg Harbor was sometimes auctioned locally at Chestnut Neck, the port on the harbor, or carried on wagons to be sold a few miles up the river at the Forks, the place where the Batsto River joins the Mullica River twelve miles from the bay. From there it would be hauled to Philadelphia, Burlington, or Dunks Ferry (the present-day Delaware River town of

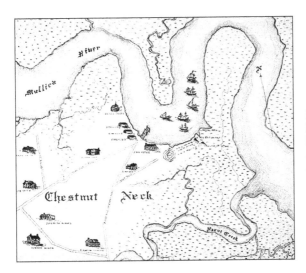

Map included in signage at Port Republic Battle Monument. *(Atlantic County, New Jersey, Commissioner of Historic Sites)*

Beverly), twenty miles south of Trenton. During the winter of 1777–1778, supplies appropriated from privateers were brought directly to Washington's troops encamped at Valley Forge.

The summer tourist mecca of Long Beach Island, with its shore towns of Beach Haven, Long Beach and Ship Bottom, forms the north shore of Little Egg Harbor. This barrier island is a narrow strip of land eighteen miles long and a half mile across. It is separated from the mainland by five-mile-wide Barnegat Bay. Heading south from the tip of the island is marshland, the island of Brigantine, and Atlantic City. Between Long Beach Island and Brigantine lies Little Egg Harbor Inlet, the entrance to the bay. When Cornelis Mey, a Dutchman, arrived in 1614 he explored the coast south of New Amsterdam and entered the inlet at Little Egg Harbor. He named the place after his crew found thousands of eggs left by the migratory birds that nested in the marshes.

The Mullica River flows into Little Egg Harbor Bay. This region was explored as early as 1637 by Eric Mullica, who gave this its name. He came to America with the Swedish settlers who settled in the Delaware Valley, and eventually bought 100 acres along the river. The Mullica, likely one of the few unpolluted streams left in the

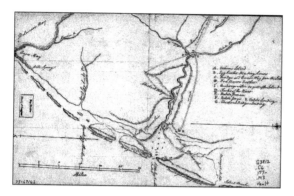

Area around Batsto and the
mouth of the Mullica River, 1777.
*(Courtesy West Jersey History
Project)*

country, is formed by the joining of streams that come together at
"The Forks" near the historic iron works at Batsto. Flowing into the
Mullica from the north are the Bass and Wading Rivers. From the
Forks to the bay is about fourteen miles. The Mullica River is the
boundary line between Atlantic and Burlington Counties.

Near the mouth of this river is a neck of land that is near to safe
anchorages in the bay. A small fishing community known as the
Chestnut Neck began there in the 17th century. The town was
located in a marsh at the edge of a dense forest of pine barrens and was
surrounded by bays, inlets, rivers and streams. At first the place was
populated by a few fisherman and livestock which grazed nearby, but
by the beginning of the Revolutionary War its location along the coast
and its deep-water harbor caused the colonial port to grow into the
largest village on the New Jersey coast. It became a thriving trade
center. By 1776 Chestnut Neck had two taverns, a dozen dwellings
and several warehouses, and its ships supplied New York City with
locally-grown food and iron products from a nearby furnace.

Soon after the war began the town became a sanctuary for the
privateers who seized British merchant ships as they hugged the
coastline. During 1778 dozens of ships full of materials bound for the
British troops in New York City were captured and taken into Little
Egg Harbor, where their cargoes were auctioned off at Richard
Westcoat's tavern at the Forks or Payne's Tavern in Chestnut Neck. In

August of 1778 alone thirty ships with cargoes destined for the British army were sold at auction. The ships carried cloth, silks, shoes, books, medicine, hardware, meat, butter, cheese, wine, salt, tobacco, sugar, molasses, coffee, ironware, nails, cooking utensils and military supplies. The most notable capture was a luxury liner of its day, The *Venus of London*. The ship itself sold for over £16000, the equivalent of millions of dollars today.

The site of Chestnut Neck today is where the Garden State Parkway crosses over the Mullica River. No trace of the town remains. The critical events that occurred there during America's most important war are often overlooked in the history of the Garden State.

Destroy That Nest of Vipers

The British could not endure the further disruption of their seaborne supply route by the privateers. On July 12, 1777, four British men-of-war were dispatched to Little Egg Harbor. Unopposed, they retrieved two of their own captured brigs (two-masted ships) which were moored at Chestnut Neck. No British troops were landed, and the British convoy returned to sea. While the Patriot forces from the area that had quickly gathered to defend the port were delighted to see them depart, they remained apprehensive. This effortless incursion made it certain that Redcoat warships would return.

During the month of September in 1777 a fort was built at Chestnut Neck to protect the port and the Batsto Iron Works, which was a few miles up the Mullica River to the west. The Batsto area had the natural resources necessary for making iron. Bog ore was dug from the banks of the streams and rivers, wood from the forests produced the charcoal for fuel, and water powered primitive machinery. The Iron Works produced household items such as cooking pots and kettles. Cannon balls and other military equipment were produced for the Continental Army during the Revolutionary War years. In fact, the Iron Works were so vital to the war effort that its workmen were exempt from military service. With the financial backing of Colonel John Cox, the owner of the Works, a small group of fortifications named Fort Fox-Burrows were erected. The first fort had placements for six guns and was located on the beach at water level, and on a nearby hill a platform was built to mount more even guns. There is no evidence, however, that any of these guns were ever actually mounted. The taking of the *Venus* may have been the single act that pushed the British to act decisively with military retaliation.

The war was not progressing well for Sir Henry Clinton, the senior British commander in America. He was ordered to evacuate Philadelphia in June 1778 to consolidate Crown forces in New York. During the march across New Jersey he had failed to defeat General Washington at the Battle of Monmouth on June 28. Politically, he could not tolerate humiliation by an unstructured gang of buccaneers from the Jerseys who operated close to his command center. Parliament was pressuring Clinton to end the disruption that was causing a shortage of supplies to the British forces in North America and causing a sharp rise in marine insurance. Privateering was becoming a major political issue and was viewed by many as the major cause of failure to end the American rebellion.

After settling his forces in New York City, Clinton made it a top priority to put an end to this menace to his vital supply line. In the last week of September in 1778 a fleet of 15 vessels mounting 152 guns and carrying 1,690 British and loyalist troops with hundreds of sailors of the Royal Navy was assembled. The task force was mobilized at Staten Island and prepared to suppress the Patriot privateers at Little Egg Harbor. Navy Commander Henry Collins of the HMS *Zebra* was placed in command of the fleet and Army Captain Patrick Ferguson was chosen to lead the landing force.

The British expedition was made up of the following units:[5]

Commanding Officer, Henry Collins

Ship	Type	Guns	Men
Zebra	sloop	14	125
Greenwich	sloop	22	200
Granby	sloop		80
Dependence	galley	7	40
Cornwallis	galley	5	40
Nautilus	sloop	18	125
Experiment	4th rate	50	150
Vigilant	armed ship	20	150
Halifax	brig	2	40
Unknown	tenders	6	60
Unknown	transports (2)	8	80

Commanding Officer, Patrick Ferguson

Unit	Men
Fifth Regiment of Foot Infantry	300
New Jersey Volunteers Infantry	100

Ferguson's 5th Regiment of Foot was combined with another 100 men of a Loyalist unit, the 3rd Battalion of New Jersey Volunteers. This Loyalist unit was under the command of Captain Peter Campbell. Their orders were simply to "clean out that nest of rebel pirates."

Captain Ferguson was known for inventing a breech-loading rifle in 1776. The weapon could fire six shots in one minute and was superior to the standard issue single-shot "Brown Bess" musket. But the so-called "Ferguson Rifle" was little used during this war. Its superior firepower was unappreciated at the time because it was too expensive, took too long to produce, and broke down easily in combat.[6]

On September 30, 1778, the fleet of Captain Collins weighed anchor and sailed from Staten Island. The expedition passed Sandy Hook with favorable winds, but the next day they ran into a severe fall storm. Captain Collins described his departure. "The King's ships, galleys and armed vessels, appointed to act under my orders, having all joined at Staten Island the evening of the thirtieth of September, and the troops being embarked on board the transports, I got under weight and stood to sea, with the wind northerly, but it shifting the day following to the southward, and blowing strong, together with some severe weather, which afterwards ensued, prevented our getting off this place before the afternoon of the 5th of the month, when the tide proving favorable."[7]

The Collins fleet had set sail during the New Jersey hurricane season. As any local shore resident knows, the tropical cyclones along this stretch of deserted coast can pack brutal winds of 110 mph or stronger. They can erode beaches overnight and push ships aground. A few years later, the Great Coastal Hurricane of 1806 packed fierce winds that uprooted trees and destroyed homes across the state. Most of the fatalities occurred aboard a ship, the *Rose-in-Bloom*, off the Barnegat Inlet. It got caught in the massive storm while traveling from South Carolina to New Jersey and lost 21 of its 48 passengers. Twenty-five-foot waves smash the shore, and tides can be six plus feet above normal during these gales. In recent years memorable tempests with benign names such as *Irene* and *Sandy* have ravaged the New Jersey Coast.

It took four days to sail just seventy-seven miles to Little Egg Harbor River. By noon on October 5 the fleet had finally arrived, but the weather continued to cause more problems. The high winds buffeting the large ships made it impossible for them to pass over the shoal water at the bar that straddled the inlet to the Little Egg Bay. Captain Ferguson knew that the delay would alert the defenders to fully prepare to repel his troops in their amphibious assault.

An Assault on a Vulnerable Fort and the Destruction of Chestnut Neck

Cresting waves smashed down on the treacherous shoal of the bar at the inlet entrance to Little Egg Harbor, turning the shallows into boiling surf. The hurricane-force winds caused Collin's fleet to shorten sail and await tide and wind conditions that would allow it to cross over the shoal. Ferguson's landing force was desperate to find a way to come ashore. Every passing hour allowed more time for the Patriots to gather reinforcements and prepare their defenses. They decided on a hazardous, yet practical, option. They row the men ashore in galleys and other shallow draft boats that could pass over the shoal, and then strike the Patriots.

This operation would require the Redcoat amphibious force to struggle through twenty miles of churning seas to reach the privateer village of Chestnut Neck. Since the fleet could be observed from shore, the element of surprise had been all but lost. All of the privateers had escaped to open sea and all valuable cargo had been removed from the town by the time the invaders arrived. Warehouses were emptied, and the citizens evacuated with their possessions to a safer place inland in the safety of the dense Pine Barrens. The place was completely deserted except for the small detachment of militia at the fort and several abandoned British prize vessels, including the *Venus of London*.

Commander Collins ordered his ships to begin bombardment on the evening before the landing was to occur. He assumed the fort had mounted several cannons that could potentially annihilate Ferguson's landing force when it approached the beach. The naval gunfire could demolish that fortification before the landing force came ashore. But the small fort, with no heavy weapons to support the Patriot resistance, was doomed.

Loyalists in the area welcomed the British invaders as they sailed into the harbor, and informed them that only a few militiamen had gathered to defend the fort. The landing force came ashore after the gunfire from their ships had pounded the defensive position. Ferguson's galleys were concealed by morning mist, and except for sporadic small arms fire, landed unopposed. When it became obvious that the American fortification lacked artillery, Ferguson's men made a frontal assault on the fort, which drove the Patriot militia into the security of the nearby Pine Barrens.[8] The outnumbered citizen-soldiers had been overwhelmed in a matter of minutes.

Ferguson's brigade spent that evening and following morning destroying Chestnut Neck. They found ten additional prize vessels that had been brought into the port, but the ships were too large to be moved further up the river, so the vessels were dismantled and set afire. The raiders also plundered and burned the twelve houses of the little town, and the warehouse near the wharf was stripped of all its contents and burned. The small fort, which had provided protection to the militia, was totally demolished.

The Vital Saltworks

Before Ferguson left Chestnut Neck to return to his convoy, he learned that he had the opportunity to destroy three saltworks only a mile upriver on the neck near the mouth of the Bass River. Salt was a vital commodity prior to the days of refrigeration. At the time, vast quantities of food needed to be preserved for use by armies and aboard ships.[9] The amount of salt needed to preserve meat was often equal to the weight of the meat itself. Without it, food spoiled for the winter, and widespread starvation became a possibility. Salt was also necessary to produce widely favored American meats—ham, bacon, and dried fish. The preservative had many other uses, including as an ingredient in medicines, fertilizers, and for curing animal skins for clothing and shoes. Few saltworks existed in the thirteen colonies on the eve of the American Revolution and the loss of the supply from Great Britain when the war began made salt production a critical issue. In 1775 the Continental Congress adopted a resolution in which it "earnestly recommended" that each colony "immediately promote, by sufficient public encouragement, the making of salt."[10]

The saltworks were located at a landing place on the Bass River owned by Eli Mathis. Folklore says that on the way Ferguson's troops were warmly welcomed with a feast provided by a Tory farmer who anticipated the British would pass by on their march to destroy the saltworks. In exchange for his hospitality the Tory farmer was "rewarded" by not being plundered. However, saltworks owner Mathis was not so fortunate; the voracious Redcoats destroyed his house and farm buildings. The saltworks were then entirely demolished, along with his sawmill and all nearby houses of known Patriots.

At this point, Captain Ferguson was tempted to continue sailing twenty miles further up the Mullica River to the "Forks," where, according to the Tories, Patriots stored a rich trove of captured goods. But the upper reaches of the Mullica River were too shallow, even for his galleys, and at that distance it would be difficult to obtain provisions from the fleet. The trip would require travel through a hostile area where aroused Americans could potentially be waiting to harass his men. When Ferguson learned that Patriot artillery was on the way to defend Chestnut Neck, he decided it was safer to return to the bay. The British action had been successful in many ways. The fort had been taken and destroyed and all prize vessels had been burned and sunk. Storehouses had been burned and the small town leveled. His victorious landing force returned to the fleet on October 7, 1778.

Upon their return, Ferguson's party found two ships of the fleet, the *Zebra* and the *Vigilant,* grounded on the bar. The next day they joined the ship's crews to help remove equipment to lighten the vessels and were successful in refloating them. With the landing force safely aboard, the fleet was ready to weight anchor and head back to New York City. But they were again deterred by weather conditions. High winds, the rising tide and shoaling kept the British expedition in Little Egg Harbor bay for another fifteen days.[11]

A message from Admiral James Gambier, the new commander-in-chief of the North American British Naval Station, arrived on a fast sloop from New York on October 10. The message ordered Collins to end the raid on Little Egg Harbor and return immediately to New York.[12] Since the Crown forces no longer held any part of New Jersey, senior British commanders believed that it was too risky for the fleet to remain on the southern coast. As the days passed, the restless Captain Ferguson and his idle soldiers on board the ships of the wind-bound fleet began to plan other ways they could harass the rebels during this inactive time.

Pulaski's Belated Rescue Attempt

The imminent invasion at Little Egg Harbor had triggered last-minute responses from the Patriots. On October 2, the military commander at Philadelphia ordered Proctor's Regiment of Artillery to Little Egg Harbor and on October 5 the Continental Congress dispatched American forces under the command of General Casimir Pulaski to the area.[13] This was a day after the fleet appeared at the harbor entrance and only a day before the British landed on the lower Mullica River at Chestnut Neck. Pulaski arrived at Tuckerton from Trenton on October 8, two days after the loss of the fort and town at Chestnut Neck. Pulaski made his own headquarters about a half- mile to the west, on the farm of James Willet and other groups of his soldiers camped nearby.[14]

At the time Tuckerton was an inland Quaker settlement off the north shore of Little Egg Harbor Bay. The Pulaski Legion settled south of the village in a position with a good view of the British fleet anchored in Little Egg Harbor Bay and awaited the next British move. One group of fifty of Pulaski's soldiers formed a large outpost near where a monument now stands, an area then known as Ridgeway Farm.

Count Pulaski was born in Warsaw, Poland, on March 6, 1745. He attained the rank of Brigadier General in the Continental Army following a recommendation from Benjamin Franklin. He quickly distinguished himself at Brandywine, where he covered the retreat of Washington's troops, preventing a total rout, and saved General Washington's life. Pulaski formed an independent cavalry unit known as the Pulaski Legion. It was comprised of Americans, Germans, some Frenchmen, Irishmen, and Poles. This was the diverse international force that rushed to defend Little Egg Harbor in October 1778.

Later, the Pulaski's Legion joined other French and American troops in an attempt to retake Savannah, Georgia from the British in the fall of 1779. Pulaski, mortally wounded by grapeshot during the attack, died two days later aboard the American ship *Wasp* while en route to Charleston and was buried at sea. Most contemporaries who met

Pulaski mortally wounded by grapeshot while leading a cavalry charge. *(Henry D. Northrup, 1901, U.S. Library of Congress)*

Pulaski agreed that he excelled as a daring and energetic equestrian. One friend described him as a soldier who fought with the force of ten. He is remembered today as the Father of American Cavalry.

The Legion gathered at the little village of Tuckerton had no way of telling exactly where the British would strike, so troops were sent to defend the most likely places for a landing.[15] William S. Stryker described Pulaski's headquarters on the farm of James Willets as it appeared in 1894:

> *The present Andrews house stands on the old foundation, and some of it once formed a part of the Willet's farmhouse. From the front of the homestead—a fine old farmhouse still standing, with cedar-shingled roof and sides—a good view could be taken of the harbor*

and of the English fleet at anchor there. Pulaski had his headquarters in this house. A few hundred yards from the doorway, and nearer to Little Egg Harbor Bay, but concealed from the bay by a close growth of timber, which still remains, the troops of horse, the artillery and a portion of the infantry of the Legion were encamped here.

Stryker stated that the site of the house was still marked by a hollow place in the ground and a cluster of trees. The Andrews homestead standing on the old Willets foundation was destroyed by fire sometime between 1935 and 1937.[16] Today, the site of Pulaski's camp on the former Willets farm is on a vacant lot on a residential street opposite 18 Hollybrook in Little Egg Harbor. There is no marker to indicate its location or significance.

The picket post was located further down the island road, near the farmhouse of Jeremiah Ridgeway, about 2,000 yards closer to Osborn Island. It was occupied by about fifty infantrymen under the command of Lieutenant Colonel Baron de Bosen, the second in rank in the Legion. Osborn Island was a small tract of land owned by the Quakers since the first settlement of the country.[17] The site of a massacre on Radio Road is marked by a stone monument which reads:

This tablet erected by the Society of Cincinnati in the State of New Jersey to commemorate the Massacre of a portion of the legion commanded by Brigadier General, the Count Casimir Pulaski of the Continental Army in the affair at Egg Harbor, N.J. October 15 1778, in the Revolutionary War

Massacre Near Osborn Island

Meanwhile, the restless ship-bound Ferguson received some amazing intelligence. One of Pulaski's junior officers, a deserter from the Hessian forces named Acting Sub-Lieutenant Carl Wilhelm Joseph

Juliat, had left the main camp to go fishing with six other soldiers. When the group did not return, it was believed they had drowned, but actually they had deserted to the enemy. The traitors rowed twenty miles to the British flagship HMS *Nautilus,* where they divulged the locations and strength of Pulaski's forces.[18] The log of the HMS *Nautilus* recorded this entry: "Came on board an officer and a deserter from the rebels." Juliat reported that American morale was low and security was almost nonexistent. He claimed that a surprise attack on the Patriots would be devastating.[19]

Juliat's critical intelligence provided Patrick Ferguson with a vital mission, an opportunity to achieve a major victory before the fleet departed. He immediately planned an attack on the post on the road leading to Osborn Island. He believed Pulaski's entire Legion was at the place when, in fact, it was an outpost. An hour before midnight on October 14, 250 of Ferguson's infantry boarded small boats and rowed ten miles to Osborn Island under cover of darkness.

They landed undetected early in the morning of October 15, at first light, and advanced inland. Ferguson ordered the flints from all muskets removed. The attack would be made only with bayonets, so the sound of gunfire would not alert the defenders. The intrepid captain was ecstatic, believing that now he would surprise the entire Pulaski Legion while their fearsome cavalry would be dismounted and slumbering.

A Quaker family named Osborn owned the island where they came ashore. The invaders traveled through the dark along a road called Island Road, present day Radio Road.[20] Captain Ferguson first sent a party to prevent anyone from escaping from the nearby house of Richard Osborn and to find somebody to guide his troops to the American post. Osborn's son, Thomas, age twenty-nine, was captured in the home and threatened with death if he refused to guide the Redcoats.

Moving across the island, the British first came to a narrow gorge and then to a bridge which crossed over what was called "The Ditch" on Big Creek. Surprisingly, this critical position was not guarded. Ferguson left fifty men there to protect the bridge in the event that it would be needed if he had to beat a hasty retreat. The creek has not changed much from that time. It is about fifty yards across, has a swift current and appears to be deep. A modern bridge has replaced the wooden structure.

Ferguson then led his remaining men over a rough road for about a mile, then across a salt meadow north of the bridge. They suddenly arrived at the first Patriot guard post, secured by only one man. This sentinel was either captured or killed before he could sound an alarm. The invaders soon came upon three farmhouses filled with sleeping American infantrymen. They fixed their bayonets and then surrounded the houses.

The shouts of the zealous Redcoat raiders awakened the outnumbered and unprepared Patriots, who found themselves surrounded. Caught off guard, the drowsy Americans attempted to snatch their unloaded muskets to fend off Ferguson's men. But they swarmed into the farmhouses and mercilessly bayoneted them.[21] A few tried to surrender, but their appeals were ignored, and they were slaughtered. Lieutenant Colonel Baron Charles August von Bose, in command of the infantrymen, attempted to lead his men out of the ambush.[22] The traitor Juliat identified him and directed the attackers to run him through with their bayonets as he slashed with his sword and fired his pistols in a futile effort to reach a door. Second Lieutenant Joseph de la Borderie, the second in command, was also bayoneted to death within minutes.[23]

All of the Patriots at the outpost were murdered, except for five men who were taken prisoner. Captain Ferguson, angered by the fact he had not surprised the main body of Pulaski's Legion, made no attempt to stop the carnage. Afterwards, he only offered this contrite comment, "It being a night attack, little quarter could, of course, be given, so that there are only five prisoners." Later, Ferguson blamed the ruthless slaughter of the Legionaires on Juliat's avarice, saying, "I have only to add that it was in consequence got from the above party [Juliat] that the infantry of Pulaski's Legion was surprised and cut off."

Different casualty numbers were reported by both sides, which is not uncommon with Revolutionary War battles. Pulaski reported

"Our loss is estimated, dead, wounded and absent about 25 or 30 men, and some horses. That of the enemy appears to be much more considerable." However, Ferguson stated there were "about fifty" American dead and added that among his own forces two were dead, one was missing and two were wounded. Douglas S. Freeman noted in his biography of George Washington that American casualties amounted to 10 officers and 40 men captured, of whom approximately 30 were killed.[24] Ferguson's men began to retreat at 10 A.M. after being warned by a Loyalist that American artillery was approaching. The captain ordered a withdrawal to the harbor and the protection of the British ships after deciding that nothing further could be accomplished on the mission.

Pulaski was only about a mile away on the Willets Farm on the road to Tuckerton. Alerted by the sounds of the clash, the startled count aroused his tired troopers and more than sixty horsemen, his entire Legion, raced toward the scene of the action.[25] The swift American cavalry charge caught the enemy by surprise as they withdrew along a narrow causeway leading to the dismantled bridge. Pulaski's men were appalled to find the bodies of many of their slaughtered comrades lying among the ruins of the burning houses as they approached the vanquished picket post.

The American cavalry pursued the marauders down the narrow, rough road. But, as Ferguson had planned, they were forced to abruptly stop at the bridge where the planking had been removed. An attempt to ford the wide creek at high tide was not successful. A few dismounted riflemen were able to climb over on the remaining bridge structure and fire at the backs of the retreating Redcoats. Their volleys were ineffective, and they were recalled since the cavalry could not support them if they overtook Ferguson's superior force.[26] By the middle of the afternoon most of Ferguson's invaders had reached the safety of the fleet.

The British raiders were staggered by the sudden pursuit of Pulaski's troopers. Several scattered and concealed themselves. These fleeing British soldiers who were separated from the main force were hidden by local Tory farmers. The last of these lost Redcoats was ferried back to the ships five days later under cover of darkness. Pulaski was enraged at the farmers who had provided protection to the enemy and threatened to retaliate against the disloyal local citizens by burning their homes. However, he decided that further disruption to the troubled area would serve no useful purpose, and instead forced the offenders to sign an oath of loyalty to the Continental Congress.

Pulaski reported to Congress on his futile pursuit of Ferguson's landing force: "We had cut off the retreat of about 25 men, who retired into the country and the woods, and we cannot find them; the general opinion is, that they are concealed by the Tories in the neighborhood of their encampment."[27] The Americans tried to assist the few gravely wounded survivors when they returned to the appalling site of the massacre. The dead were buried in a mass grave on a knoll at the southern end of the lot near where a farmhouse stood.

Thomas Osborn, the unwilling guide, was able to escape during the chaos. He hid in the nearby meadow and listened to the sounds of confusion and the pathetic cries that came from the bloodbath. When he saw the American force chasing the enemy, he came out of hiding. Everyone believed he was a spy, and the tormented Patriots, enraged at finding so many of their comrades slaughtered and not being able to prevent the escape of the invaders, tied Osborn to a tree and flogged him. Officers had to intercede to save his life.

His father, Richard Osborn, age sixty-three, was apprehended after being suspected of acting as a Tory spy. Father and son were then transported to jail in Trenton. Both of these innocent Quakers were released after two weeks and allowed to return to their homes after no treasonous acts could be proved against them. They were given a pass to ensure their safety on their perilous forty mile walk back through the pine barrens to Little Egg Harbor:

Permit the bearers, Richard and Thomas Osborn, to pass to their homes at Egg Harbour; they being examined before the Judges at

Trenton, and not found guilty, are therefore discharged and at liberty. By order of Gen. Pulaski, Le Bruce De Balquoer, Aide-de camp, William Clayton, Justice of the Peace, Hugh Rossel, Jailer. Trenton, Oct. 30th, 1778.

Both Osborns rest at Friends Cemetery in Tuckerton.[28]

After the tragedy at Little Egg Harbor, Pulaski repositioned his men twenty miles north to Barnegat. The inlet there, at the north end of Long Beach Island, led to Toms River, the strategically important saltworks port for privateer vessels.

The saga of Little Egg Harbor ended with an unfortunate event for each side. Lookouts spotted an American privateer entering Little Egg Harbor as the fleet awaited the return of Ferguson. The ship had been at sea for several days and was unaware of the British presence in the harbor. The startled American crew abandoned their vessel even though it was armed with six swivel guns and one 2-pounder.[29]

After Ferguson and his men returned, the British prepared to sail out of Little Egg Harbor on October 15, but their flagship, HMS *Zebra*, grounded on a sandbar. Rather than allow the ship to fall into American hands, Captain Collins ordered everything of value removed and then commanded it to be burned. This was a painful decision, since the formidable *Zebra* was the lead ship of the expedition.[30] Afterwards the British finally left the harbor on October 20, reaching their base on Staten Island three days later.[31]

Captain Ferguson submitted his version of the action to Senior British commander Sir Henry Clinton when he returned to New York:

Report of Captain Ferguson to Sir Henry Clinton—Little Egg Harbour, October 15, 1778

Sir—Since the letter which I did myself the honour of writing to you on the 10th instant, Captain Collins has received a letter from Admiral Gambier, signifying that the Admiral and you are both of opinion, that it is not safe for us to remain here, as the army is withdrawn from the Jerseys and ordering our immediate return ; but as the wind still detained us, and we had information by a captain and six men of Pulaski's legion, who had deserted to us, that Mr. Pulaski had cantoned corps, consisting of three companies of foot, three troops of horse, a detachment of artillery, and one brass field piece, within a mile of a bridge, which appeared to me easy to seize, and from thence to cover our retreat; I prevailed upon Captain Collins to enter into my design, and employ an idle day in an attempt which was to be made with safety, and with a probability of success. Accordingly, at eleven last night, two hundred and fifty men were embarked, and after rowing ten miles, landed at four this morning, within a mile of the defile, which we happily secured, and leaving fifty men for its defense, pushed forward upon the infantry, cantoned in three different houses, who are almost entirely cut to pieces. We numbered among their dead about fifty, and several officers, among whom, we learn, are a lieutenant-colonel, captain and an adjutant. It being a night attack, little quarter could, of course, be given, so that there are only five prisoners; as a rebel, Colonel Procter, was within two miles, with a corps of artillery, two brass twelve-pounders, one three-pounder, and the militia of the country, I thought it hazardous, with two hundred men, without artillery or support, to attempt anything further, particularly after Admiral Gambier's letter. The rebels attempted to harass us in our retreat, but with great modesty, so that we returned at our leisure, and re-embarked in security. The captain who has come over to us is a Frenchman, named Bromville. He and the deserters inform us that Mr. Pulaski has, in public orders, lately directed no quarter to be given; and it was, therefore, with particular satisfaction, that the detachment marched against a man capable of issuing an order so unworthy of a gentleman and a soldier. PAT. FERGUSON, Capt. 70th Regt.[32]

Aftermath

The massacre at Little Egg Harbor was the first battle involving the Pulaski Legion, and the only major attack on the coast of New Jersey during the war. Although it was considered a British victory, the Crown forces accomplished little by the expedition. The residents of Chestnut Neck expected the British invasion. The privateers escaped and anything of value in the town was removed. The only ships the British "captured" were their own vessels which had been taken as prizes. They held no land and failed to reach the Forks or destroy the Batsto Iron Works. The loss of Batsto would have been a severe blow to the American war effort. Normal privateering activities soon resumed after the departure of the British invaders.

Chapter 13

Massacre at Long Beach Island (1782)

*Barnegat, Ocean Township, Forked River, Tuckerton, Lacey Township,
Berkeley Township, Long Beach Island, Harvey Cedars, Burlington*

In October 1782, Loyalist Captain John Bacon and his band of pine robbers murdered as many as thirty American sailors and local residents near Barnegat Light in the middle of the night. This tragic event has become known as the Long Beach Island Massacre. In response, Patriots from all over Ocean County, then a part of Monmouth and Burlington counties, attempted to capture Bacon for several months. He eluded them until the following December, when a detachment of Burlington Militia stopped at a tavern near Cedar Bridge in Barnegat and found him behind a barricade. This action led to what may have been the last documented land battle of the American Revolution.

The final decisive battle of the Revolutionary War took place at Yorktown, Virginia, in October 1781. The surrender there by British General Charles Cornwallis was the final blow to the British army. However, the war did not officially end for another two years, although American and British armies broke off major fighting during this period as both sides waited for treaty negotiations to formally end the war.

The year 1782 was toward the end of the war, but the New Jersey coastal area was one of the few places in the country where the violence and bloodshed continued and partisan fighting raged on. The hostilities between local residents who supported American independence and those who remained loyal to Britain actually accelerated. Loyalist attacks in what is now Ocean County were led by the "Pine Robbers." These bandits were known by that name since they operated and hid out in the large area of dense wilderness in South Jersey known as the Pine Barrens.

Captain John Bacon was one of the most infamous of this group of men. He was likely commissioned a "Captain" by the "Board of Associated Loyalists." This group was formed in New York under a charter from William Franklin, son of Benjamin Franklin and the last royal governor of New Jersey.[1] Colonel Tye, another Tory leader who harassed Patriots in Sandy Hook and throughout Monmouth County, received a similar title. British military leaders valued these organized armed gangs of Loyalists because they occupied the local militia who constantly had to defend Patriot farms from their pillaging and other atrocities. This freed up the regular British army troops to conduct larger scale military operations. The Board of Associated Loyalists even provided an incentive to attract bandits. It offered a reward of 200 acres of land to anyone willing to fight for the British for the duration of the war but specified that raids were to be conducted solely against military targets. Bacon adhered to this directive by focusing his attacks on units of the Monmouth Militia,[2] but most other Loyalist guerrilla forces used the war as an excuse to plunder civilians regardless of their political affiliation.

In October 1782, the British warship *Virginia* captured a Dutch cutter. This small, swift, single-masted boat set sail from Ostend, Netherlands, with a final destination of Virginia or possibly St. Thomas, Danish West Indies. The cutter carried a rich cargo of tea which was valued at £20000. As the captured vessel was being escorted to New York, the ships two ships became separated. The *Virginia* anchored off Sandy Hook on October 29 in anticipation of seeing the cutter, but the Dutch ship had disappeared. The prize vessel had apparently steered far off course and had run aground on Barnegat Shoals on the northern tip of Long Beach Island.

The New Jersey privateer galley *Alligator* was sailing off Barnegat Bay that same week. Late in the afternoon on October 25, lookouts on the *Alligator* spotted a wreck ashore on Barnegat Shoals which proved to be the missing Dutch tea ship. This was not a great surprise to anyone familiar with this locale, since it was known to have underwater sandbanks extending from the shoreline, swift currents, shifting sandbars, and offshore shoals. Sailing near the area or entering the Barnegat Inlet challenged the skills of even the most experienced seamen.

In 1890, Edwin Salter, a New Jersey legislator and Monmouth County historian, gathered stories about the incident that had been passed down for generations by local citizens. In addition, two short newspaper articles appeared in the *Royal Gazette* in 1782 which relate to the Long Island Beach Massacre. The *Royal Gazette* was published in New York City, and since that city was occupied by the British during most of the Revolutionary War its articles were written from a British perspective. These appear to be the only known contemporary newspaper accounts. My version of events is based on those reports.[3]

After numerous wrecks too place on Long Beach Island over the next fifty years, a small lighthouse was erected at this graveyard of ships in 1835. Since that time, it has been regarded by mariners as one of the most important navigational aids for ships bound to and from New York Harbor. It was replaced in 1859, seventy-six years after the end of the Revolutionary War, by the present structure, the lighthouse known as "Old Barney." This tower was designed by George G. Meade, who was then a lieutenant in the U.S. Army Corps. Meade is better known for his later role as the Union general at the Battle of Gettysburg in 1863. The 172-foot tall lighthouse is open to the public and offers an incredible panoramic view of the area. Nearby is a visitor's center housed in a 106-year-old restored schoolhouse. The museum keeps the history of Barnegat Light alive and available to the public through the preservation of local artifacts and photographs, and it holds frequent events promoting the long history of the light and the town.

The *Alligator* sailed near the beach to investigate the wrecked vessel. Accounts list the captain of the *Alligator* as Andrew Steelman (or Stillman) of Cape May.[4] Captain Joseph Covenhoven and Lieutenant Scull were also onboard, with about twenty-two other men. Steelman went ashore with a handful of crew members. On the wreck they found the cargo of tea intact, but, strangely, there was no evidence of the crew. As remaining sailors from the American privateer went ashore and began to salvage the valuable cargo, they sent word to the mainland for help. Several local residents joined them to unload the tea chests. Among them was William Wilson, a local Loyalist. He disappeared soon after the shore party arrived.

All hands worked frantically unloading the cargo of the wrecked Dutch vessel, but late in the day the wind intensified, and the surf swirled over the beach. Many of the townsmen returned to their homes for the night and a few of the sailors returned to the *Alligator* as evening approached. The crew that remained at the wreck site set up a makeshift camp to spend the night, and the exhausted workers soon fell asleep among the dunes on the beach.

The Loyalist William Wilson, who had slipped away during the day while the stranded cutter was being unloaded, contacted the notorious Captain John Bacon and his band of Tory pine robbers. Bacon and nine of his men took out his whaleboat, the *Hero's Revenge*, during the night and sailed from the mainland across Barnegat Bay to the site of the wreck on Long Beach Island. They beached their whaleboat in a cove on the bay side of the island and before daylight moved silently across the sand toward the sailor's camp.

Bacon and his fellow robbers drew their knives and cunningly approached the camp. Suddenly, they rushed in and stabbed most of the crew to death as they slept. Captain Steelman was killed instantly. A few men, unarmed and completely unprepared, attempted to resist but were unable to defend themselves. Bacon's men hacked them to death

Barnegat Lighthouse. *(Courtesy U.S. Coast Guard)*

with bayonets. Only five of Steelman's group managed to escape alive.

Sounds from the clash and shouts for help were heard on the *Alligator* anchored near the beach. Lieutenant Scull rushed ashore with reinforcements but was wounded in the thigh by a concealed assailant as he approached the camp. Scull's men managed to drive off the raiders and they disappeared into the morning mist. The rescue party, to their horror, discovered as many as thirty dead, including Captain Steelman. A few were rescued when Scull landed and luckily another five men survived since they had left the camp to search for water.[5] The mortally wounded were taken aboard the *Alligator*. Others were left ashore to await rescuers from the mainland. This shocking mass murder of Patriots occurred on the same beach where today, thousands of vacationers bask in the sun completely unaware of this gruesome incident. John Bacon and his Pine Robbers were immediately blamed for the "Barnegat Light Massacre."

Monmouth County's history is replete with Bacon's brutal deeds during the war. His darkest deed, however, was the night of the massacre. Public outrage against Bacon intensified after the killings on Long Beach Island, and a concerted effort to capture him was undertaken. Because the attack was so outrageous and had taken place as peace negotiations were taking place, a reward of £50 was offered by Governor William Livingston for his capture. A monument commemorating Steelman and his men killed on the island stands outside the entrance to Barnegat Lighthouse State Park. Two months after the killings at Long Beach Island, an attempt to capture John Bacon led to an action at Cedar Bridge, five miles north of Barnegat.[6]

The Skirmish at Cedar Bridge: The Last Recorded Engagement of the Revolutionary War

After the tragic massacre on Long Beach Island, the Loyalist Captain John Bacon was relentlessly pursued by the Burlington County Militia. This force was led by Captain Edward Thomas and Captain Richard Shreve of the Burlington County Light Horse. Thomas and Shreve finally caught up with Bacon on December 27, 1782, two months after the massacre. They found the band of Pine Robbers at Cedar Creek Bridge, in what is today the Lanoka Harbor section of Lacey Township. The bridge lies along what was the "Main Shore Road," presently Route 9. Bacon believed that he was trapped and decided to make a stand. The robbers built a barricade across the south side of Cedar Bridge, opposite the Cedar Bridge Tavern. They waited there to ambush the Ocean County citizen-soldiers.

The militia left Burlington on Christmas Day and searched unsuccessfully for the bandits for two days. On their way back to Burlington they chanced on Bacon's barricade at the Cedar Bridge Tavern. Knowing that if caught he would be hanged, Bacon encouraged his men to put up intense resistance. After being hit with a volley of musket fire, Captain Shreve's group mounted a full-scale attack. They charged the barricade and almost overwhelmed Bacon and his men.

At that critical moment the skirmish took a surprising twist. A group of local Loyalists appeared without warning and fired on the militia from the rear. In the ensuing confusion, Bacon and his men escaped, and the Tories surrendered to the militia. One militiaman was killed in the melee and another was wounded. One of Bacon's men was killed, and Bacon and three others were wounded. The Patriots could do nothing more than arrest those who had fired upon them and transport them to the Burlington County Jail.[7] The January 8, 1783, *New Jersey Gazette,* published the only existing public account of the battle:

Cedar Bridge Tavern in 1938. *(Courtesy U.S. Library of Congress)*

On Friday, the 27th of December, Capt. Richard Shreve and Capt. Edward Thomas, having received information that John Bacon with his banditti of robbers, was in the neighborhood of Cedar Creek . . . collected a party of men and went immediately in pursuit of them. They met them at the Cedar Creek Bridge. The Refugees [Loyalists] . . . had greatly the advantage of Capts. Shreve and Thomas' party . . . but it was nevertheless determined to charge them. The onset on the part of the militia was furious, and opposed by the Refugees . . . for a considerable time . . . on the point of giving way when the militia were unexpectedly fired upon by a party of the inhabitants . . . who had suddenly come to Bacon's assistance. This put the militia into some confusion and gave the Refugees time to get off . . . Later, a number of the town's people were hanged for their part in this incident. Bacon was not brought to justice until April 2, 1783, only five months before the war officially ended.

Was this New Jersey skirmish the last battle of the American Revolution? Benson Lossing, the iconic historian who visited Revolutionary War sites in the 1850s, stated that the final action of the war was fought on September 11, 1782, at the siege of Fort Henry in Wheeling, West Virginia. Mark Boatner, a prominent historian and author of the 1970s, claimed that the last action was a successful attack against a British foraging party in the vicinity of Johns Island, South Carolina, on November 4, 1782. The engagement at Cedar Bridge occurred well after both of these actions.

Amazingly, the tavern at Cedar Bridge and the area surrounding it remain intact. The structure still sits on a dirt road surrounded by pine trees and appears much the same as it did in 1782. The wooden bar where Beacon and his combatants drank still stands inside the 18th century roadhouse.[8] Preservationists of the New Jersey Office of Cultural and Environmental Services estimated that the structure was built around 1740, close to a stagecoach route between Camden and the Jersey Shore. The wood-sided building with a long front porch has served as a hotel, restaurant and bar for travelers for over two hundred years.

Ocean County purchased the property in 2008 and it was added to the National Register of Historic Places in 2013.[9] The county is refurbishing and developing the site, which includes a caretaker's cottage and an outdoor classroom facility. Cedar Bridge Tavern sits on wooded acreage in the Pine Barrens about a mile south of Route 72. To catch a glimpse of the building, you must travel down a rough dirt road, deep into the woods. It is located on Cedar Bridge Road in Barnegat, which runs between Old Halfway Road (off Route 72) and Warren Grove Road which is between Route 539 and Route 72. A reenactment is held there each year on December 27.

Bloody John Bacon-The Pine Robber

Captain John Bacon was one of the most notorious Loyalist outlaws on the New Jersey coast. His cruel deeds can be compared to the legendary Colonel Tye, the scourge of northern Monmouth County. These desperados were certainly not motivated by loyalty to Great Britain. They were driven by what they perceived as a legal opportunity to rob and murder their fellow citizens. "Loyalist" is a misnomer for these terrorists. They pillaged, plundered and killed their neighbors regardless of their political affiliation. Bacon, like Tye and most other Tory leaders in New Jersey, gained his "Captain" title from the Board of Associated Loyalists.

Who was Bacon and what thrust him into this nefarious role? His place of birth is unknown, and no public records can be found referring to him until he was sued for debt in Monmouth County in 1775. What is curious is that he did not engage in any disruptive Tory activities until 1780, five years after the war began. Before that time, he was a shingle maker and farm worker, one of the many transient laborers who toiled in the forests and swamps of southeastern New Jersey.

Bacon worked on the Crane family farm in Manahawkin during part of this time[10] The Crane family were ardent Patriots, and several were members of the Monmouth Militia. Bacon's Tory opinions may have been a problem for his employers so for some reason he left this job. He then settled with his wife and two sons in Pemberton, an inland town about twenty-five miles from the coast[11] He is listed in the New Jersey Admiralty Court as a claimant to a British vessel that had run aground on Long Beach Island in 1779. This indicates that he had not yet switched to the Loyalist cause.

In July 1780 Bacon was described as a yeoman farmer in a Monmouth County Court record that accused him of trading with the British in New York City. An active contraband trade was carried out by many civilians of the area who supplemented their meager incomes from this illegal trade. Agricultural products, as well as the vessels to transport them, were both available in the area, and the New York market was insatiable. The hub of this illicit trade was Tuckerton, then called Clamtown. Trading with the Redcoats was a common offense and does not indicate that Bacon was a Tory activist at that time.

The early 1780s were a depressing time in the coastal and Pinelands towns of New Jersey. People were exhausted by the privations of the war. Inflation made Continental currency almost worthless. Trade with the British, although forbidden, was a frequent occurrence. At that time John Bacon joined one of Loyalist bands that plundered, kidnapped, and murdered the residents of Monmouth County.

Bacon was likely recruited for a more active role against the Patriot cause by the Board of Associated Loyalists during one of his smuggling voyages to New York. In 1780 he began plundering homes in the 25-mile area between Cedar Creek and Tuckerton. He was also accused of joining vigilantes from the pines and attempting to free prisoners from the Burlington and Monmouth County jails. The emboldened bandits extended their incursions to western Burlington County, where they pillaged the homes of several prosperous citizens.

The first plundering foray led by Bacon was near Forked River, where he and his men looted the house and mill of wealthy John Holmes. They hid in the woods near the home during the night, and at dawn they seized Holmes and held a bayonet against his heart. They demanded all his money, which he had concealed in nearby woods, but he would not disclose where it was buried. They spared his life after accepting a small amount of money that his wife kept in the house. The robbers disappeared into the pine forest after stealing everything else of value from the couple.[12]

Soon after, Bacon sent his terrorists to Good Luck, now Bayville, to raid the house of John Price. They knew that he and his brother were patriots and militiamen. Price managed to escape when Bacon's men attacked. The bandit loot included Price's musket and snare drum. The banditti began beating the drum for their amusement as they left. Bacon was hiding some distance away, and when he heard the faint drum beat he assumed the Americans were approaching. Bacon ordered his men to set up a defense line and to fire as soon as the men marching to the beat of the drum emerged from the woods. As they prepared to shoot, the bandits were recognized by their comrades and withheld the gunfire.

Three smugglers loaded a whaling ship with foodstuffs from the farms around Barnegat Bay and sailed for British-held New York City in December 1780. There they sold their produce for exorbitant prices, and after doing so they prepared for their return trip to New Jersey. John Bacon met them and asked to be taken aboard on their trip back to Barnegat. When their boat arrived at Barnegat Inlet they anchored and waited for darkness, at which point they could land without being observed. Local Patriots spotted the ship and called in the Toms River Militia to seize the vessel. When the smuggler's boat raised anchor in the darkness and entered the inlet, they were blocked by a militia boat commanded by Lieutenant Joshua Studson, who demanded their immediate surrender.[13]

The three smugglers surrendered, but Bacon refused, knowing full well that he would likely be executed if captured. Bacon fired his musket at Studson and killed him instantly. The militia crew was stunned and in the confusion Bacon and the other men escaped. The three men who had only wanted to sell their produce were now fugitives. When they later reached New York City, they were forced to join the British army. They soon contracted smallpox, but later took advantage of an amnesty offered to British deserters and eventually returned home.[14]

A Monmouth County grand jury indicted Bacon for high treason after the death of Studson. He was accused of waging war against the state, abetting enemy troops and firing on citizens of the state. Although they were scattered along the coast in several Pineland towns and were often outnumbered, Bacon's gang was never intimidated by organized forces of local militia. His men attacked Company Five of the 2nd Monmouth Militia led by Reuben Fitz Randolph at Manahawkin in December 1781. A year later he was accused of robbing the Burlington County collector of a large sum of public money and a proclamation offered another reward for his capture.

In late October 1782, Bacon led his gang in the massacre on Long Beach Island. In December he was wounded at the skirmish at Cedar Creek Bridge and accused of organizing a system to allow fugitive Loyalists and escaped British prisoners to return to New York. Another proclamation was issued that offered a reward for the capture of Bacon and two of his accomplices.

The Death of Captain John Bacon

In March 1783, after his escape from the engagement at Cedar Bridge, the infamous leader of the Loyalist Pine Robbers was finally tracked to Long Beach Island, where he was spotted scavenging a shipwreck. On April 3, a search party of six men, led by Captain John Stewart, pursued him to the tavern of William Rose, located between West Creek and Tuckerton.

What is close to an eyewitness account of Bacon's capture and death has survived. The oral history provided by the son of Captain John Stewart—Charles Stewart—recounted the event as told to him by his father. His story was recorded by George F. Fort, MD in the Pine Barrens town of New Egypt in 1848.[15]

When Stewart and his men arrived at Rose's Tavern, Stewart peered through a window and saw Bacon sitting with his gun between his knees. Stewart burst through the door and surprised Bacon, who raised his gun. Stewart tackled Bacon before he could fire the weapon and wrestled him to the ground. After both men rose from the floor Captain Stewart called for Joel Cook, a member of the search party. Cook's brother William had been killed by Bacon at Cedar Bridge five months earlier. Cook became enraged when he met his brother's murderer, and stabbed Bacon with his bayonet. Bacon fell to the floor, but soon revived and attempted to escape through the back door. Stewart blocked the door with a table, but Bacon pushed the table aside and knocked Stewart to the floor. Stewart then shot Bacon dead as he ran through the open door.[16]

Bacon's body was thrown into a cart and transported twenty miles to Jacobstown, a section of what is today North Hanover Township where his family apparently lived.[17] The soldiers would not allow him to be honored with interment in a sacred place, so they began burying his body in the middle of the road. Many local residents turned out to see the spectacle. Bacon's brother arrived just as he was being lowered into the ground and pleaded with the soldiers to allow him to take the body for a private burial. The body was then taken to be buried at the Quaker Cemetery at Arneytown near Jacobstown, but there is no evidence that a grave marker for Bacon was ever placed at the site.

This is an oral account of Bacon's demise given by Charles Stewart, the son of Captain John Stewart, to George Fort in 1848:

They traversed the shore and found Bacon separated from his men at the public house or cabin of William Rose, between West Creek and Clamtown (now Tuckertown) in the county of Burlington. The night was very dark, and Smith being in advance of his party approached the house and discovered through the window a man sitting with his gun between his knees. He immediately informed his companions. On arriving at the house Capt. Stewart opened the door and presenting his musket demanded a surrender. The fellow sprang to his feet and cocking his gun was in the act of bringing it round to the breast of Stewart, when the latter instead of his charging his piece, closed in with him and succeeded after a scuffle in bringing him to the floor. He then avowed himself to be John Bacon, and cried for quarter, which was at once granted by Stewart. They arose from the floor, and Stewart, (still retaining his hold of Bacon,) called to Cook, who, when he discovered the supposed murderer of his brother, became exasperated, and stepping back gave him a bayonet thrust unknown to Stewart or his companions. Bacon appeared faint, and fell. After a short time he revived and attempted to escape at the back door. Stewart pushed a table against it—Bacon hurled it away and struck Stewart to the floor, opened the door and again attempted to pass out, but was shot by Stewart, (who had regained his feet,) while in the act. The ball passed through his body, through a part of the building and struck the breast of Cook, who had taken a position at the back door to prevent his egress. Cook's companions were ignorant of the fact that he had given Bacon the bayonet wound, and would scarcely credit him when he so informed them, on their way home. They examined Bacon at Mount Misery and the wounds made both by the ball and bayonet were obvious. They brought his dead body to Jacobstown, Burlington county, and while in the act of burying it in the public highway near the village, in the presence of many of the citizens who had collected on the occasion, his brother appeared among them, and after much entreaty succeeded in obtaining his body for private burial. I have heard several different versions of the death of Bacon, and have for that cause been particular in detail, as I believe this statement to be substantially correct, coming as it does from the son of the principal actor in the scene. You can make such use of it as you think proper.

Very respectfully, Your obedient servant, GEO. F. FORT.

Curiously, the remote burial place of Bacon is the site of New Jersey's first state-operated veterans cemetery, which opened in 1986. It was created as "a lasting memorial to those men and women who put their lives on the line to defend our country's honor and freedom." The cemetery was named for U.S. Army Brigadier General William C. Doyle. Approximately fifteen burials occur there each business day, and the cemetery is visited by thousands of visitors each year.

The war was obviously winding down to a Patriot victory in 1783, and peace terms were being finalized in Paris. Many New Jersey Loyalists, fearing retaliation, abandoned their homes and possessions and fled to the British for protection. The Crown promised relocation to England or land grants in Nova Scotia or Canada. Bacon did not seek refuge in British held New York at this time but chose to resist until Burlington County militiamen ambushed and killed him in the tavern at West Creek on April 3, 1783. He may be the last recorded casualty of the Revolutionary War.

Bacon was a major Loyalist partisan in New Jersey, based on his impact on civilians, the number of incidents in which he was involved, and the vast area through which he roved—from Toms River to Little Egg Harbor. During the three years that Bacon ravaged southern

Monmouth County he became a type of a Loyalist phantom and was probably blamed for many depredations that he did not commit. Like other Loyalists, Bacon did not view himself as an outlaw, but as a courageous leader with a mission to punish the rebellious Americans.

Chapter 14

Redcoats on the Road of No Return (1778)

Freehold, Colts Neck, Lincroft, Tinton Falls,
Red Bank, Middletown, Navesink, Highlands

Sunday, June 28, 1778, is considered by many to be the most critical day of the American Revolution. On that day, fifty miles south of New York City at an obscure New Jersey crossroads known as Monmouth Court House, the present town of Freehold, the Battle of Monmouth was fought. The longest and hardest fought engagement of the entire war, this was the only battle of the Revolutionary War in which the main forces of both armies and the highest ranked and most renowned officers on both sides, participated.

The Battle at Monmouth Courthouse is the point in the war when the world's image of the American Army was transformed from that of a tattered band of ill-trained farmers to that of a disciplined and well-led professional military force. At Monmouth, the courage of the American soldier was exemplified, and Patriotism and valor triumphed over weakness and treason. Molly Pitcher personified the bravery of the American woman when she took the place of her fallen husband. General Washington confronted and turned around the retreating Americans led by the treacherous General Charles Lee. Baron von Steuben's relentless drilling, during the dark days of the previous winter at Valley Forge, paid off. Washington's Continentals and the citizen-soldiers of the state militias were able to stand toe-to-toe against the best army in the world.

The Patriots passed their first major test by competently repelling a series of crushing attacks that resulted in the British and Hessian professional combatants being brought to a standstill. The Americans held the field at the end of that hot summer day and the Crown forces made no further attempts to defeat the main American line. Cannons from both sides continued bombarding until 6:00 P.M., when the intense heat of the day forced both sides to disengage. The British then fell back to a position east of a ravine that traversed the field where the heaviest hand-to-hand combat had taken place.

Washington still considered taking the offensive by attacking the enemy on both flanks, but darkness brought an end to the fighting and the tumult soon subsided. The clatter of musket volleys, the frenzied roaring of commands, and the American artillery barrages that thundered from Greene's cannons on Combs Hill all went silent. An occasional musket shot, or the tormented scream of a dying soldier, may have been the only sounds to break the ominous stillness that pervaded the bloodied cornfields. A new moon cast light on the scene of carnage and silhouetted the dead, the dying and the exhausted. The dog-tired Americans slept on the ground, cradling their weapons.

The American soldiers slept soundly with their firearms. The long march from Valley Forge, the intense fighting, and the blistering heat had worn them out. The men of each regiment crumpled in their places on the battlefield when the battle ended. Several soldiers, though not wounded, died during that sweltering summer day by succumbing to hyperthermia, which set in during the intense heat of the battle. General Washington and his staff spent the night under an oak tree amid his slumbering troops. The twenty-one-year-old General Lafayette slept near his side. Most American units were within a half mile of the British lines, and everyone expected to rise at the first light of day to commence fighting again.

The first stirrings that evening came from the men sent out to gather and bury the dead. American burial parties interred most of their own dead and deceased enemies where they had fallen. The wounded were crowded either into the Tennant Church, located next to the battlefield, in the unfinished shell of St. Peters Episcopal Church in town, or in nearby farmhouses. Soldiers were treated by surgeons and nurses without anesthesia. Amputations were the standard treatment for most major wounds.

The makeshift hospital in the Tennant Church treated the wounded of both sides and buried any dead soldiers in the churchyard. The building was pierced by musket balls during the battle, and the scars remained visible for many years until it became necessary to repair the damage in order to stabilize the building. Four cannon balls were dug up in the church grounds during some grading operations in 1916. Pews scarred by the surgeon's saw are still evident, along with bloodstains of the Patriot soldiers who lie in this church cemetery.

An American soldier who was gravely wounded by a cannon ball while resting on a tombstone in the churchyard was carried into the church to die. His blood stains are still visible on the seat of the second pew from the door in the west aisle. Lieutenant Colonel Henry Monckton, the highest ranking British officer killed during the Battle of Monmouth, is buried near the old Tennant Church parsonage a few feet from the southwest corner of the church. Monckton, a grenadier commander, was struck by grapeshot during fierce action near a hedgerow. After the battle, American soldiers found him and carried him to the church where the fatally wounded officer died the same day. A British flag is still placed over his grave on Memorial Day. His gravestone reads; "Lt. Col. Henry Monckton/When on the plains of Monmouth, June 28, 1778, sealed with his life, his duty and devotion to King and Country."

Those who died in the town or in the field hospital at the Episcopal Church were buried in a pit near the center of Freehold. Today this site is on the southeast corner of Main Street and Throckmorton Street. Studies have shown that both sides probably incurred many more casualties than the modest numbers often quoted for propaganda reasons by both sides and which was repeated in history books. The Americans likely lost close to 700 men, and the British about a thousand. Close to 100 men on both sides are thought to have died of heatstroke alone.

The Redcoat army could have withstood prolonged combat, since it remained intact and had ample provisions from their ponderous wagon train. The British, however, chose not to continue to make a stand or to fight from their advantageous position on high ground. The primary objective of Sir Henry Clinton, the British commander, was to get the remaining Crown forces to New York City unharmed. His mission, to reach New York as quickly and safely as possible, turned urgent when he learned a French fleet was on its way to America. Engaging Washington in a prolonged decisive battle that could end with a British defeat was not worth the risk. Therefore, Clinton seized the first opportunity to break off the confrontation and continue the march to Sandy Hook.

To further ensure the baggage train would not fall into American hands Clinton had sent most of the supply-laden wagons on their way to the Hook early in the day, during the battle. He even appointed Hessian General Knyphausen, one of his best field commanders, to protect the convoy. The procession of wagons reached Nut Swamp, ten miles east of Freehold, while the battle raged. With a strong rear guard protecting his withdrawal, he could survive completely unscathed to concentrate all Crown forces in New York. He was successful in doing this and the city remained the headquarters of the British army for the remainder of the war. The action at Monmouth, therefore, could technically be considered a tactical British victory.

Clinton's withdrawal conflicted with the central strategy of the British expeditionary forces in America. Their plan had always been to lure Washington's Army into a decisive battle, and Monmouth provided this opportunity. Clinton must have had great reluctance about fleeing, despite his orders to deliver the Army to New York. There is evidence that he feared criticism by not making a stand; in his report to Lord George Germain, Britain's Secretary of State, he claims to have waited at Navesink for two days in hopes that the Americans would pursue him.[1] This is simply not the case.

The delay was due to difficulty loading the ships at Sandy Hook.

The Battle of Monmouth was generally considered to have ended in a draw since both sides accomplished their objectives. Washington inflicted severe casualties on the Redcoats and proved that Americans could stand against the regulars without the advantage of surprise. The British were able to protect their long column and continue to withdraw to New York with their supplies intact. But they were unable to defeat the Americans in open battle, and the Americans failed to destroy Clinton's main force. Since Washington held the field the Patriots could claim the victory, however, the question about which side was the victor still remains the subject of vigorous debate. Although it was tactically a draw, the Americans achieved a long term victory by being able to fight on equal terms with a seasoned army consisting of professional British and Hessian soldiers. This was a direct consequence of the rigorous training at Valley Forge. The exhausted British soldiers were allowed to rest for a few hours after the fighting ended.

By midnight they started marching northeast along Dutch Lane, a dusty trail that led toward Sandy Hook, fifteen miles away. The twelve-mile-long British procession had crossed the Delaware River from Philadelphia three weeks earlier to Gloucester Point, New Jersey. It then headed northeast toward its destination, New York City. This column that had trudged along the sandy roads of southern New Jersey included 11,000 Redcoat and Hessian troops with more than 1,000 Loyalist civilians and hundreds of camp followers. The baggage train had 1,500 wagons overloaded with weapons, equipment, supplies, personal baggage, and booty stolen from Patriot homes and businesses.

Sir Henry Clinton described the column in a report to Lord George Germaine: "officers coaches, draft and saddle horses in abundance; mistresses and their effects, with all the wealth and plunder from that city [Philadelphia].Under the head of baggage was comprised not only all the wheel-carriages, but also bat-horses [horses that carried officers baggage]; a train which as the country admitted of but one route for carriages, extended near twelve miles."

Also brought along were portable bakeries, laundries and blacksmith shops, large quantities of hospital supplies, boats hoisted onto wagons and collapsible bridges. All of this was followed by a vast mob of Tory refugees and camp followers. The women in the group were especially troublesome, as they frequently strayed away from the main columns to collect loot from the homes along the way. Clinton considered abandoning the civilians and jettisoning equipment but decided that it would show a strong signal of weakness to his soldiers and completely demoralize them.[2]

Later in the day, they overtook Wilhelm von Knyphausen, who had left earlier with the baggage train. During the day the enemy procession moved through the area that is today the town of Colts Neck. Hessian Captain Ewald and his Jäger brigade were in the rear guard and reported being cut off on all sides by Patriot patrols as they moved toward Middletown and the high ground to the east.[3]

Grenadier John Peebles also recorded the incident: "The line of Baggage was likewise attack'd by a small party about 10 or 12 miles from Monmouth, & had a few men kill'd & wounded. The last night's march about 14 miles NE thro' a thick wood & a sandy road almost the whole way, cross'd a creek about 5 miles from Middleton, march'd two miles further & halted till next morng. The face of the Country now changed from level to hilly." By evening the columns reached Nut Swamp, which lies beyond the present day town of Lincroft.[4] Here they encamped for the night.

Washington made the right decision by not aggressively chasing the enemy. Since he still held the field after the British retreated, he could claim a victory that would have immense propaganda value. There were other sensible reasons. Clinton's forces would soon reach the high ground at Middletown where they would have strong defensive positions. After that they would come under the protection of the guns of their fleet anchored in Sandy Hook Bay. In addition, there were many Loyalists among the population. They included the armed bands of "refugees" who could provide additional armed support. While

Clinton's army begins its march across New Jersey. (*Benson J. Lossing, 1859*)

Washington did not pursue the retreating enemy, he sent Generals Morgan and Maxwell with the New Jersey Militia units to attack the rear of the retreating enemy. This could prevent further devastation of Patriot property and encourage desertions among Hessian soldiers who had less motivation than the British regulars to continue to fight.[5]

The single lane through Monmouth County, with its surface of loose white sand, made progress difficult. The high temperature, aggravated by the heavy wool British uniforms, made life intolerable for the men. Both British and Hessian soldiers began falling out of the ranks and heading back to friends and loved ones left behind in Philadelphia.

Monmouth Courthouse to Sandy Hook-June 1778

Today, following the path of the British retreat from Monmouth Courthouse to Sandy Hook provides a fascinating trip through one of the most picturesque areas of New Jersey. The route abounds with easily identifiable reminders of the massive exodus of the British forces in 1778. In many stretches the landscape appears to be exactly as it was then.

To take the route, start out at the center of Freehold on West Main Street, a road which heads north out of town. After about a half mile, turn right onto Dutch Lane. This was the flat sandy road taken east by the British wagon train. Dutch Lane continues for about six miles east through an area once called Montrose. This is where the small party of New Jersey Militia attacked the train, as described by Peebles and Ewald. Two militia men killed in the skirmish were buried beside the road, and today a small fence encloses their graves on Dutch Lane.

The route connects with Revolutionary Road just below Vandenburg, where it falls off a few degrees to the south. Turn east onto Conover and Laird Road to the grave of Private Michael Field, located in a small roadside memorial park. Field was in the 1st Regiment, New Jersey Militia. He may have been wounded and captured in the Battle of Monmouth, and left here when the British army moved on, but whether he perished from his wounds or was slain by his captors is not known. According to local tradition, he was shot as a spy and buried at the place of his execution.[6] He died on June 29, 1778.

This is present-day Colts Neck. Originally a farming community, the area is renowned for its beauty. Its fertile fields are now covered with equestrian farms, fruit orchards, and palatial homes. The British route continues over Laird Road to Phalanx. Here the train came to a halt because the cannons and heavily loaded wagons were unable to be hauled across Swimming River. A nearby barn was pulled down and its timbers were used to construct a makeshift bridge so the train was able to continue. Swimming River is wider today after being dammed to form a reservoir. No sign of habitation is visible on either side of the river, which now forms a pristine lake. The Swimming River is upstream from the present-day town of Red Bank and is an estuary of the Navesink River.

The route continues northeast along the Lincroft-Middletown Road to Nut Swamp. The location of the British Camp there was discovered in 1992 when a deep search metal detecting team collected a number of musket balls beside the road in the Sunnyside Recreation Area. The balls appeared to be military and possibly British. The pattern and number of other artifacts collected indicated that the area was a resting place and used only for a short period, possibly overnight. It was a comfortable campsite for Knyphausen to wait for the main body of the British army to catch up with the heavily laden carriages. At that time, Nut Swamp was located in a beautiful valley with many springs and wells, but there is no evidence of any of this in what is now a residential area today.

From Nut Swamp, the army followed the course of the Poricy Brook, passed through Bamm Hollow and began their ascent to the "Heights of Middletown." On Kings Highway, the ground begins to rise towards Chapel Hill. This high ground provided the Redcoat army with a tactical advantage that could have helped them defeat pursuing Patriot forces. Colonel Peebles describes the second day of the march: "The 1st. Division march'd at day light thro' a hilly strong Country & came to Middleton about 3 miles, in the Environs of which the army Encamp'd— This little Village surrounded with hills is about two or 3 miles from Rariton Bay, and about 12 miles to the lighthouse [at Sandy Hook]-from the Hills you have a fine view of the Bay the Hook, the Fleet, Long Island, Staten Island & Amboy-In the afternoon the heavy division moved a few miles towards Neversink and about 10 o'clock at night the first Division followed, creeping & halting on a crooked road till 2 oclock of the morning. when we stop'd & took a nap which was much wanted"[7]

The column crossed over what is known today as Route 35 and followed Kings Highway East. They ascended the rise leading to Chapel Hill and then fanned out along the high ground stretching west for a mile from Chapel Hill to Garrett Hill at Middletown. This high land is about a mile away from Gravelly Point, Highlands on the Bayshore. The entire entourage of British troops, camp followers, and wagons camped in the wooded hills along the ridge on the night of June 30 and for two or three days afterwards. Sir Henry Clinton used the home of John Stillwell as his headquarters. It stood on Kings Highway at the top of Chapel Hill. Today Stillwell Road intersects

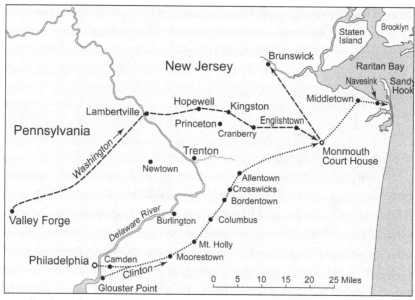

New Jersey Campaign, 1778. *(Cartography by Balefire Communications for Robert A. Mayers)*

Kings Highway, and nothing remains of the house, but its site was likely at this location.

There are a number of historic markers along King's Highway East noting that the British army camped on both sides of the road on their way to Sandy Hook after the Battle of Monmouth. This strong position along the ridge commanded a full view of Horseshoe Bay and Sandy Hook as well as the country north toward Middletown. From here British lookouts anxiously waited for the American army to appear.

Peebles describes this last camp of the army before it began crossing over to Sandy Hook on Wednesday July 1: "The army Encamp'd in a strong position, occupying the Hills from 2 to 4 miles eastward of Middleton & making a communication with the Bay in which the Fleet are lying within the Hook . . . the Enemy may be expected, who are still hovering about us, showing themselves in different places in our front & right, some popping shots, now & then. . . ."

General Cornwallis, second in command of the British forces, occupied the house of George Taylor at Garrett Hill at the other end of the ridge. No evidence of this house remains today. Other officers took over any available farmhouses nearby. Following Stillwell Road to Garrett Hill now takes you through a wooded residential area on the rear of the ridge. No evidence of the Revolutionary War era can be detected here today. Troops also occupied the area closer to the bay that now encompasses Beacon Hill Country Club and the town of Atlantic Highlands, south of Many Mind Creek. When the basement floor of an old farmhouse on Point Lookout, off of Ocean Boulevard in Atlantic Highlands, was excavated, brass buttons from a British uniform were found.[8]

Before they departed the occupiers looted anything that had any value. Household possessions and clothing were routinely taken. Teenager Jeru Patterson hid his pet colt in a nearby ravine to conceal it from the enemy troops. Surprised by the sudden approach of thousands of soldiers, he climbed a tree to camouflage himself. From this perch the boy witnessed the parade of Redcoats and watched in horror as this advancing force burned nearby homes and barns.[9]

Elizabeth Stillwell watched Cornwallis each day from her nearby home. She provided a rare eyewitness description of the famed British officer:[10] "He was a large, corpulent man, with small eyes, keen and black, he was afflicted with gout and walked very little. He sat by a table most of the time, writing and talking with his officers. In the afternoon and evening he would take his brandy freely, and by ten or eleven o'clock, a guard under each arm would assist him upstairs to bed and he would rise about ten o'clock in the morning. He was lively and talkative."

After June 30 the British army began marching from the ridge toward the bay at today's Highlands Borough. They followed King's Highway East to the village of Navesink. This tiny crossroads hamlet has changed little since that time. Where All Saints Episcopal Church now stands in Navesink, a staging area was set up where the Redcoats could prepare before moving to Bayshore for embarkation. While at the site of the church, General Clinton rode a short distance down the present Hartshorne Road to "The Portland Manor House." There he conversed with the owner, Richard Hartshorne, who was also the quartermaster of the Monmouth Militia. Clinton likely assumed he was a Loyalist.

King's Highway East becomes Monmouth Avenue and intersects with Navesink Avenue (Route 36). The British continued a few hundred yards south, then turned toward the Shrewsbury River, descending down today's Linden Avenue to Water Witch Avenue. These short streets go down a steep hill and end at Huddy Park in the Borough of Highlands. This is where Patriot Captain Joshua Huddy was hung four years later.

Advanced parties which were scouting the area ahead got a surprise. They sent word back that Sandy Hook was separated from the mainland by a narrow inlet. Captain John Montresor, Chief Engineer of the British forces, was ordered to build a pontoon bridge across the narrow channel, known locally as the "gut." The bridge was built over this waterway that had broken through the sandbar which separates the Shrewsbury River from the ocean at the southern end of Sandy Hook on its present border with Sea Bright. After the British columns reached Highlands they paused to allow the pontoon bridge to be completed. During this time some of the army was ferried over to the transport ships in Horseshoe Cove from Gravelly Point. The deep water near the shore allowed scows, barges, longboats and yawls to ferry baggage, equipment and artillery to the waiting transports.

Captain Peebles reported that the ships could be viewed by the British soldiers as they moved down the hill to the present-day Borough of Highlands. On July 5, most of the army left the heights of the Navesink and gathered on the riverbank. They followed the shore to the southeast as they made their way toward the newly-built pontoon bridge.

The last leg of the march was described by Captain Peebles: "The army march'd between 5 & 6 from yr. respective ground by different roads to the point of the Highland that joins the Hook, & there is a Gut of water across the low Sandy part next the main, a Bridge of flat boats was made for the Troops to pass some embark'd on board of flat boats & rode off to their ships but the greatest part of the army crossed at the Bridge & march'd along the Hook towards the Light House."

The entire army was able to pass over the bridge to Sandy Hook in two hours. Once on the Hook they slogged through six miles of deep sand toward the lighthouse and the safety of the fleet anchored around Horseshoe Cove. They passed through the place where toll gates now lead to beaches that swarm with thousands of sun worshipers during the summer months.

The British fleet, commanded by Sir Richard Howe, had arrived in the waters off Sandy Hook during the morning of June 29, 1778. The ships dropped anchor and prepared for the arrival of the army. The armada consisted of 11 men-of-war with up to sixty four guns, plus frigates and sloops. The warships offered a reassuring sight to the troops that evening as they descended down to the beach at Gravelly Point.

A marker on Sandy Hook near these anchorages reads, "British Embarkation-On July 5th, 1778, armies under General Sir Henry Clinton passed this point to reach British ships, at anchor off Horseshoe Cove, which evacuated them to New York. This completed their withdrawal through Middletown from Freehold after the Battle of Monmouth seven days earlier."

It took three days to move the sick and wounded, civilians, supplies, weapons, horses and wagons onto the waiting ships. The troops were the last to embark, and Peebles remarked that their process was somewhat chaotic.

While waiting their turn to board the ships the British heard the ominous sound of gunfire in the distance. What the Redcoats were listening to was the thunderous sound of the guns of the Continental Army carried eastward by the wind from New Brunswick. The Patriots were celebrating the second anniversary of the Declaration of Independence. After a generous distribution of rum, the American soldiers were parading in review in front of their Commander-in-Chief. They wore a sprig of mint in their tricorn hats as a symbol of hope. The regiments then lined up and each fired their muskets in turn, down through the ranks and back.

Peebles reported, "Saturday 4th. the weather clear'd up towards noon- all the officers horses sent off . . . great expedition this in Embarking our things so fast—hear'd a great deal of firing in the Evening Of Cannon & Small arms at a distance which we suppose is the Americans rejoicing on the anniversary of ye. Independence. The firing seems to be somewhere about Brunswick . . . orders to be ready to move at break of day."

The last of the British departed from Sandy Hook Bay by ship for New York on July 5, 1778. The fleet sailed over lower New York Bay and through the Narrows to the safety of Manhattan. When they arrived in the city, they immediately began preparing the defenses in expectation of an attack by the French fleet under Comte d'Estaing. It arrived on July 11, 1778 and anchored off Sandy Hook. The fleet arrived just a few days too late, narrowly missing a chance to trap Clinton's army at Sandy Hook and change the course of the war. New York City remained the principal base for British forces until the end of the war in 1783. The Continental Army positioned itself in New Jersey and New York on both sides of the Hudson River for the rest of the year.

New Jersey Revolutionary Campgrounds

Chapter 15

Middlebrook: The Den of the Fox (1777-1778)

I s there such a place as Middlebrook, New Jersey? You won't find it on the map. What is astonishing is that the Continental Army spent close to seven months in a place with this name during the Revolutionary War. The Middlebrook Encampment, one of the war's major winter campsites, has been overshadowed by Valley Forge and Jockey Hollow. Today, the site is in present day Bridgewater Township, just east of the junction of Routes 22 and Interstate 287.

In May 1777, and again during the winter of 1778–1779, General Washington moved the entire Continental Army, almost 10,000 soldiers, into this location in Somerset County. The presence of the American army at strategically located Middlebrook prevented the British from crossing New Jersey by land to take Philadelphia in the spring of 1777. It was where General Washington developed the strategy of restraint by not engaging in a major battle when the odds were against him. This cautious approach ultimately forced the British forces to leave the state.

A portion of this seasonal encampment, about 300 acres, has been preserved as a National Historic Site (NHS) and remains virtually unchanged since the days of the Revolutionary War. The large campground was centered northwest of Bound Brook, where Vosseler Avenue and Route 22 intersect today, and along the gap in the hills of the First Watchung Mountain, now Chimney Rock Road. Middlebrook

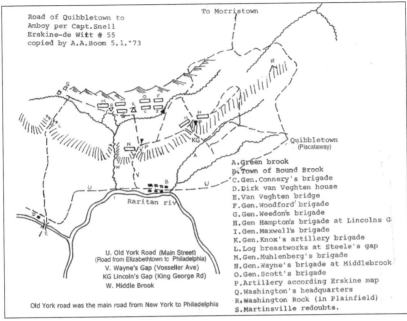

Quibbletown to Perth Amboy. A map by Captain William Scull, 11th Pennsylvania Regt. 1778. *(Courtesy of the New York Historical Society, Erskine-Dewitt Collection #55)*

was the name given to the stream that flows from the Watchung hills down through this gorge at Chimney Rock above the town of Bound Brook.[1] The army actually covered a large area in the first and second range of the Watchung Mountains from Chimney Rock Road to King George Road and up to Dock Watch Hollow Road in Warren Township. The Washington Campground Association owns twenty-five acres in the heart of this area. The garrison also encompassed the nearby colonial bridges across the Raritan River in Bound Brook. Several nearby houses in the vicinity were occupied by Washington and his generals and have been carefully restored.

Today much of this ground lies under modern Routes 22 and Interstate 287. A sign commemorating the encampment now stands in a developed area, at the corner of Chimney Rock and Gilbride Roads in Bridgewater. At present, a large portion of the remaining land has not been developed or destroyed. Much of the land used during the first spring encampment of the American Army in 1777 is owned by the Somerset County Park System. Further development of the remaining acreage is likely in the future.

The Middlebrook encampment may have been the site where the stars and stripes were first flown after the law adopting a national flag was passed by Congress on June 14, 1777. This event has been commemorated annually since 1889 at the Washington Campground on July 4 by a changing of the flag, a reading of the Declaration of Independence, and the delivery of a historical address. Also, by special order of Congress, a 13-star Flag is flown twenty-four hours a day at the Washington Campground. The first training program for army surgeons was begun in Middlebrook and the Continental Army's light-infantry corps was also formed there the under General Friedrich von Steuben. The first military training academy for artillery officers was established in present-day Pluckemin, which is located nearby.

Why Middlebrook?

The Middlebrook area was well known to General Washington; he had marched through it earlier in 1777 on his way to Morristown after the Battle of Princeton. Middlebrook had obvious logistical, topographical and geographical military advantages. The high ground made it a natural fortress that could be easily defended. In colonial days, when men and horses lugged all cannons and supplies uphill and down, its elevation made it impregnable.

The site had a 30-mile panoramic view of the no man's land that stretched over the plains of central New Jersey. Enemy troop movements could be detected from this observation post from the heights above Bound Brook, and north along the first Watchung ridge. The vista extended east and southeast to Elizabeth and the Amboys and south to New Brunswick. In that city, only eleven miles away, the British maintained a force of about 17,000 troops in 1777.

When Washington observed the aggressive activities of the British forces in central New Jersey he suspected that they were preparing to launch a campaign to control the Garden State. He would need to move swiftly to counter any assault westward. The presence of the Continental Army at Middlebrook could effectively block any overland expedition the British might attempt. If overwhelmed, the American army could survive to fight another day by hastily retreating into the safety of the hills of Morris County and the mountains of Sussex County to the west. The British master plan was to provoke the American army to move down from the high ground of the Watchung Mountains to the open plains and to engage in a decisive traditional European-style battle fought with linear tactics. Confronting a vastly superior foe would mean certain defeat for the Patriots forces, since they were less than one half the size of their opponents. The debilitated Americans had to remain intact in order to continue the war.

Middlebrook had another important asset. The population in the surrounding area was generally patriotic and receptive to providing supplies to the army. They were supported by the strong and active New Jersey Militia. The entire population of Somerset County was 10,000 residents at the time. While it could not support the entire army, the agriculturally rich countryside could contribute to ease the problems of any food scarcity. Finally, Middlebrook had plenty of trees that could be used for firewood and in the construction of huts. The area also had nearby access to a plentiful water supply.

Too Cold to Fight

In the eighteenth century, most military activity in the western world came to a standstill during the winter months. Hostilities would break off in the late fall and both sides would go into permanent winter camp for several months. A secure place was selected, cabins were built, and many officers and men would leave on furlough. Combat resumed in the spring. Although it now seems unusual that operations would be suspended for an entire season, harsher weather and energy requirements in those days made winter encampments a necessity. A season to rest, recuperate and repair equipment was essential.

Washington learned the value of this seasonal strategy early in the war when half of his fledgling army was annihilated while trying to storm the bastion of Quebec City during a raging snowstorm in December 1775. The entire Invasion of Canada proved to be a weather related disaster for the American forces, and it proved to be a lesson that they never forgot. Historians verbosely depict battles and eulogize the victories of the Continental Army, but they often miss the fact that the majority of time the soldiers were encamped.

There were a few notable exceptions to the routine hiatus taken during the winter months. Washington crossed the Delaware River on Christmas night in 1776 to surprise the Hessians at Trenton, which was followed by two more victories—one at the Second Battle of Trenton and one at Princeton. But even then, after the fighting broke off, the triumphant Patriots immediately headed to Morristown, New Jersey, where they camped until the end of May. The most notable American long-term winter encampments were at Morristown, Pompton and Middlebrook, New Jersey; New Windsor, New York; and Valley Forge, Pennsylvania. The British forces had a comfortable and festive winter in the captured rebel capital of Philadelphia in 1777-1778 and their main army spent all the other years of the war secure in New York City.

The First Middlebrook Encampment

During the winter of 1776-1777, the Continental Army made its first major winter encampment in the vicinity of Morristown. Unlike the next year at Valley Forge, the winter was remarkably mild and food supplies were adequate. In April 1777 an outpost was established at Bound Brook. This outpost garrison, adjacent to Middlebrook, was attacked by

British and Hessian forces from New Brunswick a month later. The American defenders, greatly outnumbered and outgunned, were routed, and they quickly withdrew to the high ground of Middlebrook. After this action, known as the Battle of Bound Brook, Washington moved the entire army from Morristown ten miles closer to Bound Brook. The place became known as the Middlebrook Encampment, and the American Army stayed there from May 28 and until July 2. They were now much closer to Howe's troops and could better keep an eye on them from the nearby mountains. During the entire encampment General Washington occupied a tent in the midst of this army.

During this first Middlebrook encampment the main army, consisting of the Virginia, Maryland, and Pennsylvania Brigades, accompanied by the Delaware Regiment, camped along the base of the Watchung Mountains. The Virginia troops were located at Chimney Rock, west of the gap where Middlebrook creek flows out of the mountains. The Virginian camp extended along today's Foothill Road. The Maryland Brigade was posted east of the gap, past Vossler Avenue, almost to Mountain Avenue. The Pennsylvania Brigade were posted south, at Weston, in today's Manville.[2]

While the infantry was camped along the base of the ridge, several miles northwest, at Pluckemin, the Artillery Corps was stationed in an extensive academy and barracks. The post office of the camp was on the property of what is now the Somerset Courthouse. The artificers who fabricated and repaired equipment were stationed along Old York Road in Finderne.

The Middlebrook site was described in detail by Rev. Dr. Messier, in his *History of Somerset County*. His information was extracted from the Letters from General Washington to Congress:

We may sufficiently indicate the precise place of the encampment by saying that it was on the right of the road leading through the mountain-gorge in which Chimney Rock is situated, just where it rises up from the bed of the little stream and attains the level of

Washington Valley. A strong earthwork was thrown up about a quarter of a mile to the northwest, almost in the center of the valley, as a protection to any movement approaching from Pluckamin; and the whole of the defile leading through the narrow mountain-valley was strongly guarded, while the brow overlooking the plain bristled with cannon. Just at the edge of the wood, east of Chimney Rock, huts were erected as quarters for the officers, and everything done which either safety or comfort demanded in the emergency. At Bound Brook a strong redoubt was constructed, commanding the bridge over that miry little stream, just north of the present railroad-crossing, looking to any attack to be made from the way of New Brunswick. Having taken, in this way, all possible precaution against surprise, he felt strong to abide the issue of events. The result justified his sagacity as a military tactician. . . . On the apex of the Round Top, on the left of the gorge in which Chimney Rock stands, there are yet to be seen the rude remains of a hut which Washington sometimes frequented during those anxious months of 1777.[3]

A total of 8,298 soldiers was stationed at Middlebrook during the first encampment. This included 2,660 sick or disabled men. These troops represented the entire Continental Army at that time. The presence of the American army at Middlebrook was pivotal to the outcome of the entire Revolutionary War.

In 1777, British Major General William Howe, positioned in New York City, decided that the quickest way to conclude the war would be to capture the city of Philadelphia, the new nation's capital. The easiest way to do this would be to follow a land route across New Jersey. But this plan was flawed; the Continental Army could swarm down out of the mountains from Middlebrook to take advantage of the vulnerability of his columns moving south. This threat forced the Crown forces to choose the safer but slower sea route. It resulted in a three-month delay in operations and disrupted Howe's plans to join up with General Burgoyne in northern New York. Failure to unite with Burgoyne's forces coming down from Canada resulted in the enormous British defeat at the Battle of Saratoga. This loss extended the war for five more years, until the Americans achieved victory.

After the battles of Trenton and Princeton in early January 1777, both British and Continental Army troops settled into their winter encampments, but skirmishing continued. This period, from January to March 1777, became known as the Forage War, because the British conducted raids to procure fresh provisions for themselves along with forage to feed their horses. The American forces in these actions were primarily New Jersey Militia who engaged in numerous scouting and harassing operations to attack British foraging parties of up to 2,000 men.

Howe at New Brunswick made several attempts to entice Washington to bring the Continental Army down to the open flat land of South Plainfield after American forces moved back to Middlebrook from Morristown late in the spring of 1777. Washington chose not to leave his secure position and continued to resist the temptation to engage in a campaign to liberate New Jersey.

This cautious approach earned him the name "the American Fabius." Fabius was the Roman General Quitus Fabius Maximus, who avoided decisive battles when he felt that his army was outnumbered. He achieved ultimate victory by harassing enemies in skirmishes to cause attrition, disrupt supply lines and wear down morale; he was also called "The Great Delayer" for not attacking the superior Carthaginian forces of Hannibal. Fabius is regarded as the father of guerrilla warfare. *(No.)*

Washington's cautious scheme was soon recognized and it gained respect in both America and England. Even the cantankerous John Adams began to realize the value of this tactic, writing to his wife Abigail in June 1777 that, "Our Fabius will be slow, but sure." In 1777 the London Annual Register commented, "These actions and the sudden recovery from the lowest state of weakness and distress, to become a formidable enemy in the field, raised the character of General Washington as a commander both in Europe and America and with his preceding and subsequent conduct serve to give a sanction to that appellation which is now pretty well applied to him, of the American Fabius." Washington's approach proved to be correct. By retreating and yielding he kept the beleaguered Continental Army intact at Middlebrook.

The War in Central New Jersey

By the end of June 1777, Major General William Howe, the top British commander in America, had assembled his main army in New Brunswick and its environs (today's Franklin Township and Millstone in Somerset County and part of the Raritan Valley of central New Jersey). The British had overwhelming superiority of numbers, so if Washington's Army could be lured down from the security of the Watchung Hills and into the open terrain at Millstone and South Plainfield, the Patriots could be decisively defeated. The high ground at Middlebrook, on the first Watchung Mountain, prevented a frontal assault, but feigning an overland march west toward the Delaware River might deceive the Americans.

When this failed to arouse the Americans, Howe halted his advance at Somerset Courthouse in Millstone, an eight-mile distance halfway to the American lines at Middlebrook. This British move was a defiant invitation for the Americans to come down and fight. Once again, Washington followed his Fabian strategy to avoid a major engagement and wisely remained in his secure mountain stronghold.

Howe waited one day for Washington's forces to counterattack, then decided that his strategy was futile. He withdrew all his troops back to New Brunswick and then moved them six miles northeast to ✶ Perth Amboy. The British plundered and burned Patriot homes on their march through the present-day towns of Highland Park and Edison. The New Jersey Militia and some Continental soldiers, a force of 1,200 men and two cannons, attacked the rear of the Redcoat columns as they passed through Piscataway on June 22, 1777, but failed to disrupt the British. They reached Perth Amboy the next day.

The New Jersey Militia's show of strength appeared to have

✶ THIS WAS THE "ENTICEMENT" TO DRAW WASH. OUT TO FIGHT - & PROTECT AMERICAN HOMES & PROPERTY caused Howe to give up his campaign to conquer and occupy the Garden State. On June 25, the Crown forces were observed by lookouts to be moving from Perth Amboy across the Arthur Kill to Staten Island, which was a sure sign they were abandoning New Jersey. While British sources of the time deny it, this major withdrawal appears to have been another feint to deceive the wary Americans. It was actually Howe's final attempt to coax Washington out of his mountain stronghold at Middlebrook, and this time his scheme worked.

Washington was apprehensive and hesitant about moving the army out of the mountains but yielded to criticism from his zealous officers for his lack of aggressiveness. On the day before he left the safety of Middlebrook, he wrote to Joseph Reed, his secretary and aide-de-camp, "I cannot say that the move I am about to make towards Amboy accords altogether with my opinion, not that I am under any other apprehension than that of being obliged to lose ground again, which would indeed be no small misfortune as the spirit of our troops and the county is greatly revived (and I presume) the enemy's not a little depressed, by their late retrograde emotions"

The Americans were delighted to see the withdrawal of the British. Their abandonment of central New Jersey would allow the Patriots to reoccupy the Tory-infested twenty-five-mile-square area down to Perth Amboy. Washington jubilantly observed the evacuation from his perch on the rock on the crest of the First Watchung Mountain. He became so confident that the enemy was permanently withdrawing from the state that he allowed the militiamen to disband and return home. He then intrepidly moved his American forces down to the plains at Samptown (South Plainfield) and Quibbletown (Piscataway), and fanned out his regiments in a ten-mile arc to defend New Jersey from a possible counterattack. The American lines on the plains of central New Jersey extended from Quibbletown, north to the Short Hills and Ash Swamp (now Plainfield and Scotch Plains.)

One important precaution could not be overlooked. The northern flank of the American forces needed protection. This was the critical

Short Hills-Ash Swamp area in what is today Plainfield, Scotch Plains and Edison. These hills are where the ground rises to the west of Oak Tree Road in Edison and reaches its highest point on the site of the present-day golf course of the Plainfield Country Club. The Short Hills are appropriately named since they are low and inconspicuous compared to the first ridge of the Watchung Mountains that tower above them a few miles to the west.

Washington assigned one of his most experienced combat officers to this vital mission, Brigadier General William Alexander, also known as Lord Stirling. Stirling left his post at Vermeule's farm in Plainfield on June 24 with a force of 1,798 soldiers and moved to the Short Hills-Ash Swamp area to protect the flank of the American Army. He set up his headquarters at a central location along Inman Avenue in Scotch Plains.

The British commanders were alerted by an American deserter that Washington had finally come down from the hills, so his vulnerable army was ready to challenge them on the flatlands near South Plainfield. Howe had been awaiting this opportunity. He immediately reversed course and began ferrying his British and Hessian troops back from Staten Island to begin an assault on the Continental Army. Howe planned a fast surprise onslaught using his superior numbers and artillery that would first wipe out Lord Stirling, then encircle and crush Washington's army.

Howe split his forces into two columns, one of which moved from Perth Amboy through Woodbridge while the other marched through Metuchen. The force moving through Woodbridge encountered stiff resistance from Daniel Morgan's Rifle Corps when they reached Edison. The sounds of gunfire from this skirmish cost the British the advantage of surprise. The fighting continued along Oak Tree Road, then turned west and headed up the slope of the Short Hills toward Scotch Plains. The outnumbered Patriots began to fall back to the northwest. Severe British cannon fire and the strength of the high number of swarming Redcoats forced Stirling with his retreating

Americans to lead both armies into the Ash Swamp in Scotch Plains. The Americans made a final stand there and then further withdrew toward Westfield. The British, suffering from the extreme heat of the day, broke off the fighting and continued toward Westfield. Eventually the battered Americans retreated through Scotch Plains via a gap in the Watchung Mountains at Bonnie Burn Road. From there they were able to return to the Middlebrook Encampment through Watchung and Warren, behind the protection of the first Watchung ridge.[4]

Stirling alerted the main American Army when the fighting first broke out. The alarm and his valiant stand against the entire British army at the Short Hills provided Washington with enough time for an orderly withdrawal to the more secure, high ground at Middlebrook and avoid a major battle, one that surely would have ended the War for Independence. Historians consider this battle a strategic victory for the Americans since Lord Stirling's brigades were not destroyed and the chief part of the Continental Army escaped to the security of the Middlebrook Encampment.

Later in the day, Howe arrived to assess the position of the American Army dug in at Middlebrook and decided that it was too strong to attack. Instead, he retreated north and encamped that night at Westfield. The following day the Redcoats moved to Spanktown. From there they returned to Perth Amboy, again pillaging and burning Patriot homes along the way. Finally, the Crown forces crossed back over the Arthur Kill to Staten Island, and for the first time since November 1776 no large force of British and Hessians occupied New Jersey. Two days after the British departed, Washington moved the army to an even more secure place at Pompton, sixty miles further inland. This first encampment lasted thirty-five days, from May 28 to July 2, 1777. The Continental Army did not return until November 1778, seventeen months later.

The Second Middlebrook Encampment

Washington accompanied the Continental Army north to the New York Highlands after the battle of Monmouth in June 1778. There he could guard the Hudson River from an incursion by the British army, which had moved back into New York City. As the winter approached, Washington decided to return to the Middlebrook Encampment. From this high ground, he could quickly move anywhere to protect New Jersey or become more aggressive and threaten Staten Island and New York.

On the march back to Middlebrook the Continental Army paused when a large British task force was sighted sailing up the Hudson River. This fleet had left New York with fifty-two ships and a large number of troops. The Redcoat plan was to sever the American line of march by catching the Patriots at Kings Ferry as they crossed the river to Rockland County, New York. The Americans would be caught completely helpless with their troops on one side of the river and their supplies and artillery on the other side waiting to be ferried across. Fortunately, the British were delayed and decided not to follow through with this plan, so the Americans resumed their march south to Middlebrook.

About 10,000 troops arrived at the camp by November 30, 1778. Constructing huts was the first priority, so Washington directed Rhode Island General Nathanael Greene to lay out the locations of the dwellings and to have his men collect timber, stone and other building materials.[5] Washington had standardized the hut size as 16 x 14 feet, with seven-foot walls, a peaked roof, and one fireplace and chimney. Aware of the civilian anger over billeting soldiers in their houses, the men slept in tents as they felled trees to build the huts from logs, with joints caulked with clay. Only tools, a few nails, and boards for the bunk beds were provided to the men by the army. There was no glass for windows or iron for hinges. Most components were natural materials found on the nearby wooded hillsides. The dwellings were ready for occupancy in mid-January.

The higher-ranking officers stayed in every available house in the area and were generally required to pay rent. A shortage of private homes meant that a few had to stay at some distance from the main camp. Baron von Steuben lived at the Staats House in South Bound Brook, General Henry Knox lived at the Jacobus Vanderveer House at Pluckemin, near the artillery cantonment, and Lord Stirling set up headquarters in Bridgewater at the Van Horne House on Main Street. Quartermaster General Nathanael Greene had his headquarters at the Van Veghten home near the bridge over the Raritan River south of the camp. Painstakingly restored, these homes now serve as headquarters for local historical societies.[6]

Washington set up headquarters in Somerville, five miles west of the camp on the Raritan Road. He rented the Wallace House, one of the largest homes in the area, and paid the owner $1,000 for a four-month stay. The house was owned by John Wallace, a retired Philadelphia merchant. It was built in 1776, just two years before the encampment. Aside from being spacious, the Wallace House also had the advantage of being protected behind the American lines of defense. The restored house stands today at 38 Washington Place in the town. General Washington lived in the Wallace House from December 11, 1778, until June 3, 1779, during the Second Middlebrook Encampment.

After spending only eleven days at his new headquarters, Washington left for Philadelphia to attend Congress for six weeks. When he returned in February 1779, his wife Martha accompanied him, along with servants and aides. Martha remained with him at the Wallace House for the remainder of the encampment. Washington and his staff were busy during this time hosting foreign dignitaries, preparing dinner parties, and making plans for a spring military campaign. While at the Wallace House, he and his staff planned and gathered supplies for the successful 1779 large scale campaign against the Iroquois Nations in New York State. This operation against these fierce allies of the British was launched in June and involved almost a third of the Continental Army, including the New Jersey Brigade. It was led by Generals John Sullivan and James Clinton. When the

Continental Army left Middlebrook in June 1779 it was better
equipped and trained than ever before.[7]

Life in Camp

The winter of 1778–1779 was very mild. Light snow fell in late
December and early January, but after that the temperature was
generally above freezing. Spring arrived a couple of weeks earlier than
usual. During that winter, Nathanael Greene, Quarter Master General,
managed to keep the troops reasonably well fed and clothed. There
were weeks when food was scarce, but the soldiers never starved as they
had at Valley Forge the year before, or at Morristown a year later. In the
early spring a welcome shipment of new uniforms arrived from France.

Dr. James Thatcher, a surgeon in the Continental Army, described
living accommodations at the Middlebrook Encampment during the
winter of 1779.

*February 3-Having continued to live under cover of canvas-tents
most of the winter, we have suffered extremely from exposure to
cold and storms. Our soldiers have been employed six or eight
weeks in constructing log huts, which at length are completed, and
both officers and soldiers are now under comfortable covering for
the remainder of the winter. Log houses are constructed with the
trunks of trees cut into various lengths, according to the size
intended, and are firmly connected by notches cut at their
extremities in the manner of dovetailing. The vacancies between
the logs are filled in with plastering consisting of mud and clay.
The roof is formed of similar pieces of timber, and covered with
hewn slabs. The chimney, situated at one end of the house, is made
of similar but smaller timber, and both the inner and the outer side
are covered with clay plaster, to defend the wood against the fire.
The door and windows are formed by sawing away a part of the logs*

of a proper size, and move on wooden hinges. In this manner have our soldiers, without nails, and almost without tools, except the ax and saw, provided for their officers and for themselves comfortable and convenient quarters, with little or no expense to the public. The huts are arranged in straight lines, forming a regular, uniform, compact village. The officers' huts are situated in front of the line, according to their rank, the kitchens in the rear, and the whole is similar in form to a tent encampment. The ground for a considerable distance in front of the soldiers' line of huts is cleared of wood, stumps and rubbish, and is every morning swept clean for the purpose of a parade-ground and roll-call for the respective regiments. line officers' huts are in general divided into two apartments, and are occupied by three or four officers, who compose one mess. Those for the soldiers have but one room, and contain ten or twelve men, with their cabins placed one above another against the walls, and fitted with straw, and one blanket for each man.[8]

The French ambassador visited the encampment in March and a grand review was held in his honor. During the seven months of what was became known as the Second Middlebrook Encampment, General Washington was able to mold the American Army into a disciplined fighting force of professional soldiers. This was what the army needed to match the larger, more well financed and better trained British army.

Soldiers found camp life difficult, tedious, and often boring at the large winter encampments. Life was a nonstop round of drilling, guard duty, and "fatigue work." Fatigue work included such repulsive chores as burying the remains of butchered livestock, digging latrines and making cartridges. Guard duty or "picket duty" required staying awake at night on the perimeter of the camp to watch for an enemy attack or to report suspicious activities or threats. Falling asleep on guard duty was a serious offense and was punishable by twenty lashes, or more if the enemy was near. Guard duties were assigned each day and performed in all kinds of weather.

Orderly books, the daily record of activities in camp, show that strict discipline was observed despite the primitive conditions. Parades, musters, inspections, drills and punishments were regularly held on a parade ground regardless of the weather. General Washington and members of the Continental Congress visited the inspections and camp parades, which involved the entire army.

After the Army Departed

Middlebrook saw continued use as a hospital during the following winter. After the Continental Army left Middlebrook, only one other significant event occurred in the area before the war ended. Colonel Simcoe of the Queens Rangers, a mounted dragoon troop, led a raid into the Bound Brook area on October 27, 1779. His objective was to draw out the New Jersey Militia who had remained at the encampment, and to trap them near New Brunswick with a second force. He crossed over the Van Veghten Bridge, where today's bridge on Finderne Avenue crosses over the Raritan River into Manville. Simcoe burned barges and pontoon boats left behind by the American Army, and after failing to attract militia resistance he then burned the Dutch Reformed Church and Court House at Millstone. Afterward, Simcoe became lost and was ambushed and captured when his horse was shot and fell on top of him.

The huts at Middlebrook remained abandoned and were eventually used by the local people for firewood.[9] The remains of some stone defenses can still be found on the heights of these passes where they have not been disturbed by housing developments.

A flag pole now marks the center of the Washington Campground. This 20-acre park on Middlebrook Road in Bridgewater Township, just north of Route 22, was the location of the officer's huts during the second encampment. The land was dedicated as a historic site by local citizens in 1889 and was entered in the National Register of Historic Places on July 3, 1975. The site is owned and preserved by

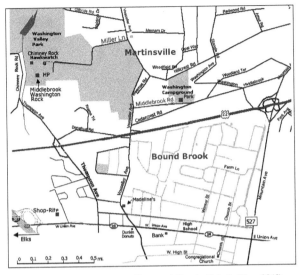

Bound Brook and Martinsville. (*Somerset County Historic Sites, 2012*)

the Washington Campground Association. Legend has it that the land was donated in the 1880s on the condition that the Declaration of Independence be read every fourth of July or the land would revert back to the heirs of the LaMonte family. A reading has been included in an Independence Day program there for the past 112 years.

The thousands of commuters who drive by these historic places in Somerset County have no idea that so many critical events of the Revolutionary War occurred there. The Middlebrook Encampment is one of the great overlooked stories of the American Revolution. Other sites related to the encampment, in Bridgewater and surrounding towns, are accessible to the public. These include Washington Rock State Park and the observation site on top of the Watchung mountain ridge in Green Brook Township. Washington Valley Park in Bridgewater is also nearby.

Chapter 16

With Knox and the Artillery at Pluckemin (1778)

General Washington forwarded a proposal to Congress on December 20, 1776, "for the establishment of Continental Artillery, magazines and laboratories." This document resulted in the authorization of General Henry Knox to prepare blueprints for the first dedicated artillery encampment and the first American military academy. Knox's plan for the artillery and officer training facility was drawn twenty-four years before the founding of the United States Military Academy at West Point. The location of the academy at Pluckemin makes this encampment unique from all others of the Revolutionary War. Pluckemin is said to have been named for a Scots village.[1] The place has been eulogized in American history, but astonishingly, its exact location has been lost to time. Perhaps this is because several bad events, including a mutiny, occurred there. Few people are acquainted with this dark side of the venerated Pluckemin, and the details are found only in regimental orderly books.

The main American army, about 8,000 soldiers, was stationed in the hills above the town of Bound Brook, about seven miles away at Middlebrook. The number of troops at Pluckemin was 675 men fit for duty in December 1778. The next spring the camp began breaking up as some regiments moved north to prepare for a new campaign, and by May 507 men remained. Their camp was nestled on the western side of the Second Watchung Mountain, about two miles southeast of the Jacobus Vanderveer House, on the road from Middlebrook to Veal

In 2012, the Friends of the Jacobus Vanderveer House unveiled "General Knox at the Pluckemin Artillery Barracks, 1779," a commissioned painting by New Jersey artist John Phillip Osborne.

Town, now Bernardsville. The Hills housing complex is located there today in this southern section of Bedminster Township, New Jersey.

The Pluckemin site had the same advantages as the main encampment at Middlebrook. It was located on a direct route to Morristown, fifteen miles away, and was at an important 18th century crossroads. The artillery would be relatively safe there from enemy attack. It was in the rear of and protected by the main army at Middlebrook. The site had natural defenses. It was elevated above the surrounding area, and behind it a mountain rose sharply. Both north and south of the camp, streams had cut deep ravines into the side of the hills and to the west and northwest was the North Branch of the Raritan River. The local roads at the time were reported to be durable enough to support gun carriages weighing up to three tons.[2] This location is now the junction of Routes 202 and 206 and Interstates 78 and 287.

An Elite Corps

The Artillery brigade commanded by Brigadier General Henry Knox functioned as an independent unit within the Continental Army. Knox set up the separate camp for his unit at Pluckemin during the winter of 1778–1779, since artillery operations and drills had little in common with the regular infantry regiments. The artillery brigade was a separate part of the Continental Army. It consisted of three battalions that were not sponsored by a specific state line and were not included in the regular army chain of command. General Knox reported directly to General Washington. Artillerymen considered themselves to be an elite corps, and they often regarded the regular infantry troops as inferiors. Needless to say, there was little fraternization between the groups.

Artillery soldiers even had a special name. An artilleryman was called a "matross." The word was derived from a German term meaning sailor, because the tasks of firing, loading, sponging and handling guns were considered to be much like a sailor's work. The skills of the matross were highly valued. Few soldiers had the expertise to compute the simple geometric calculations necessary to place a cannon ball on target. This ability was considered an art. The intricate procedure for firing and commanding a gun crew made the artillery officers essential to a successful campaign. They were often the best educated and trained leaders in the art of war, in the army. Many older, experienced men were in the artillery, perhaps because the duties were physically less demanding than those of foot soldiers.

Cannons were the kings of the battlefield and the weapons of mass destruction of the Revolutionary War. Infantry not supported by artillery was usually defeated. The artillery could often control the outcome of battles by besieging fortifications or laying down fire on a battlefield. Cannons used gunpowder to shoot a round projectile and were mounted on sturdy wooden carriages designed to support the weight of the cannon and its support structure. They were classified by the weight of the ball they fired: a 3-pounder cannon shot a three-pound ball.

Henry Knox, a young artillery officer and former Boston bookseller, gained a reputation for military brilliance early in the war. His capture of a large number of British cannons led to America's first decisive victory and caused the British army to abandon Boston on March 17, 1776. Washington had been appointed to lead the Continental Army in July 1775 and arrived in Boston less than two months after the war began. His first mission was to lay siege to the city and drive out the British forces. He was impressed by the defenses laid out by Knox, who gained most of his knowledge from reading books.

Knox proposed a plan to recover and transport the big guns that had been recently captured by the Americans at Fort Ticonderoga. His bold idea called for hauling sixty tons of cannons by ox-drawn sleds 300 miles over frozen rivers and ice-covered mountains. In one of the most awesome feats of logistics of the entire war, he was successful in getting the armament to Boston and positioning it to overlook the occupied city from Dorchester. The British were

Henry Knox. *(Charles Willson Peale, c.1784)*

stunned by the sudden appearance of these awesome weapons and soon evacuated to New York City.

The artillery brigade, with hundreds of cannons mounted on horse-drawn carts called limbers and caissons, began arriving in New Jersey in early December 1778. Of the three battalions, two were from Pennsylvania and one from Virginia. The Pennsylvanians were commanded by Colonel John Lamb and Lieutenant Colonel Ebenezer Stevens. Lieutenant Colonel Thomas Forest led the Virginia battalion. Fortunately, the complete regimental orderly books of Colonel Lamb have survived and are now part of the collection of the New York Historical Society. These records provided a detailed account of daily activities at Pluckemin, but present a less glorified version of events at the renowned cantonment than has been portrayed by historians.

The artillery, similar to the regular Continental Army, depended on the state for its financing, but other than this fiscal support they had little in common with the regular army. The cannoneers worked and drilled according to their own regulations. General Washington fostered this independence by allowing Knox to lead and administer by his own rules. It was expected that the artillery would choose their own place to set up their winter quarters miles away from the main camp at Middlebrook.

Knox ordered his men to begin building a barracks as soon as the artillery reached Pluckemin: "All carpenters, wheelwrights and joiners will join the artificers and be constantly employed with them while building the barracks."[3] The work crews were divided into groups of twelve and worked from 7:00 A.M. until 4:30 P.M.[4] As the weather grew colder, General Knox had difficulty motivating the freezing and hungry men, who were living in shabby huts, to work on building permanent shelter. The truculent gunners knew they had unique skills and resented being employed as common laborers.

Food soon became a scarce commodity in the camp, and a serious shortage of shoes exacerbated the problem. Aside from the lack of meat and bread, Knox complained that smaller food items were also missing. "Indeed, we have a scarcity of little necessaries such as sugar, chocolate, etc."[5] The desperate Knox authorized two gills of rum to be issued daily to each man as an inducement for them to work. A gill was equal to a quarter of a pint. Most of the brigade was still living in their tattered huts when a severe snowstorm the day after Christmas added to their misery.

Knox routinely insisted on cleanliness and order during the entire six-month duration of the encampment. The men complied with this directive and apparently were proud of their personal appearance. He ordered that the men "come on parade in the morning with their hats cocked, shoes blackened. Faces shaved and hair combed and tied up. The men who mount guard must be powdered." During the day the disciplined men constantly drilled and practiced their technical skills.

Construction Completed

Knox was relentless in getting the buildings completed. He punished those who shirked their duties and pleaded, "The necessity of having the barracks completed is urgent and calls for the greatest exertions"[6] Building construction was not finished until the middle of January 1779. Knox bragged to General McDougall on January 10, that his men had "got into their barracks which are comfortable and on an elegant plan"[7] Surprisingly, the artillery men had not built standard huts, but had constructed more durable larger barracks. They were spacious and built of boards, not logs, and had fireplaces and chimneys.[8]

On March 6, 1779 the *Pennsylvania Packet* described the new Artillery Camp, writing, "The huts of this corps are situated on a rising ground, at a very small distance from the road, and unfold themselves in a very pretty manner as you approach. A wide range of field pieces, Howitzers and heavy cannons make the front line of a parallelogram and the other sides composed of huts for officers and privates. This military village is superior in some respects, to most I have seen . . . although it is no more than the work of a few weeks."[9]

After the barracks were completed, a signal beacon was built on the mountain in the rear of the camp. The structure was built of logs and measured 16 square feet by 20 feet high. It was filled with brush that could be easily ignited in the event of an attack. The signal could be seen from the main camp at Middlebrook.[10] To protect the army from a surprise attack by Henry Clinton's forces out of New York, Washington ordered General Alexander, Lord Stirling, to build a series of signal beacons "on conspicuous hills and Mountains, which appear to be judicious and well disposed" on the eastern side of the Watchung Mountains. A gentleman farmer and soldier from nearby Basking Ridge, Stirling knew the local topography well. A total of twenty-three beacons was built. They stretched for over forty miles from Somerset to Bergen County. The Watchung Mountains were a natural fortress and with Lord Stirling's beacons, the hills became an impregnable line of defense. In June of 1780, two British attempts to attack Washington's encampment at Morristown failed largely because New Jersey Militia were able to mobilize quickly and move to the threatened area. The beacons proved their worth, and the British were never able to dislodge Washington or penetrate his defenses.[11]

In addition to barracks for housing the artillery soldiers, a large central building was used as the Academy. Although it functioned for only six months, Pluckemin is recognized as America's first military academy and is listed on the National Register of Historic Places. General Knox enlisted Christopher Colles, an engineer and inventor, as "preceptor" of the Academy. The establishment of the first military academy in the country focused on the training of artillery and engineering officers. Knox explained the purpose of the institute:

> *General Knox states the Academy is to be opened on Monday next when Mr. Colles the preceptor will attend every day in the week Sunday excepted for the purpose of teaching the Mathematicks & cc. . . . As the Officers of the Corps will be those means have an opportunity of acquiring a more particular and expansive knowledge of the profession and making themselves better qualified to discharge the duties of their respective stations—The General expects that they will apply themselves in good earnest to the study of this so essential & necessary Branch of Science—The duty they owe themselves——a regard for their own reputation and the just expectations of their Country: The General hopes will induce every Officer to pay the closest & most diligent attention.*[12]

Unfortunately, attendance at the lectures was reported to be very low during the entire encampment.

The Academy was the hub of Pluckemin and the encampment was built around the structure. All major activities and gatherings of all kinds were held there. The building is described in the Regimental Orderly book as follows, "The Academy was raised several feet above the other buildings and capped with a small cupola, which had a very good effect. The great room was 50 feet by 30, arched in an agreeable manner and neatly plastered within."[13] Religious services were also held at the Academy each Sunday, but few officers attended, which caused Knox to threaten them with discipline. They chose to ignore his warnings and the matter was not mentioned further.[14]

Our General-Compassionate to a Fault

General Knox had a reputation for leniency in disciplining his troops. He affectionately referred to his men as "my poor rebels." He rarely punished them for even serious offenses and when he did, he usually forgave the offenders before sentences were carried out. His compassion was taken advantage of, and his orders were routinely ignored. Knox warned soldiers multiply times ragarding minor offenses such as cutting down trees near the camp for firewood or littering the camp ground with garbage, but the habitual infractions continued. This slack approach soon caused a loss of control over the men and the authority of officers was challenged. Some of the blame for the deterioration of discipline can also be attributed to Knox's condescending policy of allowing his officers to live out of camp, so their men were without supervision.

The casual attitude toward discipline triggered a mutiny in February when most soldiers refused to work or follow orders from their sergeants and other officers. The men threatened their leaders and had to be brought under control by force. The penalty for mutiny was death. Two ringleaders were tried the next day and both were found guilty. One was sentenced to die by firing squad and the other to receive 100 lashes. As was expected, the compassionate Knox forgave both offenders a few days later, then issued a futile warning to the camp: "Mutiny is a crime of so aggravated and dangerous in nature as to place the criminal almost beyond the reach of pardon and should there be any more instances of this, the offender shall be punished with the most exemplary severity.'⁵ Discipline at Pluckemin continued to deteriorate after the uprising until the brigade left Pluckemin in June.

Liquor was regularly consumed throughout the camp despite rules forbidding its distribution. It was usually sold by suttlers (civilian merchants) outside of the camp. At Pluckemin barracks in the rear of the camp were covertly being operated as open-air bars. Spirits were available any time to soldiers who had the money to spend. Knox threatened that "this pernicious practice would not be tolerated" and ordered any liquor found in the huts and barracks to be destroyed. There is no evidence that any direct action was taken to stop this abuse.'⁶ After 8:00 P.M. taps a complete transformation took place as the formerly clean and orderly camp became a wild, undisciplined mob scene.

Gambling, mostly in the form of playing cards for money, was widespread, and cockfights were also frequently held. Knox again admonished the artillerymen and their officers with a vague threat which was never carried out. Rampant gambling continued until the encampment ended, since little was done to prevent the practice.

A Gala Affair

The social highlight of the Pluckemin Encampment took place in the spring. It was held in the Academy building and was attended by hundreds of military and civilian guests. Most senior Continental Army generals were present, as well as many prominent individuals from the state. The *New Jersey Gazette* of Trenton reported on March 3, 1779:

> *The anniversary of America's alliance with France was celebrated on the 18th ultimo at Pluckemin, at a very elegant entertainment and display of fireworks given by General Knox, and the officers of artillery. General Washington—the principal officers of the army: Mrs. Washington, Mrs. Greene—Mrs. Knox; the gentlemen and*

ladies for a large circuit around the camp, were of the company. Besides these, there was a vast concourse of spectators from every part of the Jerseies. The barracks of the artillery are at a small distance from Pluck'emin on a piece of rising ground which shews them to great advantage. The entertainment and ball were held in the academy of the Park.

About four o'clock in the afternoon the celebration of the Alliance was announced by the discharge of thirteen cannon, when the company assembled in the academy, to a very elegant dinner. The room was spacious, and the tables very prettily disposed both as to prospect and convenience–The festivity was universal, and the toasts descriptive of the happy event, which had given certainty to our liberties, empire and independence.

General Knox described the ball, writing, "We had about 70 ladies and between 300 and 400 gentlemen, we danced all night." While no guest list has ever been found the festivities likely included many of the most prominent Patriots of New Jersey.

Headquarters at the Vanderveer House

General Henry Knox used the Jacobus Vanderveer House as his headquarters from December 7, 1778 to June 3, 1779. Although the comfortable farmhouse was only a few hundred yards away from the encampment, he seemed to be oblivious to the chaos that reigned there. He was joined in the home by his wife Lucy and their two-year-old daughter. During their stay, another daughter, Julia, was born. Sadly, the child died in infancy.

The meticulously-restored Vanderveer House is the only building associated with the Pluckemin Artillery Academy that has survived. Knox continued to occupy it through the summer of 1779, when

Washington decided to move the main army north to the Morristown area. Following its occupation by the Knox family, the home underwent a series of alterations and remained in the Vanderveer family until it was purchased at auction in 1875 by Henry Ludlow. The house was subsequently owned by the Ballantine and Schley Families, who utilized the property for hunting and polo. In 1989, the neglected and decaying building and property were purchased by Bedminster Township, with the help of Green Acres funding.

This house is the only place for visitors to learn the history of the cantonment site. Built a few years before the American Revolution, it now houses a museum and is located on Route 202/206 southbound in Bedminster Township. North of the Vanderveer House stood the local Dutch Reformed Church, the heart of the little village. Although the church has been demolished, its cemetery still remains today.

In 1995 the Vanderveer house was listed on the National and New Jersey Registers of Historic Places. In 1998, the volunteer group, Friends of the Jacobus Vanderveer House, was formed to restore, develop, and operate the house as a nationally significant historic site and museum. The Friends restored the house, established historic collections there, and supported research to tell the story of General Henry Knox and the Pluckemin artillery encampment.

Pluckemin Site Rediscovered, Then Lost Again

All traces of the barracks and the academy building and other evidence of the Pluckemin encampment vanished soon after the end of the Revolutionary War. Its exact location was lost for the next 137 years. In 1916, Grant Schley, a prominent Pluckemin landowner, retained the services of Henry Schrabisch, a former New Jersey State archeologist and author. His mission was to search for the remains of the artillery park on a hillside covered with heavy foliage. The archeological work took place over eleven weeks.

Schrabisch soon discovered twenty mounds which appeared to be the remains of soldier's huts. Ashes, charcoal and rocks, discolored by fire, indicated they had fireplaces. Artifacts such as animal bones, nails and pottery were found strewn about, also suggesting the remains of the shelters. There were many ox and horse shoes in a place that appeared to have been the site of a large blacksmith shop. Schrabisch continued to excavate refuse heaps and ovens and discovered many objects that related to both the personal and military life of soldiers. He found lead shot and buttons marked with regimental numbers and the initials "U.S.A."

Schley died in 1917, and Schrabisch's work came to a halt. Schrabisch did not leave any field notes or maps but did write a series of accounts of his project which appeared in 1917 in the local *Bernardsville News*.[17] After 1917 the site was again forgotten and the clearings and excavations from the work of Schrabisch were soon covered by a forest. Only a few local residents remembered that there was a Revolutionary War site somewhere on the hill.

Artillery Camp Rediscovered

Historian Clifford Sekel first uncovered documentary references to the site in the 1960s, but he was unable to find anyone who knew exactly where it was located. After several weeks scouting the slopes of the First and Second Watchung Mountains, he finally concluded that the shells and nails he discovered on a property marked for residential development and logging were the remains of the camp.[18]

It took the persistent Sekel another ten years to raise enough interest to secure the site for his non-profit effort, the Pluckemin Archaeological Project. He then tried without success to interest other archaeologists in the site. In 1976 an engineering firm, Robert A. Brooks Associates, joined him in an attempt to obtain financing for an excavation program. Together they were able to gain the support of the property owner, the Hills Development Corporation, as well as Bedminster Township and many small local businesses, foundations, and individuals. It was a rare display of community cooperation. Sekel was joined in field work by Rutgers archaeologist John Seidel in the 1970s. They began an archaeological dig in 1979, and the project continued for the next seven years.

Sekel and Seidel were soon joined by historical geographer Bruce W. Stewart, a park historian at the Morristown National Historic Park. The team followed the 1779 drawing of the Pluckemin Cantonment by Continental Army Captain John Lillie. Lines of stone and old walls matched Lillie's image. Thousands of artifacts were recovered. Among them were a rusty bayonet and a belt buckle decorated with a cannon and thirteen-star flag, which is the earliest wartime relic that has been found that depicts the American flag. The 190,000 artifacts eventually uncovered at the site provide a rare insight into the daily lives of Revolutionary War soldiers.

The large number of artifacts unearthed during the project may be the greatest collection from a single Revolutionary War site in the country. While the archeologists worked on excavation to investigate and preserve the historic site, the developer began construction in areas where the evidence of the campsite would not be disturbed. The project continued until 1989 when it was halted due to lack of financing.

An analysis of the collection was never performed, and the objects languished in storage for the next seven years. In 2007 John L. Seidel, the director of the project in the 1980s, who trained as a historical archeologist at Washington College in Maryland, joined the Friends of the Jacobus Vanderveer House, Hunter Research (a cultural resource consulting firm), and Monmouth University to revive the project.

The group's objective was to re-examine the entire artifact collection in order to create a database and prepare publications that would serve to gain broader public recognition for the Pluckemin site. Plans were made for the Vanderveer House to become the repository for the artifact collections and records and to serve as an interpretive center for the

Pluckemin Cantonment and the Middlebrook encampment. In 2012, Dr. Seidel issued his first report on the history and archeology at the Pluckemin Continental Artillery camp. As of 2018, researchers are still cataloging the over one million artifacts that were recovered.[19]

Despite the discipline problems, what Henry Knox and his men accomplished at Pluckemin was truly impressive. Knox firmly established the necessity of organized training for officers at the nation's first military academy. His soldiers constructed barracks that were large and substantial. The archaeology of the site has enhanced the appreciation and understanding of these accomplishments and has provided an authentic account of the everyday life of officers, enlisted men, and civilian workers. Knox and his brigade departed June 3, 1779 and marched to Pompton with the Continental Army. The artillery component of the Continental Army was a key to the American victory in the War for Independence. The grounds of the artillery campsite at Pluckemin are not currently accessible to the public. There are no buildings or trails in this heavily wooded area and most of the site has been intensively developed with residential housing and surrounded by the Hills Condominium development.

Chapter 17

Forgotten Jockey Hollow
(1779-1780)

On December 7, 1779, a column of soldiers stumbled through a blinding snowstorm as they passed through Morristown, New Jersey. The village consisted of a handful of houses formed around a town green. In warmer weather cattle would graze on the green, but this was anything but warm weather. The way that led out of town was a narrow back road, slick from the rain and ice storms that had left two feet of hard-crusted snow on the ground.

After a few miles the weary soldiers trudged into a bleak, windswept 2,000-acre forest in a mountainous valley. They had reached their final destination for the year, a place known locally as Jockey Hollow. Here they would eventually suffer through more than twenty snowstorms. This was the longest and most severe winter of the Revolution and indeed the entire 18th century.

During early December, about 12,000 officers and men of the Continental Army had streamed into this camp along back roads north of New York City. Most of these men were seasoned veterans. They had fought in the Invasion of Canada in 1775 and at the battles of Long Island, White Plains, Trenton, Princeton, Saratoga and Monmouth. Some of the men had spent the winter of 1776–1777 in Morristown and were now returning. Two years earlier many had wintered at Valley Forge, Pennsylvania. At that time, the army had been smaller, and the weather less harsh. These veterans mistakenly predicted a mild winter at Jockey Hollow.

The March to Valley Forge. *(unsigned, Courtesy of Everett Historical Collection)*

The New York Brigade was returning from the 1779 Sullivan-Clinton Expedition against the Iroquois Nations. This had been a perilous six-month, 600-mile campaign deep in the rugged country of western New York State. Earlier in the year, Washington had reluctantly deployed about a third of his sorely needed troops to stop the brutal attacks and atrocities by Indians and their Loyalist allies on settlements on the frontier. During these months the Continental troops had endured hunger, frequent clashes with hostile Native Americans and exhausting forced marches over mountains and through swamps. Only about half of the soldiers who had started out in the spring were fit for duty when they arrived at Jockey Hollow. Some were killed in the fighting, while others died from illness. A few also deserted, and several men had been left behind in hospitals along the way. All of this suffering in Indian country would soon seem trivial when compared to the challenges of the upcoming winter. Orderly books of this New York Brigade, the daily record of orders and details of camp life, provide rich detail of life at Jockey Hollow during the hard winter of 1779–1780.[1]

George Washington selected this desolate Morris County location because it had obvious logistical, topographical, and geographic military advantages. It was protected on the east by three ridges of the Watchung Mountains and the impenetrable Great Swamp. Another advantage was the possibility of observing advancing troops of the main British army, stationed thirty miles away in New York City, from the first ridge of the nearby Watchung Mountains. This position also made it easy to defend the passes through the Watchungs at Westfield, Scotch Plains, Watchung and Bound Brook.

Clothing, Food and Supplies Tragically Underestimated

Jockey Hollow occupied most of the farm of Henry Wick, a prosperous farmer. Timber for the building of huts could be found in the woods surrounding his rich farmland. However, the severity of the winter and the ability to sustain the army with clothing, supplies and food were tragically underestimated. For instance, the troops needed 10,000 pounds of bread and beef every day just in order to survive.

Until log huts could be constructed, but there was no immediate shelter for the arriving men. Tents provided some protection, but the knee-deep snow had to be scraped away in order to pitch them, and both tents and blankets were in short supply. Many of the cold, hungry and barefoot men had little choice but to lie down on an armful of straw and huddle together for warmth. Most were clad only in threadbare remnants of uniforms.

The New York Brigade was assigned to the northern end of the camp, about a mile and a half north of Henry Wick's house. The site lies along the east side of Jockey Hollow Road where it intersects Grand Parade Road. This was the main road through the camp, and it led north to Morristown. The campsite is on a sloping, well-drained hillside area about one hundred yards long and three hundred yards deep. The huts stood near a footpath that led about fifty yards down the hillside to a rushing stream. The soldiers used this path hundreds of times to carry water and firewood, and to walk to the parade ground and stand sentry duty. Except for the trees and thick foliage, today this place looks exactly as it did during that winter.

A descriptive sign at the New York encampment area reads:

Brig. Gen. James Clinton with the New York brigade of the 2nd, 3rd, 4th and 5th Regiments, a total of 1,267 men, spent the winter of 1779–1780 in huts here on this hillside. They were encamped here from December 12, 1779 to May 12, 1780. The official uniform of these troops was blue, faced with buff with white buttons and linings.

John Allison was a member of the New York Brigade. By December 15 he and his comrades had begun cutting down oak, walnut and chestnut trees from the Wick land to finish and move into huts. When this supply of timber ran out, they began pulling down fences and outhouses for boards, which caused an uproar among local farmers. The few men left in most companies could be accommodated in one hut. Building huts were completed by the end of the month. These crude dwellings stretched south for a mile from the New York camp to the town of Basking Ridge.

The Arrival of the Commander-in-Chief

General George Washington arrived in Morristown on December 1, 1779, a week after the New Yorkers, and moved his staff into the Ford Mansion in Morristown. Washington was immediately confronted by a series of critical problems. Enlistments were expiring, men were beginning to desert, food supplies were not reaching camp on the impassible roads, discipline was breaking down, and officers were resigning. The Continental Army was beginning to disintegrate.

Many senior officers abandoned camp to go home to their families for several weeks. Some of them did not return until spring. The official reason offered for their absence was that they were returning to their home state to recruit replacements for their decimated units. Thus, Corporals, sergeants and lower-level officers led the army during most of the hard winter.

New York Brigade orderly books show that strict discipline was observed at Jockey Hollow despite harsh conditions. Guard duties were assigned each day, and parades, musters, inspections, drills and punishments were regularly held on the Grand Parade ground. General Washington and some members of the Continental Congress attended the camp parades. Inspections were held that involved the entire army. One day as the men stood at attention, shivering on the parade ground, General Baron von Steuben personally inspected each of the eight state brigades wintering at the camp. After reviewing the New York Regiments, the Baron reported, "The most shocking picture of misery I have ever seen, scarce a man having wherewithal to cover his nakedness in this severe season and a great number very bad with the itch."

Quartermaster General Nathanael Greene reported, "Poor fellows, they exhibit a picture truly distressing—more than half naked and two thirds starved." Washington himself criticized General James Clinton by saying that his New York troops were "in bad an order as possible." While he excused their tattered clothing, he deplored their rusty and broken muskets.[2]

A severe snowstorm hit the camp on December 28, 1779, and the weather continued to worsen into the new year. Howling winds tore apart many of the makeshift tents. Five more snowstorms hit the area in January, and their drifts reached over twelve feet high, obliterating any traces of roads in many places. Some men guarded posts in the Watchung Mountains, and others worked improving a fortification overlooking Morristown. This earthwork, started during the previous encampment in the spring of 1777, was called Fort Nonsense because it was generally believed that the project was maintained for the sole purpose of keeping the soldiers busy.

In December 1779 most of the American forces were together in one spot for the first time in six months. However, there were smaller Patriot armies in New England, New York and South Carolina. Washington ordered an immediate assessment of the state of readiness of the army. A complete muster would officially sort out those on record who had only signed up only for a three-year period. He required that "a very correct return signed by regimental commanders be made immediately to the Adjutant General of the number of non-commissioned officers and privates who were engaged for the war and whose times expired at different periods, specifying the month and year of each class."[3]

Three Years or the Duration of the War?

Many men at Jockey Hollow had now been in the service for three years, since they enlisted in early 1777. When they signed up their term of enlistment was "for three years or the duration of the war." Now that three years had passed, many soldiers assumed that their obligation was over and were expecting to leave this frozen misery. However, the Continental Congress interpreted the terms otherwise, and they expected the men to remain for the "duration of the war." This issue had never been clarified during the excitement and patriotic fervor that had overwhelmed the nation three years before.

Most men in the Continental Army that year were shocked and disappointed by the news. In February, they expected to return home with discharges in hand and soon bask in the warmth of the fireside with their families. They could easily have deserted by just disappearing into the woods and beating their way home through the bitter weather over the narrow, snow-blocked roads of the New Jersey hills. The men protested to the few officers who remained at the camp that they could prove that he had only enlisted for three years. Their pleas were ignored. Thousands were affected by these vague enlistment terms. Now, the only way to return home was to desert and risk a death penalty. Nevertheless, troops began deserting at Jockey Hollow at an alarming rate, and mutinies of entire state brigades were festering. This became a major issue for the new nation in its effort to maintain a standing army in the remaining years of the war.

Bitter Winds and Brutal Punishments

The lines of huts in the encampment offered little protection as the cruel winter raged on. Bitter winds pierced the wooden walls of the rude log cabins and froze the hands and feet of the struggling soldiers. During those weeks many regiments were reporting that only fifty men were ready for duty out of about four hundred men. Many men were unprepared to desert; they lacked warm clothing and were too far from home to survive a trip through the wilderness. Soldiers were both starving and freezing to death at the same time. Risking severe punishment, typically a hundred lashes, the suffering troops began to raid homes and steal livestock from neighboring farmers in order to stay alive.

Supply roads were all snowbound until March, and farmers refused to sell the little food that was available. Most would not accept depreciated Continental currency, which had become almost worthless. Sixty dollars in Continental script was worth only one dollar in "hard money" or Spanish milled dollars. As a result, an ordinary horse cost $20,000 in Continental currency. Joshua Guerin, a farmer whose home was only a half mile away from the cabins, demanded compensation from the army for the theft of his sheep by soldiers.

While the diaries of many officers expressed sincere sympathy for the plight of their wretched soldiers struggling to survive, punishment at Jockey Hollow was frequent and severe. Even the usually compassionate General Washington became inflexible when it came to maintaining discipline. Most offenses involved either desertion or the pilfering and plundering of livestock and other possessions from civilians. Offenders and deserters, when apprehended, were given trials by court-martial and were routinely punished by flogging, or in some cases even death. In the six months that the New York Brigade was at Morristown, the orderly books for the New York Regiments show twenty-one floggings. The reason for this appalling number is that while the army was active in campaigns, court martial trials were not held immediately, but scheduled later at permanent campsites.

Sentencing began at Jockey Hollow with the first trial on January 4, 1780. These weekly trials continued during the winter and into spring. The customary sentence meted out for such offenses was one hundred lashes. This might be the penalty for those of a seemingly minor nature, such as stealing a shirt from another soldier. At the time, however, this crime was not considered trivial, since most soldiers had only one shirt. As drummers, and sometimes fifers, laid on the lashes, they were administered to the sound of a repeated drum roll. The whip was formed of small knotted cords designed to cut through the skin with each stroke. To prolong the punishment, whippings were applied at intervals during two or three days so that the wounds would become inflamed and more painful with each application.

Executions demanded a larger audience. The punishment of death in the Continental Army was carried out by either hanging or firing squad. Being soldiers, those sentenced to this fate preferred a soldier's death—the firing squad. All the men were ordered to the parade ground to witness these tragic spectacles.

A typical record of a court-martial hearing at Jockey Hollow has these entries:

Edmond Burk. 3rd New York Regiment. Tried for attacking two officers, sentenced to be shot to death.

John McClean and William harper, 4th New York Regiment, Charged with desertion for a period over 12 months, "to receive 100, lashes on his naked back, to be inflicted at four separate times, and Harper to run the Gauntlope [gauntlet] *through the entire brigade"* [The gauntlet forced the accused to run between lines of several hundred men, all of whom ordered to lash him with switches of thin branches].

William Barrit, 3rd Pensylvania Regiment, "Deserted with his loaded musket, sentenced to death"

Joseph Waterhouse and Amous Rounds, Massachusetts Brigade, Guilt of desertion, sentenced unanimously to suffer death.

Jesse Pierce, Massachusetts Brigade, Guilty of desertion, sentenced to run the guantlope through his brigade and to be confined in a dungeon for one month on bread and water

William Straw, Massachusetts Brigade, Guilty of desertion, sentenced unanimously to suffer death.

The Commander in Chief approves each and every one of the above sentences.[4]

James Thatcher, a Continental Army surgeon who spent the winter at Jockey Hollow, observed, "However strange it may appear, a soldier will often receive the severest stripes without uttering a groan, or once shrinking from the lash even when the blood flows freely from the lacerated wounds. This must be ascribed to stubbornness or pride. They have, however, a method which mitigates the anguish in some measure: it is by putting between the teeth a leaden bullet, on which they chew while under the lash, till it is made quite flat and jagged."[5]

While the bitter cold caused much suffering, the worst problem was that the depleted Continental Army was slowly starving to death. Supply roads were snowbound until mid-March, and farmers refused to sell the little food available for depreciated currency. The entire camp often went without food for four or five days at a time. Corn used to feed horses was eagerly consumed. Pet dogs disappeared from the camp, and some men even began eating tree bark and boiling shoe leather.

In January, New Jersey officials responding to civilian complaints came to the rescue by providing a large quantity of food to the camp. This benevolent action provided a brief but welcome respite and curbed some of the plundering that was destroying the morale of local citizens. This gracious move may have saved the army from disbanding during one of its darkest hours.[6]

Colonel Lewis Dubois, commander of the 5th New York Regiment, had resigned, and General Clinton, who had departed for home in December, had not yet returned. So few New York officers remained in camp that leadership was shared with General John Stark's Regiment made up of Rhode Island, Massachusetts troops. Request for discharges because of the three-year enlistment confusion were not being answered. In desperation, common soldiers did something extraordinary—they brashly appealed directly to the Commander-in-Chief, George Washington. Incredibly, this letter has survived, and was discovered in the archives of the New York Public Library.

Camp near Morristown April 16th 1780

To His Excellancy Genl Washington Commander and Chief Of the United States of North America. The Humble Petition of John Allison Soldier in the fifth New York Regiment in the late Captain Hutchings Company Most Humbly Herewith Whereas your Excellancies Petitioner having only Inlisted for the term of three years and that time having Expired the first day of January last part and Whereas I made application to the commanding officer of the Regt for my discharge, but Could not obtain it, though I produced evidence Sworn in Writing that I was only enlisted for three years and no longer which Deposition I Inclose that your Excellancy may see the fairness and Clemency of my Inlistment——Now Please your Excellancy I implore that you would deeme justice done in this affair and your Petitioner in Duty Bound shall Pray—

N.B. As the Commanding officer of the Regt would give no attention to the produced and sworn without the evidence personally appeared-I produced them personally....[7]

There is no evidence of any replies to this, or similar pleas. After five years of combat, this was the last time that many soldiers attempted to leave the army. Most steadfastly believed that desertion was a disgrace and they continued to serve. At first, despair, disillusionment, monotony and longing for home, aggravated by the constant struggle for food, clothing, medicine, and pay, must have seemed to be more than they could bear. They became the "War Men," the label given to those who were bound to serve until the war ended. The War Men bravely accepted their fate, and willingly and loyally continued soldiering until the war concluded. During the intervening years these men became the backbone of the Continental Army. They were the corporals, sergeants and combat-hardened veterans who bonded together to form the professional army that led to the final victory at Yorktown.

At the end of the war Washington acknowledged the thousands of "War Men" who stayed on for the duration of the war, commenting, "Those gallant and persevering men who resolved to defend the right of their invaded country so long as the war should continue. For these are the men who ought to be considered as the pride and boast of the American Army."[8]

The Anger Boils Over

In May 1780 anger over enlistment terms and lack of pay for five months boiled over into a full-fledged mutiny. John Allison witnessed the suppression of a rebellion by the Connecticut Regiment. Washington, angry and deeply disturbed, fully understood the reasons for the uprising. In order to avoid large scale punishments, but still set an example, Washington ordered the execution of only one of the ringleaders. Of all the offenses committed by officers and men during the dreadful winter encampment, mutiny was feared the most. It had the potential to quickly destroy the Continental Army and the dream of independence. By spring, the entire Continental Army was reduced to fewer than 4,000 men. In June 1780, six months after arriving, the New York Brigade marched out of Jockey Hollow. They headed north on another perilous mission to the Mohawk River Valley, where Indians and loyalist raiders were devastating the settlers on the New York frontier.

Mutiny of the Pennsylvania Line Jockey Hollow.
(Edward A. Winham, 1880, Courtesy New York Public Library)

In the Shadow of Valley Forge for 150 Years

Jockey Hollow was one of those events during the war that truly tested the heart of the new nation. But for many years, it never rivaled the stories passed down about Valley Forge. New Jersey historians have always lamented that it has not been commemorated as well as it should have been. Researching original source documents and viewing both places in the context of events after the war provides some explanation as to why for many years Jockey Hollow was overlooked.

The saga of Valley Forge simply made a better story for the American public. The winter spent there, viewed by many as the low point of the war, was followed a few months later by the Battle of Monmouth. There for the first time the fledgling American Army stood up to the hardened British regulars of the best trained and equipped army in the world. This turning point in the war is popularly believed to have been achieved as a result of the training of raw soldiers by Baron von Steuben at Valley Forge. This event had great public relations value in an area only twenty miles from Philadelphia, the nation's capital for several years after the war. Valley Forge soon became a major tourist attraction. Tucked away in the back hills of New Jersey, Jockey Hollow languished for years without acclaim. It did not become a National Park until 1933.

Many disastrous things happened in Morristown, most of which were incidents which the public and the army wanted to forget in the years that followed the war. Three major mutinies by entire state brigades occurred there and in nearby Pompton. This sullied the image of quietly suffering soldiers enduring their winter encampment. The place reminded people that beleaguered troops at Jockey Hollow received meager support from civilians who often choose to sell food and supplies to the enemy rather than accept devalued Continental dollars. The avoidable breakdown of the supply chain in a bountiful country was shameful. Corporal punishment of common soldiers at the dreary camp was excessive when compared to other periods of the war. Aside from the soldiers, the local populace smarted for years over the memories of their encampments. The army brought smallpox and other diseases. They destroyed structures while searching for firewood. Finally, confusion caused by the fact that there were two major encampments at Morristown during the Revolutionary War tended to muddle their memory and commingle the history of the two events.

Valley Forge fits neatly into a single winter, and other military and political events can easily be related to that period. Jockey Hollow, purposely devoid of any large heroic monuments, is best visited in mid-winter. On a cold snowbound day, the site appears much as it did to ragged and hungry soldiers as they stood guard in the icy wind, and in fact you might sense their presence as you gaze out over the winter landscape.

Chapter 18

Pompton and the Preakness Valley: Hub of the Revolution (1780)

In June 1780, Washington led the Continental Army into an area that today encompasses Wayne Township, Pompton Plains, Totowa and Pequannock, New Jersey. It was then known as the Preakness Valley. All significant events in the state during the fight for independence radiate out from here. This place is truly the hub of the Revolutionary War at its crossroads in the Garden State. Although much has changed in this locality since that time, there is still much evidence that remains. But except for a few local residents it has been forgotten in history and its past is often unmarked and unrecorded.

Pompton, the name associated with the general area, is located at an important junction for commerce and communications. Roads intersected here that led south to Paterson, Paramus, Acquackanonk (Passaic), Newark and Morristown, New Jersey, and north to Ringwood, Suffern, Haverstraw and West Point, New York. From Pompton the American Army could quickly move twenty miles to the Hudson River if the British attempted to invade from New York City. The rich farmland of the area offered abundant sources of food and there were local iron forges for shot and cannonball.

Located on the long range of mountains that extend north across the New York state border, it is a land of fertile valleys and rolling hills with ample mineral deposits. Dutch farmers were the first European immigrants

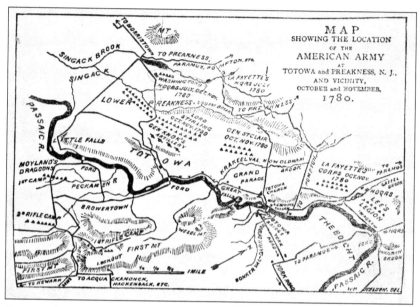

(*Charles A. Shriner in* Paterson and its Environs, *1920*)

to settle in Pompton as early as 1694, when they purchased large tracts of land from the Native Americans who were living there. Located at the meeting of the three flowing mountain streams—the Pequannock, Wanaque and the Ramapo Rivers—the area was named "Pompton," a word derived from the Lenni Lenape word meaning "Meeting Waters."[1]

General Washington experienced many problems during his stay in the area. The army was losing many men due to the expiration of enlistments and supplies were becoming more and more difficult to procure due to currency depreciation. He used the stately Dey Mansion in Wayne as his headquarters during the month of July 1780, and later returned in October through November of that year.

While in residence at the mansion, Washington received some of the best and worst news of the war. Here he learned of the momentous decision by France to join the American cause. The depressing report of the defection of Benedict Arnold also reached him there, and the tragic mutiny of the New Jersey line happened at Bloomingdale in January 1781.

The most illustrious leaders of the Revolution lived in private homes in the area during the encampments. Alexander Hamilton, the Marquis de Lafayette, and Generals Anthony Wayne, Lord Stirling and Nathanael Greene all camped here with their regiments. In 1781, the entire Continental Army and all the French forces under Rochambeau joined forces at Pompton to march south to the final critical allied victory at Yorktown. Finally, during the winter of 1781–1782 the New York Brigade, at full strength with about 2,000 men, camped nearby on the bank of the Pompton River.

Headquarters of the Patriot Army

On July 4, 1780, Washington dispersed his brigades over the valley and set up headquarters in the luxurious Georgian mansion of Colonel Theunis Dey in lower Preakness. Dey was a colonel in the Bergen County Militia, and his home would serve as the headquarters of the Continental Army from July 1 until July 29 and again from October 8 to November 27, 1780.[2]

The main body of the army was camped along what is now Totowa Road. The left wing stretched out from the Laurel Grove Cemetery to Goffle Brook Park in the town of Hawthorne. The "Artillery Park" of General Knox was located on Totowa Road at the crest of the hill that descends to the Dey Mansion. The right wing, occupied by the New Jersey Brigade, extended to Two Bridges. The Marquis de Lafayette made his headquarters in the house of Samuel Van Saun at Lower Preakness. Major General Stirling was quartered nearby at the home of George Doremus. Alarm towers were built on Federal Hill and the surrounding ridges, ready with barrels of pitch to ignite for illumination at the approach of any threat, and a cannon to sound an alert if necessary.[3]

Despite few materials and limited time, the troops tried to make themselves as comfortable as possible. Tents or huts were set on slabs of broad, flat stones and crude chimneys of stone and clay were erected on the exterior. When Totowa farmers began plowing up land at the base of the mountain in 1857 they discovered these stone floors, along with cannon balls and other artifacts from the military occupation.[4]

Food and clothing were scarce, but rum and wine taken from the British a month before at the Battle of Springfield were in abundance. All soldiers were issued a gill (four ounces) of rum each day. Officers amused themselves by giving receptions and visiting nearby Paterson Falls, which was regarded as a great natural wonder.

Glorious News and a Malicious Visitor

This first visit of the American Army to Pompton was interrupted by news of momentous events. On July 20, a dispatch rider rushed up to the Dey Mansion and to deliver this message to General Washington: "Yesterday afternoon, the long expected fleet of our illustrious ally appeared off Newport." The French Fleet had arrived in Rhode Island with 6,000 troops.

Fortunately, the Pompton location provided quick access to the French allies and was a perfect springboard for a joint attack on New York City. But this event never happened. General Rochambeau convinced Washington that trapping the British army on the Yorktown Peninsula was a more prudent strategy.

In July, General Benedict Arnold arrived in camp with a hidden agenda. This visit enabled the traitorous American officer to gather intelligence on the strength of the American forces, which he duly reported to British Commander Sir Henry Clinton in New York City. At Pompton, Arnold persuaded Washington to appoint him commander of West Point. He defected two months later and delivered the plan of the defenses of that fortress to the enemy.

Later that month the British army in New York City moved north to attack the recently arrived French army in Rhode Island. Washington promptly moved east toward Paramus and prepared to attack the upper part of New York City. This threat forced the British to abandon their plan and head south to protect the city that had served as their northern headquarters since 1776.

Washington returned to the Dey Mansion on October 8, 1780 and the troops reoccupied the encampment site of the previous summer for the next two months. In November, as the fifth winter of the war approached, the American Army marched out of the Pompton area to the Hudson Highlands.

To Yorktown and Victory

In 1781, the main forces of both the American and British armies in the north had been stalemated for two years around New York City. Washington's force was massed above New York City along the Hudson River. British troops confronted them in Manhattan. The Redcoats had held this area for six years and were well entrenched. The formidable English fleet could protect them from incursion from the sea.

The stakes for both sides at this time could not have been higher. A successful American assault against the mighty British bastion in America could win the war for the new nation. For the cautious Sir Henry Clinton, a final defeat of his northern army would end England's massive effort to control its rebellious colony. But in fact, both armies lacked the confidence and strength to face off.

The dilemma for the Americans began to lessen when a French Expeditionary Force arrived in Rhode Island a year earlier with the powerful French fleet under the command of Comte de Grasse. After conferring with Comte de Rochambeau, the Commander of the French land forces, Washington settled on a bold approach. Their combined forces would try to trap the southern British army at Yorktown, Virginia.

On August 22, 1781 the American armies began the epic march to Virginia from Haverstraw, New York. They moved south through

Paramus, Acquackanonk (Passaic) and Springfield. The French army, accompanied by the 2nd New York Regiment and Lamb's Artillery Regiment, left one day later and took a more westerly route through Pompton. General Washington rode with this column. The New York regiment guarded forty bateaux (a light, flat-bottomed river boat) pulled by oxen. They stopped for the first night at Suffern, New York.[5]

An interesting eyewitness account comes from an American who passed through the town: "In that area males are very welcome since we did not meet many of them, where one entered into a house there the first thing they did ask whether one did not want to stay with them they would hide you until the French were gone, one also encountered everywhere Hessian soldiers who had deserted."[6]

Leaving Suffern, New York the western column marched twenty miles to Pompton following present day Route 202. French officer Cromot du Bourg reported, "We went from Sufferns to Pompton, the road is superb. This is an open and well cultivated country, inhabited by Dutch people who are almost all quite rich. We arrived in good season and the camps being set and the troops arrived, I thought I could do no better than to go to Totowa to see a cataract (the Paterson falls) which is considered to be one of the most curious sights in this part of the country."[7] Baron Ludwig Von Closen, also a French officer, wrote in his diary, "The Jerseys where we are now abound in all kinds of produce. The inhabitants have kept it neat and have retained their gentle and peaceful customs, and have been very friendly towards the army. It is a land of milk and honey, with game, fish, vegetables poultry etc."[8]

American soldiers left few descriptions of the march through New Jersey. For them the terrain, towns and people were familiar since they resembled their own homes.

The columns passed through Oakland and crossed the Pompton River. They camped in Wayne Township on the Newark-Pompton Turnpike, north of the Pompton Meeting House and the Reformed Church of Pompton Plains. Washington stayed close-by that night at the Schuyler-Colfax House in Wayne. Most of these historic buildings have survived through the intervening years. The next day the French trudged twelve miles south through Pompton Plains, Lincoln Park, Montville, Lake Hiawatha and Hanover Township to Whippany. The location of their campsite in Whippany was on Whippany Road, on what was recently Lucent Technologies Park.

Rochambeau's divisions arose early the following day and tramped fifteen miles from Whippany through Morristown and Basking Ridge to Bullion's Tavern (Liberty Corner). The campsite there was just one day away from Bound Brook, where they joined the Continental Army.

From Bound Brook and Princeton, the Franco-American task force departed for Yorktown and a decisive victory. It was the last major battle for both sides on the continent of North America and is regarded as one of the most brilliant military campaigns in the history of the world.

A Comfortable Stay for the "Yorkers"

The triumphant 2nd New York Regiment returned from Yorktown to Pompton on December 11, 1781 after an exhausting 600-mile thirty-nine-day march. It began to snow when they crossed the Delaware River, and the "Yorkers" were buffeted by blizzards as they passed through Trenton, Princeton, Bound Brook and Morristown on their way to Pompton. Many of the New York soldiers were returning to a place that was familiar; they had camped there on the way to Yorktown only three months before.[9]

The snow was eight inches deep when the New York Brigade arrived on December 11, 1781. The first order of business for the weary soldiers was to build huts for the winter along a gently sloping bank of the Pompton River.

Anticipating the worst, the New York huts at Pompton were constructed more substantially than those at Jockey Hollow. Built of heavy logs with roofs of plank or timbers, each had a fireplace and housed eight men. As with previous large encampments, the incessant plundering of civilians of food and the tearing down of their fences for firewood served to diminish the image of the army at Pompton.

Unlike previous winters, the January weather turned mild, and spirits rose when a supply of new uniforms arrived at the camp, although food was still in short supply. The New York troops settled into the warm huts and began to enjoy a degree of comfort which they had not experienced in years. Orderly books show that at Pompton many available amenities enhanced the quality of life for the soldiers during that winter. Women camp followers washed clothes for two shillings and even provided their own soap. Barbers, tailors and shoemakers sold their services for modest fees.[10]

The encampment in the Preakness Valley of 2,000 of Van Cortlandt's 2nd New York Regiment in the winter of 1781–1782 has been forgotten by local historians. The details survive only in military records. Their visit is also overshadowed by the larger encampments during the previous winter.

A Visit from His Excellency and the Prussian Martinet

On March 30, 1782, George and Martha Washington arrived for a visit to Pompton from their winter quarters at Newburgh, New York, thirty miles north. They spent the weekend with the New York Regiment, and stayed in a modest local inn, known as the "Yellow Tavern," which Colonel Van Cortlandt used as his headquarters. The couple departed two days later with an armed escort and returned to Newburgh.[11] During the early spring the men of the New York Brigade were inspected by General Baron von Steuben. The formidable German martinet gave the brigade high praise for its professionalism and efficiency in parade ground maneuvers.

Muster rolls of the New York Brigade indicate that its members had served with bravery, fidelity and good conduct. Chevrons were worn on the sleeves of the men's uniforms, with one hash mark for every three years of service.

In August 1782 the New York Regiment broke camp and marched twenty-five miles to Peekskill, New York, where they joined the main army for a planned assault on New York City. This was the last military occupation of the Pompton a r e a   d u r i n g   t h e Revolutionary War.

Baron von Steuben Drilling Troops,1851 drawing by Benson J. Lossing. *(The Pictorial Field-Book of the Revolution, 1859)*

Today, the campsite where the New Yorkers bivouacked in 1781 and 1782 is an attractively landscaped commemorative park on the west side of Route 202 (Terhune Road) in Wayne, New Jersey. The road winds along the bank of the Ramapo River in an area of gracious homes in a wooded setting. This bucolic place belies its proximity to the bustling New York metropolitan area that surrounds it.

At the time of the Revolution the Ramapo River was only twenty-five yards wide. In 1836, the Ramapo River was dammed at this point to form mile-long Pompton Lake. Today, the site of the 1781–1782 encampment slopes down to this remarkably pristine body of water.

Those trying to identify this place as a Revolutionary War landmark will find it difficult. The park was the site of the home of the world-famous author, Albert Payson Terhune, who achieved fame with his many books about dogs which were written between 1900 and 1940.[12] On the ten acres his father had bought in 1860, Terhune built a large Victorian estate house. He named the home and its surrounding acreage Sunnybank. Terhune had previously discovered the grave of an American Revolutionary officer, who was buried with a British officer's sword, along with Hessian shackles and rusted cannonballs, on the property. Historian William Nelson reported that the remains of huts, together with bullets, flints, and gunlocks, had been unearthed on the wooded hillside of the estate. As with so many historic sites in New Jersey, much of the land was lost to developers in the 1960s and Terhune's home was demolished in 1969.

The War Winds Down

The location of the Preakness Valley on the southern approach to Smith's Clove, the main north-south corridor from New Jersey to West Point, ensured that it would serve as a conduit for other military events in the final months of the war. In June 1782 Pennsylvania troops mutinied over lack of pay and threatened Congress. Washington sent a detachment of 1,500 men for its protection from the New Windsor Cantonment near Newburgh, New York. This was the final movement of a large body of troops through the Pompton area.

In the summer of that year, Washington passed through on his way from New Windsor to Philadelphia to confer with Rochambeau, and after the peace treaty with Great Britain was signed in April 1783 troops released from New Windsor marched through Pompton to their homes in the southern states. George and Martha Washington again passed through Pompton on the way to Rocky Hill, New Jersey, where the fifty-one-year-old general gave his farewell address to the army.

The Valley Today

Spread over about five square miles, and encompassing several contiguous towns, many reminders of the revolutionary era events remain today throughout the Preakness Valley. Regimental campgrounds can be located on a first-rate map drawn by Washington's cartographer Robert Erskine, who was Surveyor-General in 1780. This remarkable document depicts campsites, waterways, main roads and even topography.

Physical features such as Great Notch, a gap through the hills, and Two Bridges, marking the junction of the Pompton and Ramapo

Rivers, were well known to the Continental Army. Route 202, the road used by the French columns in 1781, still follows its exact same path. Four rivers—the Passaic, Pompton, Pequannock and Ramapo—flow through the valley, and historic sites can often be located in relation to these waterways. Existing streets bear original place names; Rifle Camp Road is where 300 men under Major James Barr camped, and Cannon Ball Road passes near the Pompton forge.

The ruins of the forge at Pompton still stand above what is today the Hamburg Turnpike in Pompton Lake. Eighteenth century homes of Dutch colonists who housed Continental Army generals are now house museums which contain interesting artifacts and period furnishings. Other houses from the 18th century in the area are private residences.

The most prominent of the early homes is the Dey Mansion. This superb example of Georgian architecture was constructed between 1740 and 1750 and is considered the jewel of the historic homes in the Preakness Valley. Purchased by Passaic County from a private owner in 1934 and then restored, the brick and stone mansion is now open to the public. Seven other historic dwellings still survive in the area. (See Appendix G.)

The Pompton-Preakness Valley was the hub of continuous action during the entire duration of the Revolutionary War. Major encampments, the passage of armies and a tragic mutiny all occurred here during the eight years of the conflict.

Chapter 19

Rebellion at Federal Hill
(1781)

In January 1781 a seven-day mutiny of 200 soldiers of the New Jersey Brigade was brought to a swift and terrible end. It happened in Passaic County's borough of Bloomingdale on a rocky promontory known as Federal Hill. The leaders of the uprising were swiftly apprehended and immediately executed by their closest friends, all of whom were ordered to act as the firing squad. Every day thousands of motorists skirt along the base of this wild rock-strewn hill close to Route Interstate 287 completely unaware that one of the darkest days of the Revolutionary War occurred nearby. This tragic and forgotten incident has been referred to as the Federal Hill Rebellion or the Pompton Mutiny.

Federal Hill was lost to history and remained unknown, even to local residents, for well over a century. The hill juts upward between the west side of Route 287 and Union Avenue. Rising 560 feet above the Pequannock River to its south, it has been considered a gateway to the New Jersey Highlands. Passaic County Historians William Nelson and Charles Shriner identified it as a significant Revolutionary War site in 1920. They reported, "In a thick wood, on the bleak and desolate summit of a rocky knob of the Ramapo Mountains, overlooking the Pompton Lakes Station on the New York, Susquehanna & Western Railroad, the hearty traveler can find two rude piles of weather-beaten field-stones. These are pointed out as marking the lonely, dishonored graves of the

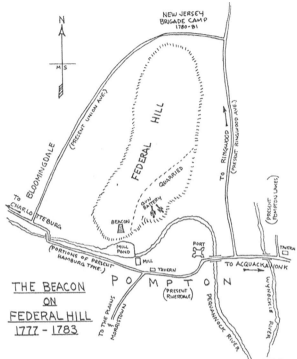

Federal Hill. *(Report by Bloomingdale Environmental Commission, 2001)*

two New Jersey mutineers."' Many people have explored the hill, but no one has ever been able to locate these graves since then.

The New Jersey Line of the Continental Army was made up of about 500 soldiers during the winter of 1780–1781. To make it easier to provide food and supplies from the local countryside, it was broken down into smaller units and stationed in different towns around Pompton (now Wayne Township). Pompton, a major Continental Army campground, served as the hub of American operations several times during the war. Units of the New Jersey Brigade were stationed at Wayne, Suffern, Chatham and at Federal Hill. The hill was about two miles away from the center of the main camp. It was a strategic place at the junctions of the Newark-Pompton Turnpike and Paterson-Hamburg Turnpike and it overlooked important routes of commerce and communication.

During the war a signal beacon was placed on Federal Hill to warn of a surprise attack by General Clinton's forces out of New York. Washington ordered a series of signal beacons to be built "on conspicuous hills and Mountains, which appear to be judicious and well disposed." Twenty-three log beacons were erected stretching for over forty miles between Somerset and Bergen Counties. They served three purposes: to call out the militia, to indicate the approach direction of the British and to direct the subsequent movements of the militia.[2]

While the winter of 1780–1781 was mild, and the soldiers were able to live in the relative comfort of sturdy log huts, the New Jersey camps were overwhelmed by many other critical problems. New Jersey had not paid its troops in over a year and they lacked warm clothing. Many men suffered from frostbite and scurvy, and the troops in the outlying base felt neglected by both their own officers and the Continental Congress. In this this fifth winter of the war, the men at Federal Hill had little to do except to dwell on their many grievances and the conditions that caused their distress.

Officers were also becoming agitated, and they petitioned the New Jersey legislature for the back pay that was owed to them. The state legislators approved their request and compensated them with all the money that remained in the New Jersey treasury. Appeasing the officers enraged enlisted men in the ranks since they received nothing. In some cases, new recruits were being paid enlistment bounties in silver as an incentive to sign up, which added to their aggression. Commissioners Reverend James Caldwell and Colonel Frederick Frelinghuysen were appointed to investigate the dissatisfaction of the soldiers, but the men at Federal Hill were not informed of this intervention.

What angered most men in the Continental Army was that they believed they had been duped by vague enlistment terms. Many had enlisted for "three years or the duration of the war" and complained that these terms implied "whichever comes first." They soon learned from Congress that they would not be going home and were compelled to continue serving "for the duration of the war." Most New Jersey soldiers had enlisted for three years in 1777 and believed that their obligations were over, but this confusion prevented them from being discharged. The congressional insistence that the men had agreed to serve for the war in effect froze the men in service. Desertion was their only way to escape, and the penalty for desertion was death.

Much of this adversity might have been contained with strong leadership. Unfortunately, Colonel Israel Shreve, the commander of the 2nd New Jersey Regiment, was not a leader who maintained discipline or inspired confidence in his men. Discontentment was especially rampant among detachments located in remote places like Federal Hill, seeing that they were located far from the main camp and the scrutiny of senior officers.

Adding to the tribulations of the New Jersey men was another revolt which had occurred only three weeks earlier and had proved to be successful in many ways. On New Year's Day 1781, a mutiny by 1,500 Pennsylvania troops occurred at Jockey Hollow, only twenty miles away from Pompton. The Pennsylvania Line mutiny gained significant concessions which emboldened the New Jersey troops and intensified their bravado. General Anthony Wayne had deployed New Jersey detachments from Pompton to help contain that revolt, but quickly learned that his men sympathized with the mutineers and were reluctant to participate.

The Pennsylvania Regiments revolted because of familiar problems: they were angry about their vague enlistment terms, they were hungry and cold, and they had not been paid. The revolt began when they killed one officer and wounded two others. The men then marched out of camp and headed to Philadelphia where they planned to appeal directly to Congress. The apprehensive Congress persuaded them to return and were granted several dispensations. While General Washington opposed any leniency, some men were awarded back pay, new uniforms and increased food rations. Of the 1,500 mutineers, 1,300 claimed that they had served over three years and were given honorable discharges. Those who swore that they had not enlisted for the duration of the war were released on their own word. The mutiny of the Pennsylvania Brigade was the largest in the history of the United States armed forces and provided a model for the New Jersey rebellion that followed.

During the first week of January 1781 a few New Jersey soldiers distributed handbills that contained threats that the men would follow the example of the Pennsylvanians. The legislature in Trenton was alerted to the possibility of a revolt and hastily tried to head off the calamity. The immediate payment of twenty dollars was authorized for each officer and five dollars for every enlisted man. Commissioners Reverend James Caldwell and Frederick Frelinghuysen visited Federal Hill and the other camps and began doling out these payments on January 15. Unfortunately, not all of the enlisted men were informed of this meager but critical stipend. Most of those who received it soon spent the cash on liquor that was being sold by camp followers and civilian vendors.[3]

Colonel Shreve was told by an informant on Saturday, January 20 that his men had decided to mutiny. Shreve quickly took the precaution of ordering the soldiers to disperse in small groups away from the center of the camp but was shocked when few men obeyed these orders. He frantically reported that many of the soldiers were "much disguised with liquor" and that he "could not prevail upon them to desist." This was the first openly mutinous act of the men at Federal Hill.[4]

Unlike the Pennsylvanians, they did not fire muskets into the air or threaten the officers. The New Jersey soldiers seized muster rolls and two cannons, and then simply walked away and headed south under the command of their sergeants and corporals. To American officers it appeared that the rebellious soldiers were on their way to Elizabethtown to join the British forces in New York City. The rebels, however, were otherwise loyal and threatened to put to death anyone who should attempt to go to the enemy lines.

Shreve then guessed that they intended to make demands on the state legislature seated at Trenton and reported this in an urgent dispatch to General Washington. The colonel and the state commissioners followed the mutineers as they moved to Chatham, New Jersey, twenty miles away. There were an additional 300 New Jersey troops stationed at Chatham and they hoped to persuade these men to join in with them.

Colonel Elias Dayton, senior officer of the New Jersey Line, commanded the camp at Chatham. He was warned that the mutineers were headed his way, so he quickly canvassed his own men to determine their loyalty. Shortly thereafter, he learned that "they had no inclination to join with the seditious part of the brigade."[5] As an added precaution Dayton sent many of his soldiers home on furlough and others to Springfield, four miles east, a place out of the path of the mutineers, while Dayton himself remained at Chatham. When mutineers marched into Chatham they were disappointed. None of the Chatham men were willing to join them in the insurrection.

Colonels Dayton and Shreve, along with Commissioners James Caldwell and Frederick Frelinghuysen, offered to meet with the rebellious troops. They began negotiating with them on January 22. A few of the more defiant men declared that unless their demands were met they would join enemy. Most, however, let it be known that they would not become traitors and would resist any attempt by local Loyalists to persuade them to change sides.

A committee of three sergeants, led by Sergeant Major George Grant, represented the soldiers. Colonel Dayton informed the sergeants that the New Jersey legislature was making an effort to work to improve their conditions but that nothing could be settled until they ended the mutiny. These terms satisfied the sergeants, but with one exception. They continued to insist on discharges for men who claimed that they had served for three years and contended that these terms had been previously granted to the Pennsylvanians. On January 23, Dayton and the commissioners refused this demand, but did offer full pardons for all the men that "immediately without hesitation shall return to their duty and conduct themselves in a soldierly manner." Dayton threatened that if the men rejected this compromise they could "expect the reward due to such obstinate villainy."[6]

The sergeants presented this offer to the men. The soldiers, now beginning to realize the severity of their actions, willingly agreed to accept the pardon. After all of them had been officially granted a general pardon, the men marched back to Pompton under the command of Colonel Shreve. To all appearances, the mutiny the New Jersey Line at Federal Hill appeared to be over, but on the way back the men began acting boisterous and renewed their threats. This time the instigators were two men—Sergeant Gilmore and Private Tuttle. Officers were threatened, and a bayonet was held to chest of a lieutenant who defended himself by knocking down his assailant. The next day the men straggling back to Federal Hill were rowdy and completely out of control. When they arrived, exhausted from their escapade and the effects of drunkenness, the soldiers slept soundly. The camp at Federal Hill was silent during the entire night.

Shreve's frantic report had reached General Washington at his headquarters fifty miles away in New Windsor, New York the previous day and he was livid. He immediately moved his headquarters to Ringwood, New Jersey, thirty miles closer to Pompton, and began assembling a force made up of men from Massachusetts, Connecticut, and New Hampshire. Their orders were to join him at Ringwood, about eight miles north of Pompton. Washington was terrified that the New Jersey mutiny, which had occurred so soon after the Pennsylvania uprising, would spread and cause the entire Continental Army to disintegrate. He wrote to Congress, "unless this dangerous spirit can be suppressed by force, there is an end to all subordination in the Army, and indeed to the Army itself."[7]

At Ringwood, Major General Robert Howe, with a reputation as a harsh leader during the suppression of the Pennsylvania mutiny, assumed command of the task force assembled to contain the Federal Hill uprising. The infuriated Washington's orders to Howe read, "You are to take the command of the detachment, which has been ordered to march from this post against the mutineers of the Jersey line. You will rendezvous with the whole of your command at Ringwood or

Pompton, as you may find best from circumstances. The object of your detachment is to compel the mutineers to unconditional submission; and I am to desire, that you will grant no terms while they are with arms in their hands in a state of resistance. The manner of executing this I leave to your discretion. If you succeed in compelling the revolted troops to a surrender, you will instantly execute a few of the most active and incendiary leaders."[8]

Howe's soldiers were slowed down by heavy snow and did not reach Ringwood until the evening of January 26.[9] From there, his 600 loyal New England troops and three cannons departed immediately for Federal Hill. As Howe's force moved south to confront the mutineers that were met by an officer of the camp who reported that the rebellion had resumed. The New Jersey soldiers continued to taunt and insult officers and to disobey orders. At Ringwood, Washington was poised to personally intercede with his Life Guard, an elite special force of 180 men. It was a difficult eight-mile march for Howe's forces on a bitterly cold night through mountainous terrain and almost impassible deep snow. They arrived at the rows of huts at Federal Hill at daybreak on January 27, 1781. Although the mutineers had returned to their huts, unrest had continued as they pressed their demand for discharging men who had reached the end of their three year enlistments. Howe, a strict disciplinarian, had no empathy for the suffering rebels and held them in complete contempt. He called their continued pleas "a tune by which I by no means am inclined to dance to." He ordered Dayton and Shreve to stop all negotiations "other than to amuse." By "amuse" Howe meant to distract the rebellious men until his entire force would arrive at Federal Hill.[10]

Dr. James Thatcher, a surgeon in Howe's force with the 9th Massachusetts Regiment, left a detailed eyewitness account of the suppression of the uprising. Thatcher reported how Howe addressed his men as they approached Federal Hill. "Being paraded in a line, General Howe harangued them, representing the heinousness of the crime of mutiny, and the absolute necessity of military subordination; adding that the mutineers must be brought to an unconditional submission: no temporizing, no listening to terms of compromise, while in a state of resistance." Howe suspected that his men might refuse to discipline their fellow soldiers. Dr. Thatcher recalled that, "some of our officers suffered much anxiety, lest the soldiers would not prove faithful on this trying occasion," but the men dutifully loaded their weapons.[11]

General Howe was briefed by Colonel Shreve concerning the layout of the camp. Howe then deployed his forces around the huts and ordered his field cannons to be trained on the insurgents. He also stationed soldiers on the road to Charlottesburgh to cut off any escape into the northern wilderness. The nearest town to Pompton was Charlottesburgh, a few miles west along the Pequanock River, but the town has since disappeared from present day maps because it is now under a reservoir.

At dawn the shocked mutineers awoke to find themselves surrounded by Howe's menacing assault force and staring into hundreds of musket barrels and the bores of the cannons. Some of the men attempted to escape but were unable to pass through the guards who were blocking the roads north. Officers then approached the huts and ordered the insurgents to come outside unarmed, form into ranks, and march to the parade field. The mutineers hesitated when they saw the cannons prepared to pour fire into the camp. Some men, recognizing their situation was helpless, followed the order but others remained defiant. The mutineers were then given five minutes to comply. Thatcher observed, "This had its effect, and they, to a man, marched without arms to the ground appointed for them."

Surgeon Thatcher, watched as the starving, barefoot New Jersey soldiers were paraded through the snow to be sentenced, wrote,

General Howe ordered that three of the ringleaders should be selected for punishment. These unfortunate culprits were briefly tried on the spot, Colonel Sprout being president of the court-martial, standing on the snow, and they were sentenced to be immediately shot. Twelve of the most guilty mutineers were next selected to be their executioners. This was a most painful task; being themselves guilty, they were greatly distressed with the duty imposed on them, and when ordered to load, some of them shed tears. The wretched victims, overwhelmed by the terrors of death, had neither time nor power to implore the mercy and forgiveness of their God, and such was their agonizing condition, that no heart could refrain from emotions of sympathy and compassion.

The first that suffered was a sergeant, [David Gilmore] and an old offender; he was led a few yards' distance, and placed on his knees; six of the executioners, at the signal given by an officer, fired, three aiming at the head and three at the breast, the other six reserving their fire in order to dispatch the victim, should the first fire fail; it so happened in this instance; the remaining six then fired, and life was instantly extinguished. The second criminal [John Tuttle] was, by the first fire, sent into eternity in an instant. The third being less criminal, by the recommendation of his officers, to his unspeakable joy, received a pardon.

This third man was Sergeant Major Grant, the apparent leader of the revolt. Grant was well respected by his regimental officers and was a dedicated, long service soldier. Several soldiers testified that he had tried to stop the mutiny once it began and had been reluctant to become a leader.

Thatcher concluded his narrative by expressing compassion for the offenders:

This tragical scene produced a dreadful shock, and a salutary effect on the minds of the guilty soldiers. Never were men more completely humbled and penitent; tears of sorrow and of joy rushed from their eyes, and each one appeared to congratulate himself that his forfeited life had been spared.[12]

The executions being finished, General Howe ordered the former officers to resume their respective commands; he then, in a very pathetic and affecting manner, addressed the whole line by platoons, endeavoring to impress their minds with a sense of the enormity of their crime, and the dreadful consequences that might have resulted. He then commanded them to ask pardon of their officers, and promise to devote themselves to the faithful discharge of their duty as soldiers in the future. It is most painful to reflect, that circumstances should imperiously demand the infliction of capital punishment on soldiers who have more than a shadow of a plea to extenuate their crime. These unfortunate men have long suffered many serious grievances, which they have sustained with commendable patience; but have at length lost their confidence in public justice.

General Howe remained apprehensive. The British had learned of the uprising from Loyalist spies and knew that the Patriot army was debilitated by these internal problems. As a result, they prepared to strike by moving 2,000 to 3,000 men from New York to Staten Island, and ordered their spies to offer bribes to any American soldier willing to defect. Uzal Woodruff, a merchant from Elizabethtown, even turned one of these offers over to Continental officers, but there is no evidence that the operatives ever approached New Jersey men directly. Eventually Woodruff became a double agent for the Americans.[13] On January 29 Howe told Washington that he had learned from encouraging intelligence that the threat of a British invasion was unlikely, so he intended to return with his soldiers to New York.[14] Washington, assured that the crisis was finally over, also returned to his headquarters at New Windsor.

In his General Orders on January 30 Washington praised Howe and his men for their efforts in quelling the mutiny. He admitted that he sympathized with the sufferings of the mutineers, but he also admonished them by stating that other armies had endured worse privations, but their nations had still been able to rely on them to serve faithfully. He added, "The General is happy in the lenity shown in the execution of only two of the most guilty," but he could no longer entertain the clemency that had been shown to the other mutineers.[15]

By crushing the New Jersey mutiny at Federal Hill with brutal force and executing the ringleaders, Washington forewarned soldiers that the Continental Army would maintain discipline under any circumstances. They understood his point. The New Jersey mutiny was the last major revolt by enlisted soldiers for the rest of the war. The next time the Continental Army faced a significant rebellion would be in New Windsor, New York in 1783, but that time the offenders were Washington's own officers.

The fact that mutinies did not spread was a sign to the nation and to the world that the Continental Army continued to be a dedicated and disciplined force capable of defeating a superior British army. The hard core of American combat soldiers that could be relied upon was the long service troops, known as the "War Men." These men had enlisted for the duration of the war and had assumed leadership as sergeants and corporals. Over time their expertise and proficiency increased as they developed self-confidence and a stanch esprit de corps. They were proud of their skills as marksmen and in their effective use of artillery. They mastered the fine points of executing linear maneuvers on the battlefield and learned to trust and depend on one another. Comradeship, enthusiasm, devotion attributed to training, and unit pride were the attributes of these successful fighting men. We see this same spirit today in many units of the armed forces special forces.

Washington ordered the chastised New Jersey regiments to Morristown a week after the executions. They remained there until July 8, 1781 and then marched to Kingsbridge, New York, now the Bronx, to join the main army. They left for the Battle of Yorktown the next month under the command of the Marquis de Lafayette. On the route south to Virginia the New Jersey men marched past Federal Hill. It was a grim reminder of their suffering and transgressions earlier in the year. The Jersey boys arrived at Yorktown after an exhausting 500-mile journey, where they completely redeemed themselves by manning the siege lines under intense bombardment and taking part in the assault and capture of Redoubt Number 10. The fall of this strong point in the British lines resulted in victory in the final critical battle of the war.

Today, Federal Hill rises conspicuously above the Pompton Valley. A marker on Union Avenue in Bloomingdale reads along its base:

Federal Hill Historic Site

The site of the Revolutionary war era Pompton Mutiny, which occurred in the cold harsh winter of 1781. It was in the eastern valley overlooking Bloomingdale that an encampment of weary troops mutinied, consequently their two ringleaders were arrested, tried, and executed in the vicinity of what is now known as Union Avenue.

The campsite on the hill disappeared from the history books of the Garden State after the War for Independence. During the 1800s a 15-foot-deep cave located on the hill was used to store blasting caps and explosives used in quarrying local stone. Nothing noteworthy happened on the desolate hill until World War I, when an ammunition storage bunker was built into the cave. The foundation of the vault and an iron door leading to it can still be seen today near the crest of Federal Hill, on the eastern side, within sight of Interstate 287. After Nelson and Shriner reported the mutineers' graves in 1920, others have explored the forsaken Federal Hill through the years, but since that time nobody has reported seeing the two stone piles marking the traitor's graves.

Camp Bergwald, a German-American Bund camp, operated on Federal Hill from the 1930s until 1941. The Bund was an American Nazi organization established in the 1930s to promote a positive view of Nazi Germany in the United States. When Hitler gained power, the Ku Klux Klan burned a cross at the camp entrance and ordered the swastika-wearing Germans to leave. They defiantly stayed on until the attack on Pearl Harbor in 1941, at which time Federal Bureau of Investigation agents evicted them. Although the former occupants left hand guns on the hill, no ammunition was discovered

Remains of bunker on Federal Hill. *(Courtesy of lostinjersey Blog)*

in the vicinity. During a brush fire on the hill in 1950 three explosions took place, all of which were likely caused by hidden gunpowder.

In 1983, two Bloomingdale boys accidently discovered documents listing a complete membership roster of Camp Bergwald. The boys found the documents inside a metal box buried beneath a rock.[16] The records gave the names, addresses, dates of birth and the members' dates of enrollment in the Deutsch Amerikanische Berufsgemeinschaft (DAB). A ledger associated with the roster recorded the hours each member had served on duty at the camp.

A great deal evidence about the Bund Camp can still be seen on the hill today: structures, cabin foundations, a concrete cistern, remnants of a swimming pool, and a dam that once formed a small lake, and many trails. Artifacts such as dishware and rusting iron bed frames have remained strewn around the camp area since World War II.

The only link to the Revolutionary War is a legend. A member of a surveying party is reported in recent years to have discovered a solid brass cannon on the hill. He hid it under some stones, but when he returned to retrieve the cannon a few days later, it was gone. Many people have searched for this treasured relic, but it has never been found.

Today, Federal Hill is privately held and has never received designation as a state or federal historic site. This historically significant

500-acre wooded tract has been under constant threat of development. In recent decades, it has become a battleground between developers who want to capitalize on its prime location, and environmentalists, historians and borough officials who want to preserve it.

The Borough of Bloomingdale and Passaic County were able to acquire 104 acres of this environmentally fragile land a decade ago by using an open space grant. A 2008 Superior Court decision forced the borough to allow for affordable housing on the tract. Despite local opposition, it was ruled that a townhouse complex must be built in order for Bloomingdale to conform with its affordable housing obligations. Recently there has been an effort to rezone much of the hill for the enlargement of an existing stone quarry. The Bloomingdale Environmental Commission has opposed all of these threats of encroachment. The tragic mutiny that occurred there has been forgotten, so if the Federal Hill site is preserved, it will not be because of its turbulent Revolutionary War history, but rather because it is environmentally sensitive.

Appendix A

Historic Houses in the Bound Brook Area

Five houses in the area occupied by senior officers during the encampments in Bound Brook have been restored and are open to the public. All can be reached by following the same roads that existed at the time of the Revolution.

The Abraham Staats House, occupied by Baron von Steuben, is located in South Bound Brook off Main Street. From Bound Brook cross the Queen's Bridge to South Bound Brook and bear left on Main Street one half mile. Turn left onto Von Steuben Lane and follow it to the end.

The Van Horne House, occupied by General Benjamin Lincoln and later by General William Alexander (Lord Stirling). From the Abraham Staats house proceed north to the Queen's Bridge over the Raritan River. At the traffic circle, proceed west on Main Street to the Van Horne House. It is located on the right just after passing Route 287 and is across from the Commerce Bank Ball Park.

The Van Veghten House, occupied by General Nathanael Greene. From the Van Horne House continue driving west on Main Street to Finderne Avenue. Turn right onto Finderne. Turn right onto Van Veghten Drive at the first stop light. The house is located at the end of the road.

The Wallace House was occupied as the headquarters of General George Washington. From the Van Veghten House return to Finderne Avenue and turn left. At the next light, turn left onto Main Street. Proceed through Somerville to the "Y" at Borough Hall. Bear left onto Somerset Street. Just after passing under the railroad underpass, look for the Wallace House on the left.

The Vanderveer House occupied by General Henry Knox at the Pluckemin Cantonment. From the Wallace House continue west on Somerset Street to Route 206. Take Route 206 north to Lamington Road. Make a U-turn and drive south on Route 206. Bear right to River Road and look for a cemetery on the right. The house is just beyond the cemetery.

Appendix B

Strength of the Continental Army in New Jersey, May 20, 1777

Major Generals	Brigadiers	Regt No.	Colonels	State	Strength	Total
Greene	Muhlenberg	1.	Reed	Virg.	120	
		5.	——	Do.	127	
		9.	Matthews	Do.	391	
		13.	Russell	Do.	——	
			Hazen	United	393	1032
	Weedon	2.	Spotswood	Do.	182	
		6.	——	Do.	223	
		10.	Stephens	Do..	295	
		14.	Lewis	Do.	——	700
Woodford	Stephen	3.	Marshall	Do..	150	
		7.	Mc Clanahan	Do..	472	
		11.	Morgan	Do.	377	
		15.	Mason	Do.	——	999
	Scott	4.	Elliot	Do.	314	
		8.	Beauman	Do.	157	
		12.	Wood	Do.	117	
		16.	Grayson	Do.	——	
		——	Patton	United	124	712
Sullivan	Smallwood	1.	Stone	Mary'd	199	
		3.	Gist	Do.	114	
		6.	Williams	Do.	118	
		——	Hall	Delaw.	79	510
	D'Borre	2.	Price	Mary'd	118	
		4.	Hall	Do.	220	

Major Generals	Brigadiers	Regt No.	Colonels	State	Strength	Total
		7.	Richardson	Do.	95	
		—	B. Arandt	Germ'n	365	798
Lincoln	Wayne	1.	Chambers	Penns'a	335	
		7.	Ja's Irvine	Do.	21	
		7.	Irwin	Do.	—	
		10.	—	Do.	231	
		—	Heartly	United	155	742
	D' Haas	4.	Cadwalader	Penns'a	150	
		5.	Johnson	Do.	241	
		8.	Broadhead	Do.	369	
		11.	Humpton	Do.	138	898
Lord Stirling	Conway	3.	Wood	Do.	150	
		6.	Magaw	Do.	—	
		9.	Morris	Do.	193	
		12.	Cooke	Do.	231	
		—	Spencer	United	186	760
	Maxwell	1.	Ogdon	Jersey	184	
		2.	Shrieve	Do.	247	
		3.	Dayton	Do.	300	
		4.	Martin	Do.	307	1038

Total Continental Army in New Jersey 7428
Total Continental Army (including regiments at Morristown and in other states) 8188

*"Arrangement and Present Strength of the Army in Jersey May 20, 1777." The original can be found in the Sparks Manuscripts, Houghton Library, Harvard University, and were reproduced in Detwiller, Frederic C. *War in the Countryside, The Battle and Plunder of the Short Hills, New Jersey, June 1777.*

Appendix C

American Forces in Battle of the Short Hills, June 26, 1777

Lord Stirling's Infantry Division

Conway's Brigade Brigadier Thomas Conway
3rd Pennsylania Regiment, Colonel Wood 150
6th Pennsylvania Regiment Colonel Magaw—
9th Pennsylvania Regiment Colonel Morris 193
12th Pennsylvania Regiment Colonel William Cooke 231
Spencer's Additional Regt. Colonel Oliver Spencer 186 (New Jersey)

Brigade Total 760+

Maxwell's Brigade Brigadier William Maxwell
1st New Jersey Regiment Colonel Mathias Ogden 184
2nd New Jersey Regiment Colonel Israel Shreve 247
3rd New Jersey Regiment Colonel Elias Dayton 300
4th New Jersey Regiment Colonel Ephraim Martin 307

Brigade Total 1098

Independent Corps Colonel Charles Armand (formerly Major Ottendorf)

Morgan's Independent Rifle Corps Colonel Daniel Morgan
11th Virginia Regiment (elements) Col. Daniel Morgan 377 (regiment)
8th Virginia Regiment (company) Capt. William Darke—
12th Virginia Regiment (elements)——

Artillery
Company of Lamb's 2nd Continental Captain Edward Archibald
    Huggs Company of Lamb's 2nd Continental Lieutenant Eli
    Elmer (West Jersey Artillery Co.)
Company of Crane's 3rd Continental Captain Benjamin Eustis
Pennsylvania Independent Company Captain Gibbs Jones
Clark's Artillery Company Captain Thomas Clark (East Jersey
    Artillery Co.)

Cavalry
2nd Continental Light Dragoons Colonel Sheldon
Elements of DeBorre's Brigade (General Prudhomme DeBorre) of
    Sullivan's Division present

*Arrangement and Present Strength of the Army in Jersey May 20,
1777. The original can be found in the Sparks Manuscripts, Houghton
Library, Harvard University, and were reproduced in Frederic C.
Detwiller's *War in the Countryside, The Battle and Plunder of the
Short Hills, New Jersey, June 1777.*

Appendix D

Strength of American and French Forces

*moving through New Jersey enroute to Yorktown August 1781
(excludes men detached and in hospitals)**

American Column	Commanding Officer	Strength**
Commander-in-Chief's Guard	Captain Caleb Gibbs	70
Rhode Island Regiment	Lt.-Col. Jeremiah Olney	360
First New York Regiment	Col. Goose Van Schaick	390
Second New York Regiment	Col. Philip Van Cortlandt	420
Combined New Jersey Regiment	Colonel Mathias Ogden	400
Canadian Regiment	Brigadier Moses Hazen	270
Light Infantry Regiment	Lt.-Col. Alexander Scammel	380
Second Continental Artillery	Colonel John Lamb	200
Corps of Sappers and Miners	Captain James Gilliland	50
Artificer Regiment	Lt.-Col. Ebenezer Stevens	150

Total: 2,720 officers and men

French Column	
Bourbonnais	811
Soissonnais	901
Saintonge	853
Lauzun's Legion	581
Artillerie	381
Royal Deux-Ponts	831
Workers (ouvriers)	33
Mineurs	23

Total: 4,414 officers and men

*The Washington-Rochambeau Revolutionary Route in the State of New Jersey, 1781–1783. An Historical and Architectural Survey. (Trenton: New Jersey Historic Trust, Department of Community Affairs, 2006). **Officers and men

Appendix E

Historic Markers Along Route of Allied Forces through New Jersey to Yorktown, 1781

(Additional details can be found at the website for the Historic Marker Database https://www.hmdb.org/)

Princeton—The Washington-Rochambeau Historic Route
Inscription: On this site, the allied American and French troops of Generals Washington and Le Comte de Rochambeau encamped August 29 to September 1, 1781 enroute to their Victory at Yorktown. American independence was assured there in Virginia by the defeat and surrender of Lord Cornwallis' British forces on October 19, 1781. Princeton Chapter Daughters of the American Revolution October 19, 1981
Location: 40° 20.83' N, 74° 39.948' W. Marker is in Princeton, New Jersey, in Mercer County. Marker is on Stockton Street, on the left when traveling south. Marker is located in front of Trinity Church. Marker is in this post office area: Princeton NJ 08540, United States of America.

Princeton- Campsite of the The Army of Louis XVI, King of France
Inscription: Commanded by General de Rochambeau during their

march to victory at Yorktown August 31, 1781
Location: 40° 20.867' N, 74° 39.95' W. Marker is in Princeton, New Jersey, in Mercer County. Marker is at the intersection of Stockton Street and Bayard Street on Stockton Street. Marker is in this post office area: Princeton NJ 08540, United States of America.

Princeton: W 3 R
Inscription: Washington—Rochambeau Revolutionary Route National Historic Trail www.w3r-us.org
Location: 40° 20.822' N, 74° 39.985' W. Marker is in Princeton, New Jersey, in Mercer County. Marker is on Stockton Street (U.S. 206), on the left when traveling north. Marker is at or near this postal address: 55 Stockton Street, Princeton NJ 08540, United States of America.

" . . . a Town laid out called Lamberton . . ." [1773]
Inscription: Historically, Lamberton was the loose-knit fishing village and port that extended along the left bank of the Delaware River from Ferry Street to Riverview Cemetery. The heart of the community lay between Landing and Lalor Streets, exactly where the park atop the tunnel is located today. . . .
Location: 40° 11.95' N, 74° 45.523' W. Marker is in Trenton, New Jersey, in Mercer County. Marker can be reached from U.S. 29. This marker is in South River Walk park which is built over top of Route 29. Marker is in this post office area: Trenton NJ 08611, United States of America.

Trenton—Ferries Across the Delaware
Inscription: Two ferries across the Delaware River in the Trenton area date from the late 17th century—the Yardley Ferry and the Trenton or Middle Ferry. Two more—the Upper and Lower Ferries—were added later in the 18th century. The Yardley Ferry, four miles above the falls, was established in 1683 and formalized through an act of the Pennsylvania Assembly in 1722. It operated into the mid-1830s. . . .

Location: 40° 11.818′ N, 74° 45.479′ W. Marker is in Trenton, New Jersey, in Mercer County. Marker can be reached from U.S. 29. This marker is in South River Walk park which is built over top of Route 29. Marker is in this post office area: Trenton NJ 08611, United States of America.

Chatham—Chatham Historic District
Inscription: Scene of Washington's Headquarters and massing of Continental troops prior to march on Yorktown August 27 - 29, 1781. Morris County Heritage Commission New Jersey Register of Historic Sites
Location: 40° 44.36′ N, 74° 22.561′ W. Marker is in Chatham, New Jersey, in Morris County. Marker is on Main Street (County Route 124), on the left when traveling east. Marker is at or near this postal address: 100 Main Street, Chatham NJ 07928, United States of America.

Hanover—A Good Place for a Halt
Inscription: " . . . *Whippany will be a good place for a halt* . . ." -Washington to Rochambeau
On August 27 and 28, 1781, a 5,000-man French Army under General Count Rochambeau encamped on grounds extending northeast from here toward the Whippany River. After resting, they marched rapidly southward, in parallel with American troops led by General George Washington, to Yorktown, Virginia. There, on October 19, 1781, the combined armies forced surrender of British General Lord Cornwallis in the final major battle of the American Revolution.
Location: 40° 48.988′ N, 74° 25.417′ W. Marker is in Hanover, New Jersey, in Morris County. Marker is on Whippany Road, on the right when traveling north. Marker is located on Whippany Road, between Vincent Terrace and Eden Lane. Marker is in this post office area: Whippany NJ 07981, United States of America.

<u>Griggstown</u>—Historic River Road and River Crossing
<u>Inscription</u>: Route of Continental Army of Morristown after Battle of Princeton, Jan. 3, 1777. Route also of armies marching from New York to Yorktown, VA. Aug. 30–31, 1781.
<u>Location</u>: 40° 26.348′ N, 74° 37.071′ W. Marker is near Griggstown, New Jersey, in Somerset County. Marker is on Griggstown Causeway just east of Millstone River Road, on the left when traveling west. Marker is in this post office area: Belle Mead NJ 08502

<u>Liberty Corner</u>—French Army Encampment
<u>Inscription</u>: General Rochambeau's troops camped here in August 1781 en route to the Battle of Yorktown.
<u>Location</u>: 40° 39.739′ N, 74° 34.684′ W. Marker is in Liberty Corner, New Jersey, in Somerset County. Marker is on Valley Road, on the right when traveling south. Marker is in this post office area: Liberty Corner NJ 07938, United States of America.

<u>Liberty Corner</u>—The Washington—Rochambeau Revolutionary Route
<u>Inscription</u>: On this site French Troops under Le Comte De Rochambeau encamped August 29, 1781 en route to meeting Gen. George Washington and achieving their victory at Yorktown, American independence was assured there in Virginia by the defeat and surrender of Lord Cornwallis' British forces on October 19. 1781. The return encampment was September 9, 1782.
<u>Location</u>: 40° 39.611′ N, 74° 34.704′ W. Marker is near Liberty Corner, New Jersey, in Somerset County. Marker is on Valley Road just south of Church Street, on the right when traveling south. Marker is at or near this postal address: 3625 Valley Rd, Basking Ridge NJ 07920, United States of America.

Appendix F

ARTICLES OF AGREEMENT,

MADE AND AGREED UPON BETWEEN CAP-
TAIN   COMMANDER OF THE
PRIVATEER   MOUNTING
CARRIAGE GUNS AND COMPANY.
(A SUMMARY OF ARTICLES TO BE SIGNED
BY SHIP'S OFFICERS, AND CREW)

ARTICLE I
THE SHIP'S OWNERS SHALL PROVIDE SUFFI-
CIENT ARMS, AMMUNITION AND PROVISIONS
FOR A CRUISE EXTENDING NOT MORE
THAN   MONTHS. IN RETURN, THEY SHALL
RECEIVE HALF OF ALL PRIZES TAKEN.

ARTICLE II
THE CAPTAIN MUST, TO THE BEST OF HIS
ABILITY, CARRY OUT THE "INSTRUCTIONS".

ARTICLE III
THE OFFICERS AND CREW MUST REPORT
FOR DUTY WHEN SO ORDERED BY THE CAP-
TAIN, THEY MUST PERFORM THEIR DUTIES
TO THE BEST OF THEIR SKILL AND ABILITY.

ARTICLE IV
REWARDS AND PUNISHMENTS--
1. ANY OF THE COMPANY LOOSING AN
ARM OR LEG IN AN ENGAGEMENT, OR IS
OTHERWISE DISABLED AND UNABLE TO EARN
HIS BREAD, SHALL RECEIVE ONE THOUSAND
POUNDS FROM THE FIRST PRIZE TAKEN.
2. WHOEVER FIRST DISCOVERS A SAIL THAT
PROVES TO BE A PRIZE, SHALL RECEIVE ONE
HUNDRED POUNDS AS A REWARD FOR HIS
VIGILANCE.
3. WHOEVER ENTERS AN ENEMY SHIP AFTER
BOARDING ORDERS ARE ISSUED, SHALL RECEIVE
THREE HUNDRED POUNDS FOR HIS VALOR.
4. WHOEVER IS GUILTY OF GAMING OR
QUARRELING SHALL SUFFER SUCH PUNISHMENT
AS THE CAPTAIN AND OFFICERS SEE FIT.
5. ANY MAN, ABSENT FROM THE SHIP
FOR TWENTY FOUR HOURS WITHOUT LEAVE,
SHALL BE GUILTY OF DISOBEDIENCE; COWARD-
ICE, MUTINY, THEFT, PILFERING, EMBEZZLEMENT,
CONCEALMENT OF GOODS BELONGING TO THE
SHIP OR HER COMPANY, STRIP OR THREATEN
ANY MAN OR BEHAVE INDECENTLY TO A WOM-
AN - SHALL LOOSE HIS SHARES AND RECEIVE
SUCH OTHER PUNISHMENT AS THE CRIME
DESERVES. SUCH FORFEITED SHARES SHALL
BE DISTRIBUTED TO THE REMAINING
SHIP'S COMPANY.
6. SEVEN DEAD SHARES SHALL BE SET

ASIDE AND DIVIDED BY THE CAPTAIN AND
OFFICERS AMONG THOSE WHO BEHAVE BEST
AND DO THE MOST FOR THE INTEREST AND
SERVICE OF THE CRUISE.
7. WHEN A PRIZE IS TAKEN AND SENT
INTO PORT, THE PRIZE MASTER AND THE MEN
ABOARD ARE RESPONSIBLE FOR WATCHING
AND UNLOADING THE PRIZE. IF ANY NEG-
LIGENCE RESULTS IN DAMAGE, THEIR SHARES
WILL BE HELD ACCOUNTABLE.
8. IF THE COMMANDER IS DISABLED, THE
NEXT HIGHEST OFFICER WILL STRICTLY COM-
PLY WITH THE RULES, ORDERS, RESTRICTIONS
AND AGREEMENTS BETWEEN THE OWNERS OF
THE PRIVATEER AND THE COMMANDER.

SHARES TO BE PROPORTIONED AS FOLLOWS-

CAPTAIN SHARES	8	STEWARD SHARES	2
FIRST LIEUTENANT	4	SAILMAKER	2
SECOND LIEUTENANT	4	GUNNER'S MATE	1½
MASTER	4	BOATSWAIN'S MATE	1½
SURGEON	4	CARPENTER'S MATES	1½
OFFICER OF MARINES	2	COOPER	1½
PRIZE MASTER	2	SURGEON'S MATE	1½
CARPENTER	2	ARMORER	2
GUNNER	2	SERGEANT-MARINES	2
BOATSWAIN	2	COOK	2
MASTER'S MATES	2	GENTLEMEN VOLRS	1
CAPTAIN'S CLERKS	2	BOYS UNDER 16 YEARS	½

9. IF ANY OFFICER OR ANY OF THE
COMPANY BE TAKEN PRISONER ABOARD A
CAPTURED PRIZE VESSEL, HE SHALL RECEIVE
A SHARE IN ALL PRIZES TAKEN DURING THE
REMAINDER OF THE PRIVATEER'S CRUISE IN
THE SAME MANNER AS HE WOULD IF
ACTUALLY ABOARD. HOWEVER, HE MUST OBTAIN
HIS LIBERTY BEFORE THE END OF THE CRUISE
OR MAKE EVERY EFFORT TO JOIN THE PRI-
VATEER, OR ELSE HIS PRIZE MONEY SHALL
BE FORFEITED TO THE OWNERS AND THE
SHIP'S COMPANY.
10. THE CAPTAIN SHALL HAVE FULL POWER
TO DISPLACE ANY OFFICER WHO MAY BE
FOUND UNFIT FOR THE POST.
11. THE CAPTAIN AND HIS PRINCIPAL
OFFICERS SHALL HAVE FULL POWER TO APPOINT
AN AGENT FOR THE SHIP'S COMPANY.
12. THE CAPTAIN, LIEUTENANTS, MASTER,
SURGEON AND OFFICER OF THE MARINES
SHALL NOT BE ENTITLED TO ANY PART OF
THE DEAD SHARES.

Appendix G

Restored 18th Century Homes in the Pompton Encampment

<u>The Dey Mansion</u>-This Immaculately restored home served as General George Washington's headquarters in 1780. Construction started before 1742 by Derrick Dey. At 1999 Totawa Road, adjoining the entrance to Passaic County Golf Course. Maintained by the Passaic County Park Commission, the Dey Mansion is now a museum, open to the public for tours. The museum is filled with furniture and paintings from the Revolutionary War era and is arranged to show the rooms as they might have been when Washington was here.

<u>Van Riper-Hopper House</u>- Museum and home of the Wayne Township Historical Commission. Built by Uraih Van Riper in 1786. On Berdan Avenue fronting on New Point View Reservoir. rooms contain 18th and early 19th century furnishings Located on its original site, the museum represents the agricultural society that dominated Wayne for over 200 years

<u>Schuyler-Colfax House</u>- Built by original settler Arent Schuyler in 1696. It is the oldest house in Wayne and was already eighty years old at the beginning of the Revolutionary War. At 2323 Hamburg Turnpike, Near Pompton Lakes line. The house was placed on the State and National Registers of Historic Places because of its construction and design. Eight generations of the Schuyler-Colfax family resided in the house, producing military, medical, legal and governmental representatives. The Schuyler-Colfax House is currently closed for restoration.

<u>Mead-Van Duyne House Museum</u>—Built by a Van Dien (Van Duyne) in 1706.—Originally at 636 Fairfield Road near Route 23 in Wayne Township, it was purchased in 1974 by the Township and moved 7 miles to a safe site at 533 Berdan Avenue, near the Van Riper-Hopper House. Private residence.

<u>Van Saun House</u> - Old Dutch home built by William Van Saun in 1869. Headquarters of Marquis de Lafayette during the 1780 encampment. The still active spring there flows into the Singac Brook At Laauwe Avenue off Valley Road and Preakness Avenue. Private residence.

<u>Ryerson Homestead</u>- Ryerson Homestead—Built in 1784 by Abraham Ryerson, who is a direct descendant of one of Wayne's first settlers. This home is at 44 Newark-Pompton Turnpike and is now a private residence that also serves as a business location.

<u>Mead House</u> - Built in 1780 at 231 Parish Drive in Wayne by Jacob K. Mead, a direct descendant of the founder of the village of Mead's Basin, this home forms the left wing of the huge mansion built in 1929 by LeGrand Parish. The house is now owned by the Lakeland Unitarian-Universalist Fellowship.

<u>Demarest House</u> - This 1760 homestead on 378 Fairfield Road,Wayne, is believed to have been built by John Ryerson, and used as a parsonage for the Dutch Reformed Church. It was dismantled and rebuilt in 1850 to rid the house of ghosts. The Demarest family bought it in 1814. It is now owned privately.

<u>Tollkeeper House</u> - Built in the 1700's at 2332 Hamburg Turnpike to house George Colfax, the toll collector on the road from Paterson to Hamburg. To supplement his income, Colfax was also a cobbler. This home currently is a private residence.

Appendix II

The New Jersey Line
and Militia in the American
Revolutionary War

<u>Regiments of the New Jersey Continental Line: (1777)</u>
1st New Jersey Regiment, Colonel Matthias Ogden
2nd New Jersey Regiment, Colonel Israel Shreve
3rd New Jersey Regiment, Colonel Elias Dayton
4th New Jersey Regiment, Colonel Ephraim Martin
Spencer's Additional Continental Regiment, Colonel Oliver Spencer
Forman's Additional Continental Regiment, Colonel David Forman

<u>New Jersey Militia Units-Year Organized</u>
1st Regiment, Bergen County Militia, 1777–78 Eastern Battalion, Morris County, 1777–78
Van Courtlandt's Battalion, 1776 Forman's Regiment of Militia, 1776–80
1st Regiment, Essex County, 1777 Hankinson's Regiment of Militia, 1777–79
1st Battalion of Somerset, 1777–81 Holmes' Battalion, Salem County, 1778
2nd Regiment of Essex County Troop, 1778 Newcomb's Regiment of Foot, 1776
2nd Battalion of Hunterdon, 1777 Smith's Regiment, Burlington Co, 1776
2nd Battalion of Middlesex, 1777 Shreve's Battalion, Burlington Militia
2nd Battalion of Somerset, 1777–80 Randolph's Company, 1782

3rd Battalion of Gloucester, 1777 Reynolds' Regiment, Burlington
Co., 1776

3rd Battalion of Middlesex, 1781 Philip's Regiment of Militia, 1777

Borden's Regiment, Burlington County, 1776 Seely's Regiment of
Militia, 1777–81

Chambers' Regiment, Burlington County, 1776 Summer's Battalion
of Militia, 1776

Crane's Troops of Horse, 1780 Thomas' Battalion of Essex Militia,
1776

Bibliography

Primary Sources

Acomb, Evelyn A. *The Revolutionary Journal of Ludwig von Closen, 1780–1783* (Chapel Hill: The University of North Carolina Press, 1958).

Acomb, Evelyn A. *The Revolutionary Journal of Ludwig von Closen, 1780–1783* (Chapel Hill: The University of North Carolina Press, 1958).

John Adams to Abigail Adams, February 17, 1777, L.H. Butterfield, ed., *The Adams Family Correspondence* (Cambridge, MA: The Belknap Press of Harvard University Press, 1963).

Lenhart, John M., "Letter of an Officer of the Zweibrücken Regiment," *Central-Blatt and Social Justice*, Vol. 28, (January 1936), (Williamsburg: Colonial Williamsburg Foundation, Vol. 15, no. 4, summer 1993).

Alexander Hamilton to Robert R. Livingston June 28, 1777, New York Historical Society Museum Collection.

Andre, John, *Major Andre's Journal: Operations of the British army Under Lieutenant Generals Sir William Howe and Sir Henry Clinton June, 1777 to November, 1778*, (The New York Times & Arno Press; 1st edition, 1968), entry for June 23, 1778.

Archives of the State of New Jersey, 1st Series. v.10. 1758.

Boom, A. A., *A report of the Middlebrook Encampment by the Continental Army in the Middle of 1777 and in the Winter of 1778–1779*. Sponsored by the Somerset Historical Society, typewritten Ms.-Collections of the Warren Township Library.
Charles Stedman, *The History of the Origin, Progress, and Termination of the American War* (London:1794).

Charles Stuart to Lord Bute, "New York, July 10, 1777," New Records, 33, 174 in McGuire, Thomas, *The New Jersey Revolutionary War Damage Claims, Claims Against the British, Essex & Middlesex Counties*, Reel 2, New Jersey State Archives.

Charles Stuart to Lord Bute, March 19, 1777 in *A Prime Minister and His Son*, Mrs. E Stuart Wortley Ed. (London:1905).

Clarke, Alured, *Lieutenant Colonel Clarke's Order Book*, British Seventh Regiment of Foot, June 21, 1778.

Clermont-Crèvecoeur, Journal, in Rice and Brown, *American Campaigns*, Vol. 1.

Clinton, Henry, General Sir Henry Clinton's official report of the battle of Monmouth reached London on August 2, 1778 and was first published in *The London Gazette*, Whitehall on August 24. The report was reprinted in the August 22–25, 1778 edition of *The London Chronicle*

Clinton, Henry, Lieutenant General to Lord George Germain, July 5, 1778. (Library of Congress, Mss. Division: PRO CO 5:96). Finigan, H.: "Montresor Papers on microfilm" David Library of the American Revolution, Washington's Crossing, PA. 42.

Clinton, Henry, *Narrative of Lieut Col Henry Clinton Relative to his conduct During part of his Campaign of the King's Troops in North America* (London J. Debrett, 1783) William L Clements Library, University of Michigan.) Entry for June 22, 1778.

Clinton, Henry, *Sir Henry Clinton's Narrative of his Campaigns 1775–1782*. William H. Wilcox, Ed. (New Haven: Yale University Press, 1954).

Collections of The New Jersey Historical Society Vols. V, VI.

Collins, Report of Captain Collins, British navy *Zebra*, in Little Egg Harbour, October 9, 1778.

Cromot du Bourg, "Diary," 124–25. *Magazine of American History*: v. 4–5, 1780–81.

David C. Munn, *Battles and Skirmishes of the American Revolution in New Jersey* (New Jersey Geological Survey, 1976).

Erskine, Robert, Field sketches and finished maps of projected battle sites in New York, New Jersey, Connecticut and Pennsylvania during the Revolutionary were begun by Robert Erskine, geographer and surveyor-general of the Continental Army, and completed by his successor, Simeon De Witt. Erskine (1735–1780) who was appointed geographer to Washington's army in 1777.

Erskine, Robert, Maps of the Short Hills and Ash Swamp. C.1779, No. 74A, 74B, 78. Collections of the New York Historical Society.

Erskine/DeWitt series Map number 55, drawn for Capt. William Scull. This map shows detailed locations of the Continental Army units during the 1776–77 Middlebrook encampment. US National Archives.

Ewalt, Johann, *Diary of the American War: A Hessian Journal*, translated and edited by Joseph Tostin. (New Haven: Yale University Press, 1979)

Extract from the log of the HMS *Nautilus* Lot 39.43, October 12 "Came on board an officer and a deserter from the rebels."

Extract of a letter from a gentleman on board HMS *Assistance* at Sandy Hook, Jan. 2, *The Scots Magazine*, March 1784, Edinburgh.

Federal Census, 1880. City of Plainfield, First District, 52. Re: John Laing.

Ferguson, Patrick "Correspondence of Major Patrick Ferguson, 1779–1780," is in Gilchrist, M. M. *Patrick Ferguson:"A Man of Some Genius"* 2003.

Ferguson, Patrick, letter, Little Egg Harbor, October 15, 1778. *The Royal Gazette,* March 10, 1779; reprinted in: William Nelson, ed., *Documents Relating to the Revolutionary History of the State of New Jersey,* Second Series, Vol. III (Trenton: John L. Murphy Publishing Company, 1906).

Ferguson, Patrick, Report of Capt. Ferguson, of the 70th Regiment, to his Excellency Sir Henry Clinton, dated Little Egg-Harbour, Oct. 15, 1778," *The Remembrancer* (London: J. Almon, 1779).

Ferguson, James E., ed. *The Papers of Robert Morris, 1781–1784,* Vol. 1: February 7-July 31, 1781, (Pittsburgh: 1973).
Hawkins, John H. *Journal of Sargeant Major John Hawkins,* (Manuscript # Am. 0765, Unpublished, microfilmed, Historical Society of Pennsylvania).

Hill, Roscoe R., ed., Journals of the Continental Congress, 1774–1789, Volume X. January 1-May 1, 1778 (Washington, D.C.: Government Printing Office, 1908).

Huddy vs. Longstreet, Writ of Replevin, November 6, 1780, Monmouth County Court.

Israel Shreve to Dr. Bodo Otto, June 29, 1777, in John U. Rees, *Colonel Israel Shreve's Journal, 23 November 1776 to 14 August 1777.*
http://www.scribd.com/doc/153790118 (accessed October 3, 2017)

Kemp, Frankin W., *A Nest of Rebel Pirates* (Batsto, NJ: Batsto Citizens Committee, 1966).

Lamb, Roger, *An Original and Authentic Journal of Occurrences During the Late American War, From its Commencement to the Year 1783,* (Dublin: Wilkinson and Courtney, 1809)

Lambs Orderly Book for 6 August 1781, The New York Historical Society.

Lauberdière, Louis, *Journal de guerre, "Lauberdière's Journal. the Revolutionary War Journal of Louis François Bertrand d'Aubevoye, comte de Lauberdière,"* Robert A. Selig, *Colonial Williamsburg,* Vol. 8, no. 1 Autumn 1995.

Lee, Francis B., Archives of the State of New Jersey, Second Series, Vol II, (Documents Relating to the Revolutionary History of the State of New Jersey / Extracts from American Newspapers relating to New Jersey) (Trenton: John L. Murphy Publishing Company, 1903).

Lincoln, Charles Henry, *Calendar of Naval Records of the American Revolution 1775–1788,* prepared from the originals in the Library of Congress by Division of Manuscripts (Washington D.C. 1906).

Lydenberg, Harry Miller, ed., *Archibald Robertson, Lieutenant-General Royal Engineers: His Diaries and Sketches in America, 1762–1780* (New York: New York Public Library, 1930).

McGuire, Thomas J., *The Philadelphia Campaign: Brandywine and the Fall of Philadelphia Volume I.* (Mechanicsburg, PA: Stackpole Books, 2006).
Messier, Abraham, D.D. *History of Somerset County* (Somerville, NJ: C.M. Jameson Publisher, 1878).

Moss, George H, "Bentinck's Log" in *Nauvoo to the Hook.* Original source was "unpublished Crown copyright material in Public Records Office printed with permission of H.M. Stationary Office.

Muster Rolls, New York Brigade at Pompton-January to June 1782.

Nash, Solomon, and Bushnell, Charles I., eds., *Journal of Solomon Nash. Soldier of the Revolution, 1776–1777,* (New York: Privately Printed, 1861).

National Archives (Class title War Office 71/86) Verdict and sentencing of two British camp followers.

New Jersey Archives, State Library, Trenton N.J. Essex County Inventories.
New Jersey Revolutionary War Damage Claims, Claims Against the British, Essex & Middlesex Counties, Reel 2, New Jersey State Archives.

New Jersey State Archives, Record Group: Military and Militia, Subgroup: Adjutant General's Office, Series: Revolutionary War Research files, Box 2.

Onderdonk, Henry Jr., *Documents and Letters to Illustrate the Revolutionary Incidents of Queens County* (New York: Leavitt, Trow and Co., 1846).

Orderly book of the 2nd New York Regiment, New York State Library #10464, Vol.10.
Peckham, Howard *The Toll of Independence* (Chicago: University of Chicago Press, 1974).

Peebles, John, *John Peebles'American War-The Diary of a Scottish Grenadier 1776–1782,* Ira D. Gruber, ed., Publications of the Army Records Society (Book 13) (Mechanicsburg PA: Stackpole Books, 1998).

Peter Wilson, comp., *Acts of the Council and General Assembly of the State of New-Jersey from the Establishment of the Present Government, and Declaration of Independence, to the End of the first Sitting of the Eight Session, on the 14th Day of December, 1783* (Trenton: Isaac Collins, 1784).

Philadelphia Campaign, Volume 1: Brandywine and the Fall of Philadelphia (Mechanicsburg, PA: Stackpole Books, 2006).

Randolph, Edward F., *Journal of Edward Fitz Randolph* (New Brunswick, NJ: Rutgers University Special Collections, University Archives).

Rankin, Hugh, "An Officer Out of His Time," Howard, H. Peckham, Sources of American Independence (Chicago: University of Chicago Press, 1978). Gilchrist, M. M., St. Andrews, Scotland, 1999 offers the best published collection of Ferguson's military writings, with a biographical introduction by Hugh F. Rankin, "An Officer Out of His Time."

Robin, Abbé, *New Travels through North America* (Philadelphia: Robert Bell, 1783).

Rodney, Thomas, *Diary of Captain Thomas Rodney, 1776–1777* (Whitefish, MT: Kessinger Publishing, LLC, 2010).

Schoepf, David, Johann, *Travels in the Confederation*, Morrison, Alfred J., ed., (Philadelphia: William H. Campbell, 1911.) cited in Edgar, Gregory, *The Philadelphia Campaign, 1777–1778* (MD: Berwyn Heights, Heritage Books, Inc., 2013).

Sekel, Clifford,"*The Continental Artillery in Winter Encampment at Pluckemin, New Jersey, December 1778-June 1779,*"(Master of Arts Thesis, Wagner College 1972) .

Shreve, John, "Personal Narrative of the Services of Lieut. John Shreve of the New Jersey Line of the Continental Army," in *The Magazine of American History with Notes and Queries*, Volume III, 1879.

Skull, G. D., *The Montresor Journals*, Collections of the New York Historical Society for the Year 1881.

State v. Huddy (1778), Monmouth County Court of Oyer and Terminer, Minutes.

Stephens, H. M. "Erskine, Sir William, Second Baronet (1770–1813)," in *Oxford Dictionary of National Biography* (Oxford University Press, 2004).

Stryker, William, *The Affair at Egg Harbor, New Jersey October 15, 1778* (Trenton, NJ: Naar, Day & Naar, 1894).

Talmadge General Orders, December 8, 1779, Headquarters, Morristown.

Talmadge, Samuel, *Orderly Books of the Fourth and Second New York Regiments, 1776–1783*, (Albany: University of the State of New York, 1932), also General, Brigade and Regimental Orders: Headquarters Morristown Dec 7, 1779 to May 31, 1780.

Thatcher, James, M.D., *A Military Journal During the American Revolutionary War From 1775 to 1783*, (New York: Arno Press, 1969).

Vail, Rebecca describes a picnic trip to the Rock from Rahway in 1847 and includes a copy of a postcard showing the Rock before the stone walls were built. (Gladys Whitehead's Memory Books Recollections 2, 1986), Collections of the Plainfield, New Jersey Public Library.

Van Brunt v. Huddy (1779), Monmouth County Court of Common Pleas, Monmouth County Archives.

Vermeule, Cornelius C. *The Revolutionary Camp Ground at Plainfield. An Address Delivered before the Continental Chapter, Daughters of the American Revolution,* January 9, 1923.

Von Closen, Ludwig *The Revolutionary Journal of Baron von Closen, 1780–1783.* (Chapel Hill, NC: North Carolina Press, Institute of Early American History and Culture, Williamsburg, VA. 1958).

Ward, Harry M., *Charles Scott and the Spirit of '76* (Charlottesville, VA: University of Virginia Press, 1988).

Ward, Harry M., *General William Maxwell and the New Jersey Continentals* (Westport, CT: Greenwood Press, 1977).

Washington to Congress, Extracted from "Official Letters of General Washington to the American Congress" vol. ii. (Boston: Manning & Loring, 1795).

Washington to Henry Laurens, President of the Continental Congress, Englishtown, July 1, 1778.

Washington Papers, Series 3, Varick Transcripts, 1775–1785, Subseries 3A, Continental Congress, 1775–1783, Letterbook 3: Sept. 1, 1777—Aug. 31, 1778.

Weelen, Jean-Edmond, *Rochambeau. Father and Son. A life of the Maréchal de Rochambeau and the Journal of the Vicomte de Rochambeau* (New York: Henry Holt Co, 1936).

William Howe to Lord George Germain. December 20, 1777, *The Pennsylvania Gazette,* From the *London Gazette,* Whitehall, August 22, 1777.

Additional Sources

Allen, Gardner W., *A Naval History of the American Revolution,* (Boston and New York: Houghton-Mifflin Company, The Riverside Press, Cambridge, 1913), Vol. 1. American Archives, Volume VI.

Andrews, John L.L.D., *A History of the War with America, France, Spain, and Holland. Commencing in 1775, and Ending in 1783.* (London: Printed for John Fielding, and John Jarvis, By the King's Royal License and Authority, 1785).

Atwood, Rodney, *Mercenaries from Hessen-Kassel in the American Revolution* (Cambridge: Cambridge University Press, 1980).

Atwood, Rodney, *The Hessians* (Cambridge: Cambridge University Press, 2002).

Barber, John Warner, *Historical Collections of the State of New Jersey: Past and Present* (New Haven CT: 1868).

Beck, Henry Charlton, *More Forgotten Towns of Southern New Jersey* (New Brunswick, NJ, Rutgers University Press, 1963).

Bierce, William, *Under the Sign of the Eagle* (Wayne Township Historical Commission, Louis Borgetts, 1964).

Blackman, Leah, *"History of Little Egg Harbor, from 1880,"* in *Old Times and Other Writings* (Tuckerton NJ: Tuckerton Historical Society, 2000).

Boom, A.A., *Report On The Middlebrook Encampment By The Continental Army During The Middle of 1777 and the Winter of 1778–1779* (Somerset County Historical Society 1975, Collection at Somerset County Library, Bridgewater, NJ).

Boyd, Paul D., *Atlantic Highlands: From Lenape Camps to Bayside Town* (Charlestown, SC: Arcadia Publishing, 2004).

Brander, Michael, *Scottish Highlanders and their Regiments* (London: Seeley Service and Co. Ltd., 1971)

Brenton, Edward P., *The Naval History of Great Brain, from the Year MDCCLXXXIll to MDCCCXXXVL, Volume I* (London: Henry Colburn, 1837).

Brubaker, Robert M., *A Wonderously Beautiful Valley, A Commemorative History of Wayne, N.J.,* (Wayne NJ: Wayne Township Bicentennial Committee, 1976).

Detwiller, Frederic C., *War in the Countryside: The Battle and Plunder of the Short Hills, New Jersey, June 1777* (Plainfield, NJ: Interstate Printing Corp., 1977).

Donnelly, Mark P and Diehl, Daniel. *Pirates of New Jersey: Plunder and High Adventure on the Garden State Coastline,* (Guilford, CT: Stackpole Books, 2010).

Cook, Fred J., *Privateers of Seventy-Six* (New York, Bobbs-Merrill Company, Inc. 1976).

Draper, Lyman C. *King's Mountain and Its Heroes: History of the Battle of King's Mountain, October 7, 1780, and the Events Which Led to It.* (Cincinnati, OH: Peter G. Thompson, 1881).

Ewald, Johann, trans., ed. Tustin, Joseph P., *Diary of the American War-A Hessian Journal* (New Haven, CT: Yale University Press, 1979).

Freeman, Douglas S., *Biography of George Washington* (New York: Charles Scribner and Sons, 1952), Volume 5.

Glenn, Thomas Allen, *William Churchill Houston, 1746–1788* (Norristown, PA: Privately printed, 1903).

Folger, Harry P., III, *The Battle of Chestnut Neck and The Affair at Little Egg Harbor, October 6, 1778-October 22,1778* (Marshallville, NJ: 2008) Col. Richard Somers Chapter, New Jersey Society, Sons of the American Revolution, www.colrichardsomers.com (accessed October 2017).

History of Monmouth County, 1664–1920 Vol. 1. (New York; Lewis Historical Publishing Co., 1922).

Hornor, William S., *This Old Monmouth of Ours* (Freehold, NJ; Moreau Brothers, 1932, republished Cottenport, LA: Polyanthos, 1974).

Kemp, Franklin W., *A Nest of Rebel Pirates* (Egg Harbor City, NJ: The Laureate Press, 1966).

King, John P., *The Making of America-Highlands, New Jersey* (Mount Pleasant, SC: Arcadia Publishing, 2001).

Kobbé Gustav, *The Jersey Coast and Pines.* (Baltimore, MD: Gateway Press, Inc., 1970).

Lossing, John Benson, *The Pictorial Field-Book of the Revolution or, Illustrations, by pen and pencil, of the history, biography, scenery, relics, and traditions of the war for independence* (New York: Harper & Brothers, 1859), Vol. 1.

Lydenberg, Harry, ed., *Archibald Robertson, His Diaries and Sketches in America* (New York: New York Public Library, 1930).

Maclay, Edgar Stanton, *A History of American Privateers* (Freeport, NY: Books for the Library Press, 1970)

Mattern, David B., *Benjamin Lincoln and the American Revolution* (Columbia, SC: University of South Carolina Press, 1992).

Menzies, Elizabeth G. C., *Millstone Valley* (New Brunswick: Rutgers University Press, 1968).

Messier, Abraham, *Centennial History of Somerset County* (Somerville, NJ: C.M. Jameson, 1878).

Miller, Pauline S., *Brief Encounter at Osborn Island: The Pulaski Affair.* (Toms River, NJ: Ocean County Cultural & Heritage Commission, 1998).

Munn, David C., *Battles and Skirmishes of the American Revolution in New Jersey,* (New Jersey Geological Survey, 1976).

Nelson, William, and Shriner, Charles A., *History of Paterson and Its Environs (the Silk City)* (Paterson, NJ: Lewis Historical Publishing, 1920).

Ott, Westley H., *1 mile x 1Mile x 100 Years=Dunellen, N.J., 1887–1987*(South Plainfield, NJ: (Pentacle Communications, 1987).

Patton, Robert, *Patriot Pirates: The Privateer War for Freedom and Fortune in the American Revolution* (New York: Pantheon Books, 2008).

Peckham, Howard H., *The Toll of Independence* (Chicago: University of Chicago Press, 1974).

Peckham, Howard H., ed., *Sources of American Independence*, vol. II (Chicago: University of Chicago Press, 1978).

Pierce, Arthur Dudley, *Smugglers' Woods: Jaunts and Journeys in Colonial and Revolutionary New Jersey* (New Brunswick: Rutgers University Press, 1960).

Ricord, Frederick W., *History of Union County* (Newark, NJ: East Jersey History Company, 1897).

Ryerson, Egerton, *The Loyalists of American and Their Times, 1620–1816, Vol II.* (Toronto: William Briggs, 1880).

Salter, Edwin, and Beekman, George C., *Old Times in Old Monmouth-Historical Reminiscences of Old Monmouth County, New Jersey* (Freehold, NJ: 1887).

Salter, Edwin, *A History of Monmouth and Ocean Counties, Embracing a Genealogical Record of the Earliest Settlers in Monmouth and Ocean Counties* (Bayonne, NJ: E. Gardner & Son, 1890).

Schleicher, William and Winter, Susan Somerset County, *Crossroads of the American Revolution* (Charlestown, SC: Arcadia Publishing, 1999).

Snell James P., Ellis Franklin, ed., *History of Hunterdon and Somerset Counties, New Jersey* (Philadelphia, Everts & Peck: 1881).

Sparks, Jared, *Correspondence of the American Revolution, vol. II* (Boston: Hale, Grey and Bowen, 1853).

Stedman, Charles, *The History of the Origin, Progress, and Termination of the American War* (London: Privately printed, 1794).

Stephens, H. M. "Erskine, Sir William, Second Baronet (1770–1813)," entry in *Oxford Dictionary of National Biography* (Oxford University Press, 2004).

Stillwell, John E., *Historical And Genealogical Miscellany: Data Relating To The Settlement And Settlers Of New York And New Jersey* (New York:1932).

Stryker, William S. *The Battle of Monmouth*, (Port Washington, NY, London: Kenekat Press, 1927).

——, "The Affair at Egg Harbor, October 15, 1778," speech given at the dedication of the Pulaski Massacre Monument, July 3, 1894 (Trenton: Naar, Day and Naar, 1894), www.babel.hathitrust.org.

Tonsetic, Robert 1., *Special Operations During the American Revolution* (Haverford, PA: Casemate Publishers, 2013).

Valentine, Alan, *Lord Stirling* (New York: Oxford University Press, 1969).

Van Doren, Carl, *Mutiny in January: The Story of a Crisis in the Continental Army now for the first time fully told from many hitherto unknown or neglected source, both American and British* (New York: Viking Press, 1943).
Volo, James M., Volo Dorothy D., *Life in 17th and 18th Century America* (Westport, CT: Greenwood Publishing Group, 2006).

Ward, Christopher, *The War of Revolution Vol. II* (New York: MacMillan, 1952).

Ward, Harry M, *Charles Scott and the Spirit of '76* (Charlottesville: University of Virginia Press, 1998).

——, *General William Maxwell and the New Jersey Continentals* (Westport CT: Praeger, 1997).

Washington-Rochambeau Revolutionary Route in the State of New Jersey, 1781–1783. An Historical and Architectural Survey. 3 volumes. (Trenton: New Jersey Historic Trust, Department of Community Affairs, 2006).

Williams, Glen, F., *The Year of the Hangman* (Yardley, PA: Westholme Publishing, 2005).

Woodward, E. M., *History of Burlington County,* (Philadelphia, PA: Everts and Peck, 1883).

Wright, Robert K. *The Continental Army* (Center of Military History, United States Army, Washington, DC: 1986).

Newspapers, Manuscripts, Pamphlets

A History and Guide to Morristown National Park (Washington, D.C., Division of Publications. National Park Service, US Dept. of the Interior, 1983).

Bebbington, George and Siegel, Alan A., "Washington Rock Is Focus of Renewed Interest" (*Warren History,* Vol. 2, No. 3, Spring 1995, Warren Township Historical Society), https://sites.google.com/a/gbhsnj.org/gbhsnj/misc/washington-rock?tmpl, (accessed October 13, 2017)

Bebbington, George and Siegel, Alan A., "Warren History," *Somerset County Historical Quarterly,* May 1, 2007.

Cedar Bridge Tavern, National Register of Historic Places

Constitutionist, Plainfield NJ, July 16, 1896.

Extract written by an officer at Amboy Feb 16 1777, *New York Gazette and Weekly Mercury,* February 7, 1777.

Fort, George F., MD, "An Account of the Capture and Death of the Refugee John Bacon," *Proceedings of the New Jersey Historical Society,* (Newark, NJ: New Jersey Historical Society, 1847).

Hyde, Murray M. C., "The Battle of the Navesink," *New York Times,* February 23, 1896.

Larsen, Erik, "Ocean County to Develop Cedar Bridge Tavern in Barnegat,"*Asbury Park Press,* February 24, 2016.

The Monmouth Democrat, Freehold, NJ: 1887, 46.

Moran, Donald N., *New Jersey and the 1777 Forage War,* Sons of Liberty Chapter, S.A.R.

Muster Rolls, New York Brigade at Pompton-January to June 1782, US National Archives http://www.revolutionarywararchives.org/newjerseyforage.html (accessed October 9, 2017).

Nelson, William, *Paterson and Its Environs* Map, *Showing the Location of the American Army at Totawa and Preakness, N.J. And Vicinity October and November* 1780.

———, "Washington's Headquarters at Preakness," in *The Magazine of American History Vol.* 3 (New York and Chicago: A. S. Barnes & Company, 1879).
New Jersey Gazette, July 1, 1778, (Burlington and Trenton, NJ).

———, January 8, 1783, (Burlington and Trenton, NJ).

New York Gazette and Weekly Mercury, February 7, 1777, (New York City).

ew York Provincial Congress, Journal, Vol. 1, Pierre Van Cortlandt, Abm. P. Lott, and John Sloss Hobart of the New York Provincial Congress to Major William Clark March 6, 1776, which appears in William Bell Clark, ed., *Naval Documents of the American Revolution* Vol. 4. (Washington, DC: US Navy Department, 1968).

Pennsylvania Evening Post, February 6, 1777.

Pennsylvania Journal and Weekly Advertiser, February 26, 1777.

Red Bank Register "Skeletons Unearthed," April 22, 1908.

Revolutionary War Sites in Manahawkin, New Jersey,
www.revolutionarywarnewjersey.com/new_jersey_revolutionary_war_sites/towns/
manahawkin_nj_revolutionary_war_sites.htm (accessed October 23, 2017).

Royal Gazette digital copies were obtained from the "Early American Newspapers" database at Seton Hall University Library. The articles are dated October 30 and November 1, 1782.

Stillman, George B., "Battle of the Short Hills. Reenactment preparations June 29 and 30, 2002" *The Brigade Courier, Brigade of the American Revolution,* Volume 18:3.

Suburban Trends Magazine, February 13, 1983. (re. German Camp on Federal Hill).

Sunnybank, Former Estate of Albert Payson Terhune, Pamphlet (undated) Wayne Township Historic Site, Wayne, NJ.

Somerville, George B., *The Lure of Long Beach,* Long Beach Board of Trade, Long Beach: 1914, 37–38.

The Pennsylvania Evening Post, July 10, 1777.

The War at the Shore 2007: Commemorating the 225th Anniversary of the Revolutionary War in Ocean County 1776–1783. Ocean County Board of Chosen Freeholders, 2007.

Wells, Charles H., "Sandy Hook Mystery Solved" *New York Daily Tribune,* April 24, 1908.

Endnotes

Chapter 1

1. Rodney Atwood, Mercenaries from Hessen-Kassel in the American Revolution (Cambridge University Press, 1980), Ch. 1.
2. Ewald, Johann, Trans, Ed.Tustin, Joseph P., Diary of the American War-A Hessian Journal (New Haven, CT, Yale University Press, 1979).
3. Swan, Harry Kels, The Military Significance of Middlebrook in 1777, June 26, 1977. Typed manuscript at Heritage Trail Association, Van Horne House. 941 East Main Street, Bridgewater, N.J. 08807. www.heritagetrail.org/van_horne_househtm (accessed October 11, 2017).
4. Schleicher, William and Winter, Susan, Somerset County, Crossroads of the American Revolution (Charlestown, SC: Arcadia Publishing, 1999), 14–25.
5. Atwood, Rodney, The Hessians (Cambridge University Press. 2002), 199.
6. Sponsors of Bound Brook historic homes: Van Horne House-Heritage Trail Association (www. heritagetrail.org); Van Veghten House-Somerset County Historical Society (www. somersethistorynj.org); Staats House-Friends of the Staats House (www. staatshouse.org).
7. Vermeule, Cornelius, Revolutionary Campground at Plainfield, N.J. (Address before Continental Chapter, Daughters of the American Revolution, January 9, 1923.)
8. Mattern, David B., Benjamin Lincoln and the American Revolution (Columbia, SC: University of South Carolina Press, 1992), 22.
9. Ewald, Diary of the American War, 55
10. Ibid., 51
11. Ibid., 52
12. Ibid., 56.
13. Ibid., 57.
14. Ibid., 56.
15. Atwood Rodney, The Hessians, 117.
16. Davis, Rev. T.E., The Battle of Bound Brook: An Address Delivered Before the Washington Camp Ground Association (Bound Brook, NJ: The Chronicle Stream Printery, 1894), 6.
17. Ewald, Diary of the American War, 57.
18. Ibid., 57.

Chapter 2

1. Moran, Donald N. New Jersey and the 1777 Forage War. www.revolutionarywararchives.org/newjerseyforage.html (accessed October 9, 2017).
2. Rodney, Thomas, Diary of Captain Thomas Rodney, 1776–1777 (Whitefish MT: Kessinger Publishing, LLC, 2010). During the war Thomas Rodney was captain of a militia

company known as the Dover Light Infantry. He was later appointed colonel of the 8th Regiment of Delaware Militia.

3. Washington to Spencer, 17 January 1777, George Washington Papers at the Library of Congress, 1741–1799.

4. Ibid., Washington to Continental Congress, 12 January 1777.

5. Stedman, Charles, The History of the Origin, Progress, and Termination of the American War (London: 1794), 1:241.

6. Smucker, Isaac, "General Charles Scott," Historical Magazine. Vol. 3., February 1874, 88–90.

7. Ewald, Diary of the American War, 56.

8. Washington to Continental Congress, 14 January 1777, Washington Papers.

9. Ibid., Washington to Continental Congress, 17 January 1777.

10. Ibid., Washington to Spencer, 17 January 1777.

11. Charles Stedman, The History of the Origin, Progress, and Termination of the American War (Printed for the author and sold by J. Murray, 1794).

12. Ibid, 1:243.

13. Philemon Dickinson Papers, New Jersey Historical Society, Newark, New Jersey.

14. Glenn, Thomas Allen, William Churchill Houston, 1746–1788 (Norristown, PA: Privately printed, 1903), 26–28. and Library of Congress Online Catalog 760.184.

15. Valis, Glenn, "The Battle of Millstone," New Jersey in the Revolution, http://www.doublegv.com/ggv/battles/millstone.1 (accessed October 9, 2017).

16. This letter is cited by Glenn and Georgeanne Valis as from "Rutgers library." Their webpage, The Battle of Millstone, can be found at www.doublegv.com/ggv/battles/millstone.html (accessed October 9, 2017).

17. Lydenberg, Harry, Ed. Archibald Robertson, His Diaries and Sketches in America (New York, 1930; reprinted 1971), 122.

18. Ewald, Diary of the American War, 52.

19. Washington to the Continental Congress, 22 January 1777, Washington Papers.

20. Peckham, Howard H., The Toll of Independence, Engagements and Battle Casualties of the American Revolution (Chicago: Chicago University Press, 1974), 29.

21. Quoted in http://founders.archives.gov/documents/Washington/03–08–02–0135 (accessed October 4, 2017).

22. Menzies, Elizabeth G. C., Millstone Valley (New Brunswick: Rutgers University Press, 1968), 86.

23. The Battle of Millstone, www.doublegv.com/ggv/battles/millstone.html (accessed October 4, 2017).

Chapter 3

1. Washington to Heath, February 14, 1777, Washington Papers.

2. John Adams to Abigail Adams, February 17, 1777, Butterfield, L.H., ed., The Adams Family Correspondence (Cambridge: Harvard University Press, 1963), 2:162–163.

3. Ewald, Diary of the American War, 51

4. Samptown is an unincorporated community within South Plainfield, Middlesex County, New Jersey.

5. Washington to John Augustine Washington, February 24, 1777, Washington Papers.

6. Pennsylvania Evening Post, February 6, 1777.

7. Stephens, H. M. "Erskine, Sir William, second baronet 1770–1813," in Oxford Dictionary of National Biography (Oxford University Press, 2004).

8. Ward, Harry M., General William Maxwell and the New Jersey Continentals (Westport CT:1997), 16–21.

9. Peebles, John, The Diary of a Scottish Grenadier, Ira D. Gruber, ed., Army Records Society (Great Britain), (Stackpole Books, 1998), 93–94,102,104.

10. Ewald, Diary of the American War, 53.

11. Ward, Harry M. Charles Scott and the Spirit of '76 (Charlottesville VA:1998), 27–28.

12. Dickinson to Washington, Febuary 9, 1777, Washington Papers.

13. Ibid., Washington to Continental Congress, January 14, 1777.

14. Ibid., Washington to Spenser, January 17, 1777.

15. Washington to Continental Congress, January 14, 1777, Washington Papers.

16. Ward, General William Maxwell, 57.

17. Peebles, American War, 97.

18. Charles Stedman, The History of the Origin, Progress, and Termination of the American War (London: 1794), 1:241.

19. Harry Miller Lydenberg, Ed., Archibald Robertson, Lieutenant-General Royal Engineers: His Diaries and Sketches in America, 1762–1780 (New York, New York Public Library, 1930), 122.

20. Charles Stuart to Lord Bute, March 19, 1777 in A Prime Minister and His Son, Wortley, Mrs. E. Stuart, ed., (London, 1905), 103.

21. Ewald, Diary of the American War, 64.

22. Ibid., 65.

23. Howard Peckham, The Toll of Independence (Chicago: University of Chicago Press, 1974), 130.

24. David C. Munn, Battles and Skirmishes of the American Revolution in New Jersey (New Jersey Geological Survey, 1976).

Chapter 4

1. James Grant to Edward Harvey, July 10, 1777 in McGuire, Thomas, The Philadelphia Campaign, Volume 1: Brandywine and the Fall of Philadelphia (Mechanicsburg, PA, Stackpole, 2006), 45.

2. Charles Stuart to Lord Bute, "New York, July 10, 1777," New Records, 33.174 in McGuire, Thomas, The Philadelphia Campaign, Volume 1: Brandywine and the Fall of Philadelphia (Mechanicsburg, PA: Stackpole, 2006), Ch. 1.

3. Archives of the State of New Jersey, First Series-1758, Vo1.10, 73.

4. New Jersey Archives, State Library, Trenton N.J. Essex County Inventories, 86.

5. Detwiller, Frederic C., War In The Countryside, The Battle and Plunder of the Short Hills

New Jersey, June 1777 (Plainfield, NJ: Interstate Printing Corp.), Chapters V, VII, VIII.

6. The Pennsylvania Evening Post, July 10, 1777.

7. New Jersey Archives, State Library, Trenton, N.J. The extensive plundering of the countryside by both British and American troops before and after the battle led to a large number of damage claims from civilians. An exact description of the property and often the dates when the damages occurred appears in these inventories. Several are dated during the week of the battle. An examination of these records provides a representative picture of the contents of farmhouses and shops, and various craftsmen's tools of the era.

8. Collections of The New Jersey Historical Society vol. VI. 99.

9. Ricord, Frederick W., History of Union County, 503.

10. Peter Wilson, comp., Acts of the Council and General Assembly of the State of New-Jersey from the Establishment of the Present Government, and Declaration of Independence, to the End of the first Sitting of the Eight Session, on the 14th Day of December, 1783 (Trenton NJ: Isaac Collins, 1784), 237.

11. New Jersey Revolutionary War Damage Claims, Claims Against the British, Essex & Middlesex Counties, Reel 2, New Jersey State Archives. There was a total of 115 individuals who filed claims for damages in Westfield during the entire war, with 92 claiming damages for June 26–27, 1777.

12. Andre, John, Major Andre's Journal: Operations of the British army Under Lieutenant Generals Sir William Howe and Sir Henry Clinton June, 1777 to November, 1778 (The New York Times & Arno Press; 1968), 42.

13. Ibid., 33.

14. Israel Shreve to Dr. Bodo Otto, June 29, 1777, in John U. Rees, Colonel Israel Shreve's Journal, 23 November 1776 to 14 August 1777. www.scribd.com/doc/153790118 (accessed October 3, 2017).

15. Alexander Hamilton to Robert R. Livingston June 28, 1777, New York Historical Society Museum Collection. This letter was addressed to Livingston while he was a member of the Committee of Correspondence.

16. Detwiller, War in the Countryside, 1.

17. Stillman, George B., "Battle of the Short Hills. Reenactment preparations June 29 and 30th 2002," The Brigade Courier, Brigade of the American Revolution, Volume 18:3.

18. Composite of Robert Erskine Maps of the Short Hills and Ash Swamp. C.1779, No. 74A, 74B, 78. Collections of the New York Historical Society. Major Robert Erskind was commissioned as the official surveyor for the American Army in 1777 and produced an extensive collection.

Chapter 5

1. Ewald, Johann, Diary of the American War, A Hessian Journal, Translated and edited by Joseph Tostin (New Haven, CT: Yale University Press, 1979), 134.

2. Montresor, John, "Journal of Captain John Montresor," Pennsylvania Magazine of History, Vol. VI, 189.

3. Peebles, American War, 189.

4. National Archives, Order Book Seventh Regiment British Foot, Lieutenant Colonel Alured Clarke, Commanding. Found on the Monmouth Battlefield.

5. US National Archives (Class title War Office 71/86), 174–175.

6. Stryker, William S., The Battle of Monmouth (Port Washington NY: Kenekat Press, 1927).

7. Schoepf, David Johann, Travels in the Confederation, Morrison, Alfred J., ed. (Philadelphia: William H. Campbell, 1911), cited in Edgar, Gregory, The Philadelphia Campaign, 1777–1778 (Heritage Books, Inc., 2013), 192.

8. The New Jersey Gazette, July 1, 1778. Burlington and Trenton, NJ, US Lbrary of Congress.

9. Lieutenant Colonel Clarke's Order Book.

10. Clinton, Henry, Narrative of Lieut. Col. Henry Clinton Relative to his conduct During part of his Campaign of the King's Troops in North America (London: J. Debrett, 1783), entry for June 22, 1778.

11. Ewald, Diary of the American War, 134.

12. Stryker, The Battle of Monmouth, 84.

13. Peebles, American War, 191.

14. Andre, John, Major Andre's Journal.

15. Woodward, E. M., History of Burlington County (Philadelphia, PA: Everts and Peck, 1883), 28.

16. Horner, William, This Old Monmouth (Freehold, NJ: Moreau Brothers, 1932), 8.

17. US National Archives (War Office, Class 71/86, Volume 86), 151–158.

18. Lieutenant Colonel Clarke's Order Book.

19. Washington to Henry Laurens, President of the Continental Congress, Englishtown, July 1, 1778. Washington Papers, Series 3, Varick Transcripts, 1775–1785, Subseries 3A, Continental Congress, 1775–1783, Letterbook 3: September 1, 1777-August 31, 1778.

20. Woodward, E. M., History of Burlington County (Philadelphia, PA: Everts and Peck, 1883), 28.

Chapter 6

1. Boom, A. A., A report of the Middlebrook Encampment by the Continental A in the Middle of 1777 and in the Winter of 1778–1779. Sponsored by the Somerset Historical Society, typewritten Ms. Collections of the Warren Township Library. In 1973–74, A. A. Boom, a local historian who conducted tours of the area around Miller Lane, did an extensive investigation of the rock walls in the area.

2. Hon. Gen. Sir William Howe to Lord George Germain. December 20, 1777, The Pennsylvania Gazette,from the London Gazette, Whitehall, August 22, 1777.

3. History of Hunterdon and Somerset Counties, New Jersey, compiled by James P. Snell and Franklin Ellis (Philadelphia: PA Everts & Peck, 1881), 50.

4. Vermeule, Cornelius C. The Revolutionary Camp Ground at Plainfield. An Address delivered before the Continental Chapter, Daughters of the American Revolution, January 9, 1923.

5. The house on 602 West Front St. Plainfield, built by Isaac Drake in 1746, is now a museum

of the Historical Society of Plainfield. Its collections and exhibits contain various Revolutionary War items.

6. Barber, John Warner., Historical collections of the state of New Jersey: past and present (New Haven, CT: J.W. Barber, 1868), 201.

7. Randolph, Edward F., Journal of Edward Fitz Randolph (Rutgers University Special Collections, University Archives), 6.

8. Ott, Westley H., 1 mile X 1Mile X 100 Years Dunellen, N.J. (Collections of the Green Brook New Jersey Public Library).

9. Lossing, Benson John, The Pictorial Field-Book of the Revolution or, Illustrations, by Pen and Pencil, of the History, Biography, Scenery, Relics, and Traditions of the War for Independence (New York, Harper & Brothers, 1859), Vol. 1, Ch. XVI, 331.

10. John Laing named in 1880 Federal Census, City of Plainfield, NJ, First District, 52.

11. The Constitutionist July 16, 1896.

12. Ibid., July 14, 1898.

13. Ibid., February 27, 1868.

14. Bebbington, George and Siegel, Alan A., Washington Rock Is Focus Of Renewed Interest (Warren History, Volume Two, No. 3, Spring 1995 Warren Township Historical Society), https://sites.google.com/a/gbhsnj.org/gbhsnj/misc/washington-rock?tmpl (accessed October 13, 2017)

15. Messier, Abraham, Centennial History of Somerset County (Somerville, NJ: C.M. Jameson, 1878), 83.

16. In 1973–74, A. A. Boom, a local historian who conducted tours of the area around Miller Lane, did an extensive investigation of the rock walls in the area, which is documented in Chapter 11 of North of the Rariton Lotts: A History of Martinsville, NJ Area, edited by Edward J. Maas, Martinsville Historical Committee, 1975. In 1974, William Liesenbein performed an archaeological investigation of the same area. He refutes some of Boom's claims that most of the walls were set up for fortifications but did admit that some may have been. He also found features which he speculates could have been huts and kitchens in 1777.

17. Lossing Vol. 1, Ch. XVI, 33.

18. Map number 55 in the Erskine/DeWitt series, was drawn for Capt. William Scull. It shows detailed locations of the Continental Army units during the 1776–77 Middlebrook encampment. US National Archives.

19. Wright, Robert K., The Continental Army (Washington, DC: Center of Military History, United States Army, 1986), Ch. 5, 91.

Chapter 7

1. Washington, Writings, Vol. 21, 439.

2. The Papers of Robert Morris, 1781–1784. E. James Ferguson, ed., Vol. 1: February 7—July 31, 1781. (Pittsburgh PA: 1973), p. 74.

3. Lauberdière, Journal de guerre, "Lauberdière's Journal. the Revolutionary War Journal of Louis François Bertrand d'Aubevoye, comte de Lauberdière," Robert A. Selig, Colonial

Williamsburg, vo1.8, no.1 Autumn 1995, 33–37, Review of journal discovered in 1978. De Lauberdière' was the youngest of Rochambeau's aides-de-camp. His views often reflect the biases of this arrogant, young aristocrat. He comments on both pleasant and unpleasant experiences and perceptions of America during the Revolution.

4. Acomb, Evelyn A. The Revolutionary Journal of Ludwig von Closen, 1780–1783 (Chapel Hill, NC: University of North Carolina Press, 1958) 89.

5. Clermont-Crèvecoeur, Journal, in Rice and Brown, American Campaigns, Vol. 1, 33.

6. Washington, Diaries, Vol. 2, 249.

7. Lamb's Orderly Book for 6 August 1781, The New York Historical Society Collection.

8. New Jersey State Archives, Record Group: Military and Militia, Subgroup: Adjutant General's Office, Series: Revolutionary War Research files, Box 2.

9. The Washington-Rochambeau Revolutionary Route in the State of New Jersey, 1781-1783. An Historical and Architectural Survey. 3 vols. (Trenton, NJ: New Jersey Historic Trust, Department of Community Affairs, 2006).

10. Abbé Robin, New Travels through North America (Philadelphia, PA: 1783), 41.

11. Acomb, Closen, 111–112.

12. Selig. Robert A., Georg Daniel Flohr's Journal: A New Perspective (Colonial Williamsburg: The Journal of the John M. Lenhart, "Letter of an Officer of the Zweibrücken Regiment," Central-Blatt and Social Justice, Vol. 28, (January 1936), 321–322. Colonial Williamsburg Foundation. Vol. 15, no. 4 (Summer 1993).

13. Nelson, William and Shriner, Charles A., History of Paterson and Its Environs (the Silk City): (Paterson, Lewis Historical Publishing, 1920). Chapter VIII, 257.

14. John M. Lenhart, "Letter of an Officer of the Zweibrücken Regiment," Central-Blatt and Social Justice, Vol. 28, (January 1936), 321–322.

15. Scott, Samuel F., "Foreign Mercenaries, Revolutionary War, and Citizen Soldiers in the Late Eighteenth Century," War and Society, September 1984, 42–58.

16. Cromot du Bourg, "Diary," 124–125. Magazine of American History: v. 4–5, 1780–81. The diary ends in October 1781, following a brief discussion that "Every thing seemed to announce a siege of New York. The establishment of a bakery and other store houses at Chatham, 4 miles distant, from Staten Island."

17. Lieutenant General Sir Henry Clinton, K.B., to Lord George Germain, July 5, 1778. State of the Forces under . . . Sir Henry Clinton, 3 July 1778, (Library of Congress, Mss. Division: PRO CO 5:96), 77.

18. Flohr's Journal, 323.

19. Cromot du Bourg, Diary, 126.

20. Finigan, H.: "Montresor Papers on microfilm," David Library of the American Revolution, Washington's Crossing, PA, 42.

21. The Revolutionary Journal of Baron Ludwig von Closen, 1780–1783, 112–115.

22. Robin, Abbe, New Travels In North America-War In America, (Philadelphia, Robert Bell, 1799) 42. The "mechanism" described, an "orrery," is a mechanical model of the solar system. It is currently housed in the Van Pelt Library at the University of Pennsylvania.

23. Weelen, Jean-Edmond, Rochambeau. Father and Son. A life of the Maréchal de

Rochambeau and the Journal of the Vicomte de Rochambeau (New York, Henry Holt Co., 1936), 256.

24. Of the five infantry regiments that made the march to Yorktown in 1781 only one copy of the orderly book of the 2nd New York that traveled with the French column in N.J. has survived. It is housed at the New York State Library (#10464, vol.10).

25. A series of field sketches and finished maps of projected battle sites in New York, New Jersey, Connecticut and Pennsylvania during the Revolutionary war was begun by Robert Erskine, geographer and surveyor-general to the Continental Army, and completed by his successor, Simeon DeWitt. Erskine (1735–1780) was appointed Geographer to Washington's army in 1777. He surveyed both sides of the Hudson River and a large area covering the adjoining states. Many of the maps are rough field sketches, from which more detailed maps were later drawn. Simeon DeWitt (1756–1834) succeeded Erskine as Geographer-in-Chief in 1780 and oversaw surveys of the roads heading south through Maryland and Virginia to Williamsburg and Yorktown, aiding in Washington's decisive victory at Yorktown.

26. Hawkins, John H., Journal of Sargeant Major John Hawkins (Manuscript # Am.0765, Unpublished, microfilmed, Historical Society of Pennsylvania).

27. Washington-Rochambeau Revolutionary Route, 199.

28. Ibid., 193.

<u>Chapter 8</u>

1. Journal, New York Provincial Congress, Vol 1, 342 Pierre Van Cortlandt, Abm. P. Lott, and John Sloss Hobart of the New York Provincial Congress to Major William Clark March 6, 1776, which appears in: William Bell Clark. ed., Naval Documents of the American Revolution Vol. 4 (U.S. Navy Department, Washington, DC, 1968), 194–195.

2. American Archives, Volume VI: 1011.

3. Journal of Solomon Nash. Soldier of the Revolution, 1776–1777, ed. Bushnell, Charles I., (New York Privately Printed, 1861), 33

4. Peebles, John, American War, 201.

5. Sir Henry Clinton's Narrative of his Campaigns 1775–1782, William H. Wilcox, ed. (New Haven: Yale University Press, 1954), 100.

6. Skeletons Unearthed, Red Bank Register, April 22, 1908.

7. Brenton, Edward P., The Naval History of Great Brain, from the Year MDCCLXXXIII to MDCCCXXXVL, Volume I (London, Henry Colburn, 1837), 261–262.

8. Extract of a letter from a gentleman on board HMS *Assistance* at Sandy Hook, Jan 2, *The Scots Magazine*, March 1784, Edinburgh. 158.

9. Bentinck's Log is quoted on page 32 of Nauvoo to the Hook by George H. Moss. Moss notes that his source was "unpublished Crown copyright material in Public Records Office printed with permission of H.M. Stationary Office."

10. This text used by Barber and Howe in their 1844 account appears to have been taken from an earlier account in the American Universal Geography published in 1789. This earlier wording was probably transcribed directly from the monument. Moss, Appendix X, 111.

11. Barber, John H. and Henry Howe Historical Collections of New Jersey, (Harvard University, S, Tuttle, 1846) 162.

12. Kobbe, Gustave, The New Jersey Coast and Pines (Short Hills, NJ: 1889), 5.

13. Wells, Charles H., "Sandy Hook Mystery Solved," New York Daily Tribune, April 24,   1908. Letter to the Editor from New York City, April 20, 1908.

Chapter 9

1. New York Gazette and Weekly Mercury, February 7, 1777

2. Hyde, Murray M. C., The Battle of the Navesink, New York Times, February 23, 1896

3. King, John P., The Making of America-Highlands, New Jersey (Mount Pleasant, SC, Arcadia Publishing, 2001), 22.

4. Extract written by an officer at Amboy Feb 16. 1777, New York Gazette and Weekly Mercury, February 7, 1777.

5. Sugar houses in New York City were used as prisons by occupying British forces during the American Revolutionary War. Out of 2,600 prisoners of war captured during the Battle of Fort Washington in November 1776, 1,900 would die in the following months at makeshift prisons throughout the city.

6. Stillwell, John E. Historical and Genealogical Miscellany: Data relating to the settlement and settlers of New York and New Jersey (New York, 1932), Vol. 5, 389..

Chapter 10

1. Van Brunt v. Huddy (1779), Monmouth County Court of Common Pleas, Monmouth County Archives.

2. State v. Huddy (1778), Monmouth County Court of Oyer and Terminer, Minutes.

3. Huddy vs. Longstreet, Writ of Replevin, November 6, 1780, Monmouth County Court.

4. Kobbé Gustav, The Jersey Coast and Pines (Baltimore, Gateway Press, Inc., 1970), 24.

5. A blockhouse is a small fort, one building, usually in an isolated position. The one Huddy was defending protected the village of Toms River and the salt works nearby. The construction of the blockhouse is described in A History of Monmouth and Ocean Counties by Edwin Salter, (Bayonne, NJ: E. Gardner & Son, 1890), 205.

6. The War at the Shore 2007: Commemorating the 225th Anniversary of the Revolutionary War in Ocean County 1776-1783 (pamphlet), Ocean County Board of Chosen Freeholders, 2007.

7. Ryerson, Egerton, The Loyalist of American and their Times 1620-1816, Vol II (Toronto, William Briggs, 1880).

8. Kobbe, The Jersey Coast and Pines, 25.

Chapter 11

1. Maclay, Edgar Stanton, A History of American Privateers. (Freeport, New York: Books for the Library Press, 1970), 70.

2. Ibid., viii.

3. Donnelly, Mark P and Diehl, Daniel. Pirates of New Jersey: Plunder and High Adventure on the Garden State Coastline (Guilford, CT: Stackpole Books, 2010).

4. Cook, Fred J., Privateers of Seventy-Six (New York: Bobbs-Merrill Company, Inc. 1976), 120.

5. Similar to modern times, the Loyalist New York Gazette and Weekly Mercury and the Patriot New Jersey Gazette often offer conflicting accounts of the same event.

6. Patton, Robert, Patriot Pirates: The Privateer War for Freedom and Fortune in the American Revolution. (New York, Pantheon Books, 2008), 160.

7. Onderdonk, Henry Jr., Documents and Letters to Illustrate the Revolutionary Incidents of Queens County (New York, Leavitt, Trow and Co., 1846), 189.

8. Tonsetic, Robert 1., Special Operations During the American Revolution (Haverford, PA: Casemate Publishers, 2013), 221.

9. Donelly, Pirates of New Jersey, 71.

Chapter 12

1. Since the engagement at Little Egg Harbor in 1778 five accounts have been written that describe the action. The first can be found in volume II of C. Stedman's The History of the Origin, Progress and termination of the American War, published in London in 1794. Stedman was a British officer who served in America during the war. It is accurate, but completely omits the embarrassing loss of the HMS Zebra, the expedition's flagship. The second reference appeared in the North American Review in 1826. This pamphlet, Judge Johnson's Remarks of an Article in the North American Review Relating to Count Pulaski, was an irate rebuke of Johnson's criticism of Pulaski. It was written by Colonel Paul Bentalou, an officer in the Pulaski Legion. Another British account was published in 1837 in Cannon's Historical Records of the British army, The Fifth regiment of Foot or Northumberland Fusiliers. The most comprehensive narrative, The Affair at Egg Harbor, New Jersey October 15, 1778, is a thirty-four page booklet written in 1894 by William S. Stryker, Attorney General of the State of New Jersey. This work renewed interest in these events that had been mostly lost to history for over a century. Frankin W. Kemp's 1966 account, "Nest of Rebel Pirates," is an exhaustive study of the battle.

2. Francis B. Lee, Archives of the State of New Jersey, Second Series, Vol II (Documents Relating to the Revolutionary History of the State of New Jersey / Extracts from American Newspapers relating to New Jersey) (Trenton NJ: John L. Murphy Publishing Company, 1903), 219.

3. The names of these vessels, their state, rig guns and number of crew, commanding officer, amount of bond furnished and owner can be found in the Calendar of Naval Records of the American Revolution 1775-1788, prepared from the originals in the Library of Congress by Charles Henry Lincoln, Division of Manuscripts, Washington DC, 1906.

4. Allen, Gardner W., A Naval History of the American Revolution. (Boston and New York: Houghton-Mifflin Company, The Riverside press Cambridge, 1913), Vol. 1, 291-292.

5. Kemp, Franklin W., A Nest of Rebel Pirates (Egg Harbor City, NJ: The Laureate Press, 1966), 15.

6. Dr. M. M. Gilchrist, St. Andrews, Scotland, 1999 offers the best published collection of Ferguson's military writings, with a biographical introduction, is Hugh F. Rankin, "An Officer Out of His Time: Correspondence of Major Patrick Ferguson, 1779-1780," is in Howard H. Peckham (ed.) Sources of American Independence, vol. II, Chicago & London, 1978.

7. Report of Captain Collins, British navy Zebra, in Little Egg Harbour, October 9, 1778.

8. Stryker, William, The Affair at Egg Harbor, October 15, 1778, speech given at the dedication of the Pulaski Massacre Monument, July 3, 1894 (Trenton: Naar, Day and Naar, 1894), 9.

9. Ibid., 10.

10. Volo. James M. and Volo Dorothy D. Life in 17th and 18th Century America (Westport CT: Greenwood Publishing Group, 2006), 122-123.

11. Folger, Harry P. III, The Battle at Chestnut Neck and The Affair at Little Egg Harbor, October 6, 1778-October 22, (Marshallville, NJ, 2008), 11, Col. Richard Somers Chapter, New Jersey Society, Sons of the American Revolution.

12. Report of Capt. Ferguson, of the 70th Regiment, to his Excellency Sir Henry Clinton from, dated Little Egg-harbour,Oct. 15, 1778, *The Remembrancer* (London: J. Almon, 1779), 153.

13. Roscoe R. Hill, Editor, Journals of the Continental Congress, 1774-1789, Volume X. January 1-May 1, 1778 (Washington DC: Government Printing Office, 1908), 290.

14. Kemp, A Nest of Rebel Pirates, 44.

15. Ibid., 24.

16. Ibid., 43.

17. Stryker, The Affair at Little Egg Harbor, 13.

18. Extract form the log of the HMS Nautilus Lat 39.43, October 12, 1778.

19. Miller Pauline S., Brief Encounter at Osborn Island: The Pulaski Affair (Toms River, NJ: Ocean County Cultural & Heritage Commission, 1998), 14.

20. The monument is located in a field on S. Pulaski Blvd., between Kosciusko Way and Kadlubeck Way.

21. Stryker, The Affair at Egg Harbor New Jersey October 15, 1778,9.

22. Kemp, in A Nest of Rebel Pirates, attempts to identify Lt. Col. Charles August Baron von Bose and includes a chapter titled "The Mysterious Baron Bose," in which he describes the thorough and painstaking research he did in trying to identify this foreign officer in the service of the Continental Army.

23. Kemp, A Nest of Rebel Pirates, 48.

24. Freeman, Douglas S., Biography of George Washington (New York: Charles Scribner and Sons, 1952), Vol. 5, 77. For his source Freeman refers to a letter of October 15, 1778, from R. H. Harrison to Joseph Reed (Reed Papers, New York Historical Society).

25. Stryker, Affair at Little Egg Harbor, 50.

26. Valentine Alan, Lord Stirling (New York: Oxford University Press, 1969), 29.

27. Stryker, Affair at little Egg Harbor, 8.

28. Blackman, Leah, "History of Little Egg Harbor from 1880," Old Times and Other

Writings (Tuckerton N.J. Historical Society, 2000), 206-208.

29. Stryker, Affair at Little Egg Harbor,50.

30. Draper, Lyman C., King's Mountain and Its Heroes: History of the Battle of King's Mountain, October 7, 1780, and the Events Which Led to It (Cincinnati, OH: Peter G. Thompson, 1881), 60.

31. Kemp, A Nest of Pirates, 51

32. Ferguson's letter, Little Egg Harbor, October 15, 1778, The Royal Gazette, March 10, 1779; reprinted in William Nelson, ed., Documents Relating to the Revolutionary History of the State of New Jersey, Second Series, Vol. III (Trenton, NJ: John L. Murphy Publishing Company, 1906), 158-159. Also in Stryker, Affair at Little Egg Harbor, Appendix, 29.

Chapter 13

1. Salter, Edwin, A History of Monmouth and Ocean Counties, Embracing a Genealogical Record of the Earliest Settlers in Monmouth and Ocean Counties (Bayonne, NJ: E. Gardner & Son, 1890), 212.

2. Ibid., 207.

3. Digital copies of Royal Gazette issues were obtained from the Early American Newspapers Database at Seton Hall University Library). The articles are dated October 30 and November 1, 1782.

4. Edwin Salter, George C. Beekman, Old Times in Old Monmouth-Historical Reminiscences of Old Monmouth County, New Jersey (Freehold, NJ: 1887), 46-47. The Monouth Democrat, Freehold, NJ: 1887, 46; Somerville, George B., The Lure of Long Beach, Long Beach Board of Trade, Long Beach: 1914, 37-38.

5. Ibid., Salter, 209.

6. Pierce, Arthur Dudley, Smugglers' Woods: Jaunts and Journeys in Colonial and Revolutionary New Jersey (New Brunswick, NJ: Rutgers University Press, 1960), 41.

7. New Jersey Gazette, Trenton, January 8, 1783.

8. Larsen, Erik, "Ocean County to develop Cedar Bridge Tavern in Barnegat," Asbury Park Press, February 24, 2016.

9. Cedar Bridge Tavern, National Register of Historic Places.

10. Salter, Edward, A History of Monmouth and Ocean Counties, 422.

11. Salter, Edward, Centennial History of Ocean County, 24.

12. "Revolutionary War Sites in Manahawkin, New Jersey," Revolutionary War New Jersey website; accessed October 23, 2017.

13. Salter, 203.

14. Ibid., 204.

15. Fort, George F., MD, An Account of the Capture and Death of the Refugee John Bacon, Proceedings of the New Jersey Historical Society (Newark, NJ: New Jersey Historical Society, 1847), 151.

16. Fort, 152.

17. Beck, Henry Charlton, More Forgotten Towns of Southern New Jersey (New Brunswick, NJ: Rutgers University Press, 1963), 260.

Chapter 14

1. General Sir Henry Clinton's official report of the battle of Monmouth reached London on August 2, 1778 and was first published in The London Gazette, Whitehall, on August 24. The report was reprinted in the August 22-25, 1778, edition of *The London Chronicle*

2. Clarke, Alured, Lieutenant Colonel Clarke's Order Book, British 7th Regiment of Foot, June 21, 1778.

3. Tustin, Joseph P., Diary of the American War, 136.

4. Peebles, Diary of a Scottish Grenadier, 200.

5. Stryker, William S., The Battle of Monmouth (Port Washington, NY: Kenekat Press, 1927), 103.

6. Hornor, William S., This Old Monmouth of Ours (Freehold, NJ: Moreau Brothers, 1932, reprinted by Cottenport, Polyanthos, 1974), 7. This account was provided by Garret Smock, a militia soldier who fought in the battle.

7. Peebles, Diary of a Scottish Grenadier, 205.

8. Boyd, Paul D., Atlantic Highlands: From Lenape Camps to Bayside Town (Charlestown, SC: Arcadia Publishing, 2004), 91.

9. History of Monmouth County, 1664-1920 Vol. 1. (New York: Lewis Historical Publishing Co., 1922), 115.

10. Hornor, This Old Monmouth, 8.

Chapter 15

1. George Bebbington and Alan A. Siegel, "Warren History," Somerset County Historical Quarterly, I/58, V/76.

2. Ward, Christopher, The War of Revolution (New York: MacMillan, 1952), Vol. II, 585.

3. Messier, Abraham D.D., History of Somerset County (Somerville, NJ: C, M. Jameson Publisher, 1878), 83. Extracted from "Official Letters of General Washington to the American Congress," vol. ii. Boston, 1796. 123,124.

4. Detwiller, Frederic C., War in the Countryside, 23.

5. Fitzpatrick, Writings, XIII, 80.

6. Sparks, Jared, Correspondence of the American Revolution (Boston, Hale, Grey and Bowen, 1853), Vol II, 266-268.

7. Williams, Glen F., The Year of the Hangman (Yardley, PA: Westholme Publishing, 2005).

8. Thatcher, James, M.D., A Military Journal During the American Revolutionary War, From 1775 to 1783 (New York: Arno Press, 1969), 161.

9. Boom, A.A., Report on the Middlebrook Encampment by the Continental Army During the Middle of 1777 and the Winter of 1778-1779 (Bridgewater, NJ: Somerset County Historical Society, 1975), 97.

Chapter 16

1. Parry, Samuel, "The Origin of the Name "'Pluckemin'" in Honeyman, A. Van Doren, Somerset County Historical Quarterly (1912), 1:196.
2. Sekel, Clifford, "The Continental Artillery in Winter Encampment at Pluckemin, New Jersey, December 1778-June 1779," (Master of Arts thesis, Wagner College 1972), 16.
3. Regimental Orders, December 8, 1778, Colonel Lamb's Orderly Book
4. Ibid.
5. Knox to McDougal, January 10, 1779, McDougal Papers, New York Historical Society.
6. Regimental Orders, December 6, 1778. Col Lamb's Orderly Book.
7. Knox to McDougal, January 10, 1779, Alexander McDougal Papers.
8. Regimental Orders, February 2, 1779, Col. Lamb's Orderly Book.
9. Moore, Frank Ed. Diary of the American Revolution, From Newspapers and Original Documents (New York: 1863), vol. II,131.
10. Regimental Orders, December 14, 1779, Col. Lamb's Orderly Book.
11. The Papers of George Washington, 19:577
12. Regimental Orders, February 23, 1779, Col. Lamb's Orderly Book.
13. Moore, Diary of the American Revolution, II, 132.
14. Regimental Orders, May 22, 1779, Col. Lamb's Orderly Book.
15. Regimental Orders, February 9 and February 13, 1779, Col. Lamb's Orderly Book.
16. Regimental Orders, February 3, 1779, Col. Lambs Orderly Book.
17. Excavations at Knox's Artillery Encampment, Pluckemin. Series of articles in the Bernardsville News, Bernardsville, New Jersey, 1917. Also see "General Knox's Artillery Park," Somerset County Historical Quarterly, 6 (3):161-168.
18. Sekel, Clifford, "The Continental Artillery in Winter Encampment at Pluckemin," 10.
19. Seidel, John L. (1983), "Archaeological Research at the 1778-79 Winter Cantonment of the Continental Artillery, Pluckemin, New Jersey," Northeast Historical Archaeology, Vol. 12, Article 4.

Chapter 17

1. Talmadge, Samuel, Orderly Books of the Fourth and Second New York Regiments, 1776-1783, (Albany: University of the State of New York, 1932), General, Brigade and Regimental Orders: Headquarters Morristown December 7, 1779 to May 31, 1780.
2. A History and Guide to Morristown National Park (Washington, DC: Division of Publications, National Park Service, U.S. Dept. of the Interior, 1983), 62.
3. General Orders, December 8, 1779, Headquarters, Morristown, Talmadge, 192.
4. Desciption of offenses and penalties are described daily in Orderly Books, 1778-1783, Talmadge.
5. Thatcher, James, M.D. Surgeon Continental Army, Military Journal of the American Revolution, 1775-1783 (Gansevoort, NY: Corner House Historic Publications, 1998), 36.

6. Cunningham, John T., The Uncertain Revolution (West Creek, NJ: Cormorant Publishing 2007), 143.

7. Letter-John Allison to George Washington from Camp near Morristown April 16, 1780, Budke Collection, George Henry Budke, 1869-1948, New York Public Library, Manuscripts and Archives Division.

8. Washington, New Windsor, New York, April 19, 1783, Writings of George Washington.

Chapter 18

1. Brubaker, Robert M., A Wonderously Beautiful Valley-A Commemorative History of Wayne, N.J., Wayne Township Bicentennial Committee, 1976.

2. Nelson,William "Washington's Headquarters at Preakness," The Magazine of American History, Volume 3 (New York and Chicago: A. S. Barnes & Company, 1879), 490-495.

3. Map Showing the Location of the American Army at Totawa and Preakness, N.J. and Vicinity October and November 1780, Nelson, Paterson and Its Environs, 236.

4. Berce, William E., Under the Sign of the Eagle (Wayne, NJ: Louis J. Borgett, 1964).

5. The Washington-Rochambeau Revolutionary Route in the State of New Jersey, 1781-1783. An Historical and Architectural Survey. 3 vols. (Trenton: New Jersey Historic Trust, Department of Community Affairs, 2006).

6. Nelson and Shriner, Paterson, 265.

7. Cromot du Bourg, "Diary 1780-81," Magazine of American History: v. 4-5, 124-125, 1880.

8. Acomb, Evelyn A. The Revolutionary Journal of Ludwig von Closen, 1780-1783 (Chapel Hill: The University of North Carolina Press, 1958), 89.

9. Muster Rolls, New York Brigade at Pompton-January to June 1782; Also, Talmadge, Samuel, Orderly Books of the Fourth and Second New York Regiments, 768-771.

10. Ibid., Talmadge, Orderly Books, 778.

11. Nelson and Shriner, Paterson, 444.

12. Sunnybank, Former Estate of Albert Payson Terhune, Pamphlet (undated) Wayne Township Historic site, Wayne, New Jersey.

Chapter 19

1. Nelson, William and Shriner, Charles A., Paterson and its Environs (New York: Lewis Historical Publishing Co., 1920), 440.

2. The Papers of George Washington, Revolutionary War Series, Vol. 19, 15 January-7 April 1779 (Charlottesville: University of Virginia Press, 2009), 555-578.

3. Shreve, John, "Personal Narrative of the Services of Lieut. John Shreve of the

New Jersey Line of the Continental Army," in The Magazine of American History with Notes and Queries, Volume III (1879), 576.

4. Shreve to Washington, January 20, 1781, The George Washington Papers.

5. Dayton to Washington, January 24, 1781, George Washington Papers.

6. New Jersey Brigade Commanding Officer to New Jersey Line Mutineers, January 23, 1781, George Washington Papers.

7. Washington to the President of Congress, January 23, 1781, The Writings of George Washington.

8. Washington to the President of Congress, January 23, 1781, The Writings of George Washington, Vol. 21.

9. Howe to Washington, January 25, 1781, George Washington Papers.

10. Howe to Washington, January 25 and 26, 1781, George Washington Papers.

11. Thatcher, A Military Journal, 302.

12. Ibid., 303.

13. Van Doren, Carl, Mutiny in January: The Story of a Crisis in the Continental Army now for the first time fully told from many hitherto unknown or neglected sources both American and British (New York: Viking Press, 1943), 224. Also Nagy, John A., Rebellion in the Ranks (Yardley, PA: Westholme Publishing, 2007), 177-178, 181.

14. Howe to Washington, January 29, 1781, George Washington Papers.

15. General Orders, January 30, 1781, Writings of George Washington, Vol. 21.

16. Suburban Trends Magazine, Feb. 13, 1983.

Index

CPSIA information can be obtained
at www.ICGtesting.com
Printed in the USA
FSHW021820161020
74800FS